God Being Nothing

God Being Nothing

Toward a Theogony

RAY L. HART

The University of Chicago Press   Chicago and London

RAY L. HART is professor emeritus of religion and theology at
Boston University.

The University of Chicago Press, Chicago 60637
The University of Chicago Press, Ltd., London
© 2016 by The University of Chicago
All rights reserved. Published 2016.
Printed in the United States of America

25 24 23 22 21 20 19 18 17 16   1 2 3 4 5

ISBN-13: 978-0-226-35962-5 (cloth)
ISBN-13: 978-0-226-35976-2 (e-book)
DOI: 10.7208/chicago/9780226359762.001.0001

Library of Congress Cataloging-in-Publication Data

Names: Hart, Ray L., author.
Title: God being nothing : toward a theogony / Ray L. Hart.
Other titles: Religion and postmodernism.
Description: Chicago ; London : The University of Chicago Press,
    2016. | Series: Religion and postmodernism | Includes bibliographical
    references and index.
Identifiers: LCCN 2015039770 | ISBN 9780226359625 (cloth : alk.
    paper) | ISBN 9780226359762 (e-book)
Subjects: LCSH: God. | Philosophical theology. | Postmodern theology.
Classification: LCC BT103 .H385 2016 | DDC 211—dc23 LC record
    available at http://lccn.loc.gov/2015039770

♾ This paper meets the requirements of ANSI/NISO Z39.48-1992
    (Permanence of Paper).

For twelve collegial friends over a lifetime

Thomas J. J. Altizer   *David L. Miller*
Henry G. Bugbee   *Robert C. Neville*
Edward Farley   *Schubert M. Ogden*
Robert W. Funk   *Mark C. Taylor*
Charley D. Hardwick   *James B. Wiggins*
Howard L. Harrod   *Edith Wyschogrod*

Contents

Preface

A writer cannot but muse privately the connection his books have with one another, if any; when the books reflect turning points, or pivots, in a career of thinking, it may justify or warrant going public with the musings. Such a project involves the sense of time acutely. When I reflect on an ostensibly pivoting or "hinging" event, I find crowding in on that reflection a reverie of timepieces. The event was one thing as anticipated, endured, and looked back upon through the measurement of sundials, shadows, hourglasses, and quite another through an electronically motived "watch" without moving "hands." Why *do* we still call our timepieces *watches* when the segments of day and night have long since ceased to be distinguished by "watches"—as in the biblical three watches of the night? A wisdom in our language chimes with that in time: one is to stand watch, particularly over pivots and hinges.

Such an event, fraught with pivoting or hinging significance, bears two distinguishable futures. When the event has not fully happened, it has or is an anterior future; and as such, as Aristotle said of any future, it can only be imagined. When the event has happened, or is concrescently collocated, it has or becomes a posterior future, which comprises the potency established in the event. This is why Bultmann claims that the meaning of an event belongs to the future to which it gives rise. Here I do not refer to how my writings were called forth by "occasions" (a conference, symposium, lecture, a festschrift, and so on) but simply seek to reckon with the two hinge or pivot books, offering a few words concerning the correlation of my first book and the present work—whether it be my last, too, is a function of time. A journal article that comprised my presidential address to the seventy-fifth anniversary annual meeting of the American Academy of Religion in 1984 falls at midpoint between the two hinge books, and substantively is itself the hinge between them. The truly avid industrious reader may wish to read it: "To Be *and* Not to Be: *Sit Autem Sermo (Logos) Vester: Est, Est, Non, Non . . .*"

This book attempts to deliver some of the unfinished business of my first book, *Unfinished Man and the Imagination*, published in 1968, almost five decades ago. During the era in which that work appeared, the blue streak of Neo-orthodoxy had flashed its course and begun to recede, having revealed the critical vulnerabilities of its doctrine of revelation. My author's foreword referred to it as an "enervating" doctrine leading to a "dead end" and opined that the American context was relatively remote from Neo-orthodoxy's "state of terminal illness" since the great vogue spawned by the European continent had never gotten its taproot down into the New World. *Unfinished Man* sought to offer an altogether alternative approach to revelation: thinking through the scope of theology and the character of revelation in tandem, and therewith establishing a framework for a fundamental theology—or a theology of culture—on the basis of the ontological potency of a "deformed imagination." This venture made bold to claim that imagination is an epistemological assumption of the cosmological argument, and further, that the only way a finite mind becomes *capax Dei* is by its power of imagination becoming *deiform*. While the argument worked through pertinent anthropological-hermeneutical issues, the theology proper—the imagining of God—was deferred to a later date. A correlative logic haunts this project: just as a humanity open to ongoing revelation is an unfinished humanity, so, a fortiori, a God revealed in ongoing revelation is and must be an unfinished God. Indeed, this book might have been titled *Unfinished God* had I not seen need for a new wineskin to associate with a thinking so many decades in gestation. Where the early book reckoned with the hermeneutical spiral and the play of theological signifiers, *God Being Nothing* attempts to reckon with the groundless ground (abyss) of the theological signified, the meontological signified, the Godhead of God.

Acknowledgments

Before turning to individuals, I wish to name the five universities in which I have taught and their presidents who befriended and supported me beyond ordinary expectations: Drew University (Fred G. Holloway, President); Vanderbilt University (Alexander Heard, Chancellor); University of Montana, Missoula (Robert Pantzer, President); State University of New York, Stony Brook (John Toll, President), State University of New York System (Ernest Boyer, Chancellor; Elizabeth Luce Moore, Chairman, SUNY Board of Trustees); Boston University (John Silber, President).

In the six decades I have taught in these universities, I have had colleagues and students in such numbers as to make it impossible to name even a fraction of them here. I limit myself to students I have known relatively recently at Boston University. My university seminars have been the primary site for the development of my thought in the period that has seen the emergence of this book. In these seminars, which have been devoted to the close reading of primary texts by major philosophers and theologians from the Axial Age to the present, students have been encouraged to read thoughtfully, to think the subjects as these figures thought them, then to "afterthink" the subjects in their own way. I have never assigned my own texts to be read in a class. But it always transpires that when we together are discussing and afterthinking a text, some small part of my afterthinking will come in to play. I may hope that with the present thought-experiment those students may now see where such lines of reference can possibly lead.

I single out for acknowledgment and special gratitude:

My research assistants in approximate chronological order, with their research interests in parentheses: "Jamie" Sandra Barkey (Flint) (religion and classics); Alina Feld (*acedia* and the Seven Deadly Sins); Sean Dempsey (religion and literature, William Butler Yeats, Wallace Stevens); Garth Green (Kant and "inner sense"); Giacomo Leoni (legacy and inheritance/"passing on"). Secretary and dear friend Christopher Tuttle (classical and Near Eastern archaeology); administrative assistant and Socratic conversationalist Eric Helmer (Emmanuel Levinas). Christopher Link (Lacan and Bataille); Kirk Wulf (William Blake); Nicholas Genevieve-Tweed (Schelling); Josh Hasler (Cormac McCarthy); Andy Linscott (Herman Melville); Gregory Stackpole (Eastern Orthodox mystics); and Elizabeth Harcourt (sommelier extraordinaire!).

My highest praise and deepest gratitude are reserved for Dr. Lissa McCullough, independent scholar, whose *The Religious Philosophy of Simone Weil* (2014) sets the standard for that most mindful of twentieth-century mystics. Without her editorial insight, craft, and skill this book would not have cried birth. I am in her debt incalculably.

For the love, patience, and forbearance of my family—my wife Fern, son Morgan and daughter-in-law Patti, son Bracken and daughter-in-law Victoria—my gratitude is without measure.

An Imperfect Overview

They said, "You have a blue guitar,
You do not play things as they are."
The man replied, "Things as they are
Are changed upon the blue guitar."
And they said then, "But play, you must,
A tune beyond us, yet ourselves,
A tune upon the blue guitar
Of things exactly as they are."
—WALLACE STEVENS, "THE MAN WITH THE BLUE GUITAR"

The present thought-experiment in philosophical theology reflects a break with the metaphysics of ontotheology—especially its idolatry of Being—but does so as a venture of metaphysical iconoclasm, not as a break with the metaphysical project itself, for that project always was (except when sidetracked) quite appropriately to think being *and* nonbeing. No less ill if not dead than the metaphysics of ontotheology is that modern philosophy of religion which, separated from all positive religion and its "divine God," sought to think, establish, and prove God as immutable perduring absolute ground—producing a putative "theism."[1] One may also cease and desist from the late-modern enterprise of heaping yet more luxuriant opprobrium on this truly dead undivine God and from generating yet more ingenious, if not ingenuous, obituaries. (The religious always already knew it.) As a task of thought it remains to be seen whether a supplanting philosophical theology can think the groundlessly renewing ground at the inmost core of the interior life of the divine God, and of all that which, qua created, is simultaneously internal and external to God: all there is *and* is not cosmically.

Everything determinate with which persons reckon ultimately is ultimately "in" God; everything indeterminate is "in" Godhead. Every determinate extrinsic to God is created by God *ex nihilo—created*, not caused, as causal relations obtain between intracosmic, intratemporal determinates. The standing or bearing of the *nihil* is one of the two most tasking and troubling difficulties besetting a theory or doctrine of God and creation. Is the *nihil* "inside" or "outside" of God? The notion of *creatio ex nihilo* arose in western monotheisms to "protect" God the Creator from a coeval power, while leaving unthought (save in esoteric theologies and pieties on the margins of heterodoxy) the standing of the *nihil*. Severely qualifying the classical *creatio ex nihilo et non se Deo*, I shall elaborate and defend the hypothesis: God creates *ex nihilo, idem est, ex Deitate ipsa* (God creates from the nothing internal to godself). If this hypothesis is sustainable, there arises the second tasking difficulty, that of conceiving or envisioning the eternal self-generation of God the determinate Creator from the abysmal indeterminacies of Godhead; that is, the task of thinking a radical monotheistic trinitarianism in ontogenesis and meontogenesis.

Sui generis is the *ad quem*—the intentional terminus—of every enterprise driven by the question "why . . . ?" The *nihil* motors both the speculations of metaphysics ("why not . . . ?") and the passions of religious practices of piety ("why the distance between the seeker and the sought?"). Western metaphysics has typically come to the full stop of "why?" with the unmoved mover (*ou kinoúmenon kineî*) or some surrogate; hence ontotheology: God identified as Being itself (*ipsum esse*). For Christians and Jews there is something deeply incongruent between God as unmoved mover and the God of biblical witness: the God of wrath in the prophets, the God of compassion in the Psalms, the God of justice contested by Job, the cry of betrayal from Jesus on the Cross, and so on. In respect of the *nihil* one can identify two extremities of religious passion: (1) the stereotypical western esoteric, as in Meister Eckhart: burn up the "not" in every created thing as the condition of entering the desert of Godhead (*reditus ad Deum*), in effect reversing the creature's exit from a primordial nothingness and thus becoming as one was when *not*, a process of deification; (2) the stereotypical eastern (Buddhist) exoteric: reduce desire and its objects by severe ascesis, and if that fails (as it did for Siddhartha Gautama after decades of trial) then inflame the *not* to the burnout of *sunyata* (nothingness, emptiness).[2] Neither of these extremities of religious passion coheres with the metaphysics of ontotheology. Neither metaphysics nor religious passion can live in an infinite regress of "why?"

To settle on these two difficulties is already to have taken *some* kind of position on a yet more primitive goad to thought, the very nerve of astonishment that there is anything at all: the "it" that occasions wonderment or astonishment that *it is* as it is: something that outstands nothing, yet is not nothing exhaustively. Is "it" one or many? Does its ultimate constitution owe to one factor or many? Religions are no less compelled by the mystery of the one and the many than are metaphysical systems, and divergences on the matter account, at least in part, for great differences between the world's religions. To stick with metaphysics: the metaphysical pluralist is prone to locate the *nihil* in the interplay of multiple factors bearing upon anything that is, hence will not have the problem of the self-generation of the *unum* from and toward a manifold; indeed, if the interplay of ultimate factors accounts for everything, and that interplay is eternal, the matter of "creation" arises not at all—no less astonishingly! Pluralism is the many in search of the one, finding the latter only episodically, in *a* being that astonishes by its presence but beckons to its many absent privatives. Metaphysical monism is less the One in quest of the many than a One bedeviled by an ostensibly palpable manifold. Here too the *nihil* is located in the many, not as the interplay of irreducible ultimate factors but as derogations of the *unum*. The self-generation of the One is in no sense *from* but always *toward* the many. But if One is the single factor, hence Being, why the otherwise-than-Being? Self-generation of One can go only one direction, toward two, more, the many. The self-effusion of One is more, but more is less than One. Here the two difficulties outlined above coalesce: as a consequence of the emanation or self-generation of the One, the *nihil* is located in the transition from one to many, the latter qua privatives, so that to be *a* being is to be deprived of Being. Both these radically different alternatives, metaphysical pluralism and monism, are already established in the West in Plato.[3]

In identifying these two difficulties, I have signaled that the problem for a theory or doctrine of creation that breaks with the metaphysics of ontotheology centers more in the one than in the many. Creation makes external difference different from the internal differentiation of God the Creator: analogous to, yet different from. Christologically, this is the difference between discarnate and incarnate Logos. In this restricted sense, and only in this sense, christology is the point of entry for a doctrine of creation, but this christology must cohere with the logically antecedent doctrine of God the Creator. Anthropologically, this is the difference between *imago Dei* and *ad imaginem Verbi* (image of God and toward the image of the Logos). In any case, if there is an essential connection between the inner differentiation of the divine life and our own inner differentiation, itself external to the divine life, the divine life is to be thought otherwise than in classical orthodoxy.

All orthodoxies require doctrinal closure. I would not speak for other religious traditions, but a Christianity rooted in the kerygmatic and didacheic theophanies of the Jesus movement gives rise to doctrines recurrently, only to be breached recurrently by a thinking that is heterodox or even heretical. How could such thinking reach *closure* when the subjects of theophany are themselves unfinished, when the sought of thought—God godself—is unfinished, when the theophany itself is "new creation"? Heterodoxy is by definition different from or other than the received orthodoxy. Not by accident do the heterodox think differently than the orthodox; they think differently the *what* of orthodox thought. Heterodoxy is essential to every living tradition, whether metaphysical or religious, because it makes lively the very questionableness of what gives itself to be thought.

The most intriguing heterodox alternative to classical trinitarianism, to my mind, in respect of the coherence of the inner differentiation of the divine and that of the created, is the line extending from Böhme (behind him, Cusa and Eckhart) through William Blake to Hegel and Schelling. This lineage, enunciated in the weird combination of late-medieval alchemical hermeticism and nascent modern sciences in Böhme,[4] embodied in the poetics and graphic arts of Blake, and brought to philosophical sophistication in different ways in Hegel and Schelling, centers in construing the divine life of the Creator as a process of dynamic differentiation (antithesis) and perduring synthesis within a unitary Spirit, a process nowhere palpable and realized, therefore manifest, except in created existence itself. It is not merely that one understands internal differentiation of the Creator from a standpoint in the internal differentiation of the creature, but that the former is only manifestly "accomplished" in the latter.

Neo-orthodox Christian theologians, especially Karl Barth, hooted this line as but one more instance of the species "mystical pantheism," as if that derogatory epithet were enough to bury it along with its carrier of the disease, the sum total of modern "idealism." Yet the thinkers of identity, whether of God or of the creature, understood that no identity can be itself that is undifferentiated by the other, an other that is internal to identity itself, however external its power in its claims. The larger point is that *ortho*doxy requires a reforming *heteros doxa* for its own *doxa* to be thinkable and believable—a point that Barth and the Barthians never got. At the very least this line of argument makes thinkable an essential relation between the inner differentiation of the Creator and the inner differentiation of the creature, even if that relation verged on one of identity—but then that was the point, how to conceive identity-in-difference, difference-in-identity?

But still the intention of classical normativity nags, and to their credit the Neo-orthodox will object: Are God and creature conflated, so theology is become anthropology and cosmology? Has the Creator disappeared in the appearance of the creature? Have the inner diversifications of identity-philosophy, shorn of their connections with the unitary divine God, flipped to their opposite, a difference-philosophy shorn of any connection with identity, yielding an interreferential play of signifiers of difference, signifying nothing but nothing, particularly as the "subject" putting such signifiers in play is "itself" but one of the counters in play, so that what began with the inner diversification of unitary Spirit and proceeded to its temporal instantiation ended in an externalization of loss and alienation, first the Creator, at last the creature? A theology become anthropology and/or cosmology is effectively nothing, and for the same reason so is "humanism."

How shall we respond? Yes and no. Yes, in the sense that no knowledgeable person can doubt that these generalizations about the directionality of mind in the West since the early nineteenth century capture its all but ineluctable "drift," both in arts and in letters (with important protests along the way). As historical report, true. But no, as well, because the thinker must position herself in relation to the pressures of the zeitgeist, as sympathizer or contrarian. While truth includes fate (here, the simulacrum of thinking's zeitgeist) in purview, truth is not exhausted by fate as embodied in zeitgeist.[5] Fate (*moira*)—or its ancient synonym necessity (*ananke*), which Plato used, especially in *Timaeus*—is one of those large matters at issue between the western classical (Greek and Roman) and the Hebrew and Christian traditions, and also within each. By the time of the Golden Age, roughly coincident with the Axial Age, Greek religion had delivered its final-stop to the question "why?" with fate, an "answer" that extended to the gods themselves, who behave as they do because suborned by and subservient to fate. Western philosophy arose in the First Academy to contest fate (*moira*) as the full stop of "why?" and explicitly so as the project of "theology" (a term coined by Plato). Philosophy qua theology is a thinking contestation of fate, in whatever form of manifestation: in Plato to cut it at the joints (analysis) and "collect" them differently by thought (synthesis) so as to get at what is manifestly "really real" (*to on*). If all the metaphysical proposals of the Golden Age—whether Academic, Peripatetic, Stoic, Epicurean, or Cynical—amounted to thoughtful reinstatements of fate on radically different terms, as arguably they are, they were nonetheless and remain thinking contestations of Greek and Roman religious fate. That they failed in Plato's project of religious reformation is historically unarguable, witness the resurgence of the mystery religions that closed the Golden Age and the rise of the New Academy—that of the Pyrrhonists. The philosophical dimensions of theological critique have reformative religious value only when internalized in the theologies of positive religions, such that they enter the ritual practice of adherents. Such dimensions function differently when the religion in question does not locate fate or its like in the gods or God. For the western monotheistic religions, Shakespeare put the problem exactly: the fault lies not in the stars but in ourselves (*Julius Caesar* 1.2.140–41). For the present heterodox variation of Christianity, that locus is insufficient: necessity, or fate, and freedom have their indeterminate antecedents in abysmal Godhead and their determinate temporal instantiations in the *betweens* of the creature: the *imago Dei* and *ad imaginem Verbi*. In any case, necessity and freedom are on the list of perduring potencies, equiprimordially in Godhead and, however differently, effective in determinate God and creature.

The thinking under way here will contest the apparently fated directionality of much modern and postmodern thought—thought that is largely nihilistic at the end of the day. Where nihilism has been evaded in the past, it has been at the cost of rendering the *nihil* harmless or otherwise nugatory. That premodern way is now permanently closed off. The challenge to thinking is: Can the *nihil* be given its due without issuing in nihilism? The phrase "radical monotheistic triniatarianism" is likely already to place us in the corps (certainly in the *esprit* de corps) of discontents that every exoteric orthodoxy generates on its esoteric underside. The first or early formulation of any doctrine is less the conclusion than the incitement of thought, and this is especially the case with "creation," for as the *creatio ex nihilo continua* is unfinished, so must be the doctrine of it.[6] This is not merely a historical but also and particularly a systematic judgment. Even if the pertinent doctrine were gotten "right" in the first place, say, at Nicaea or Chalcedon (of which I am dubious), there is the problem of how to say in different times, cultures, and worldviews the "same" thing. I take the presiding hermeneutical rule to be that under such conditions to say the same thing one must say "it" differently, and that the meaning of events (and doctrinal formulae concerning them) includes the futures to which they give rise. And if the supreme gift or "gifting" is creation itself, and our own response to the wonder of being at all takes the form of our own giving back, then the doctrinal implications of "gift exchange" must come into conceptual play, the rule of reticent delay and the rule of reserve, that of nonidentical repetition.[7]

There are ponderous difficulties in determining whether the instability and open-endedness of the doctrine of *creatio ex nihilo* owe (both historically and systematically) to the intensive and extensive problematic of making that doctrine cohere with a "settled"—hence orthodox—doctrine of the one but triune God, or whether the "settled" doctrine of God got the theophantic manifestations so wrongly as to make any theory of *creatio ex nihilo* incoherent with it. (See Topos 2: Cosmogony for an excursus on "manifestation" and "coherence" as the markers of truth, as well as of being and nonbeing.) While these two do not exhaust the field of choices, I take them to be fundamental, and I choose the latter: the problem of creation centers in God the Creator. Does, that is, if one cannot gainsay the wonderment of the persistence of the *nihil*, of which the "settled" doctrine of the triune Creator can give no plausible, coherent account. Astonishment at being anything at all is both ontic and meontic, both that we are and are not nothing *and* that our being is from, and toward, nothing—that, especially in respect of our *what*, we are *not*.

In one respect the received orthodox tradition is incontestable: the perduration of the *nihil* in creation, itself palpably manifested, is not to be rendered coherent by adducing a creator of this state of affairs and another deity to rectify it: against every such "gnosticism," the Creator-Redeemer of all creation is one, indivisibly one. Such a judgment is rendered the more ironic, if not paradoxical, by the fact that it has been precisely those esoteric discontents (whether in Judaism, Christianity, or Islam) with pure monotheism, hence flirters with the enduring gnostic temptation, situating themselves in the field of its margins who, listening to the strumming on the *doctrinal* blue guitar, insist on fretting "a tune beyond us, yet ourselves / A tune upon the blue guitar / Of things exactly as they are"—a music that sees the "Nothing that is not there and the nothing that is."

What are the routes of access to the subject matters thought in these overarching difficulties? There are three, no one of which is adequate to the subject matters without the cohering, modifying power of each of the other two: (1) ontotheological and meontological speculation, both self-standing and in concert with religious traditions, both esoteric and exoteric; (2) theological constructions and deconstructions founded on and funded by divine epiphanies variously mediated (scriptures and rituals, for example); and (3) visionary mythologies variously mediated by scriptural canon, exemplary saints or sages, bodhisattvas, for example, as well as the nondiscursive "afterlife" of scriptures, sayings, "showings" as in epic poetry, graphic and plastic arts, music, and so on, irrespective of religious cult.

A "tune beyond us, yet ourselves . . . of things exactly as they are." Exactly? *Exactly* is exasperatingly exacting. The blue guitar is the exactitude of the theological rhapsode's instrument, on which she is in peril of "things as they are" being "changed upon the blue guitar." Another blue guitar plays the music of inexactitude: "a tune beyond us, . . . yet ourselves." The theological rhapsode strums the immediacies of intellectual intuition and perception, fingers "manifestation," frets the mediacies of metaphysical and theological "coherence." From the soul palpitated by the music of the spheres, beholding "Nothing that is not there and the nothing that is," is exacted a tune on her chosen guitar of things exactly as they are, a tune that, however redolent in immediacy, in the mediacy of hearing again, is suffused with inexactitude, a fugue interminably feeding on itself, an exact tune of inexactitude. The astonishment of inexactitude and the labor of "things exactly"—the perduration of their nonadequation comprises the restless music in all theological metaphysics.

I construe Stevens's "Blue Guitar" as the symbolic placeholder for the zeitgeist that pervades the playing of any and every tune, including the tune, the performing of thinking itself, in our case the thinking of divinity. The blue guitar as instrument of the zeitgeist embodies, however unconscious the player may be of it, the referential range of the music played, where the tune starts from (*a quo*), what it takes from and what it leaves behind, what it moves toward (*ad quem*) as consonant with it. Zeitgeist frames the "time of the time," the mood, the world of the tune's parameters of resonance. As such it reconstrues presentiment, thus the very character of all re-presentations.

In this one is conscious of extending Heidegger's lead, *mutatis mutandis*, in speaking of the critical role of mood in figuring the world of one's existence (*Dasein*). The English word *mood* translates Heidegger's *Stimmung*, and the latter is worth momentary pondering. The verbal stem (*stimmen*) of the noun (*Stimmung*) means "to voice"; as poets know, poetry must be voiced, read aloud, in order to set its resonances reverberating. There is no such thing as "closet drama" in poetry: reading without vocal performance. To recall the face of an absent beloved other is all but simultaneously to hear her voice, itself sufficient to cancel absence, to invoke/evoke presence/presentiment, itself sufficient to facilitate congress. The now elderly can recall when a handwritten letter had the same effect, when voice was embodied in fingerly scrawl. It says much for the present zeitgeist that all this is effaced by the cyber bytes of electronic communication. The western Enlightenment era commonly referred to as "modern," now exported across much of planet Earth, has been supplanted though not entirely left behind by another sublatingly different zeitgeist, that of postmodernity—even if this means only "after the modern." It is this that Stevens's blue guitar comprises, and I consider him among the first and certainly the greatest of American poet-tune players on that postmodern instrument.

Back to the poems themselves. Stevens's poem begins: They said, "You have a blue guitar, / [But] You do not play things as they are." To this the instrumentalist of contemporary zeitgeist rejoins, "Things as they are / Are changed upon the blue guitar." How changed, and from what to what? Changed from the apodicities of the Enlightenment and its confidence in the anthropic principle as the base for "tuning" the full range of existence? The Enlightenment had its own guitar (although to think of Kant playing *any* instrument seems utterly whimsical), but its tune was not things as they *are* but as they are *known* (in a modern scientific sense). Changed from, but toward what? And they said, then, "But play, you must, / A tune beyond us, yet ourselves, / A tune upon the blue guitar / Of things exactly as they are."[8] We may, can, and shall contest the word "exactly." (Is exactitude the province of the arts or the sciences, or some combination of both?) What is changed on the blue guitar of the succeeding epoch, our epoch, is the mood or world of "things as they are."

For that change one must read, must *realize*, the blue guitar in conjunction with verses of Stevens's "The Snow Man": "For the listener, who listens in the snow, / And, nothing himself, beholds / Nothing that is not there and the nothing that is."[9] This is the oceanic sea change of *Zeitgeistlichkeit* from modernity to postmodernity. That change cast waves before it almost immediately in the continental successors to Kant, especially in the Romantic philosophers and artists, themselves the precursors of the mood of postmodernity. It was they who thought with greater radicality than Kant the loss of the "last enchantments" (Matthew Arnold), the demise of the plenary indulgence of all the old ipseities (things in themselves), the effacement of the comforts of all forms of ontotheology. The change on the blue guitar is the reintroduction of Being's primordial twin, the *nihil*—essential if one is to play the "Nothing that is not there and the nothing that is." It has been charged that postmodernity is marked by nihilism, which is in some senses true. The question outstanding and unresolved is whether the *nihil* can be given its due without resulting in an exhaustive nihilism, construed as utter indifference to matters of meaning and value.

Pre-facing the Divine

God is a word in the English language. Its referent is not borne on the face of common experience; it is rather a question put to its user, and for taking up this question, recourse to a dictionary is pointless. The question is the more complex for engaging the user in a quest for an answer, making the question doubly referential. The word *God* reposing in the inventory of language offers the occasion to think God, no more, no less. As long as *God* is in the language, it will be a potential goad to think God. In this, as in much else, the philosopher Karl Marx was wise. He welcomed modern atheism for lifting the burden of religion and its God as an ideological tool of oppression (*das Opium des Volkes*), but he looked forward to the disappearance of atheism itself, since the disappearance of atheism would entail the disappearance of the word *God* from the lingua franca of succeeding cultures. The word *God* still appears in language, thus meeting Plato's first mark of being, namely, that it "shows itself" (*phainomena* meaning literally "things that shine"). Two cultural phenomena today would have astonished and challenged Marx's analytical genius: the simultaneously abounding atheisms of successive generations among the "cultured despisers of religion," and the even more abounding atavistic fundamentalisms of the religious monotheisms (even if thinking God at mind's length is more evident in the former than in the latter). The word *God* is still present in the language, awaiting the actualization of its *there is*, the real-ization of its referential range.

The oldest words in a language are the most enduring and self-assertive, however used and abused. They are *signi-ficant* in the strict etymological sense of "showing pertinent signs" because they are longevous watching briefs for regions of concern that humankind has inhabited recurrently since time immemorial. Sometimes they are dismissed as "mere" words (utterly conventional, as dispensable as convention is), as dangling signifiers, to be taken or left by whim. But I repeat that they are enduring: a store of both mindful memory (*anamnesis*) and mindful forgetfulness (*Lethe*). The three principal old words used (and abused?) in this book are God, Being, and Nothingness. Each of these words has its ownmost potentiating force, and how each qualifies the others is the problematic at hand. Given that *God* is still a word in language, in the symbolism of scripture, God has not left godself without a witness, even if it is but a linguistic goad to thinking God.

Dear reader, in this thought-experiment in thinking God I cannot offer you "results," not now, nor in any possible conclusion. I can only invite you into the region of the vocative word *God*. Thinking is a solitary art, no one can think for another, and in thinking of this sort one can think only that in which one can *live*, live understandingly and mindfully. It is true that thinking is to be severely disciplined, especially through the discipline of self-wariness, for which one welcomes and is grateful for instruction by severe taskmasters. But one stands under the instructions of others, as Augustine wrote so presciently in *De magistro*, only until the "inner monitor" has been aroused, until there is evoked within that responsible voice commensurate with one's ownmost vocative, invoking, provoking thinking itself, even thinking against itself, since the distinction between the thinker and the thought loses its edgy liminality.[1]

The reason I cannot give you, the reader, *results* of thinking God owes to many factors; here I offer only the principal one. Perhaps there are some kinds of thinking in which the person gets her thoughts settled and ordered, then rummages in the tool bag of language use for communicating the lot, but thinking divinity is not that sort of venture, nor is it that of any of the old words here being thought through. Why does the thinker of God bring herself to speech at all? For only one honorable reason: to know for the first time what she thinks. We all know the dodge used by students and teachers alike, "I know what I want to say, but I don't have the words"—which effectively means they do not know and have not thought. In this dimension one writes or speaks in order to know what one thinks, or does, that is, if the indissoluble link between language and thinking is not to be denied. One speaks or writes first and foremost to apprehend, to dis-cover, to identify thinking's sought, all of which precede predication, the filling of the blanks of what is made manifest in the clearing of language coming together. The point may be scored in Maurice Merleau-Ponty's characteristically precise terms: "The reason why the thematization of the signified does not precede speech is that it is the result of it. . . . The consequences of speech, like those of perception (and particularly the perception of others) always exceed its premises."[2] What it is all about emerges only in the language itself and comes into understanding, if at all, retro-spectively. If these matters are unknown, thus not voiced in college and university departments of speech, communication, or composition, they are known by writers, poets, artists who think. Speech and writing concerned with the identity of the region of divinity are saturated with excess greater than their premises, an excess that spills over in the displace-ments of predication, the blanks to be filled by living and dying existence.

God and *the divine* are used interchangeably in these pages, and in re-spect of thinking their *what*, both are placeholders for a wide phenomeno-logical range of intentional objects of mind: the holy, the sacred, ultimate reality, matters of ultimate concern, and the like. For pure thought the phenomenological range of the divinity is indeterminate and arguably indeterminable, especially if that range is open-ended, that is, includes unfinished theophantic emergences. For the actual and active thinking of the divine, there is no such thing for the *who* of such thinking—the thinker of the divine—as pure indeterminacy, if for no better reason than that she thinks always in and through the language that is her destiny and its own determinacies. Given the relation between the signifiers and the signified of the divine within any language (which relation is yet to be mulled over), what is true in this respect of the *who* obtains also for the *what* (the signified) of the divine, the intentional object of signifiers. So near the heart of the problematic before us in thinking the divine is this: What is determinate and what is indeterminate in thinking the divine— which arguably is also Conrad's "heart of darkness"?

Thinking the *What* and the *Who*

There is no thinking divinity directly and all at once, as though "it" were a palpable object in the cosmic inventory and the task of thought were only and merely to configure the contours of mind to those of the object. As in many ventures of thought, thinking the divine involves metacogni-tion: thinking *about* thinking of God. One requires the patience of *solvitur ambulando*, one step at a time, to arrive in the phenomenological range of the *sought* of thought, which, not yet known, is unnamed. Thinking *about* thinking God is not the same as thinking God, which is why the former is called metacognition. One aspires not to think *about* the divine God but to think the divine God godself. *Who* is the one who thinks God? Who is the seeker when the sought is divinity itself? Pseudo-Dionysius the Areopagite can scarcely be improved upon: at the highest peaks of thinking divinity, "one is neither oneself nor someone else."[3]

For one thing, thinking the holy is sourced not in the lucidities of discursively determinate concepts but in the intimations on the verges of tenebrous monitions, intimations themselves at once flowing down from the upland pastures cradled in the redoubts of the mind's fells,[4] and bubbling up from the waters of primordial chaos—before God spoke all there is and is not into being-there. For another thing, what strictures from all thinking *about* the divine apply to thinking the divine solely as the subject matter of thinking? The importance of such thinking is by no means restricted to the divine: most of the things most precious to us we less think *about* than think *them*. One such stricture is critical, both to thinking those precious to us and intimately on or at hand and to thinking deity itself (which is not in any robust sense at or on hand). An incorrigible inclination of mind is to think affirmatively, to make positive affirmations in respect of the "properties" (the *what*) of the divine. But negation is essential to all determinateness, as will be much discussed hereafter. So dynamic is the impulse of the affirmative in the mind's *Tendenz* that it is alerted stricturally and reversed only by the primordial energy of the Negative in the indeterminacy of divinity itself, especially the divine self-negation, or what Hegel described as the accidents of the Negative, over which we must tarry.[5]

At the outset one does well to tarry as well over the complexities of the metacognitive in respect of holding the divine at mind's length; hence these present pre-facings of the divine. I have just mentioned the adage *solvitur ambulando* (solution or resolution step by step: thinking, like walking, proceeds in a process of morphological genesis). This homely analogy invites expansion. No hominid biped while walking thinks *about* walking; she just walks, but often thinkingly, meditatively, or speculatively. To step-by-step ambulation may be added another old observation, that if a centipede had to think about which leg to move ahead of another it would collapse in immobile stasis. None of us remembers learning to walk, but by observation of human infants one knows the morphology of walking: first one crawls on all fours, then falteringly rises on one foot, quickly puts the other one under and ahead, and advances stumblingly.[6]

Thus one understands Plato's description of man as "a featherless biped" (featherless, thus without wings, so a two-footer who walks), as one "gets" his riddle of the sphinx ("what walks initially on four, then on two, and finally on three"—two feet and a cane or staff). Walking as the body's inducement to contemplative thinking, indeed as the fleshed *speculum* (mirror) of thinking not trained on an overt goal, has attracted the attention of many philosophers. Aristotle noted that walking is the human form of locomotion by arrested falling forward: one rises on one foot but begins to fall toward the other, estopped only by quickly lifting the other foot, the while maintaining lateral balance by the swinging of arms (so we do have "wings" after all, not to bear us aloft but to keep us sufficiently upright that the next foot may reach its "ground"). Heidegger spoke of thinking's space as walking in the woods on wood-paths (*Holzwege*), in which thinking's pace is cadenced not by the goal of exiting the woods but by paths (some made by animals) within the forest itself. To exit the woods is but to return to the conventioned paths of the "they" and their goal-oriented thinking, not to mention their instrumental pragmatism governing breach of all technical obstacles to attain "the goal." The solitary thinker (thinking is not a "team sport") walks around in the woods to evade the disorientation of a thinking already set in a course and its body of settled representations, so that wandering wonderment may present to the thinker thinking's ownmost subject. So Ishmael listens in tempestuous seas to the thump of Ahab's whale-ivory peg leg on the hold of the deck above him in quiet hours, as that "old hunks of a sea captain," that "meditative Magian Rover" (Ahab) thumps the upper decks in anticipation of the presentiment of what has beleaguered the primordial depths of his thinking, the Great Whale. Finally, in a list that could go on, one thinks of Thoreau in his essay "Walking." He claims thinking that counts is not dissociable from walking, a meditative walking that is not deliberate but is rather is a *sauntering*. With whatever etymological merit, he derives *saunter* from *sainte terre*, so that a contemplative walker or saunterer is a *saint-terrer*, a pilgrim on the path to the holy land, though he know not what or where that may be. If thinking bears an analogy with walking, these metaphors (*metaphorein* meaning a carrying over) bear pondering at the outset of pre-facing the divine.

Every analogy, as historians of thought *about* analogy know, bears the burden of some disanalogy, of difference as well as similarity between the analogue and the analogate. In the present matter, the disanalogy between thinking and walking is that walking is linear (one cannot walk in all directions at once) whereas thinking is not. Thinking that is hermeneutically veridical is not circular but spiral.[7] Thinking that was linearly circular would revolve upon itself or, as in a "vicious circle," would only unpack what it assumes. For a thinking held steadfast into its subject, the image of its directionality is not that of a circle but that of a helical spiral. Technically, a helical spiral is the curve assumed by a straight line drawn on a plane when that plane is wrapped around a cylindrical surface, in particular a right circular cylinder, for example the curve of a screw or bolt thread, or the wire of a spring. Thus thinking on this image-model does not return to the thing thought at the beginning of thought's motion but to another point in the spiraling plane of thought's sought, hence an expansion of phenomenological field of both thinker and "thing" thought.

One other disanalogy between thinking and walking is noteworthy, one that amounts to a caution about *solvitur ambulando* (one step at a time). Developmentally, baby steps precede giant steps in walking. Disciplined thinking, however, moves to a different drummer. Just this difference is honored in the exhortation to attend first to the giant steps of metacognition before taking the baby steps of entering the phenomenological region of the divine, and even this honors two hoary injunctions from the western history of thought:

(1) "Like knows like." Transparently the first "like" in this adage is not and cannot be the same as the second "like," else there would be no "problem" of knowledge. In the case of thinking the divine, the thinker who is putatively mortal is to be likened to the divine *what* that is putatively not mortal. Because all "likening" proceeds through and not around a course of unlikelies, all thinking of the divine is like a set of canal locks between two bodies of water at different levels, such that the thinker is alternately raised and who/what the thinker thinks is lowered, until ideally both are progressively commensurated or "adequated." But, also, because unlikeness is never fully effaced by thinking, a certain melancholia, trauma, or perplexity of mind befalls the divine fells at mind's length.

(2) "What is first in the order of knowing may be last in the order of being"—and also, I should add, "in the order of not-being." For present purposes, this injunction is of less significance than (1). Suffice to say that it is a prime instance of thinking *about* the divine rather than having the *who* or *what* of the divine as the subject of thinking itself. It yielded the priority of epistemology over ontology/meontology, moving inductively from the best/better known to the less known, finally resting in the "that" of a first cause as *ground* with no resources on which to draw in respect of its *what*. Its yield was and always is a religiously undivine divine, as is that of all the classical "proofs" for the existence of the divine (the great possible exception being that of Anselm of Canterbury's so-called ontological argument). But this yield involves many turns of the screw and need not be tarried over now. More important is a distinction so far only implicit, one that needs now to be made explicit. I refer to a critical distinction between thinking and research.

Making, characterizing, and honoring the distinction between thinking and research do not come easily to one who has spent his adult life in a modern western research university, as I have. Such a distinction would have been unintelligible—and on their terms, unintelligent—to western premodern universities or their functional equivalent. The pre-Socratic schools, say, the Milesian and Eleatic, comprised solitaries whose thinking centered on elements that today would be thought *physical* but also included elements as much ideational as physical (such as *nous*, mind, or *apeiron*, the unlimited). These thinkers are often said to be the first scientists in the West, but that is true only by qualification. While they did think the physical elements and thus did contribute to a rudimentary taxonomy or Table of Elements, the aspiration of their thinking was to comprehend the constituents of cosmic reality as such. Their true lineage extends not to the modern laboratory scientist but to contemporary theoretical astrophysicists, quantum physicists, microbiologists, neurologists both micro and macro—those who think both the biggest and smallest "things" cosmologically and cosmogonically—those who think such things rather than thinking *about* such things, and so aspire to "the theory of everything." However, unlike many modern academic theoreticians, the pre-Socratic "naturalists" held the noun *theory* strictly to the verb within it as activated by thinking: *theorein*, to see. For an Anaximander or an Anaximines, to make an element itself the subject of thinking is *visionary*. It would scarcely be too much to claim that such thinking is *performative*, that it sees-says the world from the element's inside out. Just such a claim has been advanced and defended in its most robust form by arguably one of the greatest of modern historians of science, Gaston Bachelard, who asserts (and amplifies) that the earliest Greek thinkers performed a psychoanalysis (in the modern sense) of the elements.[8]

The successor to these solitaries, as diverse as Thales, Parmenides, and Heraclitus, was the First Academy (or Old Academy), the form of which was not an institution in either the medieval or modern sense but a symposium in its particularly Greek embodiment, whose course alternated between banqueting, ribaldry, performance of the arts, and rigorous thinking. Over such symposia Plato presided as both maestro and magister. Participants were not solitaries but colloquialists, each evincing from the other what he already knows but has forgotten and has to realize, through *anamnesis*, in order to think—Socrates being the goad of this enterprise. The surprise of *anamnesis* is that in its residue there is the recognition that one both knows and does not know, and has some vague prehension of what one does not know. In this surprise are harbored the two essential items of thinking itself, as distinct from thinking *about*: identification and predication. Suffice it to summarize what goes on in the thinking of the Platonic dialogues: when thinking is given over to thinking's subject matter, the phenomenological range is extended not only to the *what* (the subject matter) that is thought but also to the *who* of the subject (the one thinking). So the thinking under way in Plato's dialogues is elemental thinking of the elements both in subject and subject matter.

It may be useful to offer an example of identification and predication as critical to thinking's subject matter by reference to Bachelard, just mentioned. Bachelard claimed that in the history of scientific thinking there are abrupt turns in the *what* of thinking (what I have called identification) occasioned by an epistemic obstacle (*obstacle épistémologique*) the thoughtful way through and not around which is by epistemic rupture (*rupture épistémologique*, what I have called predication). A prime example is so central a notion in physics (and especially astrophysics) as that of mass. Up to and including Newton, the *what* of thinking mass was under the model of "substance," in metaphysical language a self-standing term. But incipient quantum physics could no longer think mass solely as self-standing term and had to think it rather as relations (predications), both internally and externally, as involving time and space; hence Einstein's theory of relativity. (Thomas Kuhn's theory of paradigm shifts in scientific thinking is likely indebted to Bachelard.)

Let us be so brash as to enter where some scholarly angels have feared to tread and offer a summary of the "yield" of Plato's elemental thinking of elements: those irreducible elements figuring in a "theory of everything." He aspired to think *what is there* in the world under the eye of *what there is* always and already; this is done in the middle period, largely in the *Philebus* and the *Sophist*, wherein he suggests something like a Table of Ontological and Meontological Elements. First, not in order of time but in order of identification and predication, as is the case of all primordial elements, is the "mixed," the thing presenting itself to be perceived and thought (what in later scholastic thought would be termed the *haecceitas*, the determinate thing). Second is the "limit" (*peras*) presiding over the mixed; else the mixed would not be itself but some other. Third is the "unlimited" (*apeiron*), the "womb of becoming" also presiding over the mixed; else the mixed would have no "stuff." Fourth is the cause, or artificer of the union of limit and unlimited in the mixed, however much the cause may be in flux, which he calls *psyche* (soul), with the supreme instance of *psyche* being the *demiurgos* (Plato's nearest analogue of thinking's divine *who* and *what*, which, however, is no Creator but rather an artificer or mixer of the always and already obtaining elements). Fifth is the *telos*, the end or purpose of all mixtures, which Plato identifies as the Good, and which he predicates in the *Republic* as "exceeding Being (*to on*) in dignity and power" (509b). Further, the artificer god is not omnipotent: "he persuades the unlimited to receive the limit to serve the Good as well as he can" (48a). One should note that as Plato thinks what *is* there within time and space under the eye of what there *is* always and everywhere, his table of identifications and predications is asymmetrically tilted toward *being*. He acknowledges this and promises to take up nonbeing and a similar table or taxonomy for it in a promised dialogue, the *Philosopher* (which, if ever written, has not survived). But he did not cease thinking of nonbeing, and notes toward that thinking are found in his last period, in *Parmenides*, *Timaeus*, and *Laws*. There one finds what could be a sixth element, the *chora*, or the "space" of the conditions for thinking both being and nonbeing. I shall return to reflections on the *chora* when thinking being and nonbeing in relation to the divine.

For present purposes these two examples of early western thinking (of the elements in pre-Socratic thinkers, and the elemental thinking of the elements in Plato's Academy) must suffice. The First Academy was succeeded by the Second or New Academy, which gave itself over to skeptical thinking or unthinking the thinking of the first. Indeed, were one to extend this tale from the classical period to modern and postmodern forms, one could plausibly claim that the figure to preside over its full course is that of Homer's Penelope, weaving thinking by day, unweaving or unraveling it by night. The figure itself is worth a momentary pondering, even if it cannot be followed in its full sweep. There are two matters under this figure that inhibit thinking the divine, particularly if weaving and unweaving are not kept in dialectical tension.

(1) The project of thinking the divine as the subject matter of thinking itself not infrequently has been inhibited by the tendency to issue in "the system." One well knows that this is a contentious and much contested claim, since many philosophers have claimed that the very intention of a system of thought is the divine, since the divine is putatively the very apogee of thought. The problem in this counterview is that with "the system" all thinking of the divine has been rendered determinate by the requirements of "the system," such that all primordial matters of *identification of* and *predication about* the divine have been long since settled. The dots between the lines have been drawn. Once "the system" is in place, it is uncommonly difficult to uncover, recover, discover the elemental thinking of the elements that went into the construction of "the system."

One could illustrate this inhibition almost at random from the history of western thought. I shall do so by a brief unpacking of an insight from Hannah Arendt, that "since the philosophical schools of antiquity, philosophers have exhibited an annoying inclination toward system building, and we often have trouble disassembling the constructions they have built when trying to uncover what they really thought."[9] While Arendt does not do so, let us look to Plotinus, arguably the first great thinker after classical antiquity to think within a system, and certainly the greatest as ascertained from his influence upon the first millennium of thinkers in the Christian era. Leave aside the technical and scholarly question of whether Plotinus himself was a systematician, of what he derived from Ammonius Saccas and other Alexandrians, including whether the *Enneads* are from his own hand. It is well known that Plotinus committed his insights to a plethora of notes written in an all but illegible hand, the sum of which comprised his oeuvre, and that from these notes it fell to his students (notably Porphyry) to systematize them in the *Enneads*. But how does one afterthink Plotinus? How does one think not Plotinus but what Plotinus thought, especially the divine? Surely among the most stunning of ironies in the history of western thought is the fact that among his appropriators, whether Christian, Jewish, or Muslim, all account themselves philosophically as Neoplatonists. But what of Plato's thinking of the primordial elements survives in the *Enneads*? The plurality of thinking's matter, the elements, is reduced to the One (beyond Being, saying, and *nous*); the subject, the thinker of the divine as thinking's subject matter, like any and every item in time and space, is without remainder a mere privation— indeed, is a diremption of the One. If this bold summary is anywhere near the mark, the *Enneads* is a systematization not of Plato but of a dyadic claim from Parmenides: "Only Being is; non-being is not and cannot be thought."[10] In any case, the *Enneads* offers a prime example of what Harold Bloom calls the anxiety of influence. The "system" may well have virtue as a stimulator of thinking the divine, but that virtue is accompanied by a curse, an inhibitor of the selfsame thinking. As we shall see, the system is not the only curse.

Perhaps we should step back from identifying this or that "tree" of the inhibition of thinking the divine and enlarge our vision to the horizon of the "forest" of the divine. In the cosmically short history of humankind, human persons have been both blessed and cursed by an allegedly indelible sense of that in reality, whether as ground (or origin) or goal (*telos*), which is of highest worth and which lays incorrigible claims upon human existence. The placeholder for this common human sense is the *sensus religiosus* (so Rudolf Otto in his classic *The Idea of the Holy*).[11] Otto identifies both the *what*, the subject matter of the divine or holy—the *numen*—and the *who*, the subject of the *sensus religiosus* as the fundamental *mysterium* of wakeful consciousness. To this identification he adds equally primitive predications. Of the holy in its widest horizons is characterized by him as simultaneously *mysterium tremendens et fascinans*: at once the power in reality that horrifies, disfigures, and destroys (thus is repelling if not repulsive) and the power that figures, reconfigures, and creates anew (thus is fascinatingly attractive). Otto is a prime modern exemplar of the application of critical consciousness to the conjunction of philosophy of religion and history of religions. As philosopher of religion he advanced his theory (in the classical sense of a "seeing" of the whole) of the *sensus religiosus*; as historian of religions he undertook to detail the wide and often wild variations of predications in respect of the divine Holy in their determinate variations by time and place.[12] It is of course an old and continuing modern western argument whether the *sensus religiosus* is "natural" or "cultural." For myself, I take it to be established (as far as anything can be established in matters pertaining to responsible thinking) that this sense is both, and that neither can be undertaken without the other.

(2) Having mentioned critical consciousness, I turn to that and its larger academic context as a second possible inhibitor of thinking the divine. While there can be no question of extending even this cursory review from the emergence of thinking the divine via "system" to the present in the West, it is worth pausing over developments in the career of critical consciousness as it has become the central preoccupation of the modern academy in all disciplines of thought. A giant step indeed from the second to the nineteenth and twentieth and now the twenty-first century CE! The Middle Ages of Christendom had "scholastics" to be sure, but only in a sense of schools disanalogous with modern universities. There was thinking of the divine of a high order, but largely by solitaries (Eckhart, exiled from the University of Paris to preach to noncloistered beguines at Erfurt; Nicholas of Cusa, when he could steal time from his duties as an archbishop and cardinal). Truly remarkable is that notwithstanding their solitariness these thinkers of the divine were able to think radically differently but interactively and dialogically (Aquinas, Maimonides, Ibn Sina: "interreligious dialogue" is not an invention of late modernity). Many were able and willing to think both within and against their traditions of inquiry; some were willing transgressors of "authority" worthy of admiration by any modern or postmodern thinker of the divine, willing and eager to think the *what* of the divine wherever thought led (although not a few paid the price: Savonarola, Bruno, Eckhart).

Even so, thinking consciousness in the Middle Ages was not "critical" in the modern western sense. The fundaments of the critical sense came with the apogee of the Middle Ages in its successor the Renaissance, particularly in Florence, and the *anamnesis* (not repetition but rather a sublation at a higher level) of classical humanism. The new humanism (Ficino, Bruno, Vico, and others) entailed an unweaving/unthinking and a reweaving/rethinking of Penelope's garment for the turning/returning Odysseus who was to wander the new world of the arts and sciences.

In hindsight the Renaissance seems preparatory for the most decisive step into modern western critical consciousness (not to mention critical unconsciousness![13]), that of the Protestant Reformation. However odd this turn may appear to purely secular humanists not knowledgeable of the details of the Protestant Reformation in northern Europe, the turn itself vested in the thoroughgoingly radical character of Luther's theory (or doctrine) of "the priesthood of all believers." This single idea all but encompasses the whole of his Ninety-Five Theses, and is fraught with implications for thinking anything whatever, but especially for thinking both the *what* of the divine and the *who* of that thinking. If all vocations are of equal worth in the face of that which is of highest supreme worth, no "profession" (monastic, clerical, or otherwise ecclesiastically ordered) is superior to any other. (So Jakob Böhme in the earliest days of the Reformation, a shoe cobbler, was freed for his speculations that proved powerfully influential in the lowland countries and England [William Blake], and much later in Hegel and Schelling. Not to mention Spinoza, a lens grinder in the subsequent Enlightenment.) Luther's thinking brought in its tow a radical rethinking of "authority" in all thinking. He himself recognized but two sources of authority: scripture and the individual's conscience. Well known is the fact that on scripture Lutheran Protestantism split early on into two factions in rivalry, the right wing in support of a Protestant scholasticism that outdid medieval scholasticism in stringency, and the left wing in opposition to any and all state-established religion. The unweaving and unraveling of the garment of authority is a complex and time-consuming enterprise. It was not until the Enlightenment that a thinker of the divine of highest merit under the new paradigm, Benedict Spinoza (himself an unobservant Jew), rewove the garment of scripture. And only in the nineteenth century was critical historical consciousness applied directly and fully to scripture (however incipiently the same was present *avant la lettre* in Spinoza) whether Christian, Jewish, or Muslim, and the study of scripture has not been the same since. In the interim, of course, was the Enlightenment, which applied critical thinking about conscience and so to the authority of consciousness thus governed, the apogee of which arguably was the oeuvre of the Lutheran pietist Immanuel Kant.

The cultural, social, and political residue of Luther's "priesthood of all believers" was the reweaving of the garment of the profession for the teacher/scholar, and above all its institutional embodiment, in Germany ultimately the research university, a union of but also a sublation beyond its several "faculties." If these changes of profession and institution in northern Europe were radical, they were even more so for American institutions. Since colonial days in the United States institutions of higher learning had been colleges of liberal arts, the earliest and most prestigious of which were founded for a twofold purpose, "to educate students of divinity" and "to train civil magistrates," thus to serve both church and state ("commonwealth"), as in the charter of Harvard College. In the nineteenth century America adopted the German model and transformed its colleges into research universities oriented to graduate studies under the trajectory of critical consciousness in all disciplines. With the decline and disarray of German universities following two wars in the twentieth century, America has led the world in graduate education. But even now, since the process of weaving and unweaving Penelope's garment for the turning/returning Odysseus is unending, are the needles and scissors passing from North America to the Orient, above all to China, where not only in the sciences but in the humanities, arguably most notably in the passion for the study of religion, where the teacher/scholar/thinker appears to be finding a transfigured home?

In any event, all these factors are to be kept in mind as one assesses whether in thinking the divine the distinction between thinking *of* and scholarly thinking *about* is a blessing or a curse. And another blessing cum curse remains yet to be parsed (see below), that of what the *who* brings by way of presuppositions (often largely unaware) to thinking the *what* of the divine. But immediately we must attend to the very word *God*.

God the Word

Whoever cannot seek the unforeseen sees nothing, for the known way is an impasse.
—HERACLITUS

All roads to the mind start in the soul, but none lead back there again.
—ROBERT MUSIL

All I have is a voice
To undo the folded lie . . .
—W. H. AUDEN

There is a crack, a crack in everything
That's how the light gets in . . .
—LEONARD COHEN

It is one thing to think, and another thing to exist in what has been thought.
—SØREN KIERKEGAARD

If I really want to write something, I must erase and eliminate everything that is already there; and the tablet is never so good for me to write on as when there is nothing on it at all.
—MEISTER ECKHART

Perfection is not when there is nothing more to add; perfection is when there is nothing left to take away.
—JOHN L. HENNESSY[14]

This florilegium of epigrams is offered in aid of continuing our thought-experiment, that of apostrophizing words as having a force field of their own in interrupting the vast abyss of silence that befalls every thinker of all matters of ultimate human concern. So encompassing is such a silence that it becomes compressed as "the ineffable," heralded by mystics in multiple religious cultures as the cloud of unknowing, the dark night of the soul, closing both eyes and mouth (*mystic* from *muein*, to close, i.e., eyes and lips). It was the project of modernity, starting with seventeenth-century rationalism's "substance," and especially of the Enlightenment, to reduce the ineffable to the fewest possible words (but oh! the innumerable words that took!) about the largest regions, thus ignoring the old rule or law of the inverse relation between the intension and the extension of words.[15] German luminaries of the nineteenth century reveled in the post-Kantian extension of the project to "eff" the ineffable with mounting conceptual precision by way of "system" (however oxymoronic). Of these, the three greatest philosophers were Fichte, Hegel, and Schelling, who were paralleled by the poet Hölderlin, all having been trained originally in guild theology (the last three as roommates at Tübingen Seminary). Their effect on guild theology in their day was minimal, and arguably is even less so today—sigh, a lamentable fact!

Of these it is Schelling who is most pertinent to the matter presently at issue. Having established himself early on as a brilliant *systematiker* of the philosophic sciences, a writer of furious pace, at roughly middle age he began to fall publicly silent. He wrote draft after draft of *The Treatise on Freedom* and *The Ages of the World*, finishing neither, completing only a third of the latter. His last thirty years were a time of public silence, yet he worked privately, feverously, and fervently with and against his own silences, bringing himself if but partially to speech in drafts of *The Philosophy of Mythology* and *The Philosophy of Revelation*, which were published in their rough form only posthumously.

What accounted for the turn in Schelling's thought is a contested matter among the Schellingian specialists, but there are more than hints in both *The Treatise on Freedom* and *The Ages of the World*. He came to be at dis-ease with the *results* of philosophical thinking, whether his own or that of his colleagues and their predecessors. On the one hand, they were if unwittingly extending the project begun with the seventeenth-century continental rationalists, that of taking thought to the "ground," itself irreducible, necessary and sufficient to bear the weight of thought constructed on its base. Yes, there had been some advance: he and his co-idealist identity-difference philosophers thought within the wreckage wreaked by Kant's bombs thrown into all metaphysical playpens. Still, he and they were aiming toward *results*, results following upon a ground, a repositioned ground to be sure, but a ground nonetheless. On the other hand, Schelling discerned a deeper problematic in all philosophy including his own, namely, that it proceeds invariably reductively and negatively, by erasure, until in its results it can erase and negate no more and calls that "the ground." But is a ground derived by negation anything positive at all? Anything on which to base a positive philosophy? Is it not rather a groundlessness, an abyss of nonbeing as much as of being? In these questions Schelling effectively returns to a thinker without philosophical predecessors who cared not a fig for results, Jakob Böhme, acknowledged by both Schelling and Hegel to be the father of German philosophy, whose term for the groundless abyss was *Ungrund/Abgrund*, the living in and out of which precedes any determinate or determinable ground.

Schelling was escorted to his engagement with the indeterminate abyss of groundlessness by his ruminations on freedom (in *The Treatise on Freedom*) and by his quest of the ground of historical time (in *The Ages of the World*). The latter had aspired to think the three modes of time (past, present, future). Finding no ground for their coincidence, he was to admit that his earlier thinking about identity and difference held no basis for their coincidence either. So frozen was he upon the past mode of time that he was unable even to draft manuscripts toward the present and the future (the unwritten two-thirds of *The Ages of the World*). No other thinker of historical time (the time of human *Dasein*, being-there) since Meister Eckhart was to think time so radically. He knew that historical time (despite Hegel) had escaped the net of Idea (or Concept) that he and other identity thinkers had set, yet his intuition (of Augustinian provenance) perdured that the past lives in all its opacity in the groundless ground of the present, as it harbors potencies awaiting future realization, itself awaiting the like groundlessness of human freedom. "*O Vergangenheit, du Abgrund der Gedanken!*" (Oh the past, you abyss of thoughts!)[16]

With these observations, knowledgeable readers will have brought Martin Heidegger already to mind. In some respects Schelling was indeed Heidegger *avant la lettre*. But the likeness goes further (not to speak of the differences). I have spoken of Schelling's "turn" from transcendental idealism's quest for a postrationalist, post-Kantian ground toward the groundlessness of thinking freedom and historical time. It is common knowledge that Heidegger's relatively early magnum opus *Being and Time* comprised originary (by no means the same as "original") thinking of *Dasein* (being-there) *by Dasein* thrown into a world temporally horizoned by death. As such and wholly within itself, this was a project in thinking onticity, one's ownmost being-there in one's own temporally horizoned world, thinking *existentiell*, and doing so phenomenologically, not metaphysically in any classical sense. Any hopes that Heidegger would have then turned to the relation of *Dasein* to *Sein* (from human being-there to Being as encompassing all that has being) would have been hopelessly unfounded in *Being and Time*. For one thing, in that book he had not accorded to *time* the attention he had to *Dasein* except as horizoned by time, but time itself as yet not thought through to its "ground."

After this early work Heidegger's subsequent thinking was—thinking itself. His thinking was off the beaten paths, the thinking of the *Einsamer* sauntering the *Holzwege*. But even forest trails end—in nowhere, in thickets, brambles, darkness, any of these scarcely a "ground." There one tarries and dwells until a "clearing," "lightening," "lightning" (Böhme's *Schreck*) inhabits the *choric* space (*chora*, Plato's primordial placeholder for the region of thinking the fundaments), space wherein there sounds an *alethe logon* (or *logoi*), a word or words emanating just this side of Lethe, this side of the limn of darkness and the shades, harkening to which, thinking is summoned to speech.

For this and like "turns" in his thinking Heidegger credits his rereading and afterthinking of two predecessors, Nietzsche and Schelling: on time and its groundlessness, Nietzsche on the will and the resolve to "the eternal recurrence of the same"; on freedom and its groundlessness, Schelling's *Treatise on Freedom*. In the latter, Heidegger takes as the critical sentence "Freedom not the property (*Eigenschaft*) of the human but rather the human the property of freedom."[17] Schelling progressively disassociated himself from rationalist "substance" theories of the ground, and no one ever thought Heidegger was even near to such a metaphysically loaded "result." What Heidegger came to see, what Schelling had said explicitly, is that freedom is both before and after any identifiable ground. For Schelling, freedom as pursued by result-oriented philosophy that proceeds by negation is, in the robustly pertinent sense, groundless: "How could we call it [freedom] anything else other than the primordial ground, or rather better the non- or no-ground?" (*Wie können wir es anders nennen al den Abgrund oder vielmehr Ungrund?*)[18] *Ungrund*, the very word suffusing Jakob Böhme's thinking of the Potencies and Freedom.

Let us catch up with ourselves or, rather, go behind ourselves to see where we are. Before these brief and highly selective excursions through Schelling and Heidegger we were considering that the word *God* lies there on the inventory shelf of language as a deposit, and what that fact might in itself betoken, especially in respect of its referential range. Among its characteristics as a deposit in the language, in the word *God* are the contents of the deposit exhausted by all the results of past thinking of God to which I have been exposed and which themselves comprise the presuppositions with which I initially think God? In thinking God am I to add to, or multiply, all those results? Or subtract, erase (think the Cartesian *tabula rasa*)? If erase, erase all? If some but not all, which? (What is the mathematics of thinking God? Nicholas of Cusa had much to say on that in *De docta ignorantia*). For us postmoderns, erasure bids fair to become and already to be a cottage industry, for good reason. But perhaps we should tarry at great length over the silence accompanying the word *God* and the temptation to erase, the while heeding the caution of Henry David Thoreau: "We are double-edged blades, and every time we whet our virtue the return stroke strops our vice."[19]

At this point (and arguably at any) there is no reason to extend and ramify a list of questions about the word *God*, since the very word bears its own questionableness, and if not it becomes merely a floating signifier. *God* is primarily a vocative word, and the vocation of thinking in, through, and around the oldest, most enduring words is such that one may exist in them understandingly in their ceaseless questionability. There is no thinking God without *turba*, as God godself is not without *turba*—as I hope to explicate more fully.

God the Name

Few matters have been more bruited and mooted in theology and the academic study of religion than whether God is not only a word but is also, properly speaking, a *name*. Among some of the simulacra of the divine or "the sacred realm," for example in the historically polytheistic religions (thus gods), the matter is less problematic since the discrimination of one god from another is symbolically indexed by ascribing a name to each. The name ascribed to the god is not a proper-noun name as is the name of an individual human person. However much the avatar person may be a temporal and temporary embodiment, incarnation, or trace of the named god, the god itself names a nontemporal (eternally recurring) identical power or force presiding over human and cosmic time. So in ancient Greek religion Zeus, the *primus inter pares* in the pantheon of deities, names the primordial Energy ("keeper of the lightning bolt") embodied in powerful people (kings, heroes, and similar), and likewise force and its distribution in cosmic occurrences (and so on: Aphrodite [love and the affections among mortals], Apollo [war and strife], Demeter-Persephone [nutrition and sustenance of mortal life]). So in Hinduism, which also has an *inter pares* pantheon, Brahma presides over *creation* or the emergence of what temporally is; Vishnu presides over the *preservation* of what temporally is; and Shiva, symbolized with axe and hammer, presides over *destruction* of what temporally is. The Hindu pantheon in full presides over what is and is not. In sum, in the polytheistic religions, the gods both do and do not have names, properly speaking.

On the naming of God in the western monotheisms one has a different order of complexity, a different phenomenological range of the sacred. And one needs to observe that the three dominant forms of monotheism, Judaism, Christianity, and Islam, were in origin not western in the modern sense but Middle Eastern, and that early adepts of each spread both eastward and westward and now extend to all points on the compass. (But is any religion explicable, exhaustively and without remainder, by its time and location?) To be sure, every religion or program of disciplined and coherent thinking reckons with the incorrigible problem of the one and the many, as westerners call it in respect of ultimate reality. Life itself as preciously valued, whether in humans or in the natural processes of the cosmos, is either multifaceted or multiple in number. Even so, equally valued and precious is a unity, or unifying force, driving the course of multifarious existence, whether that unity be by origin or by *telos*. The same is the case not only in religious cultures but in the cosmos itself. If the universe has such a unitary course as it has by its origin in the explosion/implosion of energy released in the big bang however distributed to the multiple if not innumerable galaxies of planets, what unitary (identical, identifiable) *telos* is served, if any? Is energy contracting through entropy, with entire galaxies (including our own) progressively disappearing into the black holes of nothingness? Or is energy self-renewing/self-aggrandizing, such that the universe is expanding in its multifariousness? The problematic of the one and the many is followed immediately by that of the inverse relation between intension and extension: the more one has of the one, the less one has of the many, and vice versa. Having been beset by the two aforementioned problematics, one then comes upon the paradox at the heart of all monotheisms, since all claim in principle that God is the *coincidentia oppositorum*, the unification of opposites without the diremptive loss of either. Here in his effort to think eternal God in time, Kierkegaard found his aspiration to think what thought cannot think.

To frame the naming of God thus in the three monotheisms just now but briefly sketched may well be thought to be prejudicial to early Christian struggles with naming God. By now it is a commonplace to acknowledge that with the receding of witnesses to the Jesus event and of apostolic remembrance, all in the early Jesus movement within Judaism, in the first and second centuries of the Common Era nascent Christian thinkers relied heavily on Greek philosophical traditions accessible to them both for words (*logos*, *hypostasis*, *ousia*, *personae*, and so on) and thought-forms to express the naming of God. As I trust will become clearer, in these pages I both continue and also robustly contest this tradition. That acknowledgment is followed immediately by another (call it a stipulation, but historically it is a fact), namely, that none of the three monotheisms is said to *derive* from philosophy or any form of human reflection.[20] All are rather said to be religions of "revelation"; that is, each is founded by and in its own theophany (appearance, showing, manifestation of God) or theophanies, transmitted (*traditio*) in its own scripture and in its own body of learned commentary (*traditum*). Thus each of the three monotheisms has its own *Heilsgeschichte* (history of the sacred), since the founding theophany of one is not reducible exhaustively to either of the other two. Even that generalization is to be qualified immediately, for of the three monotheisms only Judaism claims no relation whatever to the founding epiphanies of the other two, whereas Christianity includes the Judaic theophanies not only as preparatory to but as internally related to its own theophanies, and Islam includes both the Judaic and Christian theophanies as preparatory toward the final emendation of the Koran as delivered to and transcribed by the prophet Mohammed.

We are already more than somewhat ahead of ourselves in respect of the name God. For the world today and as far as the eye can see, there appear to be two camps of those who use the name God. In one the name God is used easily, unselfconsciously, all but familiarly, referring of course to the deity (or its simulacra) of the religious culture in which the speaker is an observant adept. In the other camp are those who use the name God because the word *God* is in the language of public discourse, but their own use of the name is suffused with intolerance of cognitive dissonance and in high dubiety about the reference of the name God in the first camp. The descriptor coined for this second camp by Friedrich Schleiermacher in the nineteenth century can scarcely be improved upon: religion's "cultured despisers" (*die Gebildeten unter ihren Verächtern*).[21] Surely it is a stunning fact that the numbers in both camps are now increasing exponentially, however paradoxically. Whereas liberally mindful theologians are alarmed that the growth in the first camp is motored almost without exception by atavistic fundamentalisms, they should be encouraged by the growth of the second, for it is in the issues there exposed that thinking God at mind's length has a future, and that notwithstanding the fact that most cultured despisers of religion are ignorant of the deepest thought in the past pertaining to those issues.

But have I been overhasty and clumsily nondiscriminating in these generalizations? (Yes.) Surely the Muslim will brook no name for God but Allah? As for the Orthodox Jew, not even the word *God* is to be voiced. It may be written, but only in Hebrew with the consonants. (There are exceptions, but only for stipulated persons, ritually purified, and only on prescribed High Holy occasions.) This proscription of the name, and prescriptions in consequence of the proscription, root in Moses's experience of theophany at Sinai, a showing that was a not-showing, since God effectively evaded Moses's plea for God to name godself. "My hind parts you shall see, but my face you shall not see." No man has seen God and lived, but that showing not-showing founded a people named (Isra-el) by one who declined naming himself, a people to live among "the nations" with their gods of many names. Is it any wonder, then, that Jews do not participate an easy, glib, familiar speech about God? And is not such easy naming of God the particular travesty of an atavistic Christianity that persists among us, especially in its most popular clergy, who at least in some theological schools seem to undergo what the French call a *déformation professionelle*, what Rudolf Otto called the development of "professional insensitivity to all things holy"?

Already in the section above, in the pre-facings of the divine at mind's length, one has adopted the heuristic processes of breaching and thinking again the phenomenological range of the sought of thought when deity is the intentionality in mind. For the cultured despiser of religion (nowadays typically the self-ascribed "humanist," whether on an Enlightenment or postmodern model), to accept or in any way honor the name God is to accept that thought has found its sought and need not think further or otherwise. Such a person will understandably deny or reject such a name as it refers to nothing, to no known reality as having intersected or cathected her own reality (never mind that what she denies may well not be affirmed by many mindful adept users of the name). Such a denial carries an indirect point not to be evaded by the thinker of divinity, namely, that all naming involves both a not-knowing and an at least incipient knowing. More exactly, naming engages a knowing not-knowing of the phenomenological range of the named over time. Even more precisely, the name should be commensurate with the sheer indeterminacy of the named as it becomes transmogrified through the determinateness of time and space, the name God not excepted. In short, the name of God is as mysterious as the *what* of God.

An incipient knowing not-knowing is not as abstruse or opaque a matter as it may seem on first blush. Many forms of knowing are initiated by the ascription of names, even if the named is at first so indeterminate and thus neutral as is *x* in equations. Persons meeting initially are introduced by someone with the giving of names or in an exchange of names, typically a family name (species, tribal, generic collectivity) and a "given" name (individuation, *this* concentration of an indeterminate unknown). Conventionally, the exchange of names is followed by the exchange of where each is from and what each does (vocation). Such markers are significant for rendering increasingly determinate something like the full phenomenological range (which hitherto had been wholly indeterminate) for the persons who are initiating mutual exposure. From this initial exposure two things have the potentiality for emergence. The first potency is that the field of indeterminacy of each becomes increasingly determinate as two previously merely external related realities "meet," from which exposure the two become "acquainted." The second potency is the possible incipience of internal relations between those introduced by name and other markers, such that two fields of indeterminacy, rendered freshly determinate, become so intercalated that neither party can be what he or she is without the other: they become "close friends" (in the nth case, lovers). All these moves starting with names are engaged in "getting to know each other."

Is *God* a name in this sense? No, not really, but in a highly qualified sense, yes. Some features of the qualification of this yes (with no intent to be exhaustive) may be mentioned: (1) Abstractly, the account given in the last paragraph but one may stand provisionally. The name God (or its surrogates) introduces the phenomenological force field of deity as distinct from any other for one thinking deity at mind's length. As such the name God is no increment of knowledge but rather is the incipience of a particular kind of knowing not-knowing; to know however vaguely the *that* of the name is not (yet) to know the *what* of the named. (The same is true, of course, with the name of a person just met.) By a "particular kind of knowing not-knowing" is meant a preliminary and provisional monition of the abyssal indeterminacy underlying the vaguely determinate name God, the very Godness (*deitas*) of God (*deus*) (see Topos 1: Theogony for the distinction between God and Godhead). The name God (and surrogates) can be and is rendered determinate in religious cultures, but Godhead, being wholly indeterminate, is not. (2) There is another respect in which the name God may be analogous to the naming of human persons, one that is also a form of knowing not-knowing. Nowadays in the West the naming of infants is largely utterly conventional, drawing from a list of currently fashionable names, or honoring family predecessors by giving the new-born the name of one of them, and so on. But in some religious cultures the naming of the newborn infant is deliberative and takes time, especially among indigenous ("aboriginal") peoples. With the Native Americans of the plains it is common even now for parents, elders, and shamans to attend the specific *what* of the newborn as evident in its spirited behavior before naming the *who*. Each newborn is said to embody or trace the spirit, the very *mana*, of something in nature, whether that of an animal or other vital power (lightning, wind) on which human life depends, of which he or she is thought to be a sister or brother. So the newborn, the child of Father Sky and Mother Earth, renews and extends the becoming not only of tribal humanity but of nature itself (etymologically, "nature" is the region of generation, of being aborning). The name initially proffered the newborn (say, Cunning-Power Wolverine, or Lightning-in-the-Sky Running Horse) is tentative, naming the reality that has emerged on first blush, but subject to the continuing discernment of spirits by those into whose care the new-born has been given. The critical point in naming comes, however, when and as the emergent reality passes through adolescence and at the limns of full self-consciousness enters upon his or her "vision quest," preceded by rituals of purification. In the vision the totem animal, or representative of the natural force, appears to the one bearing the provisional name, confirming the commensuration of the name and the named, the initially designated reality *realized* in the self-consciousness of the *who* and confirmed in the consciousness of the community.

How little of the sense of "natural philosophy" persists among us after the spinning off of that sense into the technicalities of the "natural sciences" (which Goethe so mourned)? How little of Spinoza's wandering wonderment at the ceaseless alternations at work in the becoming of things; how little persists among us of the bowing and nodding of *natura naturata* (nature natured) and *natura naturans* (nature naturing) each to the other as the real is becomingly *real*-ized? How little of Thoreau's and other American transcendentalists' project to enliven the enervated Puritan vision of America as "the new creation" by learning the "mother tongue" of nature, the very seat of becoming, having forsaken the "father tongue" of forsaken shores, how little, how much of this persists among us? Perhaps at least this much: Thoreau, Emerson, Margaret Fuller, and their lot were bent on continuing the Puritan (*mutatis mutandis*) experiment in "new creation." Experiment in two senses: (1) one sense now universally in use in natural sciences, the testing of a claim about phenomena reliably repeatable under strictures of verification, and (2) the sense now archaic but active in the eighteenth century and the time of "natural philosophy," that of *experience*—as in John Wesley's exhortation "Make experiment of God"—in which exhortation the meanings of experience and experiment were thought to be the same.

I have suggested that the matter of thinking God at mind's length is a thought-experiment. As such it cannot involve "experiment" in the first sense (above) since at least in the three monotheisms there can be no question of the controlled repeatability of their founding theophanies (save in the most derivative and recondite of ways). Besides which, each of the monotheisms has its own version of *deus revelatus et absconditus*: there is no revealing that is not also a re-veiling, no showing that is not a not-showing, no uncovering that is not a re-covering. So it is only in the second sense of "experiment," that of *experience*, that we may hope. This hope is part and parcel of the very questionableness and provisionality of thinking God. Can one think God at mind's length and *live* experientially in what one thinks?

Saying the Ineffable

As Godhead even more than God is the supreme test case of what is too awesome, sacred, or overwhelming to be expressed in words, it is apropos here to say something about saying the unsayable, the central problem of language in all theologies, whether cataphatic or apophatic. (You would have thought, the comedian Tom Lehrer once said, apophatic theologians would at least have had the sense to shut up![22]) There is no happy choice between the historical and systematic extremities, between the absolute negations of apophasis (God or Godhead is *not* . . . this or that) and the affirmations, however analogical, of cataphasis (God is . . . one, true, good, being). The extremity of the interdiction of all affirmation whatever, raised to the nth power of negation and thus rendered vacuous for want of all positive contrast terms, can only eventuate in the vow of silence, as in Wittgenstein's proposition "Whereof one cannot speak, thereof one must be silent."[23] If this is the systematic extremity of the saints' logic, historically they—positioning themselves *in* the madness of Godhead— observe the vow of silence in the breach: they give themselves to an excessive lugubriousness of language, whether for the sake of those still in the madness *outside* Godhead or for that part of themselves not yet repatriated from exile. The systematic alternative—that of cataphasis—has its own logic of inverse extremity, or does, that is, if negation is not cheated of its positive force, if it is not filtered out: in the Christian New Testament, glossolalia; in Judaism, Kabbalah; in Islam, Sufism—an unclassifiable free speech in response to an unclassifiable free God, a sacred language beyond any human language strictly conformed to the *imago Dei*.[24]

The incapacity of language to say the merely unique—language being a system for conveying the common, or relating the less common to the more common—consists in language not being sized to the theological subject, Godhead-God. The more radically monotheistic the religion, the greater the proscription of speaking the divine name, and paradoxically the greater the obligation upon the voice, through whatever indirect maneuvers of human linguistic intelligibility, to subserve that subject and no other. The locus of that simultaneous proscription and obligation is the human creature qua *imago Dei*, the force field of the linguistic play between divine and human intelligibility. In both Judaism and Christianity, each radically but differently monotheistic, the proscriptions and obligations of human language have their antecedents in the internal discriminations of the divine intelligibility itself. In rabbinic Judaism Torah is the eternal and holy, inexhaustible indeterminate (the functional equivalent of what I will call Godhead), to which in its sheer indeterminacy there is no access. Access to Torah is by the *dabar* of the Holy One who by reading Torah renders it and himself determinate, as the Holy One says "Let there be . . ." and constitutes the temporally determinate people Israel, the nation of eternal Torah. Torah is not only spoken (scripted); it speaks, lives through being danced and sung, through the commentary and argument of rabbis, prophets, priests who are instructors not only of the nation(s) but of the Holy One himself: Moses our teacher simultaneously instructs the Holy One and is rebuffed by him when asked his Name. The human saying of the unsayable but obligatory holy is a humanly linguistic afterplay of the interplay of the divine monarchial economy. Although holding to importantly different construals of the divine economy, Judaism affirms no less than Christianity *nemo contra Deum nisi Deus ipse*, or "no one against God but God himself"—whereas I shall emend this to say: *nemo contra Deum nisi deitas*, "no one against God but Godhead itself."

If one does not attempt at this point a like broad-stroke description of an essentially Christian view of the divine internal economy, that is because the same will be the burden of reflection shortly on Godhead and God. But it may be useful to note how Protestant Christianity, in the Reformation and through the person of Luther, broke with the *via eminentia*, the way of eminent affirmation that had been the hallmark of normative medieval Christianity (although not its aberrant underside, and not the underside of the Reformation either). For Luther the biblical Word has God appearing under two visages, one light and vibrant, and one dark and otiose, hence *deus revelatus* and *deus absconditus*. Attaching itself exhaustively to the light visage or appearances of God and taking light as the ruling metaphor of Being (in the long tradition emanating from Parmenides), normative Christianity had appropriated the metaphysics of light to fold God as Being itself into the totalizing power of discursive linguistic practices. Such practices did not save but lost the full panoply of appearances of the biblical Godhead of God. In this context *nemo contra Deum nisi Deus ipse* takes on another meaning in Luther's counsel: dare against God to flee to God, no less flight from light God to dark than flight from dark God to light: the only alternative to (in Bonhöffer's deeply Lutheran phrase) cheap grace. This note bears on the matter at hand in two ways. First, an independently derived ontology is not *eo ipso* suited to a theological ontology, although neither is it *eo ipso* excluded (and just such a theological ontology, emended by a theological meontology, is the larger project of these pages). Second, it marks one of the decisive ways in which the Reformation, not to mention its twin the Renaissance, fostered so many of the problematics of western modernity and its successors, notably the preoccupation with language that reached its apogee in the nineteenth and twentieth centuries, for language holds in purview both what is light and dark, familiar and strange, alluring and daunting. A brief expansion of these two points may be in order.

Concerning the first, ontology, since it is our main subject hereafter, the merest prolepsis must suffice for an initial take on the discourse of theology (saying the unsayable). One takes up again the immemorial question of being *and* nonbeing (nothingness) in the conviction that language about Being alone has lost its totalizing power in the discursive practices of late modernity. In the same breath, ours is not yet another enterprise of tongue-clucking about the resistance of human discourse to all totalizations whatever. If there is no signified that can bring all signifiers into a sanctuary of humanly secure totalization, that owes in the case of the theological signified not to its being one more in a class of otherness (which class as a whole intersects and cathects the play of signifiers) but to the very character of that signified itself. God, as exhausting the theological signified, could totalize and dominate the signifiers only on the presumption that God is exhaustively and without remainder Being itself, and further on the presumption that the signifiers themselves are forms to figure that content. If discourse were contingently insecure in its totalizations, it could still aspire to a perfection of coincidence, a coincidence of language and Being. As the preeminent source of the western metaphysics of the light of eminence (remember that the revelation came to the charioteer on the race to the Sun), Parmenides held that only Being can be, can be thought, can be said. And *who* is to think and say Being? The human being who is self-conscious divagation of/from Being, who can only *aspire* to the coincidence of Being, thinking, saying.

If all discourse whatever is thus insecure, unsafe, unfinished, and vulnerable, theological discourse is so for better reason. The theological signified is not an other among others, although if we do not understand how the other functions in *all* discourse, we surely will not understand theological discourse. But we will not move from the class of otherness—however much otherness is present/absent in discourses by reason of singularities—until we reckon the character, the *what*, of the theological signified. The disruption/interruption of the ordinariness of discourse by the divine God as signified is occasioned not by a singularity capturable in the mere differential play of signifiers. Ordinary discourse relies on the presence of the signified (so modernity) or the traces of its absence (so postmodernity) to sort and collocate, or disport, the signifiers.[25] God is the *logical* singularity with neither singularity of presence (Being itself) alone nor singularity of absence (nonbeing, nothingness) alone, but rather the coincidence of both because he is the Creator of both, which coincidence cannot be securely netted in a totalization of discursive practices.

I do not expect the bald claim that God is the Creator of both Being and nonbeing and their primordial intermediator to be convincing or even intelligible at this point. To say *creation* is to say minimally that God the Creator figures preeminently in such determinate intelligibility as the cosmos has. But just such determinate intelligibility depends on that which is itself not determinately but only indeterminately intelligible. This may be taken in the quite ordinary way in which the principle or principles of a science cannot be treated within the determinate science itself, although my claim includes a reach that exceeds the discursive grasp, that God the determinate Creator depends on inexhaustibly indeterminate Godhead. To put the matter in a Hegelian way but without ineluctably Hegelian consequences, as William Desmond has, there is a determination process more ultimate than determinate intelligibles.[26] So, to put the matter negatively, we shall be about neither a foundationalism of ontology, which could lead only to a recrudescence of premodern ontologism, or some other exaltation of the great chain of Being or one of its constitutive links, nor an extension of discursive lament/celebration of discursive meaning as the mere play of self-referential signifiers. In proleptic summation: to understand the force of theology's signified upon the play of discursive signifers, theological ratiocination must participate the lived deracination of ordinariness (and here late-modern thinking, independent of theology, notably in Heidegger, is of high value), and the lived racination (and ratiocination) of that extraordinariness unlike any other, that (theological signified) which deracinates and reracinates every other as well as the subject of ratiocination. Such discourse will not net the theological signified in a discursive totalization safe and secure from all alarm, but it aspires to render the subject a ratiocinative participant in *creatio continua*, of letting be from nothing, and so the here from which the there appears, however in a glass darkly.

Concerning the second, the modern and postmodern preoccupation with language is adduced not to summarize or comment upon it but because the central problematic in language coincides discursively with the ontological-meontological problematic in the internal relations of Godhead and God, that of indeterminacy and determinacy, and could not be otherwise in a theology that names Word as an internal differentiation of the divine life and the agential principle (= principal) of creation. It was not until the nineteenth century, primarily through the pioneering work of Wilhelm Dilthey and Friedrich Schleiermacher, that language and hermeneutics began to be severed from their theological contexts; twentieth-century construals of interpretation, semantics, and the sciences of linguistics could be prosecuted in ignorance of this theological ancestry.

One has only to think about how one says or writes a sentence to know that, in its exercise, language is the internal play of indeterminacy and determinacy. One wants to say something, a something not in the conventioned universe of labels within the language (not, say, *cat*). *What* is this something? It is known only in the exercise of saying: we can never surprise the something in its ghostly prelinguistic indeterminacy, even or especially if it is, say, an idea, something having no entitative status apart from language. Linguistic units of meaning are apprehensions before they communicate. (And when will someone blurt out, in this vaunted communications age, that a good reason one does not communicate well is that he has little or nothing to say?) Merleau-Ponty was precisely on point in claiming, as already quoted, that the reason the thematization of the signified does not precede speech is that it is the result of it.[27] This should be the standard response to the standard student complaint, eternally recurring for every teacher: "I know what I want to say, but I cannot find the words." The student will discover, when she has found, or been found by, the words that render the indeterminate *what* determinate, that this very determinateness is but episodic in the exercise of language; that every saying, if it is of an important *what*, leaves a residuum of unsaid indeterminacy, the very impulse to a fresh raid on the inarticulate.

Before some impatient scholar of linguistics lowers the boom, one must say at once that the parallel between the divine intermediation of indeterminacy and determinacy and the like play within the exercise of human language is inexact, for the reason that no natural language enfolds indeterminacy sheer. In the aural dimensions of language sheer indeterminacy could only be something like total silence, or a totally monotonic sound unbroken by unitization or other differentiation. Such indeterminacy is not evident or scrutable even in subhuman animals that have species communication.[28] The interplay between indeterminacy and determinacy in language has determinate parameters that are various and variously evident. To be bereft of the determinate parameters of human language would entail a human infant not cultured or nurtured in any system of human signs (in which case it would not be a human infant and would be nurtured in a subhuman species of system signs). No one speaks language; and everyone speaks in *a* language—English, Chinese, German. There is of course the myth of the primordial universal language, broken at the Tower of Babel into the confusion of tongues,[29] a mythological account of one of the determinate parameters of language. Or rather, of two determinate parameters, captured in the now widespread Saussurean distinction in linguistics between *langue* and *parole*. The deep structure of a language is determinate, and such indeterminacy as the speaker presides over cannot include the breach of its grammar. Nor is the fund of words within that language indeterminately deployable: even within the confines of a grammar one cannot speak wholly in neologisms.

Yes, language invariably has determinate parameters, the pricks against one cannot kick without uttering nonsense. But there are indeterminacies in the exercise of a language as well. From studies of transformative grammar we know that its walls are there but permeable. We know that words expand and contract in number and meaning, that words wear out and some are reborn. Each combination of phonemes in a word, each combination of words in a sentence, each combination of sentences in a paragraph, is an occasion for effacement or renewal of the determinateness of indeterminacy. The writer/speaker has a limited range over which to preside, but it is awesome enough to strike terror, and occasional rapture: out of what is at hand linguistically to say what is not at hand in determinate meaning. Saying/writing worth attending to is a rendering freshly determinate of some range of indeterminacy shared by writer/speaker and reader/hearer, an invocation over the troubled waters of indeterminate evocation. In such an exercise, language is put under intense pressure and so is both reserved and deliberate, such that the reader/hearer must read/listen just as deliberately and reservedly. The successful exercise of language, in its pressured precision of deliberateness, will open upon an expanded vista of indeterminacy in what is evoked from the respondent (reader response), and thus will be sufficiently volatile to betray its inadequacy to the residual impetus.[30] The Word is not estopped by words, although stops are essential to the organ of voice. The Word is instantiated by words, but words under pressure, like gases, become more volatile and trigger the law of the inverse proportion between intension and extension.[31] The greater the pressure on the intensity of determinateness in words, the greater their implosion and explosion into the extensivity of indeterminateness, and vice versa. It is the task of the poet to make intension and extension coincide in language, which is why the last poem cannot be written, nor the last theology.

Thinking Nothingness

There is merit in affirming that at a certain level in the analysis of nothingness, as well as its surrogates and constituent factors, all talk of nothingness becomes nonsense or simple silliness. That is the level at which *any* modality of nothingness is assumed to be *something* (even if not a thing, *some* kind of intention).[32] If thinking is intrinsically intentional, holds something or some "object" in view, some will claim that thinking that thinks nothing is not thinking, that it issues in nonsense. That is, the claim goes, thinking nothing appears to be riddled with contradiction and so risks becoming a self-cancelling enterprise. The fount of this reminder in the West is Parmenides, who said that nonbeing (nothingness) cannot be, cannot be thought, and cannot be said. Whether there is more than this to be said, and if so what more, is a large part of the project of thought on which we are engaged. I have already observed that if Parmenides is right there is literally nothing for the human person to think, as the human thinker is not Being in the stipulated sense, one, eternal, and unchanging. Nor is there anything for the thinker to think, since any "object" has a like partitive reality and does not have Being in the stipulated sense. Nonetheless, the Parmenidean claim has a residually incontestable point, that any attempt to think and "say" nothingness is fraught with risk.

That point becomes clear if we consider two straightforward propositions. "There is a bird in that tree." "There is nothing in that tree." I speak nonsense if these two sentences are said to have the same logical form in respect of meaning. In the first, a description of a visible state of affairs, the clear sense is that there is something called a bird perched in the tree. But the second is not about a state of affairs in the same sense. When I say that there is nothing in the tree, I precisely am not affirming that there is something, called "nothing," that is perched or otherwise located in the tree.

But is the semantic power of nothingness exhausted in the grammatical negation of something? Can "nothing" mean exhaustively just nothing? The question of "the power of nothingness," beyond the mere negation of some or any thing and beyond the lack of any entity in a state of affairs to which nothing nominally refers, nags still, unremittingly in the question itself: Why is there something and not merely nothing?[33] Every answer to this question (including every metaphysical answer) is at risk of nonsense, since nothingness is not something about which information can be gained (hence is inaccessible to the sciences), nor is it being or a modality of being (hence is inaccessible to metaphysics, except of a certain sort of which more anon). No one has thought long and deeply about nothingness who has not inhabited the dilemma: if one thinks nothingness, one is at risk of losing either *thought* or the *what* that is thought. That dilemma is what evinced from Wittgenstein the dictum, quoted earlier, "Whereof one cannot speak, thereof one must be silent."[34]

If one declines the options of the Parmenidean dilemma as exhaustive and prescinds from impalement on its horns, that in itself reflects the power of nothingness. But resolve to persist in the questionableness of nothingness carries its own peril, that of presuming *familiarity* with nothingness in the fount of its sources (a danger no less perilous than the assumption of familiarity with *being* as the negation of nothingness). So one is put on notice, and that notice might well involve tarrying longer over Wittgenstein (who to my knowledge did not tarry long over such grand old words as *being* and *nonbeing*), for no recent western philosopher has worked more rigorously to make thinkers make sense. And such a brief review may also help in part to explain why I have chosen the figures I have with whom to think and afterthink, and how I take up with them.

For Wittgenstein philosophers are obliged to do the hard thinking that makes sense, and philosophy for him is restricted to that of which sense can be made. It is a not insignificant fact that Wittgenstein encouraged none of his students to become philosophers and positively discouraged many, some of them the brightest; they were exhorted rather to do something "useful," something that would change or improve human lives.[35] They were exhorted as well in whatever they did to *think*. When thinking is most difficult and "disagreeable"—he often uses the term "nasty"—"then it's most important."[36] The kind of thinking he has in mind comprises not necessarily the perennial philosophical puzzles about certainty, probability, perception, and so on but rather thinking "really honestly about your life & other people's lives." Wittgenstein worried (to the point of contemplating suicide again and again) such life-situations as imminent death (whether in both world wars in which he participated or in recurrent situations in which he thought he would die before "completing" his thought-work), guilt over actions and thoughts he was unsure were his, the contingency of human relationships (particularly those in love), and the encroachment of the "beyond" (not his term), whether in a benign or malignant sense: life-situations that are the supreme cases of "difficult" or "nasty" thought, those occasioning what other thinkers (but not him, to my knowledge) call the experience of nonbeing or nothingness.

In the manner of Wittgenstein, one may say that whatever nothingness is, it is not *something* to be discovered. As soon as he began to have serious doubts about his contributions to "serious thinking" in the *Tractatus* (even during the composition and certainly after the publication of it), he distinguished sharply between propositions having to do with states of affairs (solely the province of the sciences) and what he called "grammatical propositions."[37] This distinction emerged in his disagreement with those mathematicians (such as his early mentor and colleague Bertrand Russell) who claimed that mathematics entails propositions about states of affairs and thus is a science. For Wittgenstein mathematics is nothing less but nothing more than a *useful* logic; its truth is tautological. To say that mathematics is "true" is to say that it has been chosen as the "rule" to govern what it is taken to govern.

He does not deny that there are "innovations" in serious thinking, but they have to do not with "discoveries" but with changes in the meanings of words. So Freud, with whose thought Wittgenstein was preoccupied for most of his adult life, did not "discover" the unconscious. Rather, Freud extended the meaning of the word *unconscious* to cover thinking about the full range of motives, which is to say that Wittgenstein extended the grammar of the word *unconscious*.[38] Within the grammatical mode one does not ask whether the unconscious exists, is a part of the state of affairs (whether it is in the inventory of what exists), but whether the extension of the meaning of the word *unconscious* is useful in construing human life.

Wittgenstein described "grammatical propositions" variously, but the key notions were (1) that such propositions are "concept-forming" and function as a "rule." We could say (although he does not put it this way) that a grammatical proposition stipulates the meaning-universe of a word, and that it establishes the rules "for what it does and does not make sense to say" when that word is used. (2) However and in addition, such a grammatical proposition is not a logical proposition (as he had thought in the *Tractatus*); it is not governed by an immutable (because tautological) form. The reason it is not tautological to use words (and perhaps notions) not used by him is the historicality of a lived grammar; it is embedded in a lived tradition. As Ray Monk says in his commentary, a grammatical proposition "is something that is always linked with *a custom, a practice* [emphasis mine]. Thus, different customs or practices would presuppose different concepts from the ones *we* find useful. And this in turn would involve the acceptance of different rules (to determine what does and what does not make sense) to the ones we, in fact, have adopted."[39] Wittgenstein himself says explicitly, "The application of the concept of 'following a rule' presupposes a custom."[40] The insistence that a grammatical proposition is circumscribed by a custom or practice indicates that there is a public meaning of its central word that is being extended or reformed in the proposition itself—in short, this insistence is part and parcel of his contention that there is no such thing as a private language (alternatively, that a private language can only speak nonsense).

What do these remarks suggest for taking up the present problematic in a Wittgensteinian manner—though Wittgenstein himself, to my knowledge, did not traffic in a grammar of nothingness? Several considerations are to be weighed.

(1) To think nothingness is not to go in quest of discovering something in some state of affairs; nothingness is not in the inventory of what is there or what there is. Whatever this "something" is as *die Sache* of thought, it is not there as things are there in any state of affairs. Nothingness is there as the accompaniment, underside, or penumbra of states of affairs, more strictly of human life-situations (as, for example, their "limit," contingency, figuring in their determinateness, and so on). Nor is this accompaniment itself something that lies in wait for discovery by thought; "it" has always and already escorted life-situations without itself ever having become a life-situation.

(2) To think nothingness is never to think "out of the blue" or "out of whole cloth" but rather is to become sensitized to the range of the word-concept (and its surrogates) within the grammar of a life-situation. Within that grammar such a thinking would crack life-situations or, more strictly, follow the fissures only partially evident on their surfaces into the recesses of what accompanies and escorts them, and puts them into question.

(3) The terrain of the grammar of nothingness (including the fact that we use this very term and its surrogates to rule over what accompanies or is the underside of life-situations) is already and always mapped by an overriding *custom* and *practice*. Thus to think nothingness is not just, or in the

first instance, to enter upon a speculative venture but requires the hard historical labor of recovering hermeneutically the custom and practice sourcing the grammar of innovation in which nothingness can be spoken and made sense of. It is important to note that the relation between custom and practice is not a settled matter, particularly in a theological grammar, and most especially in advance of the hard historical work of hermeneutical recovery (see 5 and 6 below).

(4) *That* theology uses such words as *Being* and *Nothingness* in relation to God and the human person and *how* it uses them are controlled initially by custom and practice (in the way that words are controlled by the grammar in which they are spoken). One must get inside the grammar of a custom not only to understand the *that* and *how* of a word's use but also to understand how it functions in *concept* formation. In order to speak and understand the words sensibly one must speak the language sensibly within the hearing of its public; but always at the same time, one is obliged publicly and innovatively to expand the public that can be responsibly audient.

(5) A word and its surrogates travel across boundaries of custom, from one grammar to another, always with some loss and sometimes even with gain. This is called *translation*, and the cardinal rule of translation is that one should never translate a word unless it is understood in the grammar of the language *from* which translation is made; it is not enough to know as well the grammar of the language into which the word or its surrogate is to be said. The ideal translation, arguably never achieved, would be one in which both loss and gain in the transfer were made evident.

(6) In the ordinary sense of *translation*, translation involves two languages and their grammars: the transfer of the meaning of a word-concept in one language to the same or like meaning in another, the transfer from one custom-base to another. Thus if I wanted to translate English "nothingness" into a very different custom-base, say, that of Zen Buddhism, I would need to know the custom-grammar habitat in which nothingness is most like that of the language into which I am translating. If I take Eckhart to have been a cardinal innovator in expanding the meaning of nothingness in western grammar, I would likely translate that meaning in a Zen Buddhist custom as *sunyata*, as does Keiji Nishitani.[41] But then an argument would appropriately ensue concerning whether nothingness (in Eckhart's grammar of assent) and *sunyata* are hermeneutical equivalents in their respective grammars. I have spoken here of "thinking nothingness," but everything said applies equally to the two other words, *God* and *Being*. Indeed, Christian, like Judaic, custom has been uneasy to the point of interdiction that God and Being can have formal representation

in *any* grammar. This is the very force of the subgrammar that affords the space of our problematic: the apophatic tradition.

This is to say not only that integral custom-based grammars are external to each other but also that each integral religious grammar is internally related to its constituent subgrammars, the latter differentiated by variant customs and practices. One might think (wrongly) that the present project of thought is an essay in "the" western grammar of God, Being, and Nothingness. Such an essay would be impossible. There is no more a western grammar than there is a western language, or for that matter a western religion. There is of course in each integral religion a normative grammar (or its simulacrum) that differentiates it from other integral determinate religions. In the slowly evolving normative grammar of Christianity—or rather, Christianities—the words *God* and *Being* have made sense as surrogates (even if they no longer do). But grammars change as determinate religions change, and even what counts as "normative" grammar changes, as customs and practices change within an integral tradition.[42] They may be speaking ostensibly of the "same" "thing," but Plotinus's One does not mean the same as Hegel's Absolute Spirit; Plato's *apeiron* (unlimited) is not Sartre's *néant* (nothingness).

(7) The thinking here under way is of the latter sort; it is *intra*grammatical. However specular this thinking may appear, it is not "out of the blue," nor "out of whole cloth," but is vested in some figures in theological and philosophical custom, in whose writings the grammar that rules over such words as *God*, *Being*, and *Nothingness* is extended, reformed, and potentially altered. One thinks the relation between God, Being, and Nothingness in concert with thinkers in whose texts one finds "innovations" of serious thinking on the topic. None of these spoke a private language; each made sense (of which we are obliged to make sense) within a custom; each inherited and bequeathed within a custom, however altered or innovated. De-construction and re-construction have always gone on among innovators of serious thinking within an integral custom. Only from the vantage of the dominant normative grammar do the words embodying those innovations not make sense, and, of course, those who speak only within that grammar have an *interest* that they not make sense.

Words change, as do the grammars in which they make sense, to stay in synchronicity with human life-situations. A word that has endured for many centuries is at least a watching brief for a range of reference for which it stands sentinel. I think hermeneutically true that in order to say the same thing a word once said, one must say it differently. But to do that one must discern its range of reference, especially as an activated imagination plays across its contemporary form. Accordingly, the present enterprise can be characterized as an effort in contemporary *de-struction, de-construction,* and *re-construction* of the sentinel words *God, Being, Nothing.*

A Caveat Concerning Cosmogony

The focus of Topos 2 is theological cosmogony. To manage expectations here, a caveat is due: one must emphasize the qualifying adjective *theological,* while also bearing in mind long-term historical transformations in the study of the cosmos in the West. Cosmology, once a branch of metaphysics preoccupied with the nature of the universe, was concerned with the natural order of the universe, the nature of "all there is." Cosmogony was concerned with the origin, structure, and space-time relationships of the universe. This inquiry was undertaken by "natural philosophy" and its metaphysical cosmology until the mid-nineteenth century, when it was shifted all but totally to the physical sciences, and in the twentieth century particularly to theoretical astrophysics, both macro and micro. "All there is" is now construed to include all that has emerged since the big bang, the universe as presently known scientifically, and also the possible universes (serial or parallel) inferred or extrapolated from that knowledge base. Without doubt the most demanding discipline of the modern mind, cosmogony must identify and study the most ancient masses (planets), which are ancient in the curvature of space-time (general relativity theory) but are the youngest as immediately successive physical residua of the big bang, thus are thought to hold the code for the evolution/devolution of the cosmos (quantum mechanics), for the internal interrelation of macro and micro. How this works out across a profoundly moot front that is simultaneously constructive and destructive—black holes, dark matter, dark energy, string theory, "worms"—is a process as fascinating as it is complex. The night skyscape can no longer be ignored by the daytime human landscape, nor by a theology for which the anthropic principle is cardinal.

The cognitive traffic between theology and cosmogonic sciences is mostly one-way, moving from the sciences to theology, with theologians being the learner-students. In the theology here under development God is not an item in the cosmic inventory, thus not a subject-object for scientific study, nor a causal factor in the emergence and developmental processes of the universe(s). Yet theology (this one, anyway) makes strong claims for God the determinate Creator. How can that claim be squared with the claim that God did not cause the physical universe nor intervene in it once instituted? The answer touches on how the word *creation* ought to be used. I totally reject that contemporary "creationism" promulgated by the recidivistic fundamentalisms of the Abrahamic religions. But equally robustly I affirm the old term *God the Creator*, and do so through several distinctions that we are at pains to develop, particularly the distinction between Godhead and God, which is argued in Topos 1 for the light it sheds on the self-generation of deity; is pointed to in Topos 2 as the condition for there being what is not-God—other than God—namely, the cosmos; and is extended in Topos 3 as the condition for there being what is both like God and unlike God in the human creature.

For the ordinarily mindful person the amazement is that there should be anything at all; for the religiously mindful person the wonderment is that there should be anything other than God (or the sacred). *Creation* in its most general sense refers to that which is other than God, and *God the determinate Creator* refers to that by which the conditions are established for any reality that is external to God—what cosmogonists call "the point of singularity." In an absolute, unremitting, unqualified pantheism there would be no distinction between God and world, thus no distinction between science and theology. Perhaps there is no historical instance of such a conflation, although the cult of Parmenides comes to mind as offering a possible instance. I have argued that Parmenides's thinkable, unchangeable divine One entails an acosmism, so that what is other than God (what changes) cannot be, be thought, or be said. Another more enticing possibility presents itself in the work of Spinoza, but his *Deus sive natura* is interestingly qualified by his distinction between *natura naturans* (nature naturing) and *natura naturata* (nature natured), which distinction is close to ours between the divine indeterminacy (*creatio origine*) and determinacy (*creatio continua*).

We shall have multiple occasions in these pages to ponder the polarities suffusing the dialectics of thinking being and nothingness. Among them none is more fundamental than the polarity of necessity and freedom. In the classical West, necessity (whose simulacrum was *fata*) was the catch-all word for ineluctable, binding force that prevails in both nature and human affairs, presiding over the invariable repetition of characterizing pattern (Oedipus, clubfooted by nature, will lead a clubfooted existence). Necessity in nature is sad (no construction without destruction, mutuality of predation); necessity in human affairs is tragic.

I have referred to the anthropic principle in this caveat concerning what may be expected of a theological cosmogony. The three Abrahamic faiths have a heavy investment in the great importance, if not primacy, of the anthropic principle. Each of the three religions valorizes God, the world, the human creature, and their interrelation. Remove the human creature and there isn't much left from the perspective of human meaning. The human species is one of an incalculable but finite number of species that have appeared through natural selection, transmission, and mutation and could have vanished through the same processes, since in orthodox Darwinian morphology there are no favored species and no teleology. The human species could disappear in one of two ways, one way in common with other species, the other way distinctive. The way in common: through the abrupt random distribution of natural forces removing the conditions for the survival of humans. (To give an example from the past: the collision of a giant asteroid with the planet Earth, which formed the Gulf of Mexico, is thought to have eliminated the dinosaurs and countless other species of fauna and flora. To give an example from the anticipated future: in some four to five billion years the Milky Way, the galaxy in which planet Earth is, will merge with the Andromeda galaxy; driven by the force of the supermassive black hole of the Andromeda galaxy, a hundred million times the mass of our sun, the whole of planet Earth will disappear like a speck of cosmic dust in that abyss of nothingness—all Earth's species, including humankind.)

The other way the human creature could disappear is distinctive in that it would involve decisively some form of human choice. There is clear scientific evidence of "climate change" (short for all sorts of geophysical changes) for the last roughly two centuries of human industrial civilization. What is not equally clear is the full range of causes of such changes in climate. There can be no reasonable doubt that such changes correlate with, coincide with, some industrial practices that owe to human agency. These correlations and coincidences are sufficient warrant for concluding that the human passion for survival (like that of all species) has gone the length of at all costs, including the removal of the conditions of the continuation of some species on which human survival will depend. In consequence, the human instinct for survival carried to extremity is at risk of self-inflicted moral hazard. One may survive a while at the cost of disappearing species upon which hominids depend, but the self that survives becomes a monster, bereft of moral imperatives. This is morally treacherous. Survival raised by hubris to cupidity is self-destructive.

That is ironical, of course, but there is a larger irony often missed by scientists themselves, one that displays the importance of the anthropic principle directly. It is well known that the modern scientific revolution began with the recognition (discovery) that the earth is not the center of the universe and that the human creature is not the center of the earth, effectively the humiliation or at least the diminution of the stature of each. The all but mystical irony is that that humiliation is simultaneously the grandeur of the human creature, for it is through human knowledge incrementally corrected that the universe has come to be grasped thus and so. It may well be that there are intelligences with bigger brains in other parts of the universe presently unknown to us, that we hominids will disappear, that the whole anthropic experiment will fail, and be succeeded by other universes: all these alternatives and more have been conjectured by theologians for centuries. We need to remember that the big bang was some 13.7 billion years ago, that the ancestors of *Homo sapiens* morphed in the relatively recent past, that we have only 10,000 or so years of recorded human history, that we humans are still in our infancy. Throughout that history, religions of greatly varied type have characterized every known human culture. To be human is to make meaning; it is the métier of *Homo religiosus*.

At mid-nineteenth century Ahab betook himself to "the watery parts of the world," meditating that world now perceived as both nongeocentric and nonanthropocentric. What he saw was not a dark abyss but a dazzling white blankness of indifference. The old dead God of the Romantics had painted nature like a harlot, but the new nature presented an icy silence of uncaring. In the albino whale Moby Dick, Ahab sees the agitated but random indifference of the universe focused on him, the human imposter. And imposter Ahab is, for he imposes his own difference against the cosmic indifference symbolized in the white whale. As in all contestations of necessity and freedom, the effort is tragic but noble in execution; though Ahab does not survive, his free act does as a supplement to the moral imperative.

We might say that Ahab was worrying the singularity of God and its consequences, however remote. Certainly astrophysicists are unfinished with the singularity of the big bang: Was it solely explosive (extending energy, thus expanding the universe) or solely implosive (contracting energy, thus contracting the universe), or some combination of the two? (This is why the understanding of black holes is so critical.) The comprehension of this "singularity" is unfinished, as is the process itself. We might say that Ahab was claiming a human singularity not totally incommensurable with a divine singularity—one that replaces the dead, undivine God of Romantic nature (necessity). In any case, we here engage with thinking such a parallel singularity—God the Creator—and, these caveats duly noted, may now proceed.

Theogony (Θεογονία): Godhead and God

Forasmuch then as we are the offspring of God, we ought not to think that the Godhead is like unto gold, or silver, or stone, graven by art and man's device.
—PAUL THE APOSTLE, ACTS 17:29

Thinking theogony is a thinking of the determination process of *deitas*, or so I intend to argue. The philosophical theology under development here moves toward the explicit discrimination of Godhead and God. It does so by conceiving or envisioning the eternal self-generation of God, the determinate Creator, from the abysmal indeterminacies of Godhead. This task forms the crux of the first logical step in the unfolding of a monotheistic theogony and is to be the major matter of this chapter. Here I elaborate on the two extremities of that determination process: the abyssal indeterminacy of Godhead as unsearchable Wisdom and the determinacy of determinate God as logotic Creator and salvific Redeemer. Thereafter I seek to think the intermediating space of the determination process of *deitas* through the meontologics and semiotics of the *chora* (χώρα) in Plato's later dialogues, particularly *Timaeus*.

It may be worthwhile to summarize proleptically what is to be thematized in these pages. Everything with which the human person reckons ultimately is *in* Godhead-God, whether indeterminately or determinately. Access to these elements qua purely indeterminate is by speculation alone; that is, by extrapolation backward from *some* determinate collocation. Such backward speculation toward sheer indeterminacy is entirely onto-meontological, whereas backward *determinate* speculation, by contrast, is theological: it concerns what in the Christian tradition has been called eternal creation (the self-generation of God the Creator from indeterminate Godhead), itself a backward speculation from temporal creation (what is not God and not other than God, the finite universe, created by God from nothing in and not other than God). If eternal creation is the infinite determinateness of indeterminacy—ranging from pure indeterminacy to nondeterminacy (indefiniteness) to determinateness—comprising the self-creation of trinitarian God the Creator, then temporal creation is the finite determinateness of the infinite determinateness of infinite indeterminacy. The glory and curse of temporal creation is that it delivers to the human creature, within the parameters of creation itself qua *imago Dei et ad imaginem Verbi*, responsibility for finite determinability, the range of which she or he is to discover by test and contest.

Eternal creation comprises (1) the sheer indeterminacy of the divine abyss, the very Godhead of God, which indeterminacy is rendered not determinate but nondeterminate or indefinite as the divine Wisdom, replacing the traditional Father, which indefinite Wisdom is rendered co-nondeterminate (2) as the divine Word or Logos, the traditional Son, and (3) as the divine Spirit, itself the eternal determinateness of the intermediation of Wisdom and Logos. Eternal creation comprises not only the self-generation of triune God the Creator from God's own indeterminate, abysmal depths but also the eternal generation of what is not God but not so external to the Creator as to be wholly unrelated, internally, to God: hence Adam Kadmon, or man in Paradise, the Paradise of before, *and* Satan the Archangel (whose stature in John Milton reached the Sky) in the selfsame Paradise of before. Thus eternal creation includes the divine but untested (by temporal creation) determinate parameters of God the Creator's Love *and* Wrath. The only immutability in the divine life—that of abysmal Godhead—is effaced in the triune determinateness of God, both as the Creator and as the Redeemer.

Godhead and God: Why Distinguish Them?

To come clean with it, the highest (if secret and usually unacknowledged) aspiration of theology, as impossible as it is necessary, is to write the autobiography of God. The ancient western classical theogonies were simulacra of this aspiration but amounted to mythological biographies, as philosophical theologies amounted to their literary and philosophical critique. Their own contemporary replacements (and displacements), now that late modernity or postmodernity has finished its instruction in the demythologization of history and literature, are historical and literary biographies of God.[1] For the monotheistic religions, notably Judaism and Islam, a stupefying human arrogance lies at the heart of all theology in its highest aspiration. For Judaism the Holy One gives not so much as his name, and receives instruction only from eternal Torah and the commentary/argument of the people constituted by it through his principality. For Islam, Allah speaks himself exhaustively through the Prophet in the Koran, to which its hearers are to submit (the meaning of Islam). Thus for both Judaism and Islam theology has not the standing it has in Christianity, and certainly none of its pretense to some form of an autobiography of God. For Christianity the Bible is no less crucial, yet it is, as it were, but a daybook relative to geological time—a Lurianic diary entry covering a day, perhaps a week, in temporal creation—and the Christian theologian wants to know about eternal creation as well. The Jew, having eternal Torah, has the problem of temporalizing eternity; the Christian, having the Word in time, has the problem of eternalizing time. What Jews and Christians share in common (among much they share, not to discount how they differ) is temporal creation, although they come at it from opposite directions. So perhaps it is a peculiarly Christian theological aspiration to want a penetration of the eternal interiority of Godhead apart from all temporal creation (but Judaism has its kabbalistic En Sof too), an aspiration that led to the medieval discrimination of eternal from temporal creation, issuing later, say, in the phantasmagoria of a Böhme in respect of eternal Godhead, not so much replicated as temporally supplanted by Hegel's differentiations and sublations of Spirit.

Apart from the obvious one, that the human author is not God, there are multiple reasons why the autobiography of God cannot be written, yet no one nor the sum of them diminishes the theological hunger or estops moves toward its partitive satiation. One is the way in which God is an autodidact. Human autobiographies have two functions. One is communicative, exhibiting oneself in the difference one has made in the stories of others; and when this function predominates, the autobiography is dismissed for the narcissism it is. The other is self-discovery on the part of the subject, the final instruction to oneself that coincides with the final self-(re)construction. The well-rounded human autobiography, balancing the two functions, is extraordinarily rare—and for very good reason. In the recounting or reconstructing of lived experience no precinct can be found that is exhausted by internal relations, nor a zone excavated that is exhausted by external relations (so the typical autobiography can identify only approximately where I controlled the environment and where the environment controlled me).

With God it is otherwise. God is mutually, we might say metaxalogically, autodidactive—the meaning of which depends upon the discriminations we are in process of making and elaborating. God lives two lives, neither isolated from the other nor forming an identity of conflation. There is the life of God exhausted by internal relations of immanent Trinity: there is God the determinateness of Godhead, the God who in that respect and only in that respect is external to Godhead. There is the life of God the Creator who gives rise to what is both externally and internally related to God, the selfsame God the Redeemer who does not abandon the creature to mere externality, comprised in the life of economic Trinity. Is it any wonder that for an autobiography aspiring to grasp the intercalation of these lives, intending to penetrate the divine mutual autodidacticality, the entries in the daybooks of the world's religions could but serve as palimpsest footnotes?

Thus far I have been approaching the distinction between Godhead and God, a theo-logically necessary provisioning for the trek toward creation, with the discursive stealth appropriate to elusive quarry. By discursive stealth, because the prompts are at the same time the stops; every impulse to move forward is a warning, as though the boundary sign says "Admission to Trespassers Only—Stay Alert!" So (1) the effort to say the unsayable is a venture in the transgression of language in its very exercise, to say the Sayer-Creator from the said of creation (against which Calvin railed), by one east of Eden, an alien from the Paradise of their coincidence. Having exited Paradise through the exercise of determinateness over the indeterminacy delivered into one's care, its very exercise could only be transgressive, as reentry (not back, but forward) could only be trespass. Creator and creation: each is the other's asymmetric surplus and their redemptive coincidence, if ever, is not a Paradise of before but a Paradise of after (else temporal creation is nugatory), not alone because of their incommensurability but because of the excess of reserve in each and the derangement each works on the other in the Covenant between them. So (2) the transgressive flight *from* God is a trespassive flight *toward* God. And a very large question at whose threshold we cannot avoid arriving is whether the God from which we flee is God the Creator and what we flee toward is not God the determinate Creator but indeterminate Godhead. So many of the saints or mystics (those whose eyes and mouths are closed, *muein*) thought, and do they not have the best claim (although the last to make it) to having contributed a few sentences toward a chapter in the autobiography of God, they who were submerged in the sea formed by the cumulus of God's tears, to which they added their own (and over which God brooded in saying "Let there be . . ."), making their own the auto-biography of God (again, the last so to claim), vaporizing, volatilizing, effervescing those tears in the Cloud of Unknowing?[2]

There is yet another reason why the distinction between Godhead and God is imperative. For the western monotheistic religions, God is *living*. Not, mind you, God is life, in the manner of *Lebensphilosophie*; nor God is alive, but the present progressive: God is *living*. How could what came to pass for orthodoxy have affirmed the divine immutability, which carried with it an equally unqualified divine impassibility? Christian orthodoxy could do so and did so only by being in the grip of a metaphysics driven by the need for a ground, an immutable foundation accounting for all change. To say the same thing differently: orthodox theology came under the grip of a metaphysics dominated by coherence without regard to *theophantic* appearance (manifestation). Theology first, foremost, invariably, and properly is in the grip of its sourcing theophantic appearances, and its discursive practices of coherence are in the service of saving those appearances, which *mutatis mutandis* is the aboriginal metaphysical project of Plato—who, however, worked with different appearances. In Christian (though not only Christian) conviction the paradigmatic theophanies make manifest God as *living*. The divine living is complex, as it is perplexing, and can scarcely be accounted for by what once passed as the divine simplicity; it requires indeed the theo-logical discrimination of Godhead and God. For what is living is also *dying*, God not excepted (once again, given the panoply of theophantic manifestation). The one God living and dying is also an affirmation of hitherto normative orthodoxy, although made in widely and wildly various theological forms: most soberly in Aquinas[3] and most profoundly in his contemporary resuscitator D. G. Leahy;[4] in the dialectic of living and dying in Hegel's speculative Good Friday;[5] in the tilt toward the sublation of living in dying that eventuates in the death of God, the most radical resolution of the incoherencies of orthodoxy in Thomas J. J. Altizer's absolute evacuation or kenosis of the divine immutability into the mutabilities of time.[6]

If classical orthodoxy saved the theophantic appearances—a claim that is disputable—it did so with both logical and ontological or metaphysical incoherencies.[7] It got at least the perplexity of the complex of appearances, which complex, with the metaphysical resources at hand, could be rendered only as contradictory or incoherent: God is immutable and impassible, God is mutable and passible. To get beyond such incoherence yet stay within the grip of the apparent divine God (not the God of metaphysically driven entailment) requires, most generally, a theological ontology that enfolds meontology and, based on that revision, a speculative discrimination within the reality of the apparent divine God godself. No theology intending the divine God would claim that God the Creator is mutable in the way that created, contingent realities are, so the claim for immutability must vest in an interior dimension of the divine reality other than that of God the determinate Creator. Immutability, I shall claim, coincides with pure indeterminacy. That only can change which is in some respects determinate, for change is an alteration of determinacy. The speculative name (Eckhart's unnameable name for the appearances of the desert of Godhead) for the divinely immutable indeterminacy is Godhead. Indeterminacy *vitally* sources, but does not ground, the living God; Godhead does not change into God the living Creator. Without metaphysics of any kind (*per impossibile*?), the language of ground would not arise in connection with God the Creator.[8] With metaphysics of the right theological kind, the divine ground is none other than God the Creator, who embodies the primal determinate principial rupture of the (no less divine but groundless) indeterminacy of Godhead as principal, as the agent of eternal principiality, of principial eternity. Through the primordial determinateness (of the divine abysmal but immutable indeterminacy) that God the Creator is, mutability, change, becomes possible (and through creation, actual).

One could of course go on. God is living eternally and is dying temporally. The human creature is living temporally and dying eternally (although vocated to eternal life). Indeterminate Godhead *a se* is neither eternal nor temporal, properly speaking, since nothing lacking in any determinacy whatever can be either eternal or temporal, although groundlessly sourcing both eternity and time. Godhead is the site of the eternal self-generation of God. And so on. But we cannot go on, without going back, for the distinction between Godhead and God in the one divine life has been but broached in the form that shall claim attention, and is in want of elaboration if it is to have purchase on intelligibility, not to mention persuasiveness. Ours has been an age marked by a shift from the quest for foundations to the development of genealogies, a shift in which Nietzsche has had vast effect across many fields of human inquiry. The Nietzschean project has degenerated, as he presciently anticipated in horror, into a (trivialized?) sociology of the genealogy of ideas, instead of a genealogy of what ideas are *about*.[9] The reader will have sensed long since that the project at hand participates in the shift from foundation-questing to genealogy, but to genealogy as prosecuted in Nietzsche's venerated classical antiquity, genealogy as theogony—to be sure, a theogony of different theophantic appearances.[10]

The question heading this section is: Why distinguish Godhead and

God? If on the trail of this question not many memorable reasons for the distinction have been adduced, that is itself for a very good reason. The intelligibility and force of a distinction lies in its deployment, as does its effective rationale. Moreover, the oldest rule governing distinction is *distinctio est negatio*: to distinguish is to negate or differentiate. And what is distinctionally (if not distinctively) to be negated or differentiated when the subject of distinction is God? We find ourselves immediately deposited in a test case, in a theological thought-experiment, of the claim that determinate intelligibles depend on a more ultimate determination process. How can one offer determinately intelligible reasons for making distinctions in the very midst of the determination process on which they depend? It is easy enough to pronounce *Gelassenheit* over these troubled waters, to let go of ratiocinative anxiety, to let the determination process have its way. But east of Eden one earns the bread of the mind by the sweat of the brow. And all this only because of a grand stipulation: what *is there* is finitely determinate and thus actually not (exhaustively) nothing because of what *there is*, an infinitely determinative process.

There are, of course, alternative and equally grand stipulations. Take Parmenides, for example, with whom I have decisively broken, along with all his metaphysical and Christian theological successor sycophants. There was a time when I was such a sycophant to this extent: I could affirm with Tillich that the only statement one could make of God flat-footedly is that "God is Being itself." But if God/Being/One exhausts all reality, the matter of a determination process can only be ludicrous, a bad joke. With rigor, Parmenides was entitled only to his first affirmation, that there is only One/Being—not to his second, that only Being can be thought, because thought, itself intrinsically determinate and intending a determinate that *is there*, requires negation or differentiation, nor to his third, that only Being can be said, because all saying is an act of rendering determinacy, however episodic. The first to grasp something like the full spectrum of the determination process was the incomparable Plato, who in *Sophist*, by the sheer logic of determinate intelligibles, and in *Philebus*, by the ontology of the determination process, forced the friends of the gods into a severance with Parmenides (without falling into the arms of the friends of the Many-without-a-One), who had rendered all determination and process both logically and metaphysically impossible. Oddly and famously it was the Neoplatonist Plotinus who resuscitated the Parmenidean One, but as compromised by the nagging diremptions of the One that comprise its progressive privation that is temporal ostensive reality. Even more oddly and infamously it was medieval Christian mysticism, through Pseudo-Dionysius the Areopagite, sourced importantly but not exhaustively in this Plotinian compromise of Parmenides (and of Plato no less), that kept viable the bête noire of Parmenides, the nothing or nonbeing infecting (or was it vivifying?) all being, as did the gnosticisms on the soft underbelly of orthodox Judaism, Christianity, and Islam.

The present project is to think systematically, thus determinately, the determination process on which all determinate thinking, thus saying, depends. For we cannot expect to be exempt from a simulacrum of the determination process even God godself is subject to. The divine Wisdom—who is in traditional symbolism the Father—the divine abyss of indeterminate Godhead, cannot be said without the intermediation of the determinate Word (the Son) and the determinate Spirit. The fundament of the determination process is evident in the determinative intelligibles adduced to differentiate it but is not exhausted by them. There is no way to proceed with this problematic unless one accedes to the force of this hermeneutical spiral.[11]

Emergence-y of the Divine God

The phrase "the emergence-y of the divine God" may jar for a variety of reasons, none of them inapt for what the phrase is intended to hold in view. The first is the problem of all double genitives, a problem we shall find to hound much religious discourse (as in, to cite another example, the desire of God): Does the phrase refer to the psychic state of the person occasioned by the emergence into her field of consciousness by/of God, the holy, the divine? Or does it refer to the emergence of God godself, the very coming forth of God as divine God quite apart from all psychic states of belief whatever? The two questions are not wholly externally related, of course, but it is with the latter that we are presently and throughout principally concerned.

There are, however, other nuances in the word *emergency* that trouble both references of the double genitive. (1) *Emergency* suggests the sudden, abrupt, discontinuous (with what has gone before) immediacy of occurrence. One was not prepared for this, the unexpected. (2) That is, emergency bears *contingency* on its face; what occurs with the force of immediacy did not *have* to happen, was not a necessity following ineluctably upon antecedent occasions. (3) Emergency is invariably marked by *exigency*; about what is occurring immediately one may not be indifferent; an active response is called for. (4) If emergency is thus exigent, as it is, its reference includes a straitened *crisis*, a crossing or intersection, a situation of limited options from which it is as difficult to extricate oneself as it is imperative to do so. These nuances bear more palpably upon the first sense of the emergence-y of the divine (that of the psychic state of the person) than the second, and especially so in the case of those religious traditions that mark the divine emergence-y as accompanied by conversion: the abrupt, exigent emergence of the divine God is critically responded to by a change in life that is thereafter significantly otherwise. We know well that not all emergence-ies of the divine are thus marked, that religious traditions (not to mention *intra*religious traditions) differ markedly on the matter; that the time of emergence-y takes time to take hold of ordinary time, that the time of divine emergency, however immediate, takes the otherwise time of mediate response.

We could offer an extended reflection upon emergence-y *time* but must limit ourselves to discriminating it from the ordinariness of time's flow. The time of emergence-y offers itself for meditation in its own right—the time of presentation, appearance, or manifestation that is not thick enough to receive what emerges—the in your face, ready or not, of all emergence-y. The emergent eruption of *appearance* in emergence-y time is delivered into the care of the ordinariness of time's flow, that of saving the appearances. It belongs to the creature, enfolded in time's serial manifold, that she seizes and fixes what is unfolded in time's lingering. This osmotic space, which we call *now*, holds in the instant of the moment that is otherwise than time's flow the seepage of what is arriving and what is departing; anticipating and remembering are freeze-dried in what is there, what is presented in *this* present. This what is there, what has emerged, is the residuum of what calls and the echo of receding evocation. No what there is, no *continuously* emerged what, shepherds this call; from and in the standpoint of consciousness: the world is the inventory, the cumulus of all that has lingered in my whiles. That is why saving the appearances cannot be farmed out, outsourced; it is my responsibility, as is the responsibility to check my world-inventory against that of the other in every signifying encounter with the other. Most troubling is that the creature in and of herself in the ordinariness of time's flow is the cumulative forgetting of the time of emergence-y, the forgetting of being and nonbeing as *participial infinitives* (as though being and nonbeing were nongerundive nouns to name things that are there in the inventory). That is why the religious in all traditions develop and submit themselves to disciplines of *invocation*: it is a matter not alone of saving appearances but of having appearances to save. One supposes, because of the *imago Dei*, that every human existence is graced by evocations of the divine emergence-y, which clearly can be and are variously and differently saved. Evocations recede and pale in the ordinariness of time's flow, especially when named, substantiated as some *what* is there, when added to the inventory. One's invocation is the inversion of a lingering echo of evocation: one calls upon what called, as one invites those who have invited. The religious know well that invocation does not work *ex opere operato*: the ordinariness of time's flow would not be intersected, cathected, if the divine emergence-y could be programmed by formula. That prayers typically begin with invocations indicates a watchful readiness for what one cannot, in time's flow, be ready for. As Meister Eckhart wisely said (and Socrates knew), and I repeat here often, readiness and the giving of form occur simultaneously.

Is a certain configuration of psychic state (the first sense) essential to the actualization of divine or sacred emergence-y (the second sense)? Does the divine emergence-y depend upon holding a belief or set of beliefs: that God exists, that there is (although not mine, yet) a harmonium of yin and yang, a state of desirelessness (nirvana), and the like? Many popular evangelists for many religions say so: only *believe* thus and so and God (or other blissful state) will be real for you. Here the first, psychic sense controls the second sense of divine emergence-y, what it can mean, instead of allowing for its extension of reference. Suppose one firmly holds to the belief that God exists and is wholly good and just and finds in the divine emergence-y references that are otherwise (as Job did)? One then either lives in a psychic state of cognitive dissonance, or one adjusts to the expanded referential range of the divine emergence-y itself (as Job did). Ironically (and sadly), some philosophers of religion, especially so-called Christian philosophers, are in league with popular evangelists in emphasizing *belief* as a condition of divine emergence-y. Overbelief overdetermines, and overdetermination misdetermines. The point was common in the Reformation before the reformers devolved into scholastics: intellectual formulations and their commensurate psychic states are no more essential than works-righteousness to faith (precisely not a surrogate of *belief*). Paul Tillich is only the latest of such Reformers to herald doubt as inexpugnable from the divine emergence-y. This truth is viable and widespread more in contemporary secular than in religious America, unsurprising if, as is often claimed, modern western secularity is the principal offspring of the Reformation. I do not mean the modern tradition of *dubito*: doubt everything you can and retain only what you can't. I mean that an aged secularity near the end of its modern tether (call it postmodern), when an earlier vaunted humanistic existence has played itself out, either faces despair (the effective denial of that existence) or, recognizing intellectual inadequacy to that existence (a minimal meaning of doubt), opens upon a readiness for alternative emergence-ies (whether that of a divine sponsor of human existence, a state beyond the heavy tilt of yin over yang or vice versa, a condition beyond desire, thus suffering)—any or all of which may not be free of dubeity. This says that the hermeneutical spiral obtains between the first and second senses of the emergence-y of the divine, that whatever is intensively evoked spirals around in extensivity of invocation. The process is without temporal term. Polls report recurrently that the number of Americans who affirm God increases, one may conclude empirically, in inverse proportion to the decrease among those who are religiously observant.[12] My guess, expressed without cynicism, is that the traffic from God to religion is significantly heavier than that from religion to God in contemporary America.

What seems to be essential to religion is also what often is most burdensome and sedimentary. Religion gives us (at least provisional) names for what emerges, language-maps for the territory dis-covered, what was hitherto terra incognita. But it belongs to the crisis character of emergence-y that we cannot name the participial happening; we can only name what has happened, it, what was there: in Heidegger's terms, *Dasein* as *Seiende*. Having a language is not to be despised but treasured (pity those who cannot in any sense say what they see, *per impossibile*?) for by it, at the least, we do not start from scratch. By understanding one's language, one extends one's life by proxy for centuries past, and placing that language under intense pressure to say what emerges, however flawed and incommensurate, gives to language its future. The question remains, how can the emergence-y of the divine be vivified within time's manifold flow without the fixations of the now's tyrannical ordinariness, without the like tyranny of sedimented words? This is the question that drives the audaciously speculative intelligence of the great so-called mystics in the monotheistic religious traditions. Meister Eckhart may be taken as typical: the intersection of the psychic field of emergences out of the ground of the soul by the emergence-y of the divine God at the same time cathects eternity upon time's flow in the eternal now. Fixations of temporal ordinariness can never be evaded, in any case, by resort to "this and that," to the residual what is there, the momentary deposit of the standard now.

The history of philosophy and theology in the West is the story of troubled—largely failed?—attribution in respect of the divine emergence-y as such, especially the reduction of emergence-y to some *causal* relation between two or more residua of what is there. Classical normative Christian theology always wanted to model an aboriginal emergence-y, occasioned by an absolute and unitary *what is there* who simultaneously is what there is—namely, Being itself—by reason of supervening upon all subsidiary emergenc-ies. But we have already acknowledged or implied that the divine (otherwise named God or the sacred) is not one more in the inven-

tory of what is there, as what there is includes not only being but nonbeing or nothing. The reference of the emergence-y of the divine God in
the second sense is thus not a universal constant, is not one thing among
all things that are there and distinguished from them by its constancy
and universality of presence and by its being their ground. Not alone the
psychic state but the very reference of the divine God happens in passing, in crossing, such that the selfsame reference is both ontologically and
meontologically gappy. In this respect the divine emergence-y is formally
analogous to the origin of the work of art: however constant the art object
once extruded from the artist, its reference as a work of art is otherwise.[13]

The Defaults of Being

To ponder the defaults of being is to participate actively and mindfully
in the very questionableness of being as such. In these pages there will
be ample occasions to mark and remark upon the ontological and meontological instability of everything *having* being, but (in the odd way one
must put it) without *being* Being exhaustively. This situation, having come
to or been brought to the forefront of human self-consciousness, we have
accounted as the recognition of the noncoincidence of ultimate factors
bearing on the reality of anything having being, on pain of being nothing
at all—such that one is both oneself and not oneself, and not some other.
Every viable metaphysical project (itself aroused from dogmatic slumbers
in respect of the questionableness of Being) must account for this "fault,"
the instability and vulnerability of Being, as it must account for the "defaults" of Being. Those addressing fault and default require a historically
enriched imagination that draws upon the classical western (often aided
by eastern) metaphysical options but will likely (as here) be otherwise
than them, or at least entail robust qualifications of them.

   Those who possess or are possessed of such a historically enriched
imagination are also likely to have come upon their own recognitions
of ontological and meontological instability, as every determinate thing
having being bears that nature of finitude on its face and comes to self-
consciousness in the human person. As much is by now a philosophical
commonplace. What is not commonplace but nonetheless not extraordinary is the claim in multiple western traditions (especially the medieval
Christian) that God is an *exception*, namely, that God is that reality having
being that *is* Being itself (*actus purus, ens realissimum et perfectissimum*). So
far removed from that instability of merely *having* being, God's nature is
claimed to be absolutely changeless and eternal. This position is an amal-

gam of Aristotle and Thomas (in its reception history), itself an amalgam of Parmenides and Plotinus (and so-called Neoplatonism), all in my view having lost their fecundity for a philosophical theology that aspires to join metaphysics and the monotheisms of the Book. Parmenides, because of his unremitting acosmism; only divine Being *is*, can be thought and said; nonbeing cannot be, be thought or said. Plotinus, because, while he shared a Parmenidean understanding of the divine One-Being, he acknowledged *some having* of being on the part of what is not Being (thus was not a total acosmist), that not-being was wholly privative, thus was totally lacking in positive potency.

Among their adherents, the religions of the Book take God to be one who may be counted on. Does the God counted on entail an eternally identical, changeless "nature"? Even Schelling, the most radical questioner of Godhead in late western modernity, wanted to affirm with the ancients that in the core of Godhead is an "eternal stillness."[14] But Schelling could not do so flatfootedly, and that because of his complex accounting for what can be counted on in respect of deity itself. If God in God's very Godhead is vulnerable to change, as I construe Schelling to have claimed, even though the change itself ultimately be entirely self-generated, how would such a change of counted-on God be accounted for? It has been the work of these pages at least to make a start on addressing this question. In an important article on Martin Buber, Arthur A. Cohen once wrote, "God can be counted on, but not accounted for."[15] The philosophical theologian may well agree with the first part but cannot agree with the second. If there is no accounting whatever for the counted-on, there is no comprehending of the counted-on, thus no complying with the counted-on in the first orders of life. To be sure, like all theology, philosophical theology is second-order discourse and cannot be altogether independent of first-order religious discourse. On this point, the two orders of discourse converge, for surely the remonstrations of Job in the Hebrew Bible are nothing if not a calling for an accounting of the counted-on by announcements of Torah—another instance of Plato's call, in coining the word *theology*, for a testing and contesting of "the announcements of the gods."[16]

Even so, "It was a hard thing to undo this knot"—per the Gerard Manley Hopkins poem. One reminds oneself that this section is directed toward the "defaults of Being" in relation to the "overwhelming question" toward which these pages roll (per T. S. Eliot), namely, the relation between God, Being, and Nothingness. All the ancients wanted to understand how Being *becomes* (be-comes); as the Aristotelian-Thomistic tradition has it, how an existent is and is not its essence. Is essence or form an unmoved and changeless limit, laid up in some ideal realm, but otherwise having wiggle room only as the *not yet* of any existent over which it presides? Or does essence have aboriginal blanks to be filled in by an existing person come to self-consciousness of noncoincidence in her ownmost existence? Stated otherwise, the meaning of essence is harbored in its potency, which is not the same as possibility. Possibility is what can happen, could have happened, under the conditions of essence. Potency is the power to renegotiate the range of possibility essentially.

The very recognition of noncoincidence is itself owing to a default of being, as it is the incitement of the questionableness of both being and not-being. Let us be as clear as possible about the meaning of *default* in this usage. Already we have addressed the core meaning shared by *default* and *fault* (see Appendix B on fault and fall in human existence): failure, weakness, lack, fracture, displacement. In geology, this is a breach of crust or stratum accompanied by a displacement of one side of the fracture with respect to the other in parallel direction; in hunting, it is the dog's loss of scent, thus the failure of the hunt. *Default* continues the sense of failure in *fault*, but extends and ramifies it. Thus default in law is failure to fulfill a contract, agreement, obligation, or duty. But there is another sense of *default* that is particularly intended here, one employed in computer-talk. In composing on a computer one chooses this or that application or program, say, a font. When that font fails, is lacking or displaced, the computer defaults to a "standard" font; it falls back to the default position. These are metaphors, of course, no more than that, but also no less.

The metaphor of the computer itself fails because, while the machine has a standard position to default to, in reckoning with the "defaults of being" it is precisely the standard that is in question. Each religion has its own account of the counted-on in respect of deity, the sacred, the holy, namely, the standard or measure. And what is the default of that standard, especially if that standard is not changeless, is engaged with history, thus time?

There are forms of discovery and expression other than those of discursive metaphysics and theology, which we ignore at our peril, especially in respect of the defaults of being. This is so especially in the fine arts. And as much will come as no surprise to an attentive reader, for she shall have observed already that many sections in this book have been headed by "mottoes" drawn as much from the *dicta* of the arts as from those of philosophy or theology. Practitioners of the arts (verbal, visual, plastic, musical) know intuitively what could be called the "contraction" and "expansion" joints (hinges, betweens) of the polarities that have been engaged in these pages. Philosophers identify ostensibly irreducible categories pertinent to the being and nothingness of everything with a claim to being something on pain of being nothing at all, and think *about* such categories and their applicability to life-situations. With the artist it is otherwise; the artist writes (paints, composes, sculpts) not out of thinking *about* the categories but out of the experience of the *origins* of them, and through them to the life and death that inflame them.

Above all others the artist, true to the form of her craft, inhabits the *chora* of the between: that between limit and unlimited, necessity and freedom. While bound as robustly as any discursive scientist or philosopher by the forms of nature, she is fired by that *desire* endemic to *spirit*, intimations of what discursive form cannot contain but can only provoke by evoking a certain deformation of form itself (the very vocation of the artist). From nature itself she learns that there is no creativeness without destructiveness, no formation without deformation. So Darwin and everyone who has attended nature by direct acquaintance, and so the natural *mysterium tremendum* of every life getting its life from the death of something else, and from its own death the life of something else, simultaneously horrifying and fascinating.

The very greatest art objects as works of art are possessed of making manifest and of concealing. Every serious lover of art has had the experience, once having known the double potencies conjoined, of returning to the same art object and being repotentiated differently. The work of art is episodic in its being and nonbeing, as are we. As such, it is *creatio continua*. It is also, importantly for the project of these pages, a *trace* (Schelling's *Spur*) of the default or withdrawal of determinate God (or gods) to nothingness, the abyss of indeterminate Godhead.

Defaults in the being of God are known not only in speculative (mirroring) philosophy but as well and critically in the positive religions and their scriptures: in the ancient western religions, the dying and rising gods, in plenty. In the Hebrew Bible: God creates the world and, as it defaults on its own (Noah and the flood), starts afresh; the narrative drama, both tragic and comic, in which the Lead Actor (God) is now onstage, now off; Job's contestation of the counted-on. In the Christian supplement to the Bible: the delay of the *parousia* (the annunciation by Jesus of Nazareth that the Kingdom of God is present in himself, the default to delay, to *temporization* and *temporalization*); the apex of default in the being of God, the agonistic crucifixion of Jesus, the abandonment of him by the counted-on God. Withal, the inescapable question of the being of God when God is not being God qua the counted-on, the expected.

Pertinent here is Schelling's fecund accounting for what can be intelligibly counted on—namely, change—not in the multiple manifestations of determinate God but in very Godhead itself. He took the indeterminate (my term) abyss of Godhead to comprise three equiprimordial or coeval potencies that prevail over the life and death of determinate God: (1) the potency of self-negation, the Godhead's *no* to God's "eternal stillness," requisite to the exercise of divine freedom and to a genuine Other and its freedom, the human creature over the modalities of time; (2) the potency of self-affirmation, the Godhead's *yes* to itself in the face of the Other; (3) the potency of the "triad," the potency of the three potencies in "sublimation."[17] It is critical to recognize that for Schelling each of the potencies of Godhead singly neither has being nor does not have being. Each one is potency, as are all together as triad. In Whiteheadian terms, they may be designated as potencies of relationality.

In the defaults of determinate God's own being, God recurs to and has recourse to the potencies of groundless indeterminate Godhead. More precisely, the recourse of faulted-defaulted determinate God is to the *metaxu* (μεταξύ), the between: between Godhead and God. Eternally God self-generates godself from the potencies, themselves indeterminate, *creatio ab origine*. This is not a one-time, "once upon a time" event. With indeterminate Godhead rendered determinate in the Creator-Redeemer God, time and its *creatio continua*, what is not God but by God, matter. Defaults in what is not God but by God, in the cosmos and its inventory of creatures, occasion crises in the life God, themselves provoking God's recourse to the potencies of Godhead, thus self-regeneration of determinate God, changes in the very nature of God, the "standards" of what is to be counted on.

The whole of creation, what is not God but is by God, is a trace-footnote to God. Determinate God is a trace-footnote to Godhead. Godhead is a trace-footnote to nothingness, or groundless abyssal potency. These are the several footnotes in the text of all—all that is and is not.

The Genesis and Default of God

Verily thou art a God who hidest thyself.
—ISAIAH 45:15

Everything that is and is not—that is to say, is not nothing exhaustively and without remainder, is not something else or a quality of something else—is a concentration of multiple factors. Such a formulation has had many variants in western philosophical traditions, an early classical one being the ontological schema of Plato's *Philebus*.[18] If every there-being, every being-there is a concentration, is God a concentration and so a being-there?[19] *Concentration* in this sense refers not to a marshaling of mental faculties for purposes of attention or appreciation but to the focusing of diverse factors in a unifying, actual pattern in a temporal-spatial *unum*. Concentration occurs in a scale or variety of modes, thus differently in the mode of delineated or focal actuality, that of the discrete entity, and in the mode of penumbral or regional actuality, say, that of events comprising a perduring collocation (whether actual or fictive) of ingredient focal actualities. God the Creator-Redeemer is not in any sense a focal actuality, as God is not one of the factors or powers ingredient in any spatiotemporal mix (*pace* Plato, for whom God—the World-Soul, and belonging to the order of soul—is the demiurgic cause who persuades the unlimited to receive limit in order to serve the Good as far as he can).

Wherever God is thought to be a focal actuality (as in many if not all theistic metaphysics), a fundamental confusion of creation and causality has been made. God the Creator bespeaks a cosmos he is never focally present in. If the western monotheisms in theological fidelity to biblical epiphany are preoccupied to the point of obsession with Word of God, that is for good (and sometimes horrendous) reason. The divine Word works by default of human language (and for even better reason, by recurrent default of God to Godhead). The residue of the divine Word, recurrently at the point of petering out in time (or, to say a variant, perduring only in cultic sedimented repetition), also recurs in a fresh raid on the articulate through the maneuvers of language. That is why the sacred texts of Judaism and Christianity, qua scriptures, are not stenographic reports, are not (mere) history, but rather make large drafts upon saga, myth, narrative. The central character—as a focal actuality—is not there.[20]

That the divinity whom we seek and who seeks us is not *there* as a focal actuality in space-time is advertised in scripture from beginning to end. The Bible is not the only but is the greatest western work of literary art whose central character is absent, is offstage. That is but one more reason why every symbol of God, but especially character or person, must be broken, must suffer the iconoclasm of defaulting language, for every construal of God as a there-being focal actuality is idolatrous.[21] In this respect the cultic practices of western religions have been rescued from bibliolatry time and again (kicking and protesting all the way) by the high literary arts, at least by that canon of same that extends and mediates scripture (in the Christian West, by Dante, Milton, Shakespeare, Melville, Joyce, to cite but some). For it belongs to such literary art to restore or establish those narratively destabilizing regional actualities, however fictively or poetically configured, in which the absent remains absent but has iconoclastic voice. By these remarks I by no means mean to denigrate those protective genres the cult has extruded against the deadening effect of univocalizing representative and therefore idolatrous language, notably the rabbinic Midrash in Judaism and the sermon in Christianity. Rightly done, rare as excellent, these are high arts in the pressured default of language; like scripture, they are less *about* God representationally, more *to, with, before* God the hiding seeker, a presentative language of thinking absent-mindedly.

Is God then in no sense a concentration? In the previous paragraph we took leave of Godhead momentarily, fast-forwarded to God. While not a focal actuality, is God of that other order, mode, or scale of concentration (as we have implied), that of penumbral or regional association, that of event? Addressing this question requires concentrating on concentration briefly. In the stipulated sense, concentration is not a *structure* at any point of the scale, thus is not principial. Abstractly, concentration can be thought only in its complication, its determination process. Concretely, focal actuality turns out to be less focused than reflection will bear. Take the focal actuality I know best, from the inside out: I myself. Without reflection and reflexivity, naively, I take myself to be a continuously ingressing *unum* surviving and anticipating all occasions as its carrier. But unless I am a windowless, noninteractive monad, my continuous ingression is interrupted, perturbed by a situation that exceeds my own situating. The simplest situation would be the interactive interruption of two focal actualities in a common field: I myself and you yourself. We assume such meetings to comprise much of our concrete existence, but they are high abstractions or effects of imagination. That is why real meeting between two persons, just two persons and only two persons, requires a vast labor that few are willing to undertake (the process of falling in love is a prime example): every other claiming focal actuality must be screened out of the situation. Even then, reduction accomplished, there is an emergent concentration to be reckoned with: the larger penumbral region situating our respective focal actualities constricts: now your background and foreground concentrate in the face of a like concentration on my part, and there is in our meeting thus an interlacing of regions. We may as well call a halt, for we shall not arrive at a focal actuality without regional situation (it would be empty) or a penumbral region without focal factors (they would be blind). The excursus was undertaken to say further that and how concentration is operative in a scale of modes, that these modes overlay each other interlacingly, that even the focal actuality I am is caught out of the tail of a regional eye, etc. Concentration is indeed another way of saying determination process.

And it is another way of saying reference, since nothing can be referred to that is not in some mode a concentration (which need not be this or that). In the ordinary way that language works, nothing can be referred to that is not determinate, including and especially nothing and indeterminate Godhead. The reader will rightly guess that we are sneaking up, warily, on just this realm of reference. Warily, because of the circularity of the problem. Granted that reference requires determinateness, yet the realm haunting referentiality is the determination process itself, the process that makes all determinateness possible and actual. What is referred to when *that* realm is in view? Reference will be revisited after several revolutions of just this circle. Of course, for most of those in the current climate of reference, one of relaxed comfort in correspondence and representation, the whole present enterprise will be thought bootless and probably silly. In the parching winds of such a climate the painter's oils would crust over on her palette as stonily as the common-sense philosophers' sedimented representations; the poet would break the strings of his lyre and hang himself from the nearest willow tree.

· God the triune Creator-Redeemer is the eminent economic concentration of the determination process. In this and only in this sense is God the triune Creator-Redeemer the ground of the conditions of all that determinately is and is not in cosmic space and time; as such determinate God is not the efficient cause of anything determinate in space and time. If God is thought of as "cause" at all it would be as the lure of the determination process itself, the sense of cause as *final* or teleological.

· The selfsame God the triune Creator-Redeemer is a concentration of a different, indeed absolutely unique order, without parallel (and indeed arguably without analogy, although not without traces) in the determinateness of space-time: God the Creator-Redeemer is the determinate issue of the eminent-negational, therefore wholly immanent, concentration of the foreground of creation and the background of indeterminate Godhead. *This* concentration bespeaks the groundlessness of the ground. God the Creator-Redeemer, the principal if not the sole referent of determinate Christian theology, the principal-agent of eternal and temporal creation out of principial groundlessness, the concentration of monanarchic indeterminacy and pluriarchic determinacy, includes in its reference a dimension of indeterminacy, the very Godhead of God, traced in the nimbus of space-time, the dark cloud that margins every light, the dark night of the soul in every nescient knowing.

Enough of axioms for the nonce; we have been diverted from our site as such by what inhabits it, as one invariably is in surveying any site. Godhead is the site, abode, or *where* of the genesis, the very coming forth of divinely determinate God from indeterminate abyss, as it is the locus of the default of determinate God, where God keeps godself (as Godhead) in reserve when God is not being determinate God, where God recuperates novel redemptive determinacy in his living-dying relationship with temporal creation. But have we in fact been diverted? Is there any way to think abyssal indeterminacy and the process of determinateness, other than by animadverting what arises determinately from that abyss and by marking the back-and-forth movement from indeterminacy to nondeterminacy to determinacy (*Ungrund, Abgrund, Grund*)? Philosophers are unquestionably better at cutting the joints of process than theologians (in western modernity, anyway). We have opted for a mixture of discourses, as Christian theology did in its infancy. The mixture of philosophical and theological discourses grows testy when the former analysis of the determination process yields a determinate object (matter to be thought, in the pertinent case, God) otherwise than that which theological discourse is claimed to understand thinkingly.

The test case of testiness is that philosophical discourse, metaphysics, given over to cutting being and its process at the joints. Metaphysical analysis and reflection is occasioned by two astonishments, one a commonplace, the other (alas) less so. One of many statements of the first astonishment was that calling forth from Leibniz the question: Why are there beings at all, and why not rather nothing? The very astonishment that beings are and are not null incited reflection on the question of the *ground* of their being-there. An early answer to the question of the ground engaged the mixture of metaphysical and theological (certainly Christian but also, *mutatis mutandis*, Judaic) discourses: beings are and are not nothing because God (qua Being itself) creates them *ex nihilo, ex nihilo ens creatum*, a mixture now standardly called ontotheological metaphysics. Such was the astonishment with beings, with the very glory of creation and its power to render extant the being that beings have (as long as they have it), that the standing of the nothing loses its questionableness—so powerful an astonishment that preoccupation with the splendor of beings in their (albeit tenuous) outstanding of nothingness could pass seamlessly if analogically into preoccupation with the glory of Being itself. It is difficult and perhaps impossible to say, as a historical matter, which is the more complicit in the obliviating of the questionableness of nothing, and indeed being as tinctured with nothingness—theological or philosophical discourse. However the division is made, theological ventures have borne an enormous burden of responsibility for the oblivion of nothing and its tincturing of all that is while it is (and surely it is passing odd that Heidegger, who has done more than any other twentieth-century philosopher to alert us to nothing-dyed Being, should neglect this or at least be silent about it: is this because he is, if theological, a standard medieval Catholic?). As much is the case for normative Christian theological discourse, though not for the marginal undersides, the mystical traditions of multiple theological orthodoxies: Christian, Judaic, and Islamic, wherein the second astonishment (that of nothing) has been sheltered against the allure of the first.

Metaphysical discourse for its own account is not without complicity in the oblivion of nothing-suffused Being, a claim elaborated *in extenso* and in depth by Heidegger.[22] Surely it is the case that that obliviating neglect on the part of metaphysics did not owe to an unvarying association with the ontotheological option, since other options were also available and exercised. In western classical antiquity the prevailing metaphysical response to the astonishment of there being anything at all was not *creatio ex nihilo* but rather *ex nihilo nihil fit*: from nothing can nothing come to be. This conviction seems to me Parmenidean in its root: only Being is; nonbeing cannot be, be thought, or be said. This was a metaphysical root that could not yield stem or branches: it yielded but an acosmic reality, as Plato realized in the *Sophist*. In that and subsequent dialogues Plato honored what is not Being but has being on pain of being nothing at all: the very cosmic tellurian site of human dialogue (a site that is not *eo ipso* divine, and remember that for Parmenides the news that only Being is comes as a revelation, that such Being is divine, so that only the divine truly *is*). Either Plato did not write the *Philosopher* or it does not survive, that dialogue in which he promised to expound the ontological standing of what is between *peras* (limit) and *apeiron* (unlimited), in our terms between being and nothing. It fell to the Neoplatonist Plotinus to save the appearances of beings that are somethings rather than nothings solely out of the horizon of Being, an option already eschewed by Plato. Plotinus stands at the origin, in a qualified repetition of Parmenides, of the metaphysical option that construes nothing as the privation of Being, that construes nothing solely within the horizon of Being, an option that Heidegger continues, notwithstanding his perpetual railing against the *Tendenz* of metaphysics to obliviate Being, precisely in his claim that nothing is the withdrawal, concealment, the staying-away (*Ausbleiben*) of Being as such (although my account of these matters does not square with Heidegger's).

With modernity the *ex nihilo nihil fit* took a fateful turn, once again at the instance of the great Leibniz, who construed it as the principle of sufficient reason: *nihil est sine ratio*, nothing is without grounds. This sentence could be taken in three radically different senses. (1) Nothing is without grounds. Having no grounds, nothing may be—indeed must be—ignored in proper philosophical discourse. (2) Positively stated, anything that is has grounds. The surety of a thing's being is no greater than the certainty of its ground(s), and proper philosophical discourse exhausts itself in the question of the certainty of ground(s). (3) The third is—differently punctuated—the inversion of the first: nothing is—without grounds. That says: nothing is, but without grounds.[23] And it says that nothing abridges the principle of sufficient reason, since whatever nothing is, it is groundless (in my terms, indeterminate).[24] These three construals of the ground(s) could offer a tantalizing map of the territory of all western modern (and postmodern) philosophy, and probably someone has sketched it—certainly large blocks have been done in detail. I adduce them not to contribute to the map (which would be well beyond our purposes) but to indicate the recurring somnolence alternating with insomnia in respect of the *nihil* of the *ex nihilo* (whether the *ex nihilo ens creatum* or the *ex nihilo nihil fit*) in philosophical discourse. To understand why that discourse has been given over more to ontological/meontological somnolence than insomnia in modernity, one has only to note another turn after Leibniz, and an ironical one at that. Leibniz himself clearly intended the *ratio* of *nihil est sine ratio* to refer to an ontological ground (remember that it was he who habilitated *ontology* as the substitute term for *metaphysics*). After Leibniz and beginning in Descartes, and triumphing in Kant, *ratio* came to refer not to ontological ground but to reason itself as grounding all objectivity over against subjectivity. Thus ground came to have, principally if not exhaustively, not ontological but epistemological reference. If the amnesia of ontological-meontological ground and groundlessness was broken in the nineteenth century, as it clearly was in Schelling and Hegel (not to mention their Tübingen-era roommate Hölderlin), the one Catholic, the other Protestant, that owed to the insomnia of their theological roots, particularly in Jakob Böhme and generally in German Christian mysticism, wherein nothing and its aggressive but nondeterminate force never slept. The echoes of their distant relation to the Friends of God in the High Country,[25] even if reaching them largely by intellectual hearsay, echoes that tolled the aggressive force of nothing in abyssal Godhead, reverberate in a new mixture of philosophical and theological discourses without precedent in modernity.

Lest we ourselves fall victim to amnesia of the short-term variety, it is time to call up the second astonishment said to source metaphysical (and certainly theological) discourse. The second is but the second half of the first. The first astonishment-wonder is that a finite being is, stands out from nothing (ex-ists), a matter of celebration. The second, no less astonishing wonder is that the selfsame being stands toward and into nothing. All beings come from nothing and, as we say, they come to nothing, a matter of plaintive lament. The motto of this melancholy wonderment is Ecclesiastes's vanity: all is vanity; all flesh is grass that withereth. In the individual human being, blessed or cursed with self-consciousness, the realization of coming to nothing attends the anxiety of anticipating death. What thinking of ground or groundlessness could entertain *both* astonishments? Did Nietzsche, in the thinking of the happy nihilist? This seems a crucial question for any philosophical or theological discourse, or any conjunction of them. And there seems to be a great divide on either side of which waters flow to different oceans. On the one side is plenipotentiary Being as such; atop the divide, the finite outstander of nothing is summoned to gravitate toward that oceanic plenum. On the other side is the kenary depths of privation, the lack or want of what is on the other side, whose drag or current is swift, furious, unrelenting. Suppose one lets go, slides or flows to either side indifferently—say, in the simple-minded, therefore false dichotomy, toward Being in the West and Nothing in the Buddhist East. Does one reach one ground on the one side, another on the other? (Yes, I know the metaphors are getting mixed here: ground doesn't go with ocean!) Or are both grounds groundless, all oceans forming a common abyss of indeterminacy floating all determinate grounds, however the latter heave in mountainous divides? Religions themselves divide on this momentous question, as do their commensurate metaphysics. We are trying to position ourselves to answer, to call ourselves to answer. An answer to the wrong question is always wrong—as was the supreme Being as an answer to the question: Why is there something rather than nothing? Which answer answered nothing about nothing; if it said something about why something outstands nothing, it says nothing about why something comes to nothing, or whether the nothing *from* which something comes is the selfsame nothing *to* which it goes; theologically, it says a little about God the Creator but nothing about God the Redeemer. Thinking the *ex nihilo*, the *ex nihilo nihil fit*, is unfinished. And will be when all parties of this thinking have come to nothing. Will the nothing to which we will have come be an enhancement of the nothing from which we came, a justification of our having stood out from nothing temporally or temporarily? Or will our time have been nugatory? Such is the question of a redemptive creation. Can a theological discourse itself redemptively come to nothing, an enhanced if not a plenipotentiary nothing, a graced *plenum* kenarized by the valence of the theologians thinking ex-istence (outstanding the first not)? And does coming to nothing mean something only and merely nugatory? However it is with philosophical discourse, is not theological discourse rendered serious and itself a work of praise in the realization that it too will come to nothing, and so has no investment in the perdurability of system? (Small and polite applause, Kierkegaard's one hand clapping.)

What can be tidied up, brought into focus, from the foregoing framings of questions, the *Fragenstellungen*? The overarching question is the perennial one in any mixed discourse, that of the relation of Being and Nothing to God (as tidy as that!), but that is the matter of the entire book and we are yet in its antechambers, proceeding *solvitur ambulando*, one baby step at a time. Such focusing as is possible at the present juncture is largely by reason of implicit denial or eschewal in the foregoing framings. Thus: (1) to think solely the ground or groundlessness of *either* Being *or* Nothing will not conduce to thinking the ground or groundlessness of the other, thus will not contribute to thinking their relation; (2) metaphysical discourse in service to the divine God is summoned to think the ground or groundlessness of *both* astonishments, which are only analytically *two* and as a lived realization comprise a unitary ontological-meontological amazement; (3) nothing (or nonbeing) is not to be thought solely within the horizon of Being (even Being as such, or Being itself), thus not as merely the privation of Being, or even as merely the contrast term of Being. Such a thinking does permit a thinking of *negation* but not of *nihilation* (Hegel's ingenious dialectical sublation of Nothing by Being notwithstanding). This judgment extends to (4) the disavowal of the answer to the question why there is something rather than nothing by ontotheological discourses of all stripes, namely, things are because God, construed as supreme Being or Being as such, makes them so to be. Such an avowal is the effective estopment or terminus of ontological-meontological thinking, renders closed the questionableness of both Being and Nothing, abridges the two-sided astonishment, and so goes against the fact of finite mind itself. Moreover, it does not think through the determinateness of God the Creator *and* God the Redeemer, and in particular the relation of determinate God to indeterminate Godhead, traced in the double wonderment itself. With these framings by negation and eschewal and what they implicitly anticipate, let us continue with the site of Godhead.

One should be as clear as possible about the disavowal under (4) above and the avowal that motors it. In disavowing either Being as such or the Supreme Being (or their combination) as the ground of there being beings rather than nothing, one is not giving up the avowal that God the determinate Creator is the ground of all such beings. In a defensible theological metaphysic, God the determinate Creator *is* the necessary *ratio* (condition, ground) of there being what is not nothing and not God (exhaustively and without remainder). But if God the determinate Creator is the necessary *ratio*, the selfsame God is not the sufficient *ratio* of the selfsame not-being nothing and not-being God. Such a claim introduces, if not a hiatus into, at least an amendment of the metaphysical principle of sufficient *ratio*. According to that principle, sufficient reason requires a ground that is both, equally and simultaneously, necessary *and* sufficient. I claim God the determinate Creator to be the necessary but not sufficient condition (*ratio*) of there being beings rather than nothing. Created beings necessarily involve two integers and the determinately principled principal of their relation: Being, Nothing, God (the Creator-Redeemer). Neither Being nor Nothing is spatially-temporally determinate save in created beings external to God (economically), nor determinate otherwise save in the eternal self-creation of the divine living-dying, in the rationing and spiriting of the indeterminacy of the Wisdom of Godhead. Both Being and Nothing are groundless in the common and unitary indeterminacy of Godhead. Both Christianity and Judaism (admittedly differently) declare in principle against every gnosticism (although each, differently, recurrently falls into same) that claims a god for Being and a god for Nothing, a god for creation and a god for redemption. Gnosticism is, after all, just rigorous metaphysics shorn of mythology. Strict fidelity to the phenomena of being and nothingness in the created order will lead ineluctably to metaphysical dualism. Theology no less than metaphysics is obliged to save the appearances, but it does so by setting out not from the appearances but from that by which there are appearances at all to save, and, above all to *save*: from God godself. God the determinate Creator is the necessary ground of the coinciding of being and nothingness in every being, but not the sufficient ground, for determinate sufficing melts away in the very determination process of deity whereby there is (and is not) determinate God the Creator and Redeemer. Necessary but not sufficient in metaphysical terms, determinate God is something of a metaphysical scandal, and there is no blinking it. For a purely theological thinking—and the curiosity if not the irony of this is also not to be blinked—God (the full panoply of Godhead-God) is more sufficient than necessary. That is because for theological thinking God is not ever the entailment or conclusion of a metaphysical argument, but the beginning of one. And that is because theology knows no God the Creator who is not also the Redeemer.

The matter bears a few more words since it bares the site of Godhead. In saying that God the determinate Creator is a necessary but not sufficing ground one advances no novel claim but rather rehabilitates (in an alien context?) an old Thomistic one, namely, that sufficient reason concludes to the necessity of a first cause but not to creation or to the character or nature of that first cause.[26] In subsequent, especially early modern and particularly German technical discussion of the principle of sufficient reason, a necessary but insufficiently grounded ultimate ground was called an *Ungrund*. The new metaphysical thinking of ultimate ground in the nineteenth century (certainly in Schelling and Hegel, differently but equally in Kierkegaard and Nietzsche) was occasioned by the project of thinking *Ungrund* not epistemically but meontologically: the very groundlessness of determinate being cum determinate nothing. In our terms, to think Godhead-God is to think the determination process, the metaxic crossing from indeterminacy (*Ungrund*) to nondeterminacy or indefiniteness (*Abgrund*) to determinacy (*Grund*) and back, in the eternal living-dying that comprises the divine immanence. To think God is to engage all the problems of thinking the unique, the sui generis (whether of a particular kind or of the same kind as it is, but especially the latter), the *causa sui*: self-generating determinacy from indeterminacy. To think the groundlessness of determinate God as ground is to think the insufficiency of mere Godhead. To be adequated or commensurated with its matter, theological thinking is dispatched to think sufficiently insufficiently.

God qua Determinate Creator

We have been approaching Godhead and God first by reckoning with the linguistic difficulties of such a venture, by indicating reasons for the distinction between Godhead and God, by envisioning synoptically and proleptically where such a path might lead, and by broaching the divine emergence-y itself. The first sense of the divine emergence-y, that of psychic states accompanying its actualization, received but slight attention above since there is no intention here to offer anything like an adequate psychology of the human experience of manifestation of the divine. We turn now to what is crucial for theology, the divine emergence-y in the second sense: a theological meontology of the coming forth of the divine God. With the emergence of God from Godhead, with veritable theogony, we undertake to explicate the determination process itself that antecedes any determinateness whatever. If speculative mischief is to be avoided, two things must be kept in mind: the blandishments of a part-whole metaphysics are to be resisted, and the determination process does not refer to a staged generation across serial time. The divine God that emerges, if any, does so as a unitarily determinate reality, not as serially connected parts nor as the whole of such parts. Nor are the internally discriminated dimensions of God differentiated stages in the divine life: first Godhead cum abysmal indeterminacy cum Wisdom, then Word, then Spirit. The determination process is nothing other than eternal creation, the self-creation of God.

As creation *überhaupt* is not to be thought only as something that occurred or occurs in time and space, so the life-dimensions of the Creator are not to be thought as limited to inhering only the unity of eternal creation. All elements of Godhead, rendered eternally determinate in the

73

emergence of God the Creator, are less present than traced in temporal creatures. Earlier ages, notably the high Middle Ages in the West, could be confident of a scale of such traced presence, of traced absence. At the top of the scale were angels, who are at but one remove from eternal creation and so the most presentative re-presentation of the divine life in time. (Since in medieval cosmology stars, or heavenly bodies, were thought to be angels, something of this view survives in that contemporary cosmogony in which the oldest planets are at nearest remove from the big bang.) At the bottom were sedimentary forms of matter—say, a stone—which, however embodying determinate Structure/Word, traces little indeterminacy of Wisdom, less of Spirit. But sufficient potencies of *ratio* and spirit were thought so to inhere this chunk of nature—say, a slab of Carrara marble—that, brought under the grace of a Michelangelo (note well the name itself!), both ends of the scale could be curved toward each other in an intensification of the coincidence of extremities, magnificently and awesomely in the Pietá (in St. Peter's in Rome), wherein the natural properties of stone are inverted: Structure/Word lies inert, veritably dead, in the vibrant arms of Wisdom and melancholy Spirit. To the modern western mind, in the grip of representational thinking, it is unaccountable how the formula of that age, art imitates nature, could have yielded such glorious art. But that age understood presentation nonrepresentationally, hence never understood art to copy anything. In that age of scales and their inversions, "art imitates nature" meant that art is the temporal ecstasy of traces eternally embedded in nature.

Every living (animate) thing from the smallest to the largest is marked in its core by turbulence, by what Jakob Böhme called the primoridal *turba*, even as the smallest integral units of inanimate matter center upon the particles, quanta, and charges of frenzied energy. It is not alone that everything is prey to something else, that it is unremittingly subject to exterior threat: Tennyson's Darwinian nature red in tooth and claw. Turbulence scales across the range of temporal creation from extensive macrosystem (the subject of astronomical physics) to intensive instances, whether organic (the subject of microbiology) or inorganic (the subject of microchemistry and geology). It is of course the oldest argument in the history of science whether the turbulence of space-time owes to a unitary factor or multiple factors, an argument that continues in and around unified field theory. Theology has absolutely no evidence to enter in the evidentiary hearing on causal genesis in and of the space-time universe (the only one scientists, or others, know). Theology does have the conviction that the determinate universe is there because there is determinate God the Creator. *That* the universe is evidently there is accepted by all who accept evidence in any scientific sense. The court of evidentiary hearing on all the pertinent *whys* is open and in session: why the universe is there and not exhaustively nothing, why exhaustively nothing is not there, and why in what is there *some nothing* in some sense is there. What the sciences have to bring to such an evidentiary hearing is unsettled, and is as unsettled as the evolution and devolution of the cosmos is (and theories of it). Further, theology has the conviction that although the created space-time universe is external to God the Creator, by reason of its own causal genesis (evolution and devolution), it remains nonetheless internally related to God the Creator in some sense (although, because externally related also, not internally related to God as God is related internally to Godhead). The meaning of "in some sense" must remain open-ended, and is so because of the reality of space-time and the difference that real external relation to God makes, hence the vulnerability of "in" to the sciences, the arts, and epiphanies of God godself.

This last is important for the topic at hand, the determination process itself, and specifically the divine abyss of Godhead. The turbulence evident across the continuum of the space-time universe, however external to the divine life *a se*, traces if it does not mirror the indeterminacy rendered determinate in God the Creator. Alternative accounts of the emergence-y of turbulence flourished in the origins of, if they did not constitute, Greek cosmogony. The most enduring explanation of cosmic turbulence vests in *contrariety*, the unremitting contest between opposites (say, love and hate). The Milesian naturalists were content to name multiple divinely sponsored elements party to the contest, with such unity as might be possible to be after or beyond the contest, and always to be dissolved by time, the only recurring thing to be the contest and its parties; whereas the Ionian Eleatics (notably Parmenides) championed the One before the contest of contrariety or difference, which contest could only be illusory, since a turbulent One (that is, a manifold deviant from the One) cannot be, be thought, or be said. For the ancient Greeks, what is eternally recurrent in time is itself divine; multiple eternal recurrences argue to multiple divine sponsors, hence the polytheism of typical Greek religiosity. The great and arguably monotheistic exception was (among the pre-Socratics) Parmenides, whose divine One admitted neither other deities nor a space-time world deviant from absolute Being, hence no turbulence whatever. One can therefore understand why historically Christian thought was attracted to Parmenides and why systematically it should be repulsed by him (although historically it was not, but only because its appropriation of him was through a bastardized Platonism). Attracted, because of Christianity's unremitting monotheism; repulsed, because of the evidentiary turbulent world at hand. For Christian theology (*this* one, anyway) the turbulence consequent upon the temporal contrariety of all determinate opposites is anteceded by the meontological determinateness in God the Creator of the abysmally indeterminate *turba* of Godhead, a groundless *turba* that rumbles beyond and otherwise than being and nonbeing. Its (and it is precisely no precise, no determinate, it) traces are in everything that is and is not.

Before turning directly to the abyss of Godhead, an observation about how theology has typically gained access to what I have called turbulence, and a warning (that theology has typically ignored). Mystics and saints in all traditions have known that if and when all exterior disturbance has been quelled in quiescence there remains the interior turbulence of the soul. Indeed, soul is the very self-consciousness of turbulence. Because in Christian theology the human soul has been taken to be *the* cathected *imago Dei*,[27] various readings of that self-consciousness have been possible. From the soul's self-consciousness of its own interiority Augustine could read off an entire Neoplatonic metaphysics of the Trinity. From the selfsame self-consciousness Eckhart could find in the powers of the soul only their commensurate determinates in "this and that," and counseled letting go both the powers of the soul and their determinate God the Creator in favor of the ground of the soul at one with Godhead beyond God (in my terms, the renunciation of all determinateness for indeterminacy sheer). In Böhme, the warning becomes palpable. For him, to penetrate the interior of anything whatever in nature is to gain access to the interior of everything: a drop of mercury (quicksilver) or a smidgeon of sulfur advertises the *turba* as unmistakably as does the human soul.[28] Such a view carried the danger of an unremitting panpsychism (everything is soul or soul-like), the very triumph of Neoplatonism, which led to theology offering its own evidence in forums in which it was without evidentiary value—and gave rise to charges of projection. The warning cannot be repeated too often.

Godhead qua Abyssal Indeterminacy of Divine Wisdom

Godhead is a term that has been variously used. It has signified the whole of the divine realm, as in Greek religion the full panoply of multiple deities, the pantheon. In classical Christian theology the term was the inclusive signifier of the divine reality, monarchic and triune, the common substance or nature shared equally by the divine persons. In apophatic mysticisms of several traditions, but especially in the Christian, Godhead was a conventional designator—the unnameable name—for what is beyond God in any determinate (cataphatic) sense, the directional *ad quem* of the human soul that has let go its powers. The present development of theology combines these senses of Godhead but amends them. Godhead is not the inclusive whole of the divine living-dying but rather is the groundless indeterminate turbic *energeia* of the divine living-dying, the ebullient, effervescent *fortissimo* of formless energy in the divine depths.[29] Because Godhead is abyssally indeterminant, every theology adequated to it has a large dimension of the apophatic or negative. (This is why Christian theology can and should warm to—if not embrace—all nontheistic and atheistic construals of the cosmos, and why the selfsame has a point of contact with nontheistic and atheistic religions.) However, unlike (some) apophatic or negative theologies, Godhead is not beyond triune God but in God. A reminder: we are thinking the determination process upon which all ontological and meontological determinateness and determinate thinking depend. And specifically, we are thinking the determination process of deity itself, the eternal self-creation of God (theogony). We should not have reached the end of *why?*, the *ad quem* of the determination process itself, if there were something beyond that process. Further, given the theophantic appearances entrusted to the community of Christian dangerous memory (David Tracy), one does not think the abyssal indeterminacy of Godhead sheer but only determinately as God the Creator and Redeemer, as Wisdom, Logos, and Spirit. As there is a large apophatic dimension to theology's talk of Godhead, so there is a large cataphatic range of talk about God; hence so much talk bordering on an excessive lugubriousness, so much interstitial—although contextured—silence, in taking up with the intercourse between human and divine living-dying.

Godhead is the generative indeterminacy of determinate God. Only what is determinate can ground, so Godhead is not in any sense a ground and thus is inaccessible to metaphysics, however theistic. There can be and have been metaphysics of God but not of Godhead. (If in the present aeon of time's flow the divine living-dying comprises the indissoluble union of Godhead-God bespoken in God said, "Let there be . . . ," there cannot be a metaphysics, only a meontology, of the divine living-dying.) Nor can there be a logic of Godhead, for a logic depends on the determinateness of unity (or identity) and differentiation, both lacking in indeterminate Godhead. Those thinkers who nonetheless have essayed to speak of Godhead (in my stipulated sense) have done so formally as *Ungrund/Abgrund* but materially as the superabundant excess emanating from determinate events, epiphanies of determinate God biblically narrated, events trailing clouds of generative force for both God and humankind. There is no access to the divine abyssal indeterminacy save through the determinateness of God the Creator-Redeemer, and *that* aperture is not then upon indeterminacy sheer—as there is no access to our own indeterminacy save through our own determinate acts and those to which we are party.

An overplus residue of indeterminacy infects every determinate act, as it plays across the surface of all discourse, especially discursive discourse, and forms the very seat of perplexity in all discursive discourse. The special force of poetry, for example, is so to pressure determinate words, to intensify their specific gravity, as to bring their textured indeterminacy to the fore, while not being altogether other than the words themselves. This residue accounts for the aggressiveness of force in every determinate act that can be tilted toward good *or* evil and says why resolve is not the only arbiter of the tilt, why determinate acts can and do have unintended consequences. Indeterminacy sheer, on its own terms, is discursively inaccessible because it can have no determinate referent. Thus indeterminate Godhead is not conceived but figured, and figuration is a work of the imagination (in mathematics too, for figures [integers] in the mathematical sense have no referent that are there). Figures of Godhead-God are, of course, symbols, symbols that work symbolically only as broken.[30] We can imagine nothing that has not touched us (including nothingness), nor fully realize what has. The nearer to rudiments, the purer the imagination, for imagination opens upon wholeness, not immediacy, the wholeness of coming from nothing and going toward nothing, the two nots, the wholeness of being and not-being aborning.[31] The knowledge imagination has is not science in any modern sense, is more *nescience*, such as Socrates derived from consulting his *daimon* or Paul saw through a glass darkly (1 Cor. 13:12), or getting nearer to our own time, something like William Desmond's posthumous mindfulness or Robert P. Scharlemann's reason of following.[32] I have suggested, to no roars of applause, and not altogether waggishly, that university departments of religious studies were more aptly named departments of *nescient* studies (although in this respect they are in fact often departments of *negligious* studies!).

Another and perhaps concluding word for the nonce about the accessibility and inaccessibility of Godhead (which is not a class-genus, godhood, subsuming members, gods, or even a single member, God). In some forms of theology God is said to be bipolar (or dipolar), but in such forms the polarity is taken to obtain between God and God's creation, the universe. We shall come to that relation in respect of cosmogony, what is external to God—whose simultaneously internal relation to God is at stake in the question of bipolarity. The wholly immanent bipolarity of the divine living-dying, coincident with the eternal self-creation of God, is that between determinate God and indeterminate Godhead. Just this bipolarity accounts for the simultaneous human attraction to and repulsion by/revulsion with God (Rudolf Otto's *mysterium tremendum et fascinans*); it is why for William Blake (and nervously, John Milton) Satan could stand sure surrogate for God against Newton and other sycophants of attractive order. Our present subject is the pole of the divine indeterminacy in the determination process of deity, of the eternal self-creation of the Creator. The pole of Godhead in the divine life may be called the Pole of Relative Inaccessibility (the latter phrase derived from Annie Dillard).[33] This geographical point is relatively inaccessible (actually) because it would have to be approached simultaneously (and actually) from all the starting points from which it is equidistant.[34] One of the venerable figures for Godhead was the circle. Nicholas of Cusa's *Of Learned Ignorance*, replete with mathematics, speaks of God as a circle whose circumference is everywhere and whose center is nowhere. How would one get to nowhere from everywhere and anywhere? Yet we do, for they get to us; they touch us, although we do not know how to realize them. We have the affects—and sometimes the effects—of what we cannot get to. As Annie Dillard divines, the Pole of Relative Inaccessibility is the Pole of Most Trouble but is also the Pole of Great Price. A pole-pearl, one might say, cast before metaphysical swine. Metaphysicians (bless them) are less daunted than challenged by the Pole of Most Trouble. Hegel, by all odds the greatest modern metaphysical dueler with Most Trouble, had the consummate ambition to render all indeterminacy determinately accessible, not through machinations by human design but through the dialectics of the self-mediation of Absolute Spirit. His Spirit, however, was antecedently so open-endedly determinate as to be able to sublate every accident of negation, every incursion of the indeterminate. If his Spirit could accommodate every insult of negational surprise, could be overtaken, it could not be taken over; for self-mediating determinate Spirit will raise every negational insult to a fresh and higher level of determinateness. What Hegel's Spirit did not know was its own indeterminate depths that are insusceptible of self-mediation. Without the metaxological intermediation of *ratio* and spirit, the inexhaustible groundless indeterminacy of both remains a numbing, dumbing perplexity. Hegel remarkably and monumentally exposed the determination process of Spirit, but not of Spirit's own generative depths. He spawned, whether through right-wing or left-wing Hegelianism, fascism or Marxism, some of the most intriguing perplexities affecting culture far beyond technical philosophy. And if Spirit, and all that pertains to it, is so accessible, why has it been in such palpable decline since Hegel?[35]

The thinking that would think indeterminacy must itself be commensurately indeterminate, hence apophatic and so reliant on nondiscursive forms. This is why Hegel's aspiration to have the concept sublate all metaphor or figure (which entailed his elaboration of a new logic), thus making imagination inferior to reason (against his important source in Böhme), could but compromise if not suborn the disclosive (or apparent) power of the imagination, as it did the abyssal and perplexing indeterminacy in the depths of Spirit.

The central figure upon which I have settled for the inexhaustibly generative indeterminacy of Godhead is *abyss*, yet another a-privative word in theology. *A-byssos*: without bottom, depth beyond measurement, depth unfathomable. In English the noun has had five variants: *abime, abysm, abysmus, abyssus, abyss*; I adopt the last, *abyss*, and the adjectival form *abyssal*. In premodern Christian cosmogonies it referred to the void, chaos, formless matter, infinite unconfigured space before temporal creation: thus what God the Creator in the Genesis story brooded upon in calling forth the universe. In Greek religious cosmology the abyss was the great deep, the primal chaos, the bowels of the earth or the supposed cavity of the lower world, the infernal pit. This notion survived (*mutatis mutandis*) in Greek philosophy in the notion of *aporia* (yet another a-privative), what we ourselves will later adopt and adapt in ruminating breaks in plane. Given all these nuances of the figure, the abyss of Godhead is in no sense the monarchic ground of God, is rather the monanarchic groundlessness of trinitarian God, the abyssal before or beneath of any contrast between the one and the many. Perhaps just because it suggests both space or void insusceptible of measurement and bottomlessness accessible through *some* aperture—as in Shakespeare's "dark backward and abysm of time" (*The Tempest* 1.2.50), abyss is the very archetype of a roomy figural abstraction in which not just thoughts but especially many feelings otherwise homeless find their place. *Abyss* is a word less to be read than sounded. It tolls its range.

Godhead qua Abyssal Indeterminate Desire

In the enkindling of fire lies the entire ground of all mystery.
—JAKOB BÖHME

Sweet fire the sire of muse, my soul needs this.
—GERARD MANLEY HOPKINS

One loves ultimately one's desires, not the thing desired.
—FRIEDRICH NIETZSCHE[36]

Jakob Böhme is the consummate thinker of *Ungrund, Abgrund*, and *Grund*. As such he is the source on which the major post-Kantian identity-difference philosophers unceasingly drew—notably Fichte, Hegel,

Schelling. Because his thought was presented in then alchemical, Christian kabbalistic, verging on gnostic theurgic/chemurgic figure, in my uncommonly cryptic re-presentation of him here I freely adapt his language to my own (as did all philosophical appropriators of him in their own terminology).[37]

Desire is Böhme's most comprehensive term for the restless fermentation or effervescence that comprises the internal force field of the wholly internal life of God, as *turba* (from Greek τυρβη: confusion, disorder, chaos) is the term most often used by him to characterize the simultaneity of creativeness and destruction in the indeterminate abyss of Godhead (the *Ungrund*). We spoke of the determination process, the nonserial progression from indeterminate *Ungrund* through *Abgrund* to determinate *Grund*. Using Böhme's sense of Desire, one thinks of the simple phrase "the desire of God." The matter of the double genitive raises its head again: the subjective genitive (the desire of the determinate person for something equally determinate), or God's desire for . . . what? For "something" that cannot be determinate, as in the infinite and indeterminate *Sehnsucht* (yearning) in the abyss of Godhead, there is not any determinacy, whether of God or creature. Thus we reckon presently with the "desire of God" in the sense of the objective genitive.

Desire, construed in and out of itself, is intense and intensive longing, yearning, aspiration, and is so because of the warring of *Trieben*, impulses in contrariety within the site of interior indeterminacy that comprises the abyss of Godhead. In Böhme desire is not quite what *concupiscence* was in Augustine; for the latter, in the *Confessions*, was overdetermined as erotic (and explicitly sexual). For Böhme desire as a *concupi-scienta* is a totalizing preknowing of longing itself, insusceptible of compunction, and that because it is compact of both anticipation and remorse, a concupiscence not yet sufficiently determinate to be erotically sexual. What is yearned and longed for is what is lacked, what is wanted, what is not there. What desire in and out of itself yields is, effectively, *nothing*. Here is the indeterminate prototype of all human desiring: if one desires intensively and extendedly, "something" (determinate) will present itself as a candidate for satisfying the longing, the lack. But when that candidate's satiety value has been exhausted, it recedes into the nothingness from which it emerged, and the spiraling of frenzied desiring feeds again on itself. That is why Böhme claims that Desire is the "mother" of both Being and Nothing.[38]

Böhme's figure for desire in Godhead, of abyssally indeterminate range, is fire. Who can say the word *desire* without feeling the force field of fire in both its heat and its light? But fire in all its visual resonance has been largely lost for those living in developed countries. Who now, dependent solely on the energy of electricity for light and warmth, strikes a match (Böhme's *Schreck*, the explosive precipitate of flame), lights a candle or enkindles wood? How then can the impoverished figural imagination of "developed" peoples itself be ignited by pondering fire? Böhme claimed that in the "enkindling of fire" one sees the *mysterium magnum* of the divine abyss. In this, at the dawn of modernity, he was the restauration of Heraclitus, for whom (Heraclitus) the logos of nature is the attunement ("concert") of opposites.[39] When attending flame (say of a candle) closely one observes that, while giving light and warmth, the center or base of the flame is dark and cold. From fire thus observed, Böhme generalizes the force field of desire: it enfolds the totality of binary opposites: indeterminate Nothingness and Being, Evil and Good, Wrath and Love, and so on, all moving toward the "concert" or attunement that marks their unfolding in every determinate reality. It is important to remind ourselves that these "sportings" (Böhme's term) among indeterminate opposites are not "once upon a time" but rather are traced in each and every determinate actuality, which we ourselves are.

Böhme is preeminently a thinker of "the hinge" (yet another of his figures), the thinker of the *metaxu*, the between. The vast bulk of his oeuvre is devoted to identifying those irreducible ultimates complicit in all that is and is not; that done, they must be connected, hence the matter of "the hinge." This all too brief summary could be illustrated at random from multifarious texts. Consider the following from *Six Mystical Points*: "God's wisdom has being, and yet it, wisdom is not a being. . . . God is from eternity alone all. His essence divides itself into three eternal distinctions. One is the fire-world, the second the dark world, and the third is the light-world. And yet they are but one essence, one in another; but one is not the other. . . . Each distinction shuts itself in itself in a being; and its qualification is in accordance with its property, and in its qualification is also its desire, as the *centrum naturae*. And the desire is its making, for desire makes being where there is none . . . and all is together . . . a hunger after being . . . . The right life is rooted in the fire; there is the hinge of light and darkness. The hinge is desire; with whatever it fills itself, . . . and the substance introduced in the desire's fire is the fire's wood, from which the fire burns, be it harsh or soft; and that also is the kingdom of heaven and hell. Human life is the hinge between light and darkness; to which ever it gives itself up, in that same does it burn. If it gives itself to the desire of essence, it burns in anguish, in the fire of darkness. But if it gives itself to a nothing, then it is desireless, and falls into the fire of light, and then it cannot burn in any pain, for it brings into its fire no substance from which a fire could burn."[40] From this excerpt Böhme concludes: "Then the wonderful knowledge arises, but with no perfection."[41]

Böhme's metaphor of "hinge" is paired with another, that of "separator," his term for *will*. A hinge is a device that permits a door or gate to open and close, and is at the same time a separator of spaces. Both door and gate mark limns, boundaries, and the aperture they offer affords ingress and egress, thus the potentiality of breaching and transgression of limns or boundaries. Whether that potentiality is actualized depends upon the agential separator, the will, and that across the totality of the divine economy. One can will to ingress the opening the hinged door permits, or not; but if one does, the egress will all but invariably follow as what one willed is seen to have unintended consequences, is seen to have as little satiety value as that of will's mother, desire. There is, of course, no freedom without the exercise of freedom. And there is no exercise of freedom without separation. One could make a table of separators, of which there are many: will from desire, freedom from necessity, outer world from inner world, God from Godhead, many from one, creature from Creator, and so on.[42]

In these large draughts from Böhme's corpus, all directed toward a start on the theopoiesis of desire, I am well aware of the deficiencies of that start. Withal, I have had in mind my simple daily lunch. A loaf of bread of my making, a glass of wine, a wedge of Gorgonzola cheese. The bread I eat today is both the same as and different from the loaf I made last time; the same for wine and cheese. Each food morsel or droplet of drink is a concentration, progressively determinate, of backlying or underlying indeterminacy (*Ungrund*) signaled by effervescing and fermenting yeast— that of Desire, rendered nondeterminate (*Abgrund*) by the coincidence of contraction and expansion. These processes, essential to "selving," are self-referential and remain so as the indeterminacy of Desire sufficiently "hardens" itself to separate *will* to two realms: the hardest will to the realm of Nature, that is, Necessity, which not even free will can transgress; the softest will to the realm of human determinacy, itself in its exercise not free to evade the residua (traces) of indeterminacy in the individual's ownmost potencies. So Böhme. And so the bread, cheese, and wine at my lunch plate. If *Ungrund* and *Abgrund* exegete *creation ab origine* eternally, thus the self-generation of God from Godhead, *Grund* explicates *creation continua*, the emergence-y of every determinate existent. So, to Böhme, the modulations of Desire are the backfound, the "mother," of all that is and is not.

I am well aware that these Böhmian wares are philosophically contestable, and indeed contested by no less a thinker than Hegel—who otherwise drew much from Böhme. Hegel said that those who demand "an indeterminate enjoyment of indeterminate divinity" (*unbestimmten Genüsse dieser unbestimmten Göttlichkeit*) risk getting only fog or darkness (*Nebel*). He pours contempt upon those who "abandon themselves to the fermentation of the substance" (*dem ungebandigten Gären der Substanz*), for that sort of thinking yields only dreams, and the net yield of dreams is merely edification, which is no business of philosophy.[43] But Hegel was himself inconsistent, as Böhme was. In his pursuit of plenary Being (to be sure, mindful of his new Logic or Theo-logic), he himself was aware of the ruptures of Being, occasioned by "accidents," the showings of Nonbeing or Nothingness, over which every thinker must "tarry." Hegel himself did not tarry long, so confident was he that all showings of Nothingness could be sublated by plenary Being. Indeed he could not tarry with anything apparent to mind under the form of *images* or other nondiscursive forms, forms not susceptible of subordination to the Concept. In this he broke with Böhme, and his old roommate Schelling, true to their common source in Böhme, broke with Hegel.[44]

Godhead Differently Determinate qua Creator and Redeemer

A disciplinary therefore sufficient thinking of the necessarily insufficient divine living-dying, a thinking of the very passion of God, is a theological thinking of the overplus remainder of the unsaid in the said of the tradition's principal matter, God godself. The historical abode or habitat of that taunt to thought has been the underground sinecures of the tradition itself, wherein the questionableness of the thinking of the said could be reconfigured and held open against more courageous days. The very omissions and transgressions of heterodoxies and marginal orthodoxies were themselves watching briefs for what thought hitherto had withheld from thinking; indeed, they gave shelter within their thinking to the very withholding within God godself, what we may call the staying-away of God from God the determinate Creator, the withdrawal of God in the crossing back through to Godhead, the self-refusal of God for recuperative Godhead, the very *chora* of omnipresent creativeness and destructiveness (the *chora* to come shortly into view). It is by no means easy to say what Prince of Thought kisses the withheld unthought into thinking wakefulness, either historically or as a matter of individual reflexivity. In the individual, I suspect it is the experience of the shock of the break of planes. Suffice to say that no tradition, whether theological or philosophical—especially one with a normative or orthodox core—awakens itself. One may say that the alarm clocks are wound and set not in single discourses but in their mixture; and in our own time, especially in the mixture of discourses of the diverse religions themselves.[45] As much is evident in a couple of sweeping (therefore involving egregious simplifications) generalizations, the one in theology and the other in philosophy. If early Christian theology lost the nothing of the *ex nihilo* to the Parmenidean Being-as-such, that nothing or some simulacrum of it was held only in the reserve of medieval theology's mixture with Neoplatonic discourse (even though the nothing thus reserved was merely privative Being), and an Eckhart—trying to think and preach the said of Aquinas and other schoolmen—could kiss the dormancy of Nothing into the wakefulness of Godhead beyond God, while leaving the questionableness of that kissing open. Western philosophy's long project of rendering nonbeing harmless (Gadamer) by swamping the second astonishment with the first has had its own career of interruptions, coming both from its own undersides and from discourses external to itself. An instance of the latter has already been noted: in Schelling and Hegel the theological memory of Nothing in Godhead kisses the dormancy, the reserve, of Being into a newly wakeful thinking. An example of the former, the reserve on the undersides of philosophy itself, is the inevitable Nietzsche—whose thinking of the reserve of the *nihil* exploded not just philosophical and theological but all the cultural discourses that have ensued in the phenomena of late-modern nihilism. Indeed it witnesses to the reserve in all discourses that the selfsame nihilism should have come home more in the arts than in either philosophy or theology. (It remains questionable, however, not only whether the merely destructive consequences of nihilism can be evaded but, more important, whether the *nihil* rescued from the reserve of multiple discourses in nihilism can be admitted in its positivity to thought.)

We of course are caught up in the effort to position ourselves to think again the unthought *metaxu*, the between, of Godhead and God. Why is it theologically important to do so, why the ever-pacing, sleepless furrowing of the theological brow, the mark of insomniac Ahab? Is it because we are destinately awake, summoned if not by Being then by the stretching of the *Übermensch*, the one who overcomes, while those in the village of the Motley Cow have nodded off? No, it is because of what theological thinking is summoned to think again: *the Advent and Recusal of God is unfinished*. A thinking can be no more finished than what it thinks. A theological thinking that aspires to save the appearances must think the uniform if troubled witness of the tradition, that what saves the appearances (namely, God godself) itself appears and disappears, discloses and conceals, gives and withholds, advenes and recuses. If there is a said in respect of this witness, and there is, that said bespeaks a divine advent; if there is an unsaid unthought, and there is, that unthought unsaid summons a thinking speaking about divine recusal, default, staying-away. It is not that once upon a time there was once and for all an Advent, or that once upon a time there was once and for all a Default, so that one may think the divine Advent and Recusal conclusively, however suffused the tradition is with symbolic paradigms of both. The inexhaustible indeterminacy of the divine Wisdom does not ever achieve such determinate form as to be exhausted singly either in Advent or in Recusal—indeed *could not* except in divine betrayal of the holy Covenant that constitutes creation and its redemption, which Covenant in the uniform, if troubled, witness is from everlasting to everlasting. The postcreational self-generation (intracausally) of the world is joined at the hip with postcreational theogony: this is the very economic determinateness of God the Creator, that Godhead has self-restricted its own indeterminateness, thus the becoming and unbecoming of God, vis-à-vis the becoming and unbecoming of the created order. This is so as long as determinate God Creator and Redeemer sustains a living-dying relation to creation, which is from everlasting to everlasting.

The unfinished character of the divine Advent-Recusal—roughly synonymous with the divine living-dying—is a challenge to any thinking of God, for would not such a thinking question the very reliability of the determinateness of God? Can theology as an integrally determinate process of thought be so without a stable referent? (Not to mention the affront to piety: a mother may forget her sucking babe, exults the Psalmist, but God will not forget Israel. But, as we will see, piety is closer to the thinking of the varying determinateness of God than is stiff-necked theology.) No, it cannot. But Christian theology never gets its matter so wrongly as when it takes that to be an object steadily and reliably there, whether as the Supreme Being or as Being-as-such (of which, too much already). As an integral enterprise of thought Christian theology is simultaneously indeterminate and determinate: determinate in its summons to think the divine determinateness, indeterminate in its thinking awe of the divine indeterminacy. This simultaneity or coincidence is the piety of thinking necessarily insufficiently. Because Christian theology has a large dimension of determinateness (hence the *via eminentia*), it has something to say about the intelligibility of (its) God to adherents and to those of other religions. Because the selfsame theology has also a large dimension of indeterminacy, hence the *via negativa*, it is open to the different renderings of holy indeterminate Wisdom not only in itself but in other religions as well.

As ours is a project in Christian theology, we are charged to think the divine triune determinateness within the site of the indeterminacy of Godhead. More precisely, we are charged to think the divine triune non-determinateness immanently, and the divine triune determinateness eco-nomically, within the site of the indeterminacy of Godhead. While in-exhaustibly generative indeterminate Godhead is determinately one and only one God, God the Creator and the selfsame God the Redeemer are differently determinate. Thinking this judgment further requires discrimi-nations in the immanent determinateness of the divine living-dying, the divine Advent and Recusal:

· The determinateness of God the Creator is linear and nondialectical, is monar-chic, is not and cannot be gone back on, crossed back through. Because the indeterminate Wisdom of Godhead is *ratio*ned[46] (and spirited, to come) in the determinateness of God the Creator, God creates a universe that is not random by condition and in which there is range for Spirit. The uniform witness of the (Christian) tradition is that the agential principle of creation is the divine Logos, the Word. Construed as the rationed conditions under which anything at all comes to be, comes from and goes toward nothing, *creatio ab origine* is finished, and the universe itself arising from those conditions traces the aboriginal Advent of God the Creator. That Advent is as stable as the universe itself, and it tells us little of the full panoply of the determinateness of either God or the universe. That fuller panoply engages the *creatio continua* (which involves the determi-nateness of redemption). How many times did God create the world? The right answer—once and only once, though not in time, since creation refers to the determinate conditions whereby anything whatever can be—does not satisfy, sufficiently. And does not satisfy because of the troubled state of the world in the history of redemption, a history accounted mythologically in the Bible. Not to do a full count: the Hebraic canon opens in Genesis with "And God said, Let there be . . . ," proceeds to the (near) destruction of the world in the Flood, and chronicles the making, unmaking, remaking of the people Israel; the canon of the early Jesus movement heralds a new creation, and closes in the Book of Revelation's vision of a new heaven and a new earth. Still and all, despite the faithlessness of this or that world in its comings and goings, the rainbow-sign of the divine faithfulness shines not above but out of disaster: the universe itself is the rainbow of the Advent of God the Creator. In spatial terms, we may say that God the Creator is at farthest linear unidirectional determinate remove from the indeterminacy of Godhead.

· The selfsame God (the Creator) is differently determinate as Redeemer. As the provenance of God the Creator is *creatio ab origine*, so the provenance of God the Redeemer is *creatio continua*. For redemption there is no sufficient reason; humanly received and thinkingly entertained, it is pure grace. The determinate-ness of God the Redeemer is not that of *ratio* but rather that of Spirit, which is by its nature nonlinear and metaxic, thus even more unfinished in work than that

of God the aboriginal Creator. This says that in spatial terms the determinateness of God the Redeemer is nearer the groundlessness of the indeterminate
Wisdom of Godhead than is the groundedness (in the Logos) of God the Creator.
God the Creator is the monarchic principal of temporal creation; God the Redeemer, selfsame God, is the monanarchic principal of redemption.

The determinateness of indeterminate Godhead is Janus-faced, may be
thought either immanently or economically, that wholly internal to God
godself and that external to God (i.e., from the standpoint of creation, of
God's relation to creation). In this enlightened age of aversion to speculation, thinking the former, the exhaustively immanent determinateness
of Godhead, is likely to be dismissed as theosophy or mysticism.[47] Despite
this aversion and thumbing the nose at it, we have tipped our hat in respect to the traditions honoring eternal creation as the unconditional
condition of the conditions of temporal creation: thinking the determination process upon which all determinateness depends. These remarks
edge upon expanding what it means to claim that the determinateness of
God the Redeemer is metaxic, for it is so in two respects. God the Redeemer
situates immanently between (but nearer to) the groundlessness of indeterminate Sophia and the groundedness of (and farther from) the Logos
of determinate God the Creator. And yet God the Redeemer also situates
economically between eternal and temporal creation, between God the
Creator and what ensues from temporal creation, from what goes on in
the self-generation of the universe once launched. God the Redeemer is
God freshly determinately taking account of what happens with and to his
little ones. Having granted in his mercy and grace to creatures, constituted
in the *imago Dei et ad imaginem Verbi*, the determinate freedom to preside
over their own (conditioned) indeterminacy, God the Redeemer keeps
watch, now in Advent, now in Recusal. In Recusal, because God can be and
is, granted the freedom granted to creatures, sur-prised, taken over and
a-back by the advent-ures of mankind. Without the open-ended redemptive determinateness of God, the determinateness of God the Redeemer,
we should have (if God at all) solely the logotic determinateness of God
the Creator, that of Enlightenment deism, the retired clockmaker—we
should not have the divine God.

We could of course envision the *situ* of the Redeemer differently. At
least two alternatives present themselves. One, arguably ameliorating the
speculative tinge and certainly putting the venture in more fashionable
company, would be to gender the determinateness of God. Hasn't a start
on that already been made, in the naming of the indeterminacy of Godhead the divine Wisdom (Sophia), since in all the western religious tradi-

tions the sophic dimension of deity is honored as feminine? One could be more explicit by thinking the Redeemer as feminine because determinately nearer the indeterminacy of the divine Wisdom and the Creator as masculine because determinately suffused with Logos: but such sitings would do a brisk trade in the stereotypes of the feminine as unstructured if not irrational and the masculine as Apollonic-logotic structure or *ratio*, but surely it is just the warrantability of such stereotypes that is now and rightly seriously in question.

A second alternative is indeed engagingly enticing, although it gives even fuller vent to the energies of speculation. I refer to the *tsimtsum* of Judaic Kabbalah, the where or space (*metaxu*, in my terms) of the Holy One, when/as En Sof (Godhead, in my terms) is not itself alone. The *tsimtsum* is the site of the contraction of En Sof, the site of what is and is not En Sof, the site of the beginning of difference. The citation of this parallel site in Judaic Kabbalah has its dangers in a context of Christian theological thinking, for the site occasions different forms of divine determinateness in Judaism and Christianity. While for both traditions it is the site of what I have called eternal creation, in kabbalistic Judaism it is the site of the eternal prefiguration or presagement of the breaking of vessels from which temporal creation will ensue (which has an all but exact analogue in Christianity in the eternal fall of the Archangel Michael/Lucifer [Michael: like God in being the angel of light; Lucifer: in falling into darkness], prefiguring the fall of mythologically archetypal Adam, prefiguring the temporal fall of every person). In Kabbalah, being the eternal site of what is and what is not En Sof, *tsimtsum* is the site of eternal Redemption, and reflection upon it brings the terrifying realization that God too stands in need of redemption: the pious kabbalist prays first not for his own redemption but for that of God, not so much or alone for the mending of the world but for the mending of contracted or dispersed God, for the healing of the fractured Shekhinah. Christianity in its orthodox forms has too long neglected, in its thinking of redemption, its roots in Judaism. Christian theology was right to construe its own analogue of *tsimtsum* as the site (in my terms) of the determination process of deity, the site of the divine triune self-determinateness. But orthodox Christianity has done so by construing this determinate deity as *ens perfectissimum*: as the perfect Being, God impassibly empowered to redeem the imperfect. As though God the determinate Creator were not complicit in the however free determinateness of his own creation. We ourselves have yet to think through, traverse the crossings of, redemption. And such a thinking has much, if not everything, to do with the divine Advent and Recusal.[48]

No doubt about it, the most trying of the divine determinatenesses (of the indeterminacy of Godhead) to think is that of the divine Redeemer, and both Judaism and Christianity are above all religions of redemption. Is this because humanly (is there any other way?) we can and all but invariably do take our creation, our being here/now, unthinkingly for granted in a way that we cannot take our redemption? And what is to be said of the soul nescient of the need for redemption, in the optimism of modernity said to be widely and wildly rampant? Of the soul scorning coming from nothing in the adequacy of explanation by efficient cause: I came from the loins of my parents, who came from the loins of . . . *ad infinitum regressum* (and no doubt, shortly, the medical insertion of new cassettes of *from*, a new *ad infinitum progressum*, by germline DNA genetic engineering)? If the nothing *from* is evaded in efficiently (but scarcely sufficiently) explanatory satiety, what about coming *to* nothing? Well, biologically there is the progeny of my own loins (which, in the selfsame shortly, can be done without the actual engagement of *my* loins through the selfsame cassettes, cloning, and who knows what else microbiology will come up with); and failing that, or in addition to that, there is my deposit in the accretions of human culture. Is all that of any highly redemptive satiety value? Does it justify an existence, *my* existence? These and their like are the human questions that put in question theologically the determinateness of God the Creator-Redeemer.

By these questions I by no means intend to cast aspersions on these and like questions occasioned by the rise and regnancy of the modern theoretical sciences; indeed I mean to honor them in a way that (Christian) theology has not always done. The sciences permit—nay, demand—that theology think redemption in ways it had all but forgotten. The relation between the divine self-immanence and the divine economy is not itself fixed, permanent, eternal. From a standpoint within the created universe (without which nothing, not even God the Creator)—and there is no other standpoint (which standpoint in religious sensibility includes evidences taken to be *evidentiary*)—God arises from indeterminate Wisdom as Determinate Word (Logos) and Spirit, as God the Creator (of the conditions) of the selfsame universe. The immediate but not whole (mediate) traced simulacrum of the linearity of the divine determinateness, the created universe, left God qua determinate Creator *ab origine* free to withdraw, absent himself from the universe save in logotic residua, the latter evident in the structures of intracausality and in the human mind itself. Historically, God the retired clock Designer coincided with the rise and flourishing of the modern sciences. Just this realization was potently latent in the Christian doctrine of *creatio ex nihilo* from the beginning, as some historians of science have recognized in the claim that it was the

Christian conviction of creation through the Logos that authorized or licensed (theologically) the unrestricted exercise of the human mind in respect of cosmogony and cosmology. However latent this recognition was in the Christian doctrine of creation, on the historical evidence probably only the modern sciences *could* have brought it maieutically to term (and the piteously so-called Christian creationists only advertise both their stupidity and their misunderstanding of the Christian doctrine of creation in resisting it). In any case, the recognition cannot be gone back on and won't be. There is something wonderfully liberating in the recognition, itself latent in the *creatio ex nihilo*, but often forgotten theologically in the tradition, and only incipiently thought through: God qua determinate Creator does not meddle determinately in the universe (intervene in, supravene, the intracausality of the universe): in Einstein's phrase, God does not play dice with the universe. Well then, if God the Creator does not meddle in the universe, is not there in the intracausality of the universe, we need not muddle over the nonmeddling God: surely that has been the drift of modernity. Why then did Christian reflection, which always potently but latently had this recognition—to be sure, more or less developed—always muddle over the nonmeddling God? Because determinately nonmeddling God the Creator does not exhaust the determinateness of Godhead. How to think God the determinate Redeemer who qua God the determinate Creator steadfastly does not meddle?

One honorable answer might well be: as does the Bible. If any generalization about the Bible (which comprises many books and in important respects is not a whole) is safe—and none is without qualification—it could well be the claim that from beginning to end the Bible is the witness to human exasperation, now exulting now despairing, with a now meddling now unmeddling God (despite the claim by some that the Christian canon is an exception). Having created the world by covenant with a thus constituted people, God the Creator arouses the expectation that he will be reliably present in it and to them (what I, perhaps intemperately, have called meddling). But the uniform plaint of scripture, more palpably evident in the Hebraic than in the Christian canons (although equally evident in the latter, except to literalists of all stripes), is the complaint not that God meddles but that he doesn't. More precisely, given the unvarying scriptural witness that God has not left godself without witness in God's own creation, the now meddling thus (determinately) present God along with the now unmeddling thus (determinately) absent God leaves his ostensible human beneficiaries redemptively confused, exulting in the Psalmic former, despairing in the Lamentations latter (as Job knew). This alternating ecstasy and despair is not alone or only the drama of human life; it is the very fusion and fission of the divine living-dying, the Advent and Recusal of determinate God, the very eternal self-determinateness of indeterminate Godhead. Because human confusion (on this matter, rightly placed) is sheltered in the holy fission-fusion of the endless determinateness of indeterminate Godhead, humankind has hope. Redemption is fundamentally about *hope*. It is often enough said (and by my lights rightly) of both Judaism and Christianity that creation names the origin and redemption names the end (in the sense of *telos*) of the universe; and for both the God of creation and the God of redemption are selfsame, one God. If Christianity and Judaism have few if any bones to pick over creation (and God the Creator), they divide substantively over the determinatness of one God: in Christian theology the determinateness of the indeterminacy of Godhead both immanently (internal to God) and economically (external to God, vis-à-vis creation) is diverse as between creation and redemption, with the entailment that redemption is construed differently. Redemption is not less eschatological (despite all Christian discourse about realized eschatology) than in Judaism, but it is differently so, and we are trying (again) to think this difference in the Advent, the Recusal, the Default of God the Redeemer.

A cautionary note about my use of the word *default* as a synonym of *recusal*, the staying-away of determinate God the Redeemer. Employing the simple or ordinary sense of words to do complex duty is a venture invariably perilous, and such a venture must invariably rely upon pressured context to amend their simplicity. As a term in law, *default* refers to breach of contract, a failure to keep a promise. Since God promised to be present unfailingly in and to his creation, is not default then a failure of selfsame God to keep that promise? No, because of the other resonances in the word, touched on earlier, and because of resonances in complementing words. (In principle, a singly determinate word could be adequate only to singly determinate indeterminate Godhead.) And as for *recusal*: a judge recuses herself from advention in the court when/as her interest is warranted to compromise the application of pertinent law to the case to be adjudicated: she stays-away from *that* case but does not cease to be Judge.

. Given the fact of creation, the reality of the universe external but also internal to God, the staying-away default of God the Creator (from that universe) is the economic condition of the full determinateness of God—*and* the full determinateness of the universe. Stated variantly, the staying-away of God the Creator is the condition of the Advent of God the Redeemer; just as the exercise of determinate human freedom (divinely donated in creation) issues in recognized externality to God, which takes the form of the recognition of the need for redemption—a need not *eo ipso* the negation of God but intrinsically the fulfillment of the human creature created *in imago Dei*. The human creature would have legitimate grounds for the negation of God only if the determinateness of God were exhausted in the defaulting staying-away of God the Creator, the God of origin. Every gnosticism so concludes with respect to God the Creator, as it concludes with respect to a different and superseding God, the God of end (*telos*), God the Redeemer.

· If both Judaism and Christianity have recognized in Gnosticism in all its pagan colarations a portrait to be effaced,[49] that owes—however much origin and end are to be discriminated—to the conviction that creation and salvation are seamlessly, eternally, albeit determinately intertwined in the indeterminateness of Godhead. A matter of unending awe, God creates in order to redeem godself, becomes variously determinate in order to rescue (redeem) the indeterminacy of Godhead. Immanently, as God the Creator is the determinate staying-away from indeterminate Godhead as the necessary condition of there being anything external to God, so the Default or Recusal of God the Creator is the repair or fallback of thus determinate God into the surplus of indeterminate Godhead for that determinateness which sufficiently conditions the Advent of God the Redeemer. If the determinateness of God the Creator is unidirectional and linear, thus the necessary ground of temporal creation, that of God the Redeemer is *metaxic*: engages the divine crossing back and forth (the Passover?) through the between of God and Godhead for sufficiently determinate recuperation of indeterminacy for God's reckoning redemptively with the freedom of the universe's staying-out of God. The mending of Godhead is more primordial than that of the world however much, from our standpoint in temporal creation, the two mendings are coincident—as the so-called history of redemption witnesses.

Because God advenes and recuses, appears and disappears in different determinateness, we speak of the divine living-dying. *Living-dying* in this usage of course should be scare-quoted. Or should it? Why is the death of God normally scare-quoted; and if that is warranted, why not also the life (or living) of God? Properly, univocally, literally speaking, God is not organic or animate, not even *a* Being, not an individual, not a person (nor, so we have claimed, Being as such). Notwithstanding and nevertheless, the western tradition, consistently managing a lively traffic in broken symbols, has as consistently spoken of the living God; and the Christian tradition has taken the selfsame God to be dying. We essay here to think again the divine living-dying in thinking the modalities of the determinateness of indeterminate Godhead.

The defaulting Recusal of God the eternally determinate Creator of the temporally determinate universe is a crossing back through, beyond the nondeterminacy of both nothing and Being rendered determinate by God the Creator, for a replenishment of the indeterminacy of Godhead, a metaxic trajectory that courses eternally in the repetitive determinateness of the divine living-dying, the passional crossing toward the second not of God's own salvation or redemption. God's Advent and Recusal are repetitive but episodic, because in God's own good time. *Both* Advent and Recusal are the rainbow of promise, that God has not abandoned creation, that Godhead has not abandoned God. Not creation, because the human creature too is launched on a temporal career of lurching unidirectionally from a (created) indeterminate nothingness toward a (in part, self-constituted) determinate something, a faulted lurching that redemptively defaults that something for a coursing back through all temporal determinateness for a replenishment toward his or her own second not (and simultaneously a second being). This wants a later thinking through; for now it suffices to say that the fault (in the geological sense) between *imago Dei* and *ad imaginem Verbi* in the human creature is the faint trace in temporal creation of the eternally groundless ground of the divine *metaxu*, the between of the divine Advent and Recusal.

Having been drawn into a perhaps premature thinking of the modalities of divine determinateness even though our announced site was that of the indeterminacy of Godhead and we intend to return more directly to that site, we permit ourselves a pondering of the sort of thinking under way. However sponsored and graced by our betters in the genealogical lineage of our thinking on these matters, which lineage we are all slow to discover (and we are even slower to submit ourselves to their rigorous discipline), when thinking is dispatched into thought of God it remains a lonely admission to territory without map. That territory is itself but a vestibule, something like Plato's antechamber of the Good, to which all prior thinking is summarily summoned, but from which the thinking there is simultaneously repelled, a site where what is there does not exhaust what there is, where both do not exhaust what is not there and what there is not. Thinking dispatched into and repelled by thought of the divine God is no more favored if based in revelation than in reason—save in this, that thinking summoned into thought by epiphantic (scripturally mediated) disclosure knows itself to be resisted and repelled by reservation, by what is not evident in the evidence of the *what* of theological thought. If the history of theological thinking in the main is that of thinking off the reservation, that of proper theological thinking is on the reservation—since the summons to think the divine God is simultaneously the repulsion of such thinking (an incorrigible fact known in all negative theologies: God is not . . .). Thinking simultaneously dispatched to and repelled by (often returned as undeliverable) thought of the divine God is precisely not thought of Being as such, not to mention of supreme Being.[50] It is a thinking aspiring to the thought of the divine Intellect. Theological thinking is no less audacious—even outrageous—than that, is of a piece with the aspiration to write the autobiography of God. Meister Eckhart, the most audacious of all (but then, there is Böhme to factor in), was exactly right in his Dominican (ironically, the Order of Preachers!) protest against the Franciscans: the divine intellect exceeds (as Plato said of the Good, in dignity and power) both the divine being and the divine will, indeed every divine attribute, and that because the divine intellect thinks not-being as well as being, thinks God's own becoming and unbecoming. What God thinks is his own Godhead, the eternal genesis of God. Theological thinking dispatched to and repelled by such thought audaciously thinks God's thoughts after him. And it does so under the eminent/imminent danger of idolatry, against which it is protected if at all only by a self-conscious theological iconoclasm, present above all in the astonishment of the Protestant Reformation—but which faltered and falters in every scholasticism, not less in our own. Nothing is more effectively iconoclastic than the reminder that our thinking is positioned in the *metaxu*, between the *imago Dei* and the *ad imaginem Verbi*, a *metaxu* that abridges or should abridge every venture of theological thinking. Nothing guarantees that this chasm of the *metaxu* can be bridged, crossed, thinkingly. It is the indelible but faint trace of Schelling's Cross of the Divine Intellect in the human intellect as it tries to think the divine God. Nonetheless, we too are summoned into the breach and must think bridge again.

Between Godhead and God: Pneumatic *Chora*

We are consumed presently in the effort to think the interiority, thus the immanence, of the divine God, the determination process, the motion of the abyssal indeterminacy of Godhead through modulations of the determinateness of God, very theogony. This interiority is anything but a sanctuary of impassible repose, a transcendent sinecure of quiescence. It is rather a choreograph—indeed a *perichoresis*—of trinitarian effervescence (tripping the eternal lights fantastic?). The divine interiority is marked prominently by being unsettled, a veritable *turba*, so Jakob Böhme, in which what is settled is itself unsettling. The region of the emergence-y of the divine God for humankind coincides with any region that bounds the unsettling of being settled.

Godhead as sheer indeterminacy is *anchoritic*. Not by accident were the mystics and saints who were given over in aspiration to Godhead alone (hence beyond God) called anchorites, *an-choritesm*, for they were those without a space (*chora*), without a home for their own *that in which* to be. (Plato's most straightforward discursive translation of the *chora* was "that in which.") The divine indeterminacy sheer is both anarchic and anchoritic at once. The divine living-dying, however, is not exhausted by the two extremities of its determination process, to the left the groundlessness of indeterminate Godhead, to the right the determinateness of God the Creator (the ground of all that is external to God). There is the matter of the two, the opposites, and the classical problem of mediation, that of the third, Plato's third kind (*triton genos*). In the modern German tradition of worrying this classical problem, between the *Ungrund* and the *Grund* there is the *Abgrund*. The prefix *Ab*: the staying-away from. Staying away from what? Staying away from both ground (determinacy) and groundlessness (sheer indeterminacy); staying into the crossing reserve of a third kind, which I shall come to think as the choreograph of Spirit. This *Abgrund*, abysm of nondeterminacy, Plato thought in the *chora* of the *Timaeus*. More accurately, it is through the *chora* that Plato thought the hermeneutical equivalent of what I am calling the *abgrundlich* nondeterminate within his own unfolding ontology-meontology, itself transparently different from the theological meontology essayed here, since for Plato the god or demiurgic World-Soul was but one among other multiple factors in accounting for the cosmos.

As the whole of *Timaeus* puts in evidence, the site of the discursive thinking of *chora* is somewhere in the midst of the binary opposition of logos and mythos, and that because of its very puzzling intelligibility. Not only is it of a third ontological genus, but is also of a third genus of discourse or thinking. Plato spoke of the admittance of the *chora* to a bastard reasoning, that of the waking dream—which is scarcely mythos. But it is not admitted to a logic of logos, thus not to an exactly true account, construed as a logic of noncontradiction, precisely because the *chora* gives home both to the likes and the unlikes and their passage into each other. What would be the discursive place of this third ontological kind? Although itself neither intelligible nor sensible and not even a principle, it seems *necessary* to think since (and this is the remarkable development in *Timaeus*, beyond *Sophist* and *Philebus*) the *chora* is now numbered among the eternal factors of necessity that reason (demiurgic World-Soul) must persuade in order for a many not wholly devoid of a one (namely, all that we count as cosmic reality) to be, appear, or manifest. Such a discursive thinking would be adequated to a third (in my terms) onto-meontological genus, metaxic nondeterminacy, between groundlessly sufficient indeterminacy and necessarily grounded determinacy.[51]

Incorrigible Platonist that I am in this respect, the onto-meontological genera take priority even if and especially if, as here, getting those types into the region of a true account involves a displacement of previous ontological fixations—not exempting the Platonic, but especially displacing the Neoplatonic, and above all the ontotheological. No doubt some will claim that the ontological work has been done in this or that thinker since Plato; or that—given the convolutions of the *chora*—it cannot be done; or that the ontological enterprise is misguided from the outset. The strongest claim would be that both the ontological and the discursive complexities of the *chora* (how the two remain two, yet are one, how the one remains one, yet two) are coincidentally resolved in, say, Hegel's *New Science of Logic*; the strongest voice of a theological reader of Hegel in support of this claim would be that of Thomas J. J. Altizer. The evidence against Hegel on this matter is at the very least his own discursive practices, even more the ontological warrants for them, the subordination of image to concept, indeed the subornation of image by concept. It was Plato's artful genius to reflect his own indecision as between a logic of logos (a true account) and a logic of the mimeme (the probable story) in the full range of his mixed discourses. One can abide Plato's occasional chagrin with the poets because, equally occasionally, he was one (whereas Heidegger, who adored certain poets—such as Hölderlin and Trakl, but not Rilke—was not).

In Plato's middle period, as reflected in *Sophist* and *Philebus*, any determinate thing is said to be a mixture of factors more ultimate than itself, itself being but a moving image (*eikon*) of them. According to the fourfold ontological schema of *Philebus*, any determinate thing in the cosmos is a mixture of the unlimited (*apeiron*), my sheer indeterminacy, and limit (*peras*), my determinacy of ground, and is thus mixed through the agency of a cause (*aitía*), the soul, in the service of a purpose or end, which is the Good.[52] Plato fully recognizes that every cosmic determinate thing is thus precarious. It is, against Parmenides, not nothing; but neither is it eternal being (*to pantelos on*) in the sense that the factors it is a mixture of are; it is something on pain of being nothing at all. And what kind of being is that, a being in a mirror? He promises to return to the ontological standing of the images (*eikones*), the mixed, in a subsequent dialogue, the *Philosopher*, which as far as is known he never wrote. But the problem did not go away and palpably chewed on him. The last frontal assault (to my knowledge) was in *Timaeus*, whose *chora* occasioned a fundamental amendment or addition to his earlier ontological schema. An immense literature has followed in its wake. Let it be said forthrightly that beginning to end Plato never varied from the one constant that initiates his reflections on the *chora*, the schema of the paradigm or mimeme. He takes nothing back from the *Sophist* and the *Philebus* in respect of the cumulus of the paradigm(s) and that they are mixedly, determinately mimed in every cosmic reality. But what holds, gives shelter to, the mime? Whatever it is, it has not the constancy of the eternal determinates (form, soul, Good) nor the constant inconstancy of the eternally indeterminate Unlimited. What is it itself?

This pointed question is taken up in a vast project indeed. The *Timaeus*, says Plato, is the totality of discourse concerning the universe (92c); as such it is a general ontology, a theology, a cosmology, a physiology, a psychology, a zoology—the whole shooting match, as we say, an ambition few modern thinkers have entertained. There in the middle of the dialogue . . . pause . . . does one read too much into the discursive placement of the *chora* in the middle, the between, of the dialogue? In any case, there in the middle is the there of the mime, a kind of aperture on every thing's cosmic abyss. Mind you, if the *chora* is an abyss, it is not to be confused with that chaos also named at the beginning of the dialogue which demiurgic Reason is to dispel or supplant through the very constitution of the cosmos by persuading or overcoming it with necessity. No, if *chora* is abyssal it is so not as akin to the primordial chaos but as a strange feature of necessity. (Strange, because necessity cannot function without it, yet it by itself is not necessary. Necessary to the determination process, in my terms it is between necessary ground and sufficient groundless.) This strangeness, so alien to the other factors of necessity (and not exempting the unlimited), is triggered whenever the *chora* is put into play, which is whenever one is seized both by the solidity and the tenuousness of anything there. Where the *chora* is brought into play, which is every cosmic where, the *da-* of *Dasein*, it coincides with something like an abysm, or *aporia*, but a strangely although nondeterminate necessary one because it cradles the *eidola* (hence having *some* features of determinacy), all those mimemes that comprise the totality of the beings of the cosmos (while at the same time being insufficient in respect of intelligibility, as we shall come to, hence indeterminate). This choric abysm is not itself a mere feature of the cosmos itself, thus not a fault *in* the cosmos, but a condition of there being a cosmos at all, a condition of things that have *some* being on pain of being nothing at all. Thus the *chora* itself is beyond cosmology and anthropomorphy. That says that the abyssal *chora* is itself eternal, is numbered among the factors of necessity with which demiurgic reason must conjure in order to subdue chaos into some service of the Good. But the itself of the *chora*, how is *that* to be thought? In itself it seems out-nothinged only by the blank nothingness of the unlimited. If the *chora* is abyssal and thus veers toward nothing, it is not *that* kind of nothingness it reaches to. It appears rather to be a chasm, to be chiasmic, the *metaxu*, the between, the place between the sheer unlimited and those other eternal factors and conditions that solicit and summon the mixed, the mimemes, into cosmic being. But perhaps we get too far ahead of ourselves. We need to get a summation of the middle part of *Timaeus* into view.

At roughly midpoint in the *Timaeus* Plato pauses to recapitulate the germ of the treatise thus far and to announce a new beginning. The force of what had gone before is summarized in the claim that the generation of this universe was a mixed result of the combination of necessity and reason (48a).[53] Hitherto he had reckoned with reason's contribution (which of course included the causal agency of soul and the eternal forms) to any mixture, and now he must begin again by attending to what is factored in necessity, above all what is termed errant cause. Since this factor (or factors) is not pliant to reason, he will not be able to speak of it in terms of the first principle or principles (48c) but rather, venturing still on the worth of a probable account, he will offer an explanation no less probable than another, but more so (48d) (and in so doing when essaying proba-bility, continuing a tradition unbroken from the pre-Socratics, he invokes the aid of a protecting deity). Reason has delivered two radically different kinds (genera) of being: the intelligible invisible model (the paradigm), which is eternal and unchangeable, and the copy or mimeme (*eidolon*), which becomes, is visible and changeable.

It is necessary to admit to thought a third kind, and it is this thinking that comprises Plato's new beginning in the middle. He is slow, even ago-nizingly slow, to name it (and does not do so, as *chora*, until he reaches his new summary statement at 52a). Slow because the thing to be thought is difficult and obscure (49a) and free of all qualities (or characters) of its own (50c–51b). Why difficult and why obscure? As a third kind of being and giv-ing housing or hospitality to the mimeme, as entertaining the mimeme's participation of the eternal paradigm(s), it cannot itself be totally unreal, thus not nothing. But it manifestly has not the same kind of being as the paradigms in themselves, but of a kind no less constant and thus coeternal with them. Plato in fact stalks his quarry by query and largely through metaphor/symbol. His first such is a quasi-abstract one, immediately fol-lowed by a concrete one: it is the receptacle—as it were, the nurse—of all becoming (49a). And his most straightforward discursive indication of what it is, is that in which all things come to be (49e), the *that in which* without which there would be no this or that.[54] Stated in my terms, there

can be no determinateness without the intermediation between indeterminacy and determinacy, without nondeterminacy as the receiver or
host of that intermediation.[55] Plato appears to be saying that while there
is no material counterpart to the ideal forms, thus no eternal material substance, there is, because of qualities concatenating in this or that as this
or that comes to be and vanishes, something like a substantial recipient
or guesthouse—an always-there home for transients. (Here begins an old
argument about substance, and Aristotle will pounce on it.)

Something like a substantial recipient because "it must be called always
the same; for it never departs from its own character" (50bc). The *that in
which* is difficult and obscure because its character is: to have no character. It never takes on the character of anything it gives room to. It neither
receives nor gives. All applicants at the cosmic guesthouse are registered;
no passports, no visas, no credit checks, all welcome, none expelled. It is
matrix, mother, nurse, womb; when we reach its name, *chora*, it is space
and synonyms: location, region, site, situation. Without character itself, it
can and does receive any character or combination of characters. Had it a
nature or character itself, it could not receive things of a contrary nature;
had it a character, it could not host both the eternal and the temporal.
Plato's summary statement before the naming of *chora*: "we shall not be
deceived if we call it a nature invisible and characterless, all-receiving,
partaking in some very puzzling way of the intelligible and very hard to
apprehend" (51b). The *that in which* is apprehended by a sort of bastard
reasoning, and hardly an object of belief (52b), a statement made in the
first naming of *that in which* as *chora*. Prior to the naming of it as space,
Plato had approached it through metaphor, sensory detour for acceding
to intelligible meaning.[56] As the kind of reality the *chora* has is a third kind
between the sensuousness of becoming and the intelligibility of pure
Being, so the discursive thinking appropriate to it must be between the
logic of logos and that of the dream, hence a bastard reasoning. My own
summation: not Being and not Nothing, yet sheltering determinate becoming (itself the concatenated determinateness of Being and Nothing),
the *chora* is nondeterminate and as a characterless such is coeternal with
both Being and Nothing.

Plato's Timaean *chora* is sighted and sited in every (determinate) particular as speculative intelligence is engaged, a site that while offering
shelter to that particular also shelters an internal *aporia*, abysm or gap. Of
course, every thinker of note has thought *aporiae* and abysses and in doing
so has sighted/sited them variously. At least three such sites have been
perennial candidates. Whether and how the abyss can be bridged depends

in large measure on the site: (1) the abyss/*aporia* between Creator and creation (or between ground and what arises from and on the ground); (2) the *aporia*/abyss within temporal/created things; (3) the *aporia*/abyss within the ground, or between the ground and the groundless. Each site has and all sites have claims upon such thinking as is here under way, especially in the thought-experiment: God-Godhead. None can be dismissed, nor can any be evaded save as it folds into a more encompassing abysm.

In a radically monotheistic Christian thinking of the *creatio ex nihilo* the abyss between Creator and creature (1) is not (and cannot be) indissoluble, however much orthodox Christianity may have made it so (out of a paranoid fear of pantheism). If the nothing from which every temporally determinate thing stands out is not exhaustively external to the Creator (as here acknowledged, by the *creatio ex nihilo*), then the nothing is *internal* to the creating God, and such abysm as the creature participates is folded back into (3). Further, the selfsame abysm obtains not in respect of the creature's *esse*, since any creature *is* (exists, *esse*) as fully as any other creature and indeed as fully as the creating God. Such abysm as the creature participates thus must obtain in respect of its essence, which owes to its degree of nothing—and if that nothing is internal to the god, we are back to (3). But perhaps (2) yields the primary range of abyss(es) to be thought, as in Plato's *chora*?

Indeed that site (that of the created, or mixed) has its own perplexing *aporiae*/abysms beyond the disjuncture between the *esse* and *essentia* of classical representational realistic metaphysics. First is the space or habitat of any hecceity or mixed, exactly the *that in which* the later Plato thought by bastardly reason through the *chora*. Thinking just this *aporia* alone carries its own difficulty—as Plato saw—for this *aporia* doubles or triples itself. When philosophical thinking encounters a perplexing *aporia*, the intrinsic nisus of such thinking is to bridge the gap through all the available maneuvers of discursive logic. One has only to think the space (*chora*) of a particular bridge—whose nature is to connect this with that (typically one body of land to another, over water or air, over a literal chasm—to see that this *aporia* multiplies itself doubly or triply. The space of the Brooklyn Bridge is the particular place of that bridge and no other: because of where it is it (among many other factors, in number probably indeterminable) renders Manhattan and Brooklyn determinate in relation to each other; it is but one of innumerable ways in which those boroughs are determinate, ways in which the gap between them is bridged. *This* bridge could have been located at other points on the East River: the possible space of bridge was actually placed as the *that in which* of the Brooklyn Bridge, habitat of *this* bridge, thus bridging the (second) *aporia* between bridge and the Brooklyn Bridge, and simultaneously bridging the *aporia* between this determinable Brooklyn and that determinable Manhattan.

The abysm sighted in the site of the temporally determinate (or determinable), the *aporia* between existence and essence as representational metaphysics had it, thus doubles or deepens itself as the site of bridge itself heaves into view. That site (of the determinate or determinable) is sighted as the temporal trace of a more primordial *aporia* within the ground of all that determinately is and is not. (If Plato did not think this expanded [or is it concentrated?] *aporia*, that was because his metaphysics had no space for a unitary ground.) Classical representational realistic metaphysics sought to bridge the expanded chasm through a claimed coincidence of essence and existence in God: in medieval Christianity by thinking God as *ens realissimum et perfectissimum*. Once the pandoric abysm is opened as in Plato's *chora*, that way of tracking *aporiae* to their lair is not viable even if one's problematic is not that of Plato (as here).

Bridge-itself triples the abysmal space (to the third) from which we set out in contemplating that of any *hecceitas*, that of the Brooklyn Bridge. The Verrazano Bridge connecting New York and New Jersey, the Ponte Milvio spanning the Tiber in Rome, the Ponte Vecchio arching the Arno in Florence, all are determinate bridges (which could have been placed elsewhere). But the *that in which* of any actual (determinate) bridge, as well as an alternative potential place for the selfsame bridge (but then, would it be *this* determinate bridge?), is different from the *that in which* of bridge-itself. The abysm underlying each of the three sites is at once internally unitary and diverse. Thought is solicited if not compelled in the contemplation of any determinate thing downward into the vortex of a helical spiral, so that each abysm or *aporia* is enfolded in a more encompassing abysm, arcing from determinacy toward indeterminacy. The differences between the planes of abysm must itself be bridged, an enterprise of thought held in fidelity to the determination process itself, a thinking at least aspiringly adequated to that process. For some pages now we have been edging upon the intermediating bridge between indeterminacy and determinacy in the divine living-dying, upon upwardly spiraling helical theogony, from indeterminate Godhead to determinate God.

The place of the ideal forms (bridge itself) has not the determinateness of any temporally-spatially located thing. That place is itself nondeterminate, is the *Ab-grund* between *Ungrund* and *Grund*; it stays away from both absolute indeterminacy and from absolute determinacy; in the divine self-constitution, it is the place of Spirit, the place of the very body of God. One may of course be invited into the antechamber of the choric abysm at any level of the determination process, through any gap, break, or caesura of plane that puts itself upon us. Any entrance thus for any standing, for the reflective mind, will lead to recessive-progressive breaks, gaps, *aporiae*, if what is beyond them is to be reached. Little wonder, then, the speculative fascination with the bridge! Little puzzlement too why I have settled so much attention at this point upon Plato's *chora*, since it is through reflection upon the standing of the *that in which* of any particular thing that we are inserted into the maelstrom of interlocking *aporiae* and driven into the ground and its groundless beyond to thinking necessarily insufficiently: from necessary standing to insufficient understanding.

Cosmogony (Κοσμογονία): God and Creature

> The starting point of critical elaboration is the consciousness of what one really is, and it is "knowing thyself" as a product of the historical process to date, which has deposited in you an infinity of traces, without leaving an inventory. Therefore it is essential at the outset to compile such an inventory.
>
> —ANTONIO GRAMSCI, *THE PRISON NOTEBOOKS*

This chapter is a modest first step toward rethinking a Christian theological understanding of *creatio ex nihilo*.[1] In such ventures one does not begin from scratch but aspires to insert oneself in discourses in which the *a quo* (from which) is clear but the *ad quem* (toward which) is not, discourse that promises the potency of allowing voice to what is sought, discourse sufficiently volatile to betray its inadequacy to the residual subject about which the words are in play, to echo Thoreau.[2] Such discourse I have found to beckon in theologians more concerned with beacons than boundaries, whose beacons transgress boundaries. Almost as old as the *creatio ex nihilo* itself is the ascription of nonbeing as one of the names of God by the Greek Cappadocian Fathers in the fourth century CE, a lineage that extends in the Latin West through Marius Victorinus in the same century, Pseudo-Dionysius of the sixth century, Maximus the Confessor in the seventh, John Scotus Eriugena in the ninth, Meister Eckhart in the thirteenth and fourteenth, Nicholas of Cusa in the fifteenth, and Jakob Böhme in the sixteenth and seventeenth centuries, not to mention William Blake in the eighteenth and F. W. J. Schelling in the nineteenth.

Any reference to *the* Christian doctrine of creation is already overdetermined. If one takes the irreducible core of such a doctrine to be the claim that God created all that is not God from nothing (*ex nihilo*)—all that is on pain of being nothing at all—that is but the *a quo* and certainly not the *ad quem* of theological thinking on creation. Between the *a quo* and any sustainable *ad quem* there is much hard and plain historical work to be done: Why was an irreducible core of the *ex nihilo* slow to emerge and gain acceptance? And there is the even harder not-so-plain thinking of a theological and metaphysical sort: What of the *nihil*, the nothing or nonbeing of *ex nihilo*; is the *nihil* external or internal to God? Such a thinking is rendered both difficult and necessary by the assimilation of the *ex nihilo* to a metaphysical tradition of Being, bent on, in Gadamer's apt phrase, "rendering nonbeing harmless" or nugatory, whether in classical antiquity the eternity of Parmenides's acosmic One, or in late modernity the temporality of traces, the temporally endless play of signifiers. As much does not mean that Jerusalem should have nothing to do with Athens's Being and its stiff-arming of nonbeing, anymore than it means that Jerusalem should now have everything to do with Benares's *neti neti* or Kyoto's *sunyata*. Christian theology is as intellectually embedded as all forms of Christian religion are culturally embedded. That says that Christian theology and Christian religion are evolving, and have been since their origin. *Creatio ex nihilo*, the doctrine no less than the actuality of creation (*creatio continua*) is unfinished; and the doctrine arguably is unfinishable, or is so if the *nihil* is not to be cheated of its claim and force.

The venerable distinction between *creatio ab origine* and *creatio continua* arose in early Christianity and was developed extensively in the rigor of medieval thought for a variety of reasons of which two may be mentioned: (1) the effort to discriminate the divine reality from its modalizations, eternal and temporal, as monarchic and as trinitarian; and (2) the effort to discriminate yet relate the divine reality to what is *not* God; that is, the relation between Creator and creation. It was the latter that brought the distinction into fresh importance with the dawn of modernity, occasioned in the seventeenth century by the rise of the new sciences, above all astronomy. Earlier geocentric theologians, taking creation essentially to be exhausted by earth and the heavens visible from it (the latter inhabited by the remnants of eternal creation, the angels), could construe creation to be essentially finished in one fell fiat. The new heliocentrism and its successors, such as the expanding/contracting universe, exploded that old trope without possibility of repair.

Now, whether or not one holds with the divine creation of the universe but especially if one does, one must account for the perpetuity, the process of finite creation, given the big bang (or a surrogate construct), the process of the self-aggrandizing, self-contracting universe. Thus is revivified in new cosmological and cosmogonical frames the venerable distinction between *creatio ab origine* and *creatio continua*, a distinction enfolding the determination process itself: eternal creation as determinate God the Creator from indeterminate Godhead; temporal creation, as determinate letting be on loan (hence not God and not other-than-God) toward a *not* that is the province, within determinate parameters, of self-causation (whether of gain or loss). While initially in this chapter we are to be reminded of the *scène* of creation in eternity, we must turn hereafter to the *scène* of time, particularly the remarkable time-consciousness that has marked modernity and postmodernity. For we will need to ponder Thoreau's homely counsel that you cannot kill time without injuring eternity.

As one undertakes to rethink *creatio ex nihilo* in the eternity and time of nonbeing (and being), one does not do so because one has gotten back to first base, some foundation or ground, to what Leibniz called "necessary and sufficient reason." Early western modernity in philosophy largely exhausted itself (if not the subject matter) in such a foundationalism, just as postmodernity seems bent on establishing the groundlessness of the primordial words in play (*God, being, nothing, creation*). On the other hand, no one should delude herself by thinking that in thinking anything of high importance she begins from scratch. Augustine found in the *Confessions* that he had not to begin but to take up with a conversation he had overheard within himself, one to which he had not hitherto been audient and in which he had not been actively a participant. Thinking of this order is less a beginning, is more a resumption (see my remarks on the impossibility of an absolute beginning in Appendix B).

Christian theology can have done with neither being nor nonbeing because both God and the human home are doubly *located* and *vocated* in eternity and time. The two topics in each pair, eternity and time, being and nonbeing, are not two topics but one; that is, each is bound to the other. They are so if Christian theology is sourced by epiphanies and hierophanies that are incorrigibly apocalyptic, as I take them to be. By this I do not mean—but rather dispute—that eternity correlates with being, time with nonbeing, while recognizing that some of the Christian theological traditions argue just that strict correlation. These matters and their corollary doctrines (God, world, anthropology) are at stake in the doctrine or theory of creation—especially the *creatio ex nihilo*, the doctrine that the present reflections aspire to unthink, rethink, and afterthink.

Antonio Gramsci observed in his prison notebooks that to know ourselves on a topic is to recognize that the historical process has left an infinity of traces pertinent to it but without an inventory, and that critical elaboration of the topic awaits making such an inventory.[3] Within the scope of this chapter it is not possible to make an inventory of the traces in the discourses of all theologians—nor even in the theologians just named—on the topic of creation. If I here concentrate for the most part on Eckhartian traces, even that will be by virtue of discriminating them according to *problematic* in something like Louis Althusser's sense: some determinate unity given rise to by analysis. The two unities utilized here to inventory the traces of creation are eternity and time, and the problematic of *their* unity, mindboggling in its infinity of traces, is broached only toward the end in underdeveloped references to the apocalyptic.

The One and the Many

Recall that the burden of the previous chapter was to think the self-generation of the divine life, itself a condition of the distinction between Godhead and God. Closely interconnected with that distinction is consideration of the classical philosophical-theological problem of the one and the many. In Judaism and Islam, God is severely and unambiguously one—except when God *is not*, that is, in Kabbalism and Sufism, respectively. In most traditional Christianity, God is ambiguously one: one substance or nature in three persons; christologically, two natures in one person. All three monotheisms claim the oneness of God to be the deliverance of revelation, however different each may be from the other. And what of the standing of what is not-God, the mortal creature? Is the creature a one or a many, and in what respects? Is the creature one because it is *like* the one God, but different because *unlike* God in its manyness?

If the oldest philosophical problem is the one and the many, the oldest incitement to thinking is the wonder or astonishment that anything is: Why is there anything at all, why not rather nothing? As noted repeatedly in these pages, nothing, the *nihil*, hovers over everything existing as that from which existents stand out temporarily and into which they dissolve. Nothing is not a *something* that presents itself to mind as existing things do (but then, neither is Being such a something). Is the nothing that hoveringly surrounds the one the same nothing that hoveringly surrounds the many? Is the one determinate (one thing), is the many determinate (as in many things)? Enfolded in this question is the ultimate question about ultimate matters: Are both one and many indeterminate in their very natures? Our unfolding answer is yes, because each is equiprimordial in the abyssal eternal indeterminate Godhead *ipsum*.

Of the two diverging alternatives, I essay to combine the virtues of both, resisting but submitting myself to the blandishments of the vices of both. To be sure, classical Christian orthodoxy had the same intention, but we are given to question, was it an intention that failed of fruition? Normative Christian theology aspired to accord both one and many their due through the doctrine of the Trinity. It vested one and many in the divine God by construing God's interior life as exhausted by three subsistent persons related through a common (therefore unitary) substance or essence (*ousia*). While there is not a scintilla of such a doctrine per se in the Bible, the doctrine of the Trinity arose in early Christianity to make multiple sacred epiphanies, as reported by biblical witnesses, cohere with the one divine God, and further to make those epiphanies cohere with the scene of all manifestation: creation itself. If normative orthodoxy succeeded in part with the first coherence (of which I am dubious), it did not with the second. The second coherence would require an essential connection between the internal differentiation of the divine life (the Creator) and the external differentiation of what is by God but not God and not mere nothing (*ouk on*): creation. The orthodox account failed in this coherence because the divine inner differentiation of Trinity, or God in three persons—Father, Son (Logos), Holy Spirit—was conceived to be immutable, omniscient, omnipotent, and so on.

Consider omniscience, for example: rather than being the contemplation of what is at hand, divine knowing is rather a kind of "making" (*poiesis*), as the Book of Genesis has it. For God to know "all" unchangingly is to know everything in principle through God's internal differentiation as Logos, as agential principal, thus as both the *quo est* and *quod est* of creation. But such an *omniscientia* is incomparably less rich than the *scientia* of "this and that" of creation (as any poet knows, including the poets of the Psalms). What the vaunted omniscience lacks, and ill-fits it as characterizing divine knowing, is the difference that making qua *creating* makes. Here omniscience connects solidly with immutability—knowing all eternally means an unmoved mover—whereas the biblical God qua Redeemer is moved by the movings of creation, the fortunes of Israel, and all the peoples of creation. For mutable creation, to be is to reverse the emanation from the One, to reverse the *exitus* by *reditus*, shedding oneself of privations in an ascent back up the ladder of descent to plenary Being, itself below the One that is "beyond Being." Is what we commonly construe as "creation" such an unqualified disaster?[4] And why, oh why, did western Christianity attach itself to such a view for a millennium and more, as did Judaism and Islam in esoteric forms for lesser periods?

Presently, in addressing cosmogony, we ask: How to connect the one and the many in the self-generation of God godself—conceived as on-going rather than as a once-upon-a-time settled event—with the one and the many in the *creatio continua* of the cosmos? This thought-experiment proposes that the classical Christian affirmation that God creates from nothing, not out of God, be emended to the affirmation that God creates from the nothing that is internal to God godself. If this emended affirmation answers the *why* of what is not-God—that is, the creature—what is the *why* of God godself? The regress of the question "why?" is alleged to stop with God godself, hence the matter of the self-generation of determinate God from the nothingness of the indeterminate potencies of God godself, the Godhead, *deitas ipsum*: God in onto-meonto-genesis, *ab origine et continua*. Godhead thus understood, like the human creature in Meister Eckhart, "lives without a why."

In the groundless abyss of the divine indeterminacy, one and many are equiprimordial and prevail over everything that determinately is and is not—whether determinate God or determinate creature. In the *Ungrund* of indeterminacy from which all divine things are manifest, God godself, the Godhead, self-generates its life, harboring internal to itself the potencies of the indeterminate *Ungrund* become the *Abgrund*, the latter become non-determinate. These potencies themselves shelter what are normally taken to be contraries: being and nothingness, one and many, freedom and necessity, principle and principal. They are held eternally in the Godhead in ready pertinence to the giving of form, the actualization of determinacy in time in the manifestation of "this and that." Each this or that is the actualized determinate coincidence of opposing potencies; presiding over each is the logos of Heraclitus, as is the Logos of the gospels: Jesus on the Cross.

Principle (*quod est*) and Principal (*quo est*)

Metaphysics is often said, and venerably so over the course of western traditions, to be the *scientia* of first principles, the elaboration of those irreducible principles involved in the being and the ways of being of anything whatever that is. Such principles are to be established without *petitio principii* (one must not "beg the question," assuming what is to be proved): the probative demonstration of first principles themselves is otherwise than the demonstration made through their use. Adherence to this injunction has fostered an unending scurry across the metaphysical cartography of principles, a scurry alternately of contraction (in extremity, monism) or expansion (in extremity, pluralism). Do not all metaphysical systems operating solely under their own head of steam commit *petitio principii* in respect of the *that* of what is to be accounted for? That is why Aristotle said that metaphysics (philosophy) begins with the astonishment (wonder) that there is anything at all, rather than nothing. If the story or history of metaphysics is the unfolding of the trivialization, dissipation, forgetting of this astonishment (which many now claim as the bankruptcy of metaphysics), that owes to the methodological rigor of the injunction disallowing *petitio principii*, and more important, the even greater astonishment not only *that* something is but that nothing is in and of it, that anything that *is* is compounded of being and nonbeing.[5] What this says, and means, is the project of these pages.

Christian theology too is concerned with principle(s) (*archē, archai*) and has been since its earliest alliances with metaphysical philosophy. From the standpoint of metaphysics alone, however, there is something anarchic in the way theology derives its *archai*. This is so for multiple reasons. First, the labor of metaphysics begins in the afterglow of astonishment; theology begins by dwelling in and dwelling upon the astonishment itself for what may be said responsibly in its afterglow. Second, theology does not exalt to methodological preeminence the injunction against *petitio principii*. Even if that is so, as I think it is, however, it is not the positive point at stake. The injunction against *petitio principii* is incontestable: surely one who assumes what is to be proved does not understand the grammar of proof. But is the grammar of proof commensurable with the grammar of ontology, of meontology, of there being anything at all and not nothing—and the perduration of nonbeing in all that is there? That something *is* is *shown*, not proved.[6] That is why the first mark of being is said to be that it appears, is manifest. Spirited being is showing that speaks, in which showing the said and the sayer, the spoken and the speaker, are inseparable.[7] Persons are not manifest to each other in their being as persons until they speak: we outstand nothingness by bespeaking manifestation.[8]

The positive point is that theology is founded and funded by *revelation*, a term that, if its weary and wearying history is any clue, beggars both description and explanation.[9] One invokes the hoary term not to lob a bomb into the playground of the metaphysicians (to paraphrase Karl Adam on the early Barth), which it could be taken to be only if comprising the deposition of a body of knowledge *senkrecht von oben* into human synapses, a view credited by no contemporary theologian worthy of the name. Minimally, the term *revelation* signals that the primal astonishment (*that* there is) bears as ineluctably the first mark of truth as it does the first mark of being/not-being. (We shall come to the second mark of truth, coherence, anon.) The first marks of truth and being are effectively the same, however differently they may be parsed in ontology and epistemology, which is why in classical realistic metaphysics truth is taken to be one of the transcendentals—along with one, good, being. That first mark of truth is manifestation, disclosure, showing, being put in evidence, which is apparent in the Greek a-privative word for truth, *aletheia* (ἀλήθεια), meaning not in the shade, not dead, not beyond the pale, not concealed, uncovered (hence its resonance with the German word for existence, *Dasein*, therebeing).

For Plato the first mark of the being of something, and so of the truth of it, is that it is there, that it appears, that it shows itself, that it is manifest. In Greek mythology Lethe was the penultimate river to be crossed in the soul's journey and marks the boundary between light and increasing darkness; the ultimate river to cross is the Styx, utter darkness in which the soul is but a shade of itself. As all that is "appears" in its uncovering, it "shines"; hence the value attached to gold immemorially by the ancients, as gold was thought to have captured and concentrated the brilliance of the sun. When retrieved as metal from the bowels of the earth's internal darkness, when excavated as truth from beyond the Styx and Lethe in the basement of the human soul, gold's brilliance once again reflects the sun—not as adornments for head and fingers, but as uncovering what is there in the light of what there is, adornments of the human mind attached to the upper reaches of Plato's Divided Line.

One remembers a hoary epistemological dictum, of which much was made in the Middle Ages, that "like knows like," so that knowledge is a process of likening mind and the thing to be known (hence another medieval dictum: "to know a thing is to be it in an intellectual way"). It is sometimes quipped that for Aristotle light is in things presenting themselves to a darkly blank mind, and the mind induces such light as is there in them to enlighten the mind, whereas in Plato light is internal to mind, and only under its beam are they "there." Although this is an unwarranted oversimplification of both thinkers, without doubt for Plato light is internal to mind itself, else he would not have become the source of the great western illuminationist tradition as he was for Augustine and his progeny (indeed, German scholars often account Plato's metaphysics as *Lichtsmetaphysik*). Because there is light in both mind and thing, mind and thing can be likened; what is there and what there is can be made cognitively commensurable.[10]

All appearances, "shinings," epiphanies, hierophanies, and the like are experienced with immediacy. Their significance putatively extends well beyond their longevity yet cannot be grasped within the time of immediacy. To grasp the significance of such manifestations the mind's forces of mediacy must be brought into play, else they are not re-presentable for reflection and reflexion. We can say of immediate appearance in relation to mediate reflection/reflexion what Kant said of percepts and concepts: immediacy without mediacy is empty, mediacy without immediacy is blind. Therefore, in speaking of the priority of manifestation, one does not indicate an exclusive preserve of theology but of all ventures with a claim to truth. No amount of marshaling of evidence in support of an argument without a prior *putting in evidence* conduces to the truth of the matter, which is why merely circumstantial evidence is suspect in the law.

All religions originate and perdure in "showings" taken to be paradigmatic—as not just the manifestation of this or that to these or those people, but as a pattern bearing upon any and every showing. Religions vary widely and wildly on *what* (*quod est*) is shown, and in the ways or media of manifestation (a person, a stone, a rainbow, a war or other contest, and so on). No less variegated and varied are the ways those showings "back then"—which may have been in historical time or may have been *in illo tempore*, Eliade's "time that never was but always is"—are related to showings *now*. Just as varied are the forms for the transmission of "showing" deemed paradigmatic: to take the "literate" religions alone: myth, legend, saga, prophetic oracle, priestly law, narrative of war and contest, parable, story, etc. No religion, however "literate," depends solely on the inscription once-for-all of its funding/founding showings. Every religion constitutively relies on *ritual* for the vivification and restauration (indeed aggrandizement) of showings in souls otherwise bereft of manifestation. This is why seeing what is shown requires the discipline of ritual. In these important respects, theology is a thinking handmaid to religion (*some* religion) and in that sense derivative, funded in and by a showing at second remove.[11]

These observations have been entered in order to mark differences (however much they otherwise might share in common) between two enterprises of mind—those of metaphysics and theology—taken historically to be soul-siblings in reckoning with "principles" of being. And there is one yet more critical: that is, for the western monotheistic religions, what occasions the astonishment *that* there is anything at all to be accounted for by principles however derived and ordered is a—or rather, *the*—principal (or principals, in the case of polytheistic religions). Christian theology ventures to speak principially of the principal of there being anything at all, of God the Creator. Such a theology in its Christian ramifications is tasked to speak of the evolution and devolution of "principles" as constituting the life (*quod est*) of the Principal of Creation, the internal and determinate principles of the divine creativity arising from the indeterminate abyss of Godhead (the divine Wisdom)—the eternal self-creation of

God from Godhead—and the external and determinate principles of all that is not God and not mere nothing, the created itself. Most tasking of all is the *nothingness* that perdures in anything that is, creature or Creator. Perdures, that is, if we credit as we must the second critical mark of truth: coherence. What shows itself irreducibly "here" must cohere with (which is not to say, be identical with in all respects) what manifests itself "there," although to "cohere with" does not imply "is adequated to" or "is commensurate with."

The great premodern age of speculation about what may be called "scenes of origination" (always accompanied by "scenes of redemption") in Christianity, Judaism, and Islam encompassed the Middle Ages from beginning to end. In Christianity that speculation was fed by the interfructification of metaphysics (commonly Neoplatonist) and biblical commentary. From Augustine and Eriugena through Meister Eckhart and Jakob Böhme, reflections on the being of what there is proceeded in tandem with meditative commentary on three canonical manifestations or epiphanies of "scenes of origination," two from the Hebrew Bible, one from the Christian: Genesis, Exodus, and the Gospel of John. No doubt the joining of these two sources of reflection was immeasurably assisted by their availability in a common language, Latin, a condition not repeated in the same way since, or likely ever again to be.[12] As much was evident in the currency of "principle," of "principal." Genesis 1:1–3 was rendered, "*In principio*, God created . . . and God said, Let there be. . . ." *Principio* was construed to have both a temporal and a substantive sense: in the beginning and in/through principle God (we may say, the agential principal) created. Exodus 3:14 made manifest the coincidence of principle/principal with being, destinate for doctrinal closures in the tradition under examination here: when Moses asks of God his name, God answers: "I am that/who/what I am," which the Jerome Vulgate renders *Ego sum qui sum*.[13]

But the ontotheological tradition had its dissenters long before their progeny in late modernity and postmodernity, and did so because of a third scriptural manifestation or epiphany which Christian reflection took to be both continuous and discontinuous (both coherent and incoherent) with the preceding two: that of John 1:1–5. Eckhart noted that the Prologue to John's Gospel did not say *in principio* was *esse ipsum* but rather *in principio* was the Word (*Verbum*), that the Word was what God was, that all things were created through him, that what came to be was alive with his life. This had the effect of calling in question the ontological coherence of epiphantic manifestations, of cracking open any closure on doctrine of creation. One must think through again, honoring both manifestation and coherence, both the "by-which-it-is" (*quo est*) and the "what-it-is"

113

(*quod est*), both the *principio* and *principium*, of anything whatever, Creator or creature. The manifestation of Word requires a revisiting of the scene of origination, and especially the *mise-en-scène* of deity itself, a veritable theogony, the emergence of deity from Godhead (*deitas*), the eternal self-creation of God the Creator.

We put ourselves on notice that a rethinking of "principle" is not a matter of metaphysical resolve alone, not a resolution of will to attend to principle as one more of the things *there* in what there is to appear. We have not somewhere else to go to think what principled thinking thinks, transporting ourselves to a realm other than the one we already inhabit. But there are what a modern person might call conditions in the subject of thinking (which scarcely are merely subjective conditions) for thinking principle, originating scene, conditions that a medieval person would likely call spiritual discipline. If principial origination is the self-constitution of spirited being, the thinking of the spirited being we are is to be aligned or cohered with what is thought. Hence Eckhart's insight that "readiness and the giving of form occur simultaneously," Böhme's claim that if all being (*Wesen*) is a birth, a principle (*Princip*, *principium*) is understood only in "rebirth," and nearer our own time, Husserl's phenomenology of meaning as a function of the *origin* of meaning: *Sinn ist als Sinngenesis*.[14]

Taxonomy of Finite Modal Wholes

Drawing on a metaphorical reading of Genesis and the Gospel according to John, Meister Eckhart identified four integral modal wholes of creation in time, of which the first three merit notice, and especially the third. "The first . . . is those that are mere beings [things that merely exist], the second . . . is living beings, the third . . . is the human intellect [living, conscious soul], and the fourth . . . is the angelic intellect and any other that might be separated, free from matter and image."[15] In discriminating the inorganic, organic, and "spirited" realms or finite wholes, Eckhart did not diverge significantly from other major medieval thinkers. Such thinkers as diverse as Al-Ghazali, Eckhart, Aquinas, and kabbalistic authors agree on the point.

Eckhart claims furthermore that to exist, to live, and to understand "exhaust and complete the totality of being" for the temporal creature. What is to be said of the totality of temporally created reality will depend on which of its intended constituent modal wholes is intentionally foremost, and on the position of the speaker (the whole standpoint of vision). Thus if I speak of the whole of temporal creaturehood as such, therefore in maximal logical extension, that is, abstractly and universally, I will take as intentionally highest or most perfect what is indeed lowest or least perfect, namely, the *existence* or modality of being of the creature.[16] In the same modality of extension toward another whole that is fewer in the number of what it comprises than mere existence, yet more capacious in respect of the *kind* of being thus embraced, *life* is higher than intellective soul or understanding.

If I substitute intensiveness for extensiveness, attend to the wholes of temporal creaturehood not abstractly but concretely, the situation will be reversed or inverted, in what Eckhart called intellective *conversio*. I thus gain access to a whole concretely (not to all flowers but to this geranium on my windowsill) at the highest level of its perfection, at the furthest reach of its temporally arrested helical orbit.[17] In the intensive apprehension of a creature (for that matter, anything whatever), *that* it is is a poor clue—necessary, but insufficient—to understanding *what* it is. If we want to grasp the extension of a thing, we look to its participation "down" and "out"; if the intension, its "up" and "in." The maximal extension of any temporal whole involves what is lowest and least perfect about it, namely, mere existence; maximal intension involves what is highest and most perfect about its *kind* of being as instanced and concretely present. So while abstractly or extensively being is the highest virtue of temporal creatures, concretely or intensively it is the lowest.[18]

In a book on God, the reader may be rightly curious that in the schema of mutually participative modal wholes identified from high scholasticism there is no mention of God. Surely in a medieval plenary schema God would either head the schema or end it, and God would be the "highest" modality? Why then have I not included God at this point? This is because the schema refers only to temporal modalities of being, and God has never been thought within the Abrahamic faiths to be exhaustively and without remainder temporal. Moreover, referring to the temporal modalities (and, arguably, to all modalities whatever), the mode of being common to them all is *existence*, the lowest and least perfect of their virtues. The consensus of the high scholastics in the main was that God is not a modality of being so much as *ipsum esse, ens realissimum et perfectissimum* (Being itself, most real and perfect). As such, on this high scholastic view, there is no distinction between God's essence and God's existence, so that God's essence *is* to exist, and it is this precisely that distinguishes God from all temporal creatures.

We have seen that all temporal modes of existence are marked by a distinction between their existence and their essence, between their mere *that* and their *what*, whether actual or potential. What basis does the human creature, who livingly inhabits the distinction, have for understanding the one modality not subject to it? Is the mere *existence* of anything whatever (God included) a sufficient clue, however essential as a condition of its being at all, to *what* it is? On Eckhart's part, he virtually alone among the high scholastics discerned the problem with God as *ipsum esse*, whose essence it is to exist. If one thinks of a modality of being merely as existing, one may think of God as of an existing cow (or any "this and that"), namely, as something from which one can get what one wants of it (from a cow, say, milk and cheese). For Eckhart, the existence of God was not only insufficient for knowing what God *is* and *is not* but also a positive deterrence. Hence his prayer to God to be rid of God (so conceived), so that one might enter into the desert, the abyss of the Godhead.

Historically, every taxonomy of modal wholes comprising the totality of temporally finite realities has been presented in a scale, whether from highest to lowest or vice versa, with the higher subsuming all that is below it but adding something else that distinguishes it from what is below. Any such taxonomy has always indirectly reflected the state of the sciences upon which any taxonomy draws. Thus in the spectacular advances of the modern physical and biological sciences, modern taxonomies of modal wholes contain finer (more determinate) distinctions within modal wholes than did medieval taxonomies. For example, the line within the modal whole of "organic" between the "animal" and the "human" was much cleaner and less problematic than it now can be. For us now because of ongoing research in the neurobiological sciences, particularly on the central nervous systems of animals and the brains of humans, we have reason to be much less certain that intellective soul can be imputed only to humans and not to other animals. Further, from the astrophysical sciences, we have reason to qualify the imputation of intellective soul only to humankind, proscribing it to any higher modal reality, given the open question whether there are intelligences in the cosmos superior to humankind. (Could just this have been an *Ahnung* in the Middle Ages guiding the common ascription of the highest model reality to the order of "angels," notwithstanding that this order was not a temporal mode but rather a visible eternal (by reason of inhabiting "stars," taken as traces of eternity)?

Another matter: we have yet to consider the human creature's relation to the *nihilo* in the hoary doctrine or theory of *creatio ex nihilo*. In all the Abrahamic faiths, God is "living." But in the human creature's understanding of living, all that lives also dies. Does God also live and die? Nietzsche and Hegel said yes, and much of the philosophical genius of nineteenth-century—especially German—continental philosophical thinking was expended on developing a metaphysical framework rendering this affirmation coherent with affirmation of a religiously divine God. In this context we may also cite the twentieth-century American thinker in like mold, Thomas J. J. Altizer, and if one turns to the arts, the novelists Herman Melville (*Moby-Dick*) and Joseph Conrad (*Heart of Darkness*), the poets Blake, Hölderlin, and Rilke, and the artists Rothko and Pollock, to mention but a few.

Creatio ex nihilo

Temporal creation encompasses exhaustively and without remainder all in finitude that is there, determinately, in the universe. What can be said of God the Creator of this universe is from a standpoint in God's creation and God's epiphanies in the selfsame creation. The maximum divine reality, Godhead, encompasses exhaustively and without remainder all there is and is not (an affirmation of Eriugena) indeterminately, nondeterminately, and determinately. Everything determinate with which persons reckon is ultimately in God; everything indeterminate is ultimately in Godhead. Every determinate external to God is created by God from nothing (*ex nihilo*)—created, not caused, as causal relations obtain only between intracosmic, intratemporal determinates. Much thought lies in wait for the development and expansion of these two claims.

The ultimate standing or bearing of the *nihil* is one of the most troubling and vexing difficulties besetting a theory or doctrine of God and creation. This difficulty became evident (although not immediately) with the adoption in the second century CE of the formula *creatio ex nihilo*. In simplest terms, is the *nihil* inside or outside God? Even those of minimal familiarity with the history of doctrine will know that theories have arisen and reached closure for multiple reasons. Unquestionably, one motivation was to protect a stipulated religious institution (in the case of Christianity, the Church in Rome); another was, for a burgeoning system of thought, to exclude some options available to any active and free-ranging mindfulness. The theory or doctrine of *creatio ex nihilo* arose early in the Common Era (roughly, second century CE) in both Christianity and rabbinic Judaism to "protect" God against any coeval divine power, any competitor for agency in the emergence of the universe. Specifically, the *ex nihilo* doctrine arose to exclude a rampant Marcionism and all forms of gnosticism, the view that *this* universe is to be ascribed to an ultimate Evil principle that is in contention with an ultimate Good principle, a contention to be resolved only in an eschaton beyond this universe. The only matter the formula (*ex nihilo*) itself settles is that the *nihil* from which God creates is not evil exhaustively and without remainder, thus that the universe created by God is not intrinsically evil. The only matter the formula itself establishes, granted that God is the Creator, is that there is no power coeval with God in the emergence of the universe. It leaves unsettled and to be thought recurrently how both God and creation are good, and evil.

A venerable conundrum: Given creation and its Creator—and the ungainsayable manifestations of both good and evil in the former—how to render those manifestations coherent with the Creator otherwise putatively manifested as Good? And *is* God epiphantically manifest as exhaustively *the* Good? Even if all good and evil in creation were ascribable to determinate acts by human agency, so that all good and evil within finite reality are works of human hands, those hands and their capability are the work of the Creator, so does he escape culpability (granting praise, where warranted)? And what if not all good and evil in the created order are ascribable to human agential determinateness? What of the aperture on indeterminacy opened by determinate acts, immediately good and/or evil, an opening upon indeterminacy capable of yet more terrifying or exalting determinateness, and so on, finitely ad infinitum—a determinacy freshly configuring indeterminacy? Do not intentional acts of good have unintended evil consequences and—even more oddly—vice versa?[19]

The intelligibility of good has no claim of priority over that of evil, and without the intelligibility of both the intelligibility of either is at the least in question. Intelligible, of course, is not a surrogate for likeable or nice—as Job found out. It is humanly impossible not to raise his questions, and humanly impossible to answer them. Having delivered responsibly on the determinateness given into his care, and seeing where it got him, Job called the Creator to account for what we have called the divine determination process. So do we; every theologian is first Job. God stonewalled Job, and it is part of the *imago Dei* to contest what we are separated from but belong to. Against God, to God. So we take our stand with the theological Job and call God to account for his autodidacticality: Is God's creation of the cosmos and of the agents of his purposes but a maneuver-moment of self-instruction in how to make the Good determinately good, coincident with his own abysmal indeterminacy?

If we posit that all elements and energies with which the person reckons ultimately are reducible to two, they are the benevolent and the malevolent, the good and the evil. Both are in all, everything, and so in God—but in God differently according to the infinite determinateness of indeterminacy, according to whether in God eternal or God temporal. Every effort to make God wholly good or wholly evil crashes on this theopoetic, ontic-meontic fact. The one God is Love *and* Wrath, not in ontic-meontic fact alone but in the history and mythology of epiphanies: in the unending story of the nation Israel among the nations, in the Cross, in Dante, Milton, Blake, and in latter days (to make an arbitrary end) in Melville's *Moby-Dick*, which, like its Old Testament–Calvinist background, is the death of God qua exhaustively Good—where dark Word becomes light flesh.

The two poles of the divine comprise light and darkness, right hand and left hand of God, the daunting *numinosum tremendum* and the attracting *numinosum fascinosum* (Otto). If metaphysical philosophy is the intellectual effort to establish the homogeneity of reality largely through abstract forms of totality (being, nothingness, infinity, the absolute, and so on), religions at the level of their adherents' lives are efforts, more of praxis than speculative thought, to *locate* both homogeneity and heterogeneity.[20] The western religions (or is it only garden-variety Christianity?) typically sequester homogeneity in a realm celestial and divine, heterogeneity in a realm demonic and infernal (classically in Augustine's two cities, in Luther's two realms). When religion degrades to the point where God is the simple sign of homogeneity, it betrays the needs (those of homogeneity *and* heterogeneity) it was supposed not only to regulate determinately but to satisfy determinately. Is the divine determination process itself exhaustively homogenous?

It is more than passing curious that the Christian tradition could have settled for long on the original formula of *creatio ex nihilo* alone, since it only secured that the *nihil* was not a separate coeval power and otherwise in no way addressed the bearing of the *nihil* on the divine creativity. Such a situation could not long endure. What is known is that in due course the original formula of *creatio ex nihilo* was emended and added to in a second and so far abiding formula: *creatio ex nihilo et non se Deo*, that is, creation from nothing and not from God.[21] But this emendation settles nothing; more precisely, it settles nothing about *nothingness* in relation to God. The emendation strictly implies that, nothingness having been excluded as coeval with God, the nothingness from which God creates is internal to God godself. Another surpassing curiosity is that the tradition did not think this emendation through, and one can only conjecture two possible reasons for its not doing so. First, by the time of the hegemony of the emendation, mainstream Christian theology had allied itself with a metaphysics of Being bent on rendering nonbeing nugatory or "harmless," as Gadamer never tired of saying. And second, denial of the emendation—that is, affirmation of the claim that God creates from nothingness internal to godself—construed rigorously would lead to pantheism, the latter always *trop outré*. (Why "trop" outré? Because of its invitation to a pantheism that would be in effect a pan-cosmic idolatry?)

By no means is it the case that the *ex nihilo* remained unthought beyond these premature closures. While neglected by the canonical (exoteric) theologians of the Middle Ages, the *ex nihilo* remained near the center of reflection by the neglected ones, the esoteric mystics in the Middle Ages who preserved the very questionableness of both being *and* nonbeing (nothingness). And, astonishingly, this thinking of the *nihil* reemerged in their distant heirs, the nineteenth-century so-called Romantic philosophers of identity and difference: Goethe, Hegel, Schelling, and others. The *nihil*—and correlative adjustments in respect of Being—reemerges now in the thinking under way in this thought-experiment. The intent is to think, and invite the reader to think, the contrary of the emendation (*creatio ex nihilo et non se Deo*) by substituting for it a further refining and intentionally defining emendation: *creatio ex nihilo, idem est, ex Deitate ipsa*, or God creates from nothing, that is, from the very Godhead itself. This claim builds on another rigorous distinction—that between Godhead and God, as argued already—in which Godhead comprises the eternally indeterminate potencies of both Being and Nothingness, from which arise all that determinately *is* and *is not*.

Thinking of every fundamental sort is metaxic, between an *a quo* and an *ad quem*, between a *from which* and a *toward which*—and either may be unitary or multiple. The primordial *a quo* of thinking divinity is Godhead, which, being wholly indeterminate, is neither unitary nor multiple. Thus Godhead *a se* (solely in itself) offers no indications of its con-sequent possible and actual determinate forms (as God or gods in the positive religions and/or philosophical systems), thus no determinate *ad quem*. As the *a quo* of thinking divinity, Godhead offers the imaginative rendering of the eternal internal generative process that is more ultimate than any determinate intelligible. From such a *from which* multiple *toward whiches* are possible and, given the potencies available from what the western tradition has called "necessity" and "freedom," they are actualizable under the conditions of determinacy (time-space, the influences of human culture, and so on). They are not only actualizable but actualized, as the history of religions attests.

That said, it is uncommonly difficult (some hold arguably impossible) to take indeterminate Godhead as the *a quo* of thinking divinity with a clean slate, as difficult as thinking anything whatever without presuppositions. Without question, all thinkers of God and other matters of ultimate concern do so with *interest*, as that concern is taken to bear on the meaning of the thinker's determinate existence. The Hindu polytheist will think of the multiple traces of Godhead, each requiring a symbolic determinate deity. The atheist has a compelling interest in denying the referentiality of anything that could be construed as traces of divinity. And so on. There is an all but ineluctable tendency in human thinking to think backward, from the desired *toward whiches* back to the "from which" that will allow and nurture the *terminus ad quem* one has already reached unthinkingly. The animus of such thinking is to espy "goals," however vaguely envisaged, then retrace the steps of the path leading thereto until one reaches the trailhead and take that as the *a quo* of thinking (the special passion of American pragmatism?). The most that a retrogressing from goals to locate the *a quo* of one's thinking can achieve is the individualization of one's own path. But if the subject matter of thought is divinity, such a thinking backward from goals is beset by a searing irony, namely, that working backward from an *ad quem* of "goals" (however vague) all but invariably delivers one into the hands of religious conventions in respect of the *a quo* that leads to them. The irony is that (at best) in a backward individualizing path from *ad quem* "goals" to the *a quo* of thinking divinity, the thinker ("I did it my way!") only confirms her solidarity with the "they" (Heidegger's *das Mann*) or with James Joyce's H.C.E. (Here Comes Everybody). If I have dwelt on such backward thinking overlong, that is but to illustrate the power of presuppositions in thinking divinity (presuppositions I referred to earlier as both blessing and curse). Whether derived from one's own thinking, imbibed with mother's milk religiously, or learned from philosophy, the total hegemony of presuppositions must be broken if the *a quo* of thinking divinity is Godhead itself.

In the introduction, "Pre-facing the Divine," I spoke of the *who* of the thinker and the *what* of thought in a radical theology (a theology of the radices), the subject and the subject matter of theology. The sought *what* of theological thought requires of its thinker-who a self-awareness made acute by the discipline of self-wariness, a self wary of her interests. And wary not only of her interests but of any presumed settled relation between the *a quo* and the *ad quem* of theological thinking. Indeed, for any authentic thinking of Godhead and God the relation between the *a quo* and the *ad quem* remains questionable, thus open. The substantive reason for this is that the relation between primordial abysmal Godhead and con-sequent determinate God(s) remains questionable, thus open. Such openness is endemic to the symbolic re-presentation of God as both "living" and "dying."

Self-wariness on the part of the person holding God at mind's length thus entails evading the temptations of a fixed course and its body of settled re-presentations, the latter a sure way of missing the presentations or manifestations of the subject matter sought. Only by avoiding the temptations of evasion (the sum total of presuppositions) can one participate imaginatively the phenomenological extension of the range of divinity in its intensive *Ungrund* and *Abgrund*. How that very extended intensiveness itself extends toward the *ad quem* of the thinker is itself a matter of individual history, thus of freedom and destiny.

But let us pause and, as Kierkegaard counseled constantly, not get ourselves in too great a hurry. The present cosmos (or the *cosmoi*) as currently known and knowable did not emerge from the *nihil* in an instant, in one day or six days, is in fact in process of emergence or creation, a process both continual and continuous, a process into which the thinker of God and creation inserts herself mindfully—though, nota bene, this process does not obviate the mind's distinction between *creatio ab origine* and *creatio continua*, for reasons to be detailed later in this chapter. Since time-space emerges coincidentally with the cosmos, all references to God or the world as a temporally "before" *a quo* commit a category mistake, for both God the Creator and the cosmos are rendered determinate only by the processes of creation and destruction necessary to continuing creation.

The *Mise-en-scène* of Creation

What being and nonbeing (or nothingness) mean in and for a doctrine of creation depends on the most inclusive horizon or *scène* in which they are parsed, whether in that of eternity or that of time. To take eternity as the *mise-en-scène* of creation, to state the matter negatively, is not to explain, argue for, or otherwise speak of God and God's creation from a standpoint in time. As Eckhart said, the merely temporal person will invariably attempt to see God the Creator with the same eyes with which she or he sees a cow and for the same reason—for what she or he can get out of both.[22] The proper *scène* of creation is that in which the eye with which one sees God and all that is created is the same eye as that with which God sees.[23] Thus, eternal creation is about what God sees, creation as it is and is not, *before* actualized temporal creation. It is about the interior dynamics of Godhead, the wholly immanent and emanationist procession of Trinity as eternal prefiguration of temporal creation, itself the prefiguration of external creation in time. If the fundamental theological claim about the creature is, as Eckhart thought it was, that "if God took back all that is His, all creatures would perish," then the fundament to be thought through is what God is and is not, what is and is not God's. In essaying to think creation within the *scène* of eternity, we are immersed for the most part in a premodern discourse; within the *scène* of time, in a modern or late-modern discourse. In what follows, I shall attempt both *scènes*.

The Middle Ages from Augustine through Meister Eckhart is an epoch in theology whose discourse is suffused, whatever the topic addressed, by the horizon of eternity. I mention Eckhart and Augustine because both, however much their thought was embedded in the horizon of eternity, have proved to be bridge figures to the modern horizon of time: Augustine for the surplus of his thought that did not enter doctrinal closure, Eckhart for the surplus of his thought that doctrinal closure could not contain. I shall dwell initially and briefly on and in the language of Eckhart, for while he shared eternity with all other major medieval theologians as the context of creation, he did so otherwise than they. He would not, like the so-called ontotheological tradition hardening before his eyes, locate being essentially in eternity and thus in coincidence with Godhead, or restrict nonbeing or nothingness to time and the creature. What he did do was refresh the questionableness of being *and* nonbeing, whether as attributed either to God or the creature, just as he also imploded what one might call the "origi-nariness" of origin.

The problem of origin is the problem of the *other*: How can an effect be genuinely other than its cause? However other, the effect must also be like its cause, since nothing can be in an effect that is not in some mode first in its cause. According to the *ex nihilo* doctrine, nothing is in the creature as effect, since the creature is a compact of being and nothing. In the regnant ontotheological tradition, God as Being itself calls the creature forth from nothing; and as long as the creature is, it is other than mere nothingness and other than God as Being itself. If otherness is otherwise in the major medieval meontological abridgments of that tradition, this is due to sustained reflection on the *nihil* and especially to the conclusion that nothingness is not time-bound but suffuses eternity as well, that nothingness is the deepest nature of God godself. The question of otherness then rides on the question of the relation, as I term it, of the two nots or nothings: the nothingness that the creature stands out of and the nothingness of God the Creator; more exactly, the nothingness internal to Godhead from which determinate God the Creator emerges. Are these the same or different nothings? Is the nothingness of the creature external or internal to God the Creator? John Scotus Eriugena, whose *Periphyseon* presents arguably the most comprehensive and systematic meontology of the Middle Ages, presents one clear answer. For him all nothingness (whatsoever, whensoever) is internal to God: "All things that are and all things that are not" are modalizations of the divine nothingness, of that "super-essential nothingness" beyond "all things that are and are not."[24] There is one reality, "all things that are and are not."[25] *Sub specie aeternitatis* their name is God; *sub specie temporis* their name is creature. Eriugena does allow for difference or otherness, but as the modalization of identity in a way that anticipates Nicholas of Cusa's coincidence of opposites and Hegel's concrete Absolute as the identity of identity and difference. Eckhart presents another option, but one that leaves the question of the two nots unthought but eminently questionable.

Given that Eckhart used Godhead (*Gottheit*) and God (*Gott*) interchangeably, the reader has to rely on context to determine the reference of each. He never relates them to each other coherently, and did not do so, I opine, because of the limitations of Neoplatonic metaphysics from which he, like other major medieval Christians mystics, drew in construing God, particularly in relation to nonbeing or nothingness, which was understood to be exhaustively *privative*. If the *quo est* ("that-by-which-it-is") of God is different from that of the creature, in what does the difference consist? If not, in what does the difference between God and creature consist? And what of the *quod est* ("what-it-is") of God and the creature? What does the "is" of each *stand out of*—the same or a different nothingness? All such questions are complicit in the larger question of the two sets of the two nots.

If the *creatio ex nihilo* alone does not account for the two nots and such otherness as they permit or entail, neither does it answer the question that so mesmerized the medieval and especially the Christian Neoplatonic mind, namely, why should there be anything other than God?[26] Eckhart has at least two answers. As pastor, as preacher and shepherd of souls, he says: live your time so detached from time that you are "without a why."[27] The first answer is, don't ask "why?": every *why* is a mark of the nothingness from which one comes.[28] The second answer comes from Eckhart as theologian, speaking from the vantage of eternity: "If the creature could have known God without the world, the world would not have been created."[29] The intelligibility of this answer awaits some large Eckhartian conclusions, which I shall state summarily and then indicate how Eckhart reaches them. For the creature to know God is for both the creature and God not to be, is for both creature and Creator to egress both time and eternity into Godhead indeterminate and uncreated. As the eternal finality of temporal creation salvifically reverses or inverts cosmogony, so the finality of eternity reverses or inverts the genesis of God. By the "genesis of God" I mean that for Eckhart, God the Creator and creation are correlative realities. God *is* when the creature says "God," according to Eckhart. God "becomes and unbecomes" (*Got wirt und entwirt*) correlatively with creation's becoming and unbecoming.[30] Eckhart's final answer to the question of why there is anything other than God appears then to be: God eternally creates the world in order that eternity may be rid of God and time of the creature, indeed, that eternity may disappear as the horizon of anything determinate, God or creatures.[31]

There is call to unpack these Eckhartian claims. Eternity as the *scène* of creation requires looking at creation as eternal exit or egress and as eternal return, the latter, indeed, as eternal transgression. The creature as *creatio continua* is the coincidence of a double exit: inheringly existent so long as temporally existent, she or he exits nothingness or nonbeing when she or he exits the divine life. What sustains the creature from relapse into nothingness sheer is the eternal boiling over, flowing, or breaking out (*exitus, efflux, ebullitio, uzgienc, uzvliezen, uzbruch*) of the divine life into its other, into what is distinct from it. As said just now, the finality of creation as eternal is the return (*reditus, refluxus, wider ingan, inganc, duzchbrechen*) of the creature to the divine life: a return beyond the divine life as determinate Creator to that (indeterminate) Godhead from which God the Creator is *efflux*.

Thus Eckhart sternly counsels the human creature to "return." Return to what? "To be as you were when you were not," which can be (in my terms) only the first not, the state of nothingness sheer. Is this a return to God? On this matter Eckhart is conflicted, and within the limitations of a Neoplatonic metaphysics he is incapable of making the distinctions conducive to coherence. As for all Neoplatonists, for Eckhart the only being a creature can have or be is privative; the person's place in being is determined by what she lacks or is in want of, namely, full being. To rid oneself of the "this and that" of existence is thus a condition of return to the state before one was a "this and that," namely, nothingness. Such would be a return to God only if God and nothingness coincide. But Eckhart claims in some texts that God is *ipsum esse et simpliciter*, that God is simply Being itself. In other texts he claims that the human person must become nothing in order to be rid of God thus conceived, and thus to enter the "desert of the Godhead," which is beyond both being and nothingness. I judge these texts not capable of cohering with each other within the metaphysical resources available to Eckhart.

The "beyond" that sources God and to which both God and creature return, which precisely is not a "this or that" (redolent of Paul Tillich's "God beyond God"), Eckhart names the *nomen innominabile*, the unnameable name, nothing or nonbeing.[32] But the problem persists: What is the relation of the nothingness of Godhead beyond God ("upside" nothingness) to the nothingness out of which the creature exists/exits ("downside" nothingness)? Are they the same or different? If they are the same, it would appear that temporal creation is not only gratuitous but wholly adventitious. If they are different, that difference would have to be accounted for in one of two ways. If construed wholly within the *scène* of eternity, the difference would entail the contest between Godhead and God the Creator (*per impossibile*: How could indeterminacy and a determinate contest each other?) and its consequent trivialization of actual temporal creation, as in every form of gnosticism. If the difference between the two nothings is accounted for by the difference between eternity and time, the *scène* of eternity would have to be qualified by the *scène* of time in order to think that difference.

In this, one of several ways Eckhart renewed the questionableness of being and nonbeing, he left the matter of the relation between the two nothings unthought and unsaid; it is one of the reasons those who think being and nonbeing in the horizon of time find in him a precursor, notwithstanding his aspiration to think creation from a vantage in eternity.

Creation within the *Scène* of Eternity

I am aware of skirting many steps of exegetical logic in these generalizations about and from Eckhart and of rendering him more straightforward than his corpus warrants. So complex is his thought that not a few interpreters have found at least two largely irreconcilable Eckharts: on the one hand, the scholastic epistemologist of analogy, predication, and/or attribution, the metaphysician of the Vulgate Exodus 3:14 (*Ego sum qui sum*, or "I am who/what/that I am" = *Deus est esse ipsum*), the theologian of the academic treatises and scriptural commentaries; on the other hand, the epistemologist of dialectic and the metaphysician of Neoplatonic indistinction, the theologian of the vernacular sermons. Such a bifurcation is exegetically unwarrantable, and it is as ideologically driven as were his interlocutors and judges. There is one Eckhart, a profoundly original thinker who so interwove the key terms as applied to deity (being, nothing, intellect) that they came to *mean* otherwise than among his predecessors and contemporaries, an inheritor and a bequeather of the questionableness of those signifiers and their signified. He was at home with all the Thomistic transcendentals (one, being, true, good) and, like most of his contemporaries, could provisionally favor *being* as the transcendental comprehensively comprising God and creature. This favoring, however, abridges the regnant ontotheological tradition. All talk of being depends on *what* is in view. If just *being* is in view, without regard to that to which it refers, and if being is construed exhaustively as *existence*, then a fly has as much being as does God.[33] If *a* being and its kind of being is in view, thus "this or that," God is by contrast not-being, nonbeing, or nothing. If the sense of being derives not from being formally inhering in "this or that" or *a* being, hence not *existence*, however, it bears the sense of being as such or Being itself. As *esse simpliciter* or *esse absolutum*, God is neither the *being of beings* nor *a being*; and in relation to such being-itself, all beings (creatures) are entirely nothing (*luter nihts*). From the vantage of eternity, the "nameable name" (*nomen nominibile*) of God is being and that of the creature is nothing—all of which sounds very much like the ontotheological tradition he received. Why was Eckhart not content to rest the matter there?

There are primarily two reasons: First, his radicalization of the Dominican understanding of intellect, involving an unprecedented elevation of the transcendental *verum* over the transcendental *esse*, and second, a like radicalization of what Emilie Zum Brunn has called "the metaphysics of the Word."[34] These two moves are as essential to reaching the "unnameable name" of God as they are to Eckhart's critique of—and meontological substitutions for—the ontotheological tradition. His critique shares little, however, with contemporary postmodern exceptions to ontotheological thinking. The latter center in attacks on logocentric thinking itself, whereas Eckhart's implicit claim is that logos-centered thinking has been rendered impossible by the exhaustive priority of *being* in the ontotheological tradition stemming from Parmenides.[35] A genuine logos-centered thinking will require the subversion of that tradition through the elevation of truth (*verum*) over being (*esse*), more strictly the elevation of truth's organon, intellect, over being, even more strictly a thinking through "intentional nihilism" (the coinage is Vladimir Lossky's) in order to speak the "unnameable name" of the Godhead of God.[36]

In speaking of the Word or Logos in connection with this elevation, I have not forgotten that our present topic is creation within the *scène* of eternity, as Eckhart did not. God the Father-Creator is the principal, the "by-which-it-is" (*quo est*) of anything that temporally is, and Eckhart never tires of saying that the first thing God creates is being;[37] but God the Logos is the principle, the "what-it-is" (*quod est*) of anything temporally created as it virtually is. Now, John the Evangelist did not say "*In principio* was being, and being was with God, and God was being," but rather "*In principio* was Logos, and Logos was with God, and Logos was God."[38] But word, words, and truth have reference solely to (are the exhaustive intentions of) intellect, not being. What is in the mind *as it is in the mind* does not have the nature of being. What intellect intends, qua intellect, is otherwise than being, is indeed nonbeing. (And one may suggest that this Eckhartian sense of intellect is construed as "imagination" in such modern poets as Coleridge and Hölderlin and in the nineteenth-century German identity-difference philosophers, notably Schelling.)

So Eckhart can and does affirm that God in God's *deitas* (which I construe as Godhead) is intellect and thus nothing, that the divine intellect intends nothing while it creates what it knows and sublates what it creates (namely, being and beings), but eternally only as their *quo est* and *quod est* cause and not as effects. I pause over the latter, however, because I am unsure that God is the *cause* of anything, and that for two reasons: first, because God qua determinate Creator *quo est* is not a (as in first) cause, and second, because of freedom imputed to the human creature, the *quod est* of the human creature has blanks that only the human person can fill in? Eckhart can affirm that God is intellect and nothing at the same time that he speaks of God as "purity of being" (*puritas essendi*).[39] Eckhart can do so without contradiction, for by "purity of being" he clearly means that God in God's deity (*deitas*) is free *of* and *from* being. "Without contradiction" clearly requires the distinction between God and Godhead that Eckhart could not complete, the afterthinking of which is here under way. The *puritas essendi* allows Eckhart to continue to affirm the "I am who I am" of Exodus, while continuing as well the concealment that accompanies all disclosure of deity, the covering over again of all uncovering (the enigma suffusing the Mosaic experience). In this, the highest pitch of Eckhart's assimilation and radical modification of his theological predecessors, in the asymmetrical priority of intellect over being, the identification of the core of God's Godhead with intellect, and in the orientation of intellect to nonbeing or nothingness, we have the very ecstatic reversal of Parmenides, whose thought had so long dominated and indeed constituted western ontotheological consciousness. Parmenides had held that only being can be, while nonbeing cannot be, be thought, or be said. For his part, Eckhart maintained, although for the divine intellect alone, thus infinitely distancing Godhead and the ontological order, that only nonbeing can be thought, and only those words that say not, say truth. In the beginning was, in the end will be, and in the eternal now is this, the Word.

In this brief overview of Eckhartian eternal creation, I have spoken of being and nothing largely in relation to God and Godhead. Meanwhile, back at the ranch in time, how is it with the human soul viewed from the vantage of eternity? From eternity the soul is not abandoned to its temporal aseity, for solely *a se* the temporal creature is not only *from* nothing but *for* (or toward) nothing. As such it has or is merely *indicative* being; without the sustenance of the eternal "that-by-which-it-is" (*quo est*), its creator, it would be nothing at all. If so much attention is lavished on the soul in the Middle Ages, that is because in the soul the contest between being and nonbeing (downside nothing) is both reflected and reflexive: here, *imperative* being battles *indicative* being over a meontological field; the virtual *what* accuses the actual *that*; and the *quod est in quantum* of Zion troubles every distinct pleasure in Egypt, Babylon, Charlottesville, Boston, or Polebridge. Temporal deliverance from the clutches of downside nothingness, the bare fact of creaturehood, of being *a* being on pain of being nothing at all, this *quo est* is a "first grace" of eternal creation tabernacling in time and as such is the condition not of being but of becoming a child of the Creator God.

A "second grace" is less a work of creation in time than a trace in the soul's fundament of the uncreated.[40] This "second grace" as the birth of the Son or Logos in the ground of the soul is not a superadditum to the "first grace" of creation in time; it is not something superimposed upon a human nature individuated in the first. This "second grace" is not actualized in temporal creation except as trace, as the *capax Dei* in the soul's ground, which is inaccessible to will, knowledge, distinction, time—to all the "powers" of the soul. The ground of the soul is ordinated not to God the Creator, hence not to *indicative* being *from* nothing *for* nothing: not to anything in time or eternity or to their dialectic, hence neither to God the Creator nor to the distinct effects of creation. Eckhart avers and avows that the soul is made *in* the image of God the Creator, but there is in the soul's ground that which is not made because not created, an image *to* or *toward*, an image toward the Logos (*ad imaginem Verbi*).[41] When the soul in its ground is wholly detached and released from all downside nothingness, hence from all creatures, the *capax Dei* is rendered effervescent through the inversion of the overflowing of creation or emanation. This actualization of the birth of the Son (Logos) in the ground of the soul inverts the flowing out of God from Godhead. The soul's salvific career is marked by detachment from temporal creation's downside nothing, indifference to the dialectic of being and nonbeing in eternal creation, and releasement into upside nothing, into indeterminate Godhead cum nothingness inexhaustible.

This career is summarized tellingly in two of Eckhart's most famous sermons. The first meditates Saul's vision, the vision that made Saul Paul.[42] Blinded by a light from heaven, Saul fell to the ground; and when he arose he saw nothing. In seeing nothing, Eckhart says, Saul saw four "things": the nothing was God, it was nothing but God, he saw all things in God, and he saw all things as God. In another sermon on the same Pauline vision, Eckhart comments, "When grace had finished its work, Paul remained that which he *was*."[43] This means to say that when Saul saw God and all things as nothing, he saw as when he was not, "before" the first grace of creation and the second grace of redemption, "before" he was created and was still indeterminate in Godhead. In yet another sermon, Eckhart tells of a man (some scholars conjecture that Eckhart himself is the subject) who dreamed that he was impregnated by nothing. "In this nothingness God was born. He was the fruit of nothingness."[44]

The Problematic of Time

I want at this point not so much to enter upon a critique of Eckhart thus so briefly and incompletely summarized as instead to think the question-ableness of several problematics in a Christian understanding of creation that he bequeathed. I do so out of a different context, that of the radically temporal and this-worldly consciousness of modernity and late modernity, and having but little part (and that wholly respectful) in the effort of some to uncover in Eckhart a postmodern thinker in a premodern epoch (as in Reiner Schürmann's reading of Eckhart as a medieval Heideggerian)[45] or of some to see in him *the* western nontheistic thinker of *nothing* parallel to eastern modes of thought, as in Rudolf Otto and Keiji Nishitani.[46]

What, simply put, are the deepest Christian convictions about the world created in time? That the temporal world is *real*, is not illusory. Having actually begun, it can actually end; but as long as it is, it is not nothing without remainder and has its own reality distinct from its Creator. As such, the world in time is troublingly and imperatively good, although not wholly or purely so indicatively because of the potencies in the structure of what is made and the actualities of human making for the coalescence of good and evil. The world in time, contingently good and contingently evil, is not the highest good, for such a good comprises the telic relation of the creature to God, of God to the creature—a relation salvifically *realized* neither in time pure nor eternity pure but instead in their apocalyptic coincidence or togetherness in the "eternal life" of the Kingdom of God, which, in respect of time, is both *already here/now* and *not yet*. The Kingdom of God of the Jesus movement was seen from the vantage of the Cross (the crucifixion of Jesus), in which pure eternity was emptied into the immanence of time, and pure time as distant from eternity was emptied into eternity. Just this coincidence of a self-negating eternity and a self-negating time Eckhart sought to bespeak by the "eternal now."

Against the backdrop of these (what I take to be) Christian convictions about the world created in time, I turn now to comment on three problematics in the thought of Eckhart. The first is the standing of time itself in the schema of creation; the second is the two nots: the nothingness of the creature in time on the one hand, on the other the nothingness of God the Creator and for Eckhart ultimately the nothingness of Godhead; and the third, Eckhart's christology—or lack of it—in relation to the schema of creation and redemption. We shall see that these problematics, which suffuse each other, can scarcely be fully treated seriatim.

The first is the problematic of time. From this brief overview of Eckhartian eternal creation, one might be tempted to conclude summarily that for him creation in time is nugatory, is an eternal distraction or rather a distraction from eternity, and so that from which the soul is to be eternally distanced. We need not pile quotations on those already cited, but Eckhart unquestionably spoke of the "malady of time" and vivified the recollection that "Scripture always exhorts us to go out of this world."[47] The sermon usually placed first in most collections as summarizing the thrust of Eckhart's thought begins "here in time," as though all speech in time from the vantage of eternity is that of an alien.[48] He says again and again, "Close your heart to all that is created," "annihilate all created things," "hate the soul" that likes to be like what is unlike eternal God.[49] Consequently, Nietzsche could have relied on Eckhart alone to fuel what he called Christendom's *ressentiment* against time and the earth—but not without distortion both of Eckhart and of Nietzsche himself. It would be a distortion of Eckhart because for him one must exit mere existence in time, be released and detached from the world in time, in order to let the world be, and be as *not*. Releasement from the timely world's, the worldly time's "this and that" is scarcely *hatred* or *denial* of the world in time. It is a translation of the gospel saying "Who would save his soul must lose it." The temporal loss of the soul coincides, however, with the birth of the Son/Word in the ground of the soul[50] and is essential to the "breakthrough" beyond time and eternity into uncreated Godhead.[51] The time of the celebration of this birth or rebirth is not anything modern consciousness can recognize as temporal; it is the eternal now. It would be a distortion of Nietzsche because his love of time is exceeded only by his love of eternity: "*For I love you, O eternity!*" is the recurrent exclamation of Zarathustra, the overcoming, the coming *übermensch*.[52] Nietzsche's eternity—no mistake about it—is not Eckhart's; it is the willed eternal return of the same, the eternal return of time's "this and that."

The temptation to say that temporal creation is finally denigrated and thus nugatory in Eckhart would be an anticipation of saying that he finally understands what is in time to be not *created by* but *emanated from* God. One can and must "let things be," be detached from them, by releasing them to and keeping them "where they are eternal," letting them be as they are by accident or contingency while possessing them as they are eternally, as *God* (that is, negating them as negated God).[53] What is eternal in the creature is the image *in* or *of* God and is an emanation of the divine nature. No *will* is involved in this emanation; it "flows out" as does a branch from a tree.[54] Will arises only with *purpose*; and will and purpose arise simultaneously ("readiness and the givenness of form occur simultaneously"[55]) through the potency of the void between eternity and time, in the void between the *imago Dei* and the *ad imaginem Verbi*. Solely as there, as *Dasein*, as indicative being, as released from temporal being and as eternal being, is the world emanated as estranged God. However "first" this emanation of God the agential Father is in respect of time, the *logical* first is the principial emanation of God the Logos. Between these two emanations is held the potency for creation in time. Eckhart can be read otherwise, but at his most radical it is emanation that is eternal, once and for all, and creation in time that is potential and unrealized (I return to this issue below under "The Problematic of Christology").

The Hebrew Bible and the history of the Jewish people witness to a unique valorization of time in the sacred fact of the actual manifestation of eternal Torah in time to the eternal people Israel in time. Modern biblical scholarship construes the account in Genesis of creation to be logically dependent on and chronologically subsequent to the giving of Torah, the oral Mosaic covenant. Only within the context of God's actual manifestation through eternal Torah to the people Israel in time does the congeries of such questions as "Why the creature?" "Why what is other than God and resistant to God?" and "Why time?" make sense. Time is valorized because it is *where* eternal Torah claims and blesses, charges and corrects its people. Eternity is valorized because Torah itself is eternal. The temporal Shabbat reading, saying, and singing of Torah is the conjunction of eternity and time, the realization of the eternal Torah and its eternal people in time. Despite occasional attempts in the history of Judaic mysticism to construe the creature in time solely from a vantage in eternity (or better, the eternal prefiguration of the creature), as in Lurianic Kabbalah—attempts paralleled in Christian mysticism—religious Judaism has never forsaken the conjunction of time and eternity taken to be endemic to living Torah.

A like simple summary of Christianity is impossible without entering upon tortuous and tortured matters, such as Christian distinctions between old and new Israel, Law and Gospel, and so forth—all matters that arise when two peoples read one Book and hear and practice two different religions. The fundamental difference between Judaism and Christianity concerns how eternity is present in and to time and how time qualifies their conjunction or togetherness. It says nothing not screaming for commentary by each to say that for Judaism eternity conjoins time through Torah's ritual (Shabbat) manifestation, while for Christianity eternity conjoins time through the Incarnation and its ritual repetition in the Eucharist. Both religions can and do affirm that the *realization* of the conjunction of time and eternity is in a *person*, the person at worship. Nonetheless, the exhaustive *referent* of *person*, especially in respect of eternity and time, differs in the two cases. There is never any question about what is eternal in Judaism: it is Torah. One could say that for Judaism the giving and receiving of Torah *eternalizes time*: there is no question of God's becoming man or of man's becoming God, only of man as she or he is in time before eternal God. For Christians, on the other hand, the Incarnation *temporalizes eternity*. Lacking Torah's clear voice of eternity, Christianity must construe eternity from its temporalization. That could mean and has meant many things, all centering in Trinity and christology—to which we will come momentarily. It could mean, as it has for some Christians in all times, and does especially for so-called Evangelical fundamentalists today, that Jesus of Nazareth as temporally incarnate God delivered certain teachings that function as the Christian equivalent of Torah (and where those teachings are incomplete, the magisterium of the Church serves as the equivalent of Torah). Still, it could mean and has meant otherwise; and arguably what it means depends on whether the doctrine of creation has trumping priority over other doctrines, such as Trinity and christology. The argument over doctrinal priority emerged early on in the Christian movement, and it continues.

It continues because the Christian construes eternity from its temporalization, the Word made flesh in time. What Christian theology can and must say about the eternity and time of being and nonbeing is subject (not exhaustively and without remainder, since it is the *Word* made flesh in time) to what happens in time and how time is construed. No religion is more vulnerable to time than Christianity, if any is as much so or in the same sense, that is, if Christianity is not reducible to Torah or some historical revision of it. Christianity in all forms has been deeply vulnerable to the alterations and exacerbations of modern time-consciousness, as most especially western liberal Christian theology has been. It has not mattered that the sources of modern time-consciousness were not identifiably Christian as long as they have been conducive to understanding the Christian reality, since God has not left godself without a witness, however other this other. Any list of the shapers of modern time-consciousness would include at or near the top Marx, Freud, Einstein, and Husserl, all of them Jews. To my knowledge, these figures have neither individually nor collectively had much effect on religious Judaism, except negatively (that is, in some cases dividing the religious from the nonreligious Jew). Whatever time is for the Judaist, Torah conjoins eternity and time by eternalizing time. For Christianity, whose central reality is the conjunction of time and eternity through the temporalization of eternity, the character of time is scarcely inconsequential.

I am far from claiming that Christian theology constructs a doctrine of creation or of christology out of the *New York Times* science section, only that both doctrines are vulnerable to self-correction out of the history of time itself, as the Word it knows is the Word made flesh in time. The meaning of that affirmation lies in the future to which it gives rise. We have not something to recover, regain, or return to but instead something to go forward to, to gain, to become; then, because it is future and thus merely temporal, something to lose, to negate, to resign anonymously in favor of a temporalized eternity. Time for the Christian is incremental; the "eternal life" of a twentieth-century Christian is not that of a Christian in the second or the fourteenth century.[56]

There are both deontological and meontological dimensions to human being; and neither dimension is ascribable exhaustively to time or to eternity. Time conjoined with eternity—temporalized eternity—maintains their coincidence in human life. The anonymous second-century author of the *Letter to Diognetus* said that the Christian is obliged to make of every homeland a foreign land, of every foreign land a homeland.[57] This means that the human creature lives in a bicameral house with connecting doors. With temporalized eternity one takes leave of Eckhart, however much his thought stimulates the questionableness of "eternity," "time," "being," "nothingness." For him, creation in time is schooling for the negation of temporal existence, preparation not for the affirmation of the eternal plenary being of the Creator but for the negation of that being as well. It is schooling for the eternal now of Godhead: not the eternalization of time or the temporalization of eternity but the realization of the oblivion of both time and eternity in uncreated Godhead.

The Problematic of the Two Nots

I have begun to broach matters best treated under the second problematic in this afterthinking of Eckhart, that of the two nots, the two nothings. Creator and creature in covenant, creation in time as the labor and ecstasy of the not, signify that both God and humankind pass through the not in order to realize the covenantal intention. Each stands out of a primordial not beyond initiative: the creature out of the abyss of temporally horizoned nothingness, itself external to the interiority of Godhead; God the Creator out of the abyss of Godhead. Each is possessed as well of a primordial being, but a primordiality of being that is merely eternal, an untested, ahistorical contest of being and its abyss, a primordiality of unexercised freedom. Biblical covenant obtains not between a Godhead of pleromatic indeterminateness and a human determinate automaton of the nought; both come into being, asymmetrically so. God the Creator and woman the creature are covenanted, both as having exercised freedom— and that exercise is creation in time, east of Eden, away from all innocence, whether of Godhead or of the creature eternally prefigured.

The being that God the Creator has vis-à-vis the creature, like the being that the creature has vis-à-vis God the Creator, is *metaxic*, is *between* not only being and nonbeing but between two nots or nothings. God the Creator is between the purely eternal indeterminate nothingness of Godhead and the purely temporal nothingness from which the creature is called forth. Creation in time renders determinate both God the Creator and the creature, one from one nothingness, the other from another. They meet and stand before each other in covenant, in the *metaxu* of eternity and time, in temporalized eternity, in the apocalyptic "between." To speak for the nonce only of the human creature's two nots: the *creatio ex nihilo* says only what the creature is *from*, not what, exhaustively, it is *for*. Eckhart was right to distinguish the *that* of creation in time from the *what*. The *that* of something in time is a temporary outstanding of purely temporal nothingness; but the *what*, this, too, is a nothingness, for we are created *from* nothing *for* nothing, yet for a different nothing. Everything—by which I mean the meaningfulness of time, time eternalized—depends on whether the nothingness from which we come is the same nothingness toward which we go, whether time comprises nothing but a return to the nothingness from which we come. Solely within the horizon of time, it is such a return. The nothing toward which we go, precisely not to which we return, however, is the Word made flesh in time, the self-negation of God, the temporalization of eternity.

In all talk of the two nots, one struggles to say in what respect the human creature is external and in what respect she is internal to God, how she is other and how not-other than God. The Christian tradition has wanted to say that the person is external to God by creation and internal to God by redemption or salvation. The temptation in that tradition, acceded to in some doctrinal closures, has been to focus on one reality, the creature out of nothing and not out of God (*creatio ex nihilo et non se Deo*), hence exacerbating its otherness, the doctrine of creation. Since that creation—on all empirical evidence—is messed up ("failed" by human agency; see Appendix B on fault and fall), the focus shifts to another reality, albeit an eschatological one, a "new creation" that corrects the botched-up first. There is *something* right about this, the something that compels all Christian theologians to speak of a first and a second grace, of a first and a second birth, and so forth. That something, however, cannot allow two doctrines of equal standing, those of creation and redemption. Eckhart was right to make creation primary and christology subordinate, just as he was right to combine the *quo est* ("that-by-which-it-is") and *quod est* ("what-it-is") in the divine creativity, although he got much else wrong in both the notion of creation and that of the Christ. Even in being wrong, however, he serves theological passion well in rendering thinkingly questionable what had become closed and destinate. It is always better to be profoundly wrong than superficially right.

Eckhart is profoundly wrong, at the end of the day, in explaining creation in time and God the Creator by explaining them away, by delivering both to uncreated indeterminateness and therewith to oblivion. I hope I have said enough that such a peremptory and edgy conclusion will not betray the subtlety of his thought; but the entire *Tendenz* of his thought is that creation and its Creator are an ontic-meontic catastrophe from which both creature and Creator are to return to a condition as when they were not. This is so because Eckhart, however suggestively he breached the inherited ontotheological closures, was unable finally to break with that Neoplatonism in which all nothingness is privative. Even that judgment, however, is not quite correct. He did break with Neoplatonic nothing as merely privative being and accorded to nothingness real power—and in this emphasis modern nihilism finds a genuine ancestor. But what being and its modalizations had served in the regnant ontotheological tradition, nothingness and its modalizations serve in Eckhart.[58] The nothingness from which the creature comes and verges on falling back into is but a modalization of that nothingness from which God the Creator emerges to call the creature forth; both nots are emanations of the nothingness of indeterminate and thus uncreated Godhead. For Eckhart, God the Creator and the creature are diremptive, privative, and diminished nothings, are not-other than nothing while not being other than nothing. (See Nicholas of Cusa, who learned so much from Eckhart, who argued in *De li non aliud* that the most comprehensive name of God is "not other"!)

If Eckhart schools us in the questionableness of nothingness, we must think nothingness otherwise than he. First and foremost is the distinction between the two nots, between the nothing from which we arise and that toward which we go, a distinction not evident in the *creatio ex nihilo* alone.

The first nought we do not get to choose; the nothingness from which we come is incorrigible. That we exist at all owes to a divine power of negating that first nought in the abyss of Godhead, neither now nor ever to be our own. The indicatively existing creature stands out from a downside nothing solely by the creating act of determinate God, stands out of the nothingness wholly internal to indeterminate Godhead, as does determinate God the Creator, so that the existing human creature is external both to Godhead and God. The *nihil* of the *ex nihilo* is a numbing mystery; and arguably not much more of it can be said than that (as D. G. Leahy has said[59]) it is not reducible to the ideal source of itself, is not reducible to God the Creator, but instead emerges with that which emerges from it. The Christian tradition has concluded only what it is not: it is not some power coeval with God the Creator, so that every form of gnosticism is closed off. (More could be said, arguably, were one afterthinking not Eckhart but Böhme.) On the distinctiveness of this *not* hangs the externality of the creature to God the Creator.

For analytical purposes we may discriminate two sets of two nots. In each set one is *from* nothing and *for* (or toward) nothing; and in each the crucial question is whether the nothingness one is from is the same as that toward which one goes. The two sets are discriminated in that nothingness in the first set is horizoned solely by time, in the second by what I have called temporalized eternity. (A third set has been treated implicitly in Eckhart, who views nothingness from the vantage of eternity, looking toward nothingness beyond the togetherness of eternity and time.) One set, located wholly in time, is indicative that-being from the *not*, deontologically charged to cast *what-being* toward the *not*: human temporal existence is a deontological suspension bridge over the meontological abyss. If the *creatio ex nihilo* alone explains the *quo est*, the indicative *that* of the creature's being from downside nothing, it does not by itself explain the creature's *what*, its *quod est*. To be sure, there is no human *that* without a *what*; and as modernity has understood only too well solely within the horizon of time, one need not be a Christian to experience a deontological claim laid on a meontological ground. The *what* accompanying the human *that* emerges with will, and will, as Eckhart said, emerges with purpose, or, as Böhme said, with want or desire.

Let us meditate this set of the two nots through some language from Edmond Jabès and Maurice Blanchot, two late-modern indwellers of the solely temporal *metaxu* of the two nots.[60] Existence as the interweaving of the two nots that I outstand is one of *want*, just as time is the medium of want. One is in want of what is not or no longer there, the *loss* of a primal good sensed somehow still to hover over and beckon my existence, a missing or failed *what* that verges every missing and failing. One's name was inscribed in the Book, but the Book is blurred: my existence is an outstanding palimpsest to which I add erasure and deformation. My soul's longing is for the constituted text, the Book in which I am named or called, but my standing out of the text is but my contribution to its effacement. The Book of which I am in want is lost and I am, to the extent that I am, a loser. Existence is the exacerbation of loss, is a list of grievances. Of such stuff, we can hear William James saying in the wings, are all sick or melancholic souls made.[61]

However this may be, or in addition thereto, existence is suffused with another kind of *want* or *what*, not the loss of the Book that was in a time not my time—in the "before" not—but the *lack* of the text not discovered because not yet written—in the "after" not. It is the palpitations of the *not yet* or the "after" not that sets the souls of the "healthy-minded" aflutter: what I am to do and be between the two nots is to write the text that has not been lost but can only be written and thus found out of the *that* I am, so long as I am, graced by the plenary and kenary visitations creation affords. It says much about the hold of late-modern time-consciousness that so few have exercised the option of healthy-mindedness, whether in philosophy or the arts. With the want of what is not, not because it is lost but because it is not gained and is one's responsibility to gain, one is even nearer the heart of darkness. Worse than paradise lost is paradise not gained even though the *what* of my existence be the expenditure of existence for or toward its gain. This expenditure is the agony of composition that is the bitter foretaste of the Work unwritten, the Work it is my destiny to add as an excursus to the lost Book.[62]

The faint *invocations* of the lost Book are met by the palpitating *evocations* of the unwritten Work in the suspended existence that I am. They threaten unceasingly to choke each other off and me with them. The constant conjunction of *invocation* and *evocation*, of the two nots, that is the agony of composition yields a human will so overdetermined by *desire* that the Book is proleptically dirempted by my Work. Such is the risk and discontent of existence unwilling to live out its days in pining loss, willing to outstand that loss by outstanding the other lack, that of the text whose weaver I am on Goethe's infamous roaring "loom of time" to which I am uniquely vocated. Indeed, let us consider the transcendingly great Goethe, arguably the greatest of modern healthy-minded souls, whose love of time and the earth was the model for Nietzsche: his Faust would gladly hand over his eternal soul to Mephistopheles could he but present one moment of time to which Faust could say "*Verweile doch*" (Tarry, it is enough). Toward the end of his life, Goethe persisted in refusing to file grievance against existence, affirming: "I will say nothing against the course of my existence." The selfsame Goethe in the following sentences then declares: "But it has been nothing but pain and burden, and I can affirm that during the whole of my seventy-five years, I have not had four weeks of genuine well-being. It is but the perpetual rolling of a rock that must be raised up again forever."[63]

In this first set of the two nots, horizoned solely by time, does the mere *I-that-am* return to the selfsame nothing from which I come? No sooner asked than denied. I know no mere *I-that-am*, only an *I-that-am-what*, a *what* willed either in piecemeal restitution of loss or in piecemeal anticipation of gain, a *not* that puts something (my existence) between the two nots, qualifying the *not* from which I come and constituting the *not* toward which I go. Every human person's existence between the two nots relegates the strands of her temporal nothingness. The nothingness I inherited in 1929 at birth is not the nothingness I shall bequeath on *x* date at death, anymore than the nothingness Eckhart inherited from Augustine and Pseudo-Dionysius in the fourteenth century was the nothingness he bequeathed to Nicholas of Cusa and Jakob Böhme, or that Plato in the fifth century BCE inherited from Parmenides and Heraclitus and bequeathed to Aristotle. Modern time-consciousness instructs us afresh on the *creatio continua* through its temporalization of the *ex nihilo*: the nothingness from and toward which we go is temporally refunded. It may be cold comfort, this valorization of time, but it is not nothing (in the odd way one must put it) that human existence adds (something?) to nothing.[64]

The Problematic of Christology

Why speak of yet another set of the two nots? Why not remain solely within the horizon of time, its one and only birth, its one and only death? After all, the Christian inhabits that set to the full. East of Eden she or he participates in the labor and the ecstasy of the two temporal nots and their refunding of nothingness from and toward which every human existence is oriented. She or he is also deontologically (imperatively) claimed to make a *what* bridging the meontological abyss. The short answer, requiring a different analytic, is that—however episodically—she or he inhabits not time alone but rather time conjoined with eternity, living in temporalized eternity, in the New Testament's "eternal life." The *what* toward which she or he lives is both willed and not willed, or rather is willed as not; the being she or he becomes between the two temporal nots refunds not only the pool of downside nothingness but moreover the nothingness of temporalized eternity. These negations and inversions lived in an existence temporally eternalized require the Christian theologian to enter upon an analytic of a first and recurrent *birth*, a first and recurrent *death*, a first and second set of the two nots. It is to the second set that I turn briefly in conclusion.

I have proposed that God is determinate being from indeterminate Godhead who as Creator is the *quo est* and as Redeemer is the *quod est* of the creature. This much agrees with Eckhart, *mutatis mutandis*, but then one takes leave. The human creature is not nothing but rather is a *that*, solely through that divine creative act by which she or he is determinate being from indeterminate nothingness (and for that matter, from indeterminate being). The creature is external to God not only by virtue of its *that* but also by virtue of its *what*; and it is above all the human creature's *what* that requires, for the Christian, a second set of the two nots. This is the reason I can scarcely afterthink Eckhart in any of his construals of the birth of the Logos in the ground of the soul, given that an Eckhartian condition for the birth of the Logos is my negation of "*my*," my *that*, indeed every "this and that," the negation of every externality, whether of the creature or of God. For Eckhart, moreover, the Logos born in the ground of the soul under that condition is internal not to God but to Godhead; its actualization is oblivion.

External to God in the freedom of the *in imago*, I may render my *what* further determinate wholly between my temporal birth and temporal death, exacerbating my otherness and externality to God. Within the same time, but a time eternalized—a time Eckhart wanted to say but could not say in his "eternal now," still external to God, in a way Eckhart could not recognize but gave us the language for saying—in the freedom of the *ad imaginem Verbi*, I may render my *what* further determinate by negating the what between my temporal birth and death (which does not free me of the responsibility of attaining it) in favor of the *what* of my second birth, that of temporalized eternity, that of God's negation of godself, in my existence, in my time. Creation entails the externality of the creature to God, yet it permits the creature to be internal to God, not internal to the eternal Godhead but to the negation of that Godhead in the temporalization of eternity, internal to the Word made flesh, in my own flesh. However much modern time-consciousness may have enriched the sense of negation and nothingness, it has scarcely made easier the negation of the first in favor of the second birth. Much greater surety vests in the negations and affirmations that go with external relations than in those that go with internal relations. The pathos of existence verging on the new birth, according to Kierkegaard, is "increased by the fact that the nonbeing which precedes the new birth contains more being than the nonbeing which preceded the first birth."[65]

It is the Christian witness that there is a temporally eternal *what* for the human person that exceeds the *what* of mere time alone; Christians in all times, Eckhart not excepted, have associated such an exceeding *what* with the Logos of God. Eckhart is wholly orthodox in affirming that both the *quo est* and *quod est* of the creature owe ultimately to the one God. One doctrinal closure, that of a high christology based on the prologue to the Gospel of John, identifies the Logos with God the Creator and signals implicitly that the Logos is made flesh in the Jesus of the gospels, so that the *what* of creation is identified with the *that* of a particular person in time. If Eckhart's christology is culpable—which it is—it is so not because of his neglect of Jesus of Nazareth as incarnate Logos but instead because his Logos is finally related neither to God nor to the creature; it is a trace in the ground of the human person's soul of the uncreated and uncreatable nothingness of Godhead, of which both God and creature are emanations. His neglect of Jesus had at least this merit: it would not deliver him into the modern oddity of questing for a Jesus whose historically warrantable words, his discoursing on the proper human *what*, would oblige my *that*. (Was Jesus a cynic, a liberationist, a Marxist? Then that is what I am supposed to be!) The *what* of no other person in time—Jesus (though he be incarnate Logos) not excepted—can serve as the *what* of my *that*.

Eckhart is profoundly right on this count: the Logos nowhere becomes flesh if not in my own soul.[66] If this is so—as I believe it to be—Eckhart leaves unthought not just a possibility but a historical actuality pregnant for systematic thinking that is not fixated exhaustively and without remainder upon the realization of the Word made flesh in Jesus of Nazareth. If the Logos, the *what* of a person exceeding the dialectic of the two temporal nots, is actualized only in the person's apocalyptic temporalization of eternity, there is a temporalization of the *ad imaginem Verbi* well beyond Roman Catholicism's claim for the Church to be a continuation of the Incarnation. Just as there is a temporalization of downside nothingness, that of the first set of the two nots, so too is there a temporalization of upside nothingness, that is, of God's being not merely eternal God and of man's being not merely temporal *metaxic* man, a temporalization of the second set of the two nots. This rudimentary insight, available only as not being thought through in Eckhart, comes to flower in the potencies of the Protestant Reformation and its direct offspring: modernity and its time-consciousness.[67]

Oddest of all in afterthinking Eckhart, given his enrichment of the vocabulary of being and nothingness, is the utter absence in his thought on the Logos of the idea of the kenosis of God, of seeing with the eye from the Cross. Did he not take the kenotic step because, on his own terms, it would have involved a further diremption, a further exinanition? For the early Jesus movement, however, God godself took just this risk, and it is the good news of Good Friday. Withal, in afterthinking Eckhart—while thinking his several problematics otherwise than he did through the being and nothingness he rendered perduringly questionable—we may well heed his counsel on prayer: "When I pray for aught, I pray for nought; when I pray for nought, I pray as I ought."[68]

From all determinateness, God the Creator's not excepted, follows mutability, hence suffering; this truth is not limited to Buddhism. Were God's suffering redeemable wholly within the scene of eternal creation (*creatio ab origine*), there would not have been the *mise-en-scène* of temporal creation (*creatio continua*). This point is well taken in religions other than Christianity, notably in Buddhism, in which all suffering is ascribed to determinateness as such, relief from which is attained only by the discipline of its evacuation into emptiness, what I have called sheer indeterminacy or absolute nothingness. The selfsame de-realization of created determinateness is the project of Neoplatonist Christian mystics, including Eckhart; hence the *reditus* to indeterminate Godhead, the nothingness beyond Being. In the view under development in the present thought-experiment, however, nothing (like its contrastive twin, being) is not itself sheer indeterminacy. Both nonbeing and being are nondeterminate creations of the divine Wisdom and subject to the determinateness of the divine Word and Spirit. Properly did F. Scott Fitzgerald write in *Tender Is the Night*, "The strongest guard is placed at the gateway to nothing," and I should add that an equally strong guard is placed at the gateway of being, and that the guard of both gateways is God the Creator. The eternal suffering of God the Creator of this universe is redeemable in, *only* in, the temporal suffering in his creatures *in imago Dei et ad imaginem Verbi*. Pray for us sinners now and in the hour of our dying in the death of God!

Anthropogony: Creature and God

For in fact what is man in nature? A Nothing in comparison with the Infinite, an All in comparison with the Nothing, a mean between nothing and everything. Since he is infinitely removed from comprehending the extremes, the end of things and their beginning are hopelessly hidden from him in an impenetrable secret; he is equally incapable of seeing the Nothing from which he is made and the Infinite in which he is swallowed up. . . . Who will follow these marvelous processes?

—PASCAL, *PENSÉES*

We have already noted in some depth that to think the human person, the world, and God is to participate in anthropogony, cosmogony, theogony. In this chapter we venture to think theologically the human creature, reconnoitering the territory of human being using the maps at hand (though many areas are marked "terra incognita" and "unexplored"), centering on the person's ontological instability, the very fragility of human outstanding of nothingness. Every move is to be made that *real*-izes this reality. For there is no simple standpoint from which to surprise the human phenomenon in its totality; one's reflection is engaged by that totality in its complexity from the beginning or not at all. But that totality is, in Gabriel Marcel's sense, a *mystery*: not a problem to be solved by being dissolved but an intractable fact inaccessible to revision, one that sources at once the greatness and the baseness of humankind. As such it instantiates Kierkegaard's passion of reason to think what cannot be thought through perspicuously, or as I prefer to put the matter, the passion to think a limit that is not itself the product of thought. What gives itself to be thought in this *aporia* is reflexively the very bathos of reason, more exactly the bathos of the thinker, and ultimately the very abyss of *what* is thought. One needs to mark the intercalation of God and the human person when thought is engaged.

In what follows about the human creature, we need to be aware of our own nescience and how that nescience is being constantly shifted and corrected by the natural and human sciences. If it is still the case in biology that ontogeny recapitulates phylogeny (meaning, for example, each of us is vestigially fish and fowl), we cannot know too much about what is quite literally incorporated in us ontogenetically. The same is to be said of the human intellective soul, given the hardwiring of the human brain, as well as all its culturally instilled software. We cannot remind ourselves too often of Husserl's insight, noted already, that *Sinn ist als Sinngenesis*: meaning is a function of the origin of meaning. We need to attend to the *from* from which we have become as much as to the *to* toward which we go.

We are arrived then, summarily, to the threshold of undertaking a theory or doctrine of the human creature, a theological anthropology. Turning away from the extensiveness of doctrinal and specular discursions, the intensiveness of the individual person's lived experience is to be at the fore. My hope is to expose a basis in the average reflective (and reflexive) person's lived experience for understanding the internal dialectics and polarities of her modal whole—as a living, organic, intellective soul—and its interplay with other modal wholes comprising temporal creaturehood (recall the discussion of finite modal wholes in Topos 2: Cosmogony). Certainly we cannot consider the whole of the human creature in itself, in isolation, since we ourselves are set in a context of situating wholes; we do not merely situate ourselves but are situated as well.[1] Though I employ a variety of approaches, in all of them a major question recurs: What is the relation between the kind of being we have as existing persons to the *not* or nothingness, and how does that relation toll in the chambers of our lives? The first approach will be to consider three scenes taken to play out in the drama of each individual person's life: (1) the scene of its suspension between a primordial and a consequent nothingness; (2) the scene of its suspension between factual actuality and essence or potency; and (3) the scene of its renewal or redemption.

Human Existence between Two Nots

It is the peculiar anxiety of thinking about them that neither being nor nonbeing is sufficiently determinate as to be the subject of mindful intention, hence of phenomenological reduction. That being is more privileged than nonbeing in this respect is nothing more than a metaphysical conceit. No *something*, whether finite hecceity or infinite Being, so determinately *is* as to be free of the margins of nonbeing. Everything living is margined by two nots: the nothing it is *from* and the nothing it is *toward*. Such thinkable intelligibility as being and nonbeing may have depends on a determination process more ultimate than both.

While I borrow the phrase "scenes of . . ." from contemporary Freudian psychoanalytic theory, notably Lacan and Bataille, I construe scenes themselves in a theological, not a psychoanalytic, sense: scenes of origination pertain to creation, scenes of renewal to redemption (or salvation-health). Because in Christian theology the scene of origination and the scene of renewal are both externally and internally related, they are ultimately referred to their determinate Creator (thus a doctrine of God coherent with a doctrine of creation). As previously, I shall not cavil to use philosophical language at hand, although I do not doubt that there are other languages in which the selfsame matters arguably may be brought better to expression. In respect of "scenes of origination" we shall think, first, humankind's suspension between nontemporal *ouk on* (nonbeing or nothingness) and temporally qualified *me on* (relative nonbeing or nothingness), out of both of which we *ex-ist* (stand out of and are other to), and, second, humankind's suspension between and noncoincidence with two kinds of being ("existence" and "essence"), both rendered determinate by the time and space of the individual human person. This meditation is offered not as the conclusion but as the initiation of our work, thus is in the theatrical sense a *mise-en-scène*.

Scene 1: We cannot remind ourselves too often that to exist involves a double negation. To exist means literally to "stand out of." Out of what? Out of nonbeing or nothingness. Thus to exist is to negate nonbeing or nothingness, is to exit nonbeing in favor of being existently (existentially). The scene of the human person's origination is what may be called the first not, and the exit from that state of absolute and blank nothingness (*ouk on*) is in favor of being existently on pain of being nothing at all. In this exit from the first not the individual human person is not complicit at all; one's will is not involved (although that of one's parents is or may be); by the time the human person comes self-consciously to the astonishing recognition that "I am (existing)" (to which astonishment we shall return) one has exited the first not. But that very recognition is simultaneously tinged with a twin recognition of the second not. The "I am" is escorted by the recognition that *there was* when I did not exist and *there will be* when I shall not exist. My existing, however, a kind of being on pain of my being nothing at all, is between two states, conditions, or kinds of nonbeing, for I did not exist and shall not exist. My temporal-temporary existing is *between*, in Plato's language μεταξύ, from first not toward second not. But whether the nonbeing from which I come is the same as the not-being toward which I go is an inescapably stunning question on which the meaning of my temporal-temporary existence hangs, since if they are the same my existence itself seems to count only for nought. That they are the same or different, and how, are matters on which religious mythologies (stories of primordial or archaic states and consequent ends) differ sharply.[2] In any case, such being as I temporally have or am is a suspension, is in suspense, between two nots: a nontemporal "before-not" and a temporal "after-not" (if my existence is to have meaning, the latter cannot be solely nontemporal), a primordial and a consequent not.

Existence as the interweaving of the two nots I outstand is one of *want* (lack), as time is the medium of want. But human existence is suffused with another kind of want (in the sense both of lack and desire), not the loss of the Book that was in the time not my time but the lack (and desire) of the text not discovered because not yet written. This want is even nearer the heart of darkness. It were bad enough that the text is lost in which I was and dumbly intuit that I may still be inscribed, and will not know until it is recovered readingly. Worse still is the agony of composition that is the bitter foretaste of the Work unwritten, the Work it is my destiny to add as an excursus to the lost Book. The faint *invocations* of the lost Book are met by the palpitating *evocations* of the unwritten Work in the field of existence that I existently am, and threaten to choke each other off—and me with them. The constant conjunction (as Hume said, not to be confused with causality) of *invocation* and *evocation*, of existing between the two nots that is the agony of composition, yields a human will all but immobilized by *desire* and *lack*, such that—what shall one say? The Book is further diremted by my Work?[3] This is the risk and discontent of existence unwilling to live out its days in pining loss, that outstands that loss by outstanding the other lack, that of the text (web) whose weaver I am and to the loom of which I am uniquely vocated. *This* Not-text, this sequent or con-sequent Not, what is its warp, what its weft? All writers, especially poets, musicians, or other rhapsodes, know the agony of composition, metaphor for human existence itself, as each human person is the composer of her own symphony (rather, as is usually the case, cacophony). One exclaims with Franz Rosenzweig: "I wish I were a symphony by Beethoven, or something else that has been completely written. What hurts is the process of being written."[4] One lacks the Work, which, even if and when written, never substitutes for the Book.

In the present *mise-en-scène*, I have spoken of being qua existing in the human person as coinciding with nonbeing, or rather of one's swinging in time between two kinds of not-being on the verges of time. It belongs to the kind of being I am that I coincide nonbeing at both termini, the *terminus a quo* and the *terminus ad quem*. Effectively, that kind of being is a noncoincidence; neither of the kinds of nonbeing or nothingness is reducible to the other, and such being as I am/have qua existing seems distributed exhaustively and without remainder to neither alone, nor in any obvious way to both. Does this signify, for the human person, that "mere existence" cannot exhaust the dialectic of being and nonbeing (nothingness), even if the only basis one has for understanding that dialectic is one's own existence, one's own becoming?

Scene 2: There is another noncoincidence in respect of human existence to be considered. If I do not know *which* nonbeing is the more powerful lure (or "drag") of my existence, I have or am a like difficulty in respect of *being*. I am ontologically as well as *ouk*ontologically/*meon*tologically, cataphatically as well as apophatically, plenarily as well as kenarily noncoincident. This noncoincidence evoked the distinction in the western metaphysical tradition between existence and essence, and in modernity between the ontological and the deontological (between what I am and what I ought to be). Thus to say that I do not coincide with myself in respect of plenum (fullness of being) is to say that I am not what I am, that I am not in my existence what I ought to be in my essence.[5] Still and nonetheless, as long as I am (exist), I know *that* I am. (Do I indeed know that I am? See the interlude below, "The Sur-prise of 'I exist, here, now.'") But what *what* goes with that *that*?

If we take the *existence* of *a* being (such as I am) to be the full surrogate of being, we are trapped in a certain form of ontological noncoincidence (*a* being is not other beings and, in the way indicated under (1) above, is not even itself). The modality of being an existent being is that of *determinate* being. And if we attend to the mere *existence* of something, its existence (as long as it exists) must be said to be as absolute as that of any and every determinate being. Thinkers as disparate as Meister Eckhart and Søren Kierkegaard are in agreement when the latter writes, "A fly, when it is, has as much being as the God."[6] If being is nothing but existence, we are left with Hamlet's question and no other: to be *or* not to be. But the reason that is not *the* question, or not the only question, is that being is not reducible to the facticity of existence, to the being (existing) of *a* being, not forgetting that that is the kind (or one of the kinds) of being I am.[7] Indeed that is at bottom the principal reason why, in extremity of frustration with our own ontological instability, we do not kill ourselves, take ourselves out of existence, the humanly ultimate "standing out" not only of not-being but of being.

We rage at the precise determinateness of being—it, our existence. So insistent can that rage become that one is tempted to put an end to one's only determinateness of being known from the inside out. Such a putting to an end would be the flame-out of desire itself at the hand of all but fortuitous will: the passion for some kind of determinate other that, in aspiration, would embody the infinity of the indeterminate. Among Freud's most profound insights was the claim for an internal connection between infinite—or should one say indeterminate—desire (the "pleasure principle") and the death instinct: suicide as the subpsychic, unconsciousness statement of the relation between being and nothingness. Suicide is desire's rampage against the refusal of determinateness to yield, is the existentially ultimate and hopeless reassertion of the rights of will over desire, the aspiring leap into indeterminateness pure.

Why then does a rational person enmeshed in the snares of noncoincidence not *commit* (as we say) suicide? Is it because one harbors a nagging suspicion (*Ahnung*, hunch) that thus suicidally to coincide with nonbeing (to cease to exist) would scarcely end one's being, or rather one's unstable career of coinciding with being? (But then, what would "one" or "our" mean since the determinateness of being *a* human person would be lost?) One has the presentiment as well (is it the same or a different *Ahnung*?) that just as existence does not exhaust being, so not existing does not exhaust nothingness. On such a slender reed, in extremity, does the volitional continuity of a reflective and reflexive life hang.

It may well be that there is a scale of determinate things in a considerable segment of which *existence* is a more or less adequate surrogate of *being*, where a thing's existence, so long as it exists, permits the negation of the nought, the affirmation of the non-nought. Thus this piece of stone serving as a paperweight on my desk: to exist as *this* stone it has only to be not everything or anything else (including every other piece of stone) *but* this stone in this cosmos to be. I cannot imagine that this piece of stone could be *more* this piece of stone than the piece of stone that exists here, now. Fulfilling the negations necessary for this-stoneness, or in affirming the full range of the non-nought, it cannot be more or less than itself.

But the human person, fulfilling those conditions equally and existing in the same sense, can "fail" or "succeed" in her or his being (see Appendix B: Fault and Fall in Human Existence). That is because a human self is not only externally but also internally determinate in respect of her or his being and not being.

Our *mise-en-scène* of origination has supplied two of those possible internal determinations: (1) suspension between a primordial and a sequent or consequent nothingness, and (2) suspension between factual actuality (existence) and a claiming essence or potency (*potentia obedientalis*). In matters ontological and meontological one might refer to external determinations as those of nature and to internal determinations as those of temporal selfhood, of history.

Scene 3: The scene of renewal or redemption. Taking the determinations of being and nonbeing (nothingness) within time to comprise the order of *creation*, incompletely described in the preceding scenes of origination, we turn now to a range of determinations that is the central preoccupation of the religious, the order of redemption or salvation, which may be accounted (again, incompletely) as scenes of renewal.

The first coming to be is the order of creation (*creatio ab origine*), and I understand both Judaism and Christianity to affirm, at least mythologically, that while creation establishes the structures of determinateness for all that is not God, human being qua created is unfinished, and this involves the critical distinction between *creatio ab origine* and *creatio continua*. Creation does not mean that everything in the world is fully or finally fashioned in the modality of its true being; for Christians and Jews creation leaves something to be *done*. In the biblical mythological accounts God creates the world, names mankind, then in effect says to humankind "*do* something" (name the other creatures, replenish, multiply, take dominion, and so on), all the while remembering whose the world is, the Lord's and all the fullness thereof. The command to "do" is, to be sure, laced with interdicts, what *not* to do (don't eat of forbidden fruit of the garden, listen to snakes, and the like). The common Christian opinion that "not doing" takes precedence over "what to do" in the Hebrew Bible doubtless reflects a fundamental misunderstanding of Torah. In Christian conviction, what humankind *does* often skews creation, so that humankind always has imperatively to do something about what has already been done. Because we have to do something about what has already been done, both by God and by humankind, Christians and Jews distinguish between orders of creation and redemption.

Immediately one must pause, lest confusion ensue. To establish this critical distinction between *creatio ab origine* and *creatio continua* one must understand that there are two sets of two nots, the first set pertaining to theogony, the second to anthropogony; the first nought of theogony is not the first nought of anthropogony. Always and everywhere *creatio ab origine* ought to refer to the self-generation of God from the abysmal indeterminate nothingness internal to Godhead, the negation of that nothingness that God may be determinate Creator. The second not (of the first set), that of *creatio continua*, is a partial negation of determinate God. This assumes that God the Creator is not *ens perfectissimum*, for if God is such perfection nothing else can be, except as illusory simulacra. The set of two nots bearing on creation therefore deals with how there can be other than God, the universe and its inventory

We resume the set of two nots touching anthropogony. The first nought we outstand we do not get to choose; we are created creators. That we exist at all, that we factually become, owes to a power of negating that primordial, ungrounded nought, a selfsame power of affirming the non-nought, a power not now or ever to be our own. For us any further coming into being will presuppose a grounding in which we are not complicit, the grace of being the being we are on pain of being nothing at all. That grounding, however, is a necessary but not sufficient ground of *my* being. My human life, as the unity of determinations over which I preside as the created élan of determinability, properly begins with the temporal funding and regrounding of *my* not: not God, not anyone or anything else in the cosmos, in short, my ownmost *ad quem*, my ownmost *toward*.

The religious are they who center their redemptive being in the religation of the two pools of the not and in the invocative-evocative inversions between the "already" indicative facticity of existence and the potencies of the temporally funded and imperative not-yet. This involves nothing less than dying to the life that makes us merely other than (and thus negates) the first nought, the life that affirms itself merely as an existing non-nought; and it involves nothing more than birth (commonly called rebirth) to a new life that is the negation of an existence correlated with an ungrounded second nought. There is a first and a second coming to be, as there is a first nought to come from and a second nought to come toward.

Existence that has become conscious, says Kierkegaard, is bathos, "for is it not a most pathetic thing to come into existence from nothing?"[8] To be sure, for Kierkegaard, existence that has become conscious of itself as shot through with nonbeing is so by virtue of what he calls the "Moment." In this eternal now bathos reaches its apogee as the existing one is intersected by its absolute unlike, its absolute unequal, its absolute other; this fragile existence in time is thrown out of an ungrounded uncreated nought, meeting in time what time cannot yield: eternity. In one of his feebler attempts at irony (of which he normally is the consummate master), Kierkegaard calls the bathos of recognition the "new birth." The difficulty with the new birth, he writes (putting it as a question), is "increased by the fact that the nonbeing which precedes the new birth contains more being than the nonbeing which preceded the first birth."[9]

What might these reflections suggest, not in a Kierkegaardian framework but in the presently proffered scene of renewal? That the human creature enhances the pool of being by taking responsibility for the creaturely dialectic of being and nothingness? That wresting of being from nothingness, simultaneously replenishing the pool of nothingness (but of a different kind), constitutes the unfinished character of the human mode of being? From the divine negation of the first and ungrounded Not and the divine affirmation of the non-nought, I came into a first being, that of mere existence. The pathos of my existence is not just that it is a coming from nonbeing but that it goes toward another: my first being qua existent is also an e-ject of the death I pro-ject. Yet this coming death has more of being in its nonbeing than the nonbeing from which I came: this is the "good" of Good Friday. To advance knowingly into death is to have retrieved the nonbeing behind one that is the eject of the advance, as the advance is the project—the coincidence of far countries, the far before and the far yonder or far-after. The coincidence of being and nonbeing that is human life is surely not a matter of *one* new birth but of the recurrence of birth, whenever time is both mortified and revivified by the eternal, when life is "eternal life," or in Eckhart's language the eternal now. William Blake inscribed himself (allegedly for his tombstone) thus: "William Blake, one who is very much delighted with being in good company, born 28 Novr 1757 in London & has died several times since."[10]

One has spoken cryptically thus far of scenes of origination and renewal for the human creature (cryptically: from the crypt, from the recesses) and scarcely at all of the *mise-en-scène* for deity. Blake and other visionaries of the religious West (Luria, Böhme, Coleridge, to name but a few) were at some pains to speak of that energy by and through which creation and creativity are exercised in all scenes, by God and humankind, namely, the imagination. Böhme (and in this his follower Blake) no less than Coleridge construed the primary imagination to be, in Coleridge's words, "the infinite repetition in the finite mind of the eternal act of creation in the infinite I AM."[11] Drawing upon Böhme, Schelling, and Blake, we have had occasion to note the divine conversion of velleity into sublime desire, the mutation of that desire back again to will, the incessant task of embodied imagination.

Interlude: The Sur-prise of "I exist, here, now"

Sur-prise means to take over, overtake; to be surprised is to be taken over, overtaken, the initiative lying elsewhere, astonishingly. I shall never forget a lecture by my colleague (now deceased) whose office was but a few doors from mine, a Nobel laureate in literature, Saul Bellow. He was in his mid-eighties at the time, and one of his public lectures comprised a long meditation on his career as a novelist. What arrested me early on and evoked my own recognition was a plain statement: "At a critical point in my writing I had a sudden burst of self-awareness that was the closest thing to a metaphysical insight I have ever had. It was, simply: I exist, here, now."

Why should such a realization be as astonishing as it is infrequent? After all, the reality of the ordinary (that I am, here, now) is the condition of the appearing of all ordinary things to me. Why then so infrequent the realization of this reality? I do not doubt that Bellow's sudden realization/recognition of his own existing here and now suffused his entire oeuvre. His genius was to coax the extraordinary from the ordinary in his characters and their lives (among many books, see *Henderson the Rain King*).

In this as in many respects Saul Bellow embodied an ancient Greek view of things (although he was learned in Judaic, Christian, and oral and "primitive" cultures as well). His métier was that of novelist, but as such he had the soul of a poet (and as noted earlier, for the Greeks religion and the arts were at one in the importance of the *realization* of the ostensibly *real*). Like two other modern artists with sympathetic proclivities for the Greeks, Wallace Stevens and William Butler Yeats, Bellow viewed poetic prose as the artifice of eternity for illumining the ordinary (so Stevens's "An Ordinary Evening in New Haven"), as the *alethe logon*, the uncovering word illumining all otherwise ordinary words. For him, as for Pindar among the Greeks, "the poetic statement is *itself* the religious *realization*."[12] Moreover, the poetic or poetic prose statement (or painting or sculpture or music) is inseparable from the awareness (in the reader or viewer) it elicits. It is for this reason that artists stand in the lineage of "the announcers of the gods" to truly attuned religious adepts. As artificers of eternity, as announcers of the eternally recurrent "coursing powers" presiding over and suffusing all things temporal and transient, the artist in her work and in the awareness it elicits brings to bear an eternal light upon the light ("shining") emitted by all ordinary temporal *phainomena* ("the things that shine"). Every phenomenon requires to be "collected," according to Plato, in order to be an object or intention of the mind. As such it "shines" and is reflected in the human mind, to be met with and by the superior light of immortal recurrence, giving to the phenomenon a gravitas and dignity transcending itself. The work of art is not a translation of something expressible otherwise; it is itself an apprehension of, in, through a transient thing or person (for Michelangelo, the phenomenal figures Moses or David; for Stevens, an ordinary evening in New Haven).

It is often and truly noted that for the ancient Greeks the all-embracing reality was nature (φύσις, *physis*). Within nature's embrace the "immortals" and the "mortals" were sharply distinguished. For the mortals, each and every determinate identity dies, whereas the immortals are eternal. But no sense of eternity connected with the sense of eternity in the western monotheisms (in which the divine is putatively a separately existing entity) can be imputed to the Greeks. In Greek mythology there was a pantheon of identifiable immortals or gods, to be sure, but they have not that determinate identity that defines all natural things in time (namely, they do not die). The eternity of the gods consists in this, and only in this, that they name the nondiscursive and nondeterminate forms that repetitively preside over and suffuse any and all of nature's mortals. There are as many gods as there are discriminable sorts of mortal life in nature. These sorts center on the emergence of life and its sustenance (so sex and love, Aphrodite; warfare and strife among competitors for life, Athena; food, Ceres, Persephone, and so on). So the gods are immortal by reason of being names for the "coursing powers" repetitively ingredient in every determinate mortal life, and rendering each such life luminescent and plangent.

No ancient western culture, not even the Egyptian, was more sensitive to the fact that each and every identity *dies* and that every human identity knows this. No ancient western civilization was more given over to the memorialization of death than the Egyptian, yet for them as for the Greeks the fundamental reality was human life in all its blazing phenomenality. In a culture of death bidding to become an all-pervasive industry, as is the whole of western modernity and postmodernity, life itself is the miracle to be accounted for and memorialized. From Greek philosophy alone one would gain the impression that the Greeks were interested first and foremost in grand generalizations about mortality and immortality, being and nothingness, knowing and not knowing, etc. But from the Greek poets (say, Pindar) one would know that they were engaged all but exclusively with specific, concrete persons (say, Castor and Pollux, the simultaneity of the identity of each, their difference from each other, and their sameness): "the miracle of being in its only knowable mode, the miracle of individual existence." "Never, not even in birth or sex, is that sense of given form and its given expressiveness more poignant than in death: that he or she should never see or speak again is the most moving definition of how marvelous it is that someone should speak or see."[13]

These observations about the Greeks are not a digression from beginning this interlude with Bellow's "metaphysical insight" but rather indicate a path for returning to it with enhanced understanding of its importance. One can see why in a lecture on his career as a writer Bellow began with his acute realization "I exist, here, now." This affirmation carries implications for the writer of fictional prose, who must create or devise characters that convince the reader of their reality and in whom the reader can and does recognize something of herself or himself. Moreover, the "I am, here, now" carries a co-implicate, namely, the *realization* that the very meaning of "I am" depends critically upon the existence of other persons who have intersected my own existence in both external and internal ways, since knowing and being known by other persons is part and parcel of one's ownmost existence. However much one's existence internally is an awareness of being between two solitudes, between a first and a second not, one's "I am, here and now" is not a solitary affair since our existence is externally constituted by intercourse with other persons who in their idiosyncratic (the Greek word, unfortunately now much abused, was "idiotic") ways are preciously ingredient in one's existence, here, now.[14] In the great instances of the novel as art form, the same is to be said of fictive characters. Who that reads Herman Melville can but think that his or her own existence is described and enhanced by Ahab, Queequeg, Ishmael, Billy Budd?

I allude to the astonishment of realizing "I am, here, now" in the context of the arts deliberately, as I have avoided the context of philosophy equally deliberately, for reasons I think warrantable. Every competent reader of this book will know that what is *modern* about modern philosophy began with Descartes's meditations on the "I am." Why then not enter Descartes into the lists of this interlude? Because his meditations on the "I am" are of a different order than those of Bellow. Leaving aside many problems not relevant to present purposes (his intent to ground philosophy in the human subject, the centering of certainty in thinking and its proofs both rational and empirical, and so on), Descartes's concern was not the sheer astonishment of "I am" but the certification of the warrants for affirming it, so that one can affirm "I am" indubitably (see Appendix A). If anything about human beings is indubitable, it is that once one was not and there will be when one is not. The astonishment of the "I am" is that, here and now, I "exist." Far more promising than Descartes's *cogito ergo sum* (I think, therefore I am) is Augustine's *dubito ergo sum* (I doubt, therefore I am)!

If modern philosophy was marked by its extension of the Enlighten-ment, locating "enlightening" in the human subject, postmodern philos-ophy is marked by the darkness that horizons everything finite (and, as we claim here, God godself). While this recognition is so far scant in American guild philosophy, it is fulsome in modern and especially postmodern arts. The sur-prising recognition and realization that one exists, however fleet-ingly and temporarily, is surrounded by an encroaching tenebrous edge, is simultaneously a recognition that one comes from nothing and goes toward nothing, that all existential outstanding of nothingness is frag-ile. Further, one's surrounding creatures are themselves entering into and exiting existence, and did they not I would not be. So my existence, and that of everything else, at its highest moment of self-recognition, is an ig-nominious existence. Intellectual as well as moral virtues have their dark, vicious (and viscous) underside.

The recognition "I *am*, here, now" is escorted by a sharp pang of ontic humility, by an accompanying recognition that my existence is enabled by the sacrifice of other existences, as my own exit from existence will enable the advent of other existences.[15] We come thus upon both the grandeur and the ignominy of self-conscious human existence. To *realize* that "I am, here, now" is also to realize that, as long as I am here and now, I tolerate gratefully this profound yin and yang (the grandeur and the ignominy).[16]

Having underscored the importance of *realizing* "I am, here, now," it is well to take account of a snare (if not a delusion) in the "now." *Now* of course focuses on the present, the time of immediacy, and it has been said already that immediacies without mediacies are not to be trusted. Aristotle said that the present is the least real of the modalities of time, that it can only be imagined, that no sooner has one recognized the present than it is already the most recent entry into the past, and that the future is simply the next candidate for entry into the (specious) present. Marcel Proust made a career of this fact novelistically (*À la recherche du temps perdu*). Phi-losophers may forget that the surprise of "I am, here, now" depends for its recognition on the cumulative effect of the coincidence of all three modes of time (past, present, future), but poets and novelists do not.[17]

As the bell has not yet rung for us to return to our seats from this in-terlude to the concert (symphony or cacophony?) of the human person's careering with the modes of being, let us linger over the "I exist, here, now" as a situation of e-merging, of e-mergence-y. To e-merge: to come forth from a surrounding obscurity or hiddenness. Emerging in this sense is a presencing of something of import that has claiming initiative. I spoke earlier of this as *alethe logon*, a word that so enlivens what it names (human existence) as to root and make flourish all its other uses.

A fundamental thesis of this study is that we live out of the future but understand out of the past; recalling Schelling, the living opacity of the past, present in the deposit of old words (Heidegger's drawing near of the distant) is the groundless ground of the present. A certain diachronicity, even anachroncity, conduces to a startled synchronicity. It is not easy to know in what time to live, or how to extend or distend one's own available time by proxy, the project of all earnest learning. The pertinent available time is not the time we are in, as Augustine said, but the time in us, the morning to which we awake whatever the time of day, the time of dawning, the time of Thoreau's inward morning, the time of the sun's rising over the Mount Katahdin of the soul's dark valleys.

It belongs to the human creature, the one enfolded in time's manifold, that she seizes and fixes what is unfolded in time's lingering. The osmotic space and time of "here, now" holds temporally-temporarily the seepage of what is arriving and what is departing: anticipating and remembering are freeze-dried in what is *there*, what presences in this present. It is the residuum of what calls and the echo of receding vocation ("the receding sound of what you had relinquished . . ."[18]). No evident "what-it-is," no what there is, shepherds the call: the world is the inventory, the cumulus, of all that has lingered in my whiles. For the most part, the human creature in and of herself is the cumulative forgetting of e-mergence-y. Hence, absent the enlivening "I exist, here, now," one has the standard perception of the world's inventory as ordinary (Heidegger's *das Mann* and the perception of *Alltäglichkeit*).

It further belongs to the crisis character ("critical state") of e-mergence-y that we cannot immediately name *what* is happening, since that adheres to the lingering whiles that follow, though they do not linger long. The history of philosophy and theology in the West is the story of failed attribution in respect of e-mergence-y as such, especially the reduction of e-mergence-y as such to some causal relation between two or more residua of "what is there" ordinarily. High classical Christian theology always wanted to model an aboriginal E-mergence-y occasioned by One "what is there" who simultaneously is "what there is" by reason of supervening upon all subsidiary emergencies. Thus the great medieval Christian mystics spoke of two creations, eternal and temporal. *Mutatis mutandis* (necessary adjustments having been made), we shall do the same; but the necessary adjustments are radical, involving as they do reimaginings of Godhead-God and creation.[19]

The modern person has forgotten—and forgotten he has forgotten— the state of e-mergence-y, a state or condition that was the soul's yearning of the late-medieval mind. How can e-mergence-y be vivified within time's manifold without the fixations of the dead now's tyrannical ordinariness? I think this the prime driver of Eckhart's audaciously speculative intelligence. The answer can never be found by resort to "this and that," by what there ordinarily are, by pursuing the archaeology of ontic artifacts. It was the conditions—ontological and meontological—of e-mergence-y as such that claimed him. (Let us leave aside the question whether Eckhart's Neoplatonism had the metaphysical resources to elaborate those conditions coherent with his other claims, as I think he did not. The reader will have ample opportunity to judge whether *we* do.)

For Eckhart the standard world is that of time, the residual *whats* of successive lingerings. In such a world of beings ("this and that") nothing can emerge but nothing. He recognized "powers of the soul" oriented thus and thought them not only worthless but harmful. What is to be understood is e-mergence-y itself: of being from nothing, of nothing from being. This is not the standard business of ordinariness. Of course Eckhart got himself into serious trouble for rendering nugatory the powers of the soul (sensing, thinking rationally, conceiving, and so on) and exalting the soul itself, rather its ground in the groundless abyss that traces not God but the Godhead, in which ground the very Logos is born, traced in every human soul (and for this he was condemned as a heretical pantheist). If I refer to Eckhart at all in this context it is to say that in the serial and episodic experiences humans have of e-mergence-y, one grounds another, and to have no such experience of e-mergence-y is to have no "grounds." If one has no experience whatever of the astonishment at "I exist, here, now," how is one to understand being or not being at all?

The first bell has rung, and there is shuffling of feet to return to the concert (however disconcerting). Repetition is one of the rules of learning.

Saul Bellow: "I exist, here, now."

There are times, too rare, when nothing is more important than the fact, the *realization* of existing. Why is the *re-cognition* and *real-ization* of this fact such a sur-prise, such an astonishment? As if one had never existed before, but now suddenly does, now stands out of nescience conscientiously? And in that moment of vitalized prescience, there is nothing whatever to do but *live*—to see, hear, taste, touch, smell, think and afterthink the profuse and temporary-temporal efflux of being, for once and almost for the first time to understand being as participle, one's being as be-ing. (Standing out of nothing is not to be counted on, is not some sort of ontological entitlement. How many times have we to learn this?)

And then, with the last bell, one remembers Ahab with his quadrant (sextant) shooting the sun to determine the "here" of the *Pequod* in the vastness of the sea, with the result that he destroys the instrument: "Thou sea-mark! thou high and mighty Pilot! thou tellest me truly where I *am*—but canst thou cast the least hint where I *shall* be? Or canst thou tell where some other thing besides me is this moment living? . . . Science! Curse thee, thou vain toy . . . !"[20]

The Bicameral House of Human Being

It were well to take stock of where we are at this point in framing a view of the reality that is a human person, attending mostly to her or his existence and the pertinent modes of being most complicit in the valorization of that existence. One has spoken extensively (about human existence as such), though not intensively (thus not about the existence of John or Mary Doe, although if the extensions are veridical John and Mary must be able to recognize herself or himself in them). The most *extensive* claim is that human existence is an existence between two nots: the power to outstand (stand out of) both the first and the second not while living between them is the meaning of a person's existence. It has been the labor of unpacking this claim that has commanded attention so far, and much remains to be said. For example, in the *mise-en-scène* of origination (above) the first not was ostensibly identified as *ouk on*, blank nothingness, about which nothing can be said. Nothing to be said until one speaks of the *nihil* in the *creatio ex nihilo* and all necessary attendant theories (of Godhead, God, creation, and so on). The same is the case with a further explication of the two nots by reference to, if not in analogy with, the classical modal categories of essence and existence. I have already claimed that essence in respect of the two nots, and particularly as regards the second not, is not just a class-universal (although assuming it) but is a temporally tinged specific essence for each individual human person in which she or he is complicit. The full-orbed meaning of this claim awaits the further distinction developed in the next section: that between *in imago Dei* and *ad imaginem Verbi* (in the image of God and toward the image of the Logos), a distinction patterned on the metaxic between of *creatio ab origine* and *creatio continua*, and one critical for the scene of renewal outlined above.

Any student of medieval thought will know that argument raged concerning the respective rank of the four transcendentals (being, unity, truth, goodness) and especially whether, of these four, being could so sublate the other three as to claim hegemony in anything whatever that *is*. But to think being is to engage truth, assuming that thinking is essential to ascertaining truth in respect of being. If the being to be thought is that of the human person, as it is in the present chapter, one encroaches upon "unity": is the person's existence stably unitary or numeral? And is that existence exhaustively and without remainder "good"? Are we prepared to *think* human existence? More importantly, are we prepared to *live* in what is thus thought, no matter how many hares are scared up—running in all directions? Well did Kierkegaard write, "It is one thing to think, and another thing to exist in what has been thought."[21] If the analytic of human unstable existence presented so far is troubling, leaving a picture of the person in dour mood, perhaps we have to learn again how light espouses— indeed is espoused to—darkness, how the stiletto of silence must enter the heart to become words of truth. If there is a bone of oneness (unity) in us, its marrow is made of a wealth of differences.[22] Such unity as the person has and is is not simple.[23] It is rather marked by numeral or distinctional being, as thinking itself is initiated by drawing warrantable distinctions.

In a further "raid on the inarticulate," that of the territory of human existence, we may proceed through the much used, sometimes abused, metaphor of the "house of being." The house of human being is a single citadel, but a duplex one—and that not in a dualistic Marcionite fashion, as though the person has two ontic/ontological halves, each inhabiting different quarters without connecting doors. Rather, the whole of the human person is vested temporally/temporarily in a bicameral house of being. One says what is distinctive about the temporal creature that a person is by saying that he is self-consciously *a* being be-ing (a being participially) who *is*.[24]

The twofold manner of human being, requiring a bicameral habitation in time, may be explicated in a variety of ways. For an orientation, it will be useful to draw upon Eckhart, while more adapting than adopting some of his ideas. (1) The person is more a compound than a mixture of being (*ens*) and being "this and that" (*ens hoc et hoc*). She is a compound of being human and being this or that human (Diana, not Paul), existing between the *extension* and the *intension* of being human. (2) She moves back and forth between imperative virtual being (what she is *toward*), hovering in one of her two rooms, and indicative or formally inhering being by which she is, as a "this or that," in the other room; she has been brought into a bicameral existence in time out of the cold of sheer nothingness (out of the first not). (3) She is "*a* being be-ing" whose mere existing serves only to exacerbate the questionableness of being anything at all. The only sure modality of her being is that of her indicative mode (hence the importance of the "I exist, here, now"), but she (as the "this" of Diana) shall not exist. How shall she, within her limited time and space, participate the further ranges of her being *imperatively*, both extensively and intensively; has she a key to the other room? (4) In respect of her existence, her standing out of the blank nothingness of the first not, she (Diana) is *made*: she is born into the room of indicative being, and the key to get out, although certain to be used, is not at her initiative (save by suicide). It is otherwise with the other room, that of virtual and imperative but potential/possible human being: the contours of that room, its furnishings, and its key are of her *making*. Whether there are other creatures in the cosmos who have the responsibility of determining in part their range of being and its meaning, we cannot now know enough to know. But the human creature is one such, a created creator (which entails, of course, the distinction between *creatio ab origine* and *creatio continua*). Because of this the western monotheisms have a special commitment extensively to the "anthropic principle," and intensively to every individual human person.

Of course, no individual human person exists indicatively in and of him- or herself, as each of us exists in dependent relation to nonhuman existents as well as other humans (indicatively, especially the parents who gave us life). So we continuously need a realizing sense of the realities upon which our living and dying depend (animal, vegetable, mineral, viral, and so on), all life depending on the death of other things, their life depending in part on our death, so also a realizing sense of the modalities of their being as well. Every thinker of "being" and its modes has done so through a scale of being differentiated according to level or grade, usually with the modes most stable at the bottom, and the least stable at the top—unless the scale is a Neoplatonic one, in which case the order is reversed, so that the most stable is at the top (the One, Being itself), and the least stable is at the bottom (those things that are at farthest remove from stable Being itself, thus have the most privative—lack of—being). Since I resist all Neoplatonist (but not Platonic) metaphysics, I follow the "bottom up" gradation, and thus do not denigrate the bottom inhabitants of the scale, as they comprise the bodily basis of my own existence.[25]

There is of course a scale of bicamerality of being according to level or grade in the created order. Barring external agency, the being of a piece of stone is more or less stable; it may be effaced by wind or water, or faced by Michelangelo, but left to itself it manifests little of the twofold (this is addressed in Appendix B on fault and fall). With rise in the scale, instability rises;[26] in the human case, instability owes to the unsettled proportion of one's existence lived in one room (that of indicative standing out of blank nothingness, the first not) and lived in the other (that of imperative virtual or potential existence toward the second not). One can quit neither in favor of the other, as they are co-conditional, so one exists in both simultaneously. Even so one's time, blood, and tears are limited and must be proportioned between the two rooms of the single citadel of existence. The proportion itself never reaches stability, so with self-conscious intellective soul ontic/ontological instability becomes *anxiety*.

We are examining the range of being open to the human person existing between two nots. There are of course multiple metaphysical construals of the place of human beings in the larger scheme of things, as there are comportingly multiple religious cultures to go with those construals. While not all religious cultures are theistic, and not all work within a gradient ontic/ontological structure of the sort under development here, all recognize differentiated planes of reality, and that in at least three respects. First, all honor an extraordinary segment in reality at the highest plane: gods, sponsoring and eternally recurrent powers, the sacred, the holy, "heaven" (Confucianism), perhaps most neutrally called "ultimate reality," a state that models the lure for all other instances of ordinary reality.[27] Second, all discern and venerate certain persons whose thought and practice are beacons but not boundaries, who embody extraordinary participation in the higher plane of reality (sage, teacher-scholar, seer, medicine man, priest, prophet, saint, "holy person," and similar). Third, all religious cultures have soteriologies (to use the western term, which literally means ways or paths of moving toward the holy, the highest plane of reality). These methods of ascent to the highest plane vary widely, from intense meditation ("sitting" in yoga) to the suspension of discursive thought ("no-mind" in some forms of Buddhism) to pragmatic counsel (the prudent sage in Confucianism) and so on. Most such forms of "deliverance" from ordinariness are prescribed through ritual practice.

These are broad generalizations, and qualifications are necessary for any particular religious culture, as well as within one, according to the historical period of its development. On soteriology another generalization is warranted, even if hazardous. For present purposes religious cultures may be differentiated according to whether their soteriologies are ones of "return" to an aboriginal state or oriented to the linearity of time, thus toward a future end-time. However hazardous, the ascription of the former to eastern and the latter to western religious cultures is no doubt overly simple, yet there is *something* to it. Generally, the soteriologies of "return" involve a cyclical or circular view of time, whereas those of future-oriented religious cultures involve a linear notion of time. But there definitely are part-whole metaphysical construals in the West. It is not only in classical Hinduism that all partitive existence (including the human) is either simply illusory or a matter to be overcome religiously by ritual practice through "return" to some aboriginal state (even if that state be one of regeneration/reincarnation for another run at time); this is also the case with Neoplatonism and all the western religious cultures it has influenced, not excepting Christianity. Still, it is generally the case that the western monotheistic religious cultures are committed to linear time. Certainly it is so for Judaism and Christianity, as both are deeply messianic and so committed to the "toward," the end-time, notwithstanding that there are radical differences in how these are construed. (Far less certain for me is Paradise in Islam: Is this an aboriginal *before* or an eschatological *after*?)

The present thought-experiment in respect of the human person has chosen for its framework the linearity of time, thus the *telos* of the second not, and not a *return* to the first not (the sheer blankness of nothingness out of which the person stands qua existent). To be sure, there are thinkers within the framework of the linearity of time who opt for return as the salvific or redemptive *conversio*, the most striking instance being Eckhart himself. I judge that they cannot do so in coherence with other features of their onto-meontological thought (as was argued in Topos 2: Cosmogony). What seems common to all religious cultures is that for the human person in the present plane of being, that of existence, there is want, lack, privation of, desire for something missing, something essential to ultimate meaning. Does this *something* that is lost need to be found and returned to; or does it lie ahead, yet to be discovered, created, emergent? In any case, it seems incontestable that one's between-existence is suffused with an appetition (to use the western medieval word) for a plane of being/nonbeing not now our idiosyncratic ownmost. We have spoken of this thirst and hunger in all modalities of being and nonbeing under the rubric of the "desire of God" (that double-entendre double genitive: Is it the desire of the creature for God, or God's desire for creation, or both?).

The present project on the human person essays an analytic ("cutting reality at the joints") of his or her appetition for such a plane, the existential situation in which he or she desires completion of the human project, the inescapable forces, thwarting or encouraging, that bear on that project that is her or his life. Contending with this complexity justifies the appeals made to contemporary theorists of complexity, chaos, and stability and instability in mathematics and the sciences generally. While the individual person yearns for the equilibrium of the plane aspired to, the individual in time, this Diana, is what the selfsame theorists call a "disequilibrium system," is continually if not continuously in a "critical state," always at a "tipping point." Ours is always a crisis e-mergence-y. In this respect as in all others the human person traces what infuses and suffuses all determinate modalities of being, God not excepted, namely, the indeterminate *turba* of indeterminate Godhead (the sacred, the holy). Without *Turba* (whence turbulence, instability), there would be nothing determinate, including our own determinate selves. It is the price of being anything at all, and not merely nothing. All that notwithstanding, the human intellective and appetitive soul aspires to a plane of being deemed better than that of mere conflicted existence and essential to the person's fruition, what may be called the "angle of repose." A technical phrase in geology and construction engineering, "angle of repose" refers to the angle of incline/decline at which dirt, rocks, or any and all debris cease to roll, thus is just before the "tipping point." The phrase may be adopted as metaphor for the person's careering through the planes of his reality and episodically reaching those rare points at which countervailing forces attain some harmony without loss of their tensive strength.[28]

Creatio in imago Dei et ad imaginem Verbi

Pascal's question in the epigraph to this chapter ("In fact what is man in nature?") is the right first question; the question about human nature must be premised on what humanity is *in* nature.[29] *Homo sapiens* is neurologically a larger-brained, opposable-thumbed, bipedal primate who subsumes characteristics of several strands of primates such that, in roughly the last two hundred thousand years, through the processes of random mutation and natural selection, these characteristics have been concentrated in one or two primate strands who are thought to comprise uniquely the attributes of the "human" animal. As two hundred thousand years is a minuscule fraction of the approximately thirteen billion years since the cosmic big bang occurred, it is likely premature to call the present era of cosmic time with full confidence the Anthropocene—as has been proposed by some. Throughout the present thought-experiment I have urged the problematicity of the anthropic principle, including whether humans are in any sense principals on the cosmic scene. Without question, the Abrahamic monotheisms have a heavy affirmative investment in this matter. Such investment includes living with many paradoxes and ironies. Modernity has known since Galileo and Copernicus that the cosmos is not geocentric, and since Darwin that planet Earth is not anthropocentric. The irony is that this fact is escorted by its opposite: the fact that man has no special standing on planet Earth is known (so far as we know) by no other species, but if that is so the identical fact discloses that human powers have a reach that exceeds their (human) grasp. To be sure, this exceeding reach of consciousness of states of affairs is the work of big-brained primates, not (necessarily) the work of a divine afflatus. But the human is not limited to mere "consciousness of" states of affairs, although most of the natural sciences are committed to extending human

163

consciousness of, say, the physical eco-environment of planet Earth in a particular geological era. So, in the late Anthropocene era (to use that nomenclature for the nonce), one is aware not only of "consciousness of" but also of human acts, whether intended or not, that have effect *in* nature: the effect, so to speak, of *human* nature *in* nature. I take it to be established that some of the current environmental degradation is owing not to random mutation and natural selection but to human agency, and that remediation of *that* degradation will require like human agency. I agree with William James that from the reality of effects we may safely reason to the reality of causes.

By no means does this address adequately the complexity of "human nature," a project broached in Appendix B—to which I add here, as another instance of irony and paradox, that the experience of the abject baseness of human nature ("fall and fault in human nature/nurture") is inextricably bound up with the experience of the moral grandeur and exultation of human nature. In short, human nature is metaxic; it is the lived *between* of two extremities, between utter self-aggrandizement at all costs (the hell with other species, and other individuals in the human species) and utter self-ascesis at all costs (a nonpredatory attending to the needs of other species and individuals in one's own species); in ordinary language, between rank selfishness and caring altruism. Further, one noted that Pascal's was the right first question since it asks the prerequisite question, what is human nature as embedded *in* nature itself, nature as external to the human reality? As important as to know that humans are subject to the variabilities and invariabilities of the body, as are all animals, is to know as fully as one can how hominids are otherwise *in* nature. Pascal is impatient of taking all the steps necessary to a mindful answer to his own question; he overleaps them to conclude: "What is man in nature? A Nothing in comparison with the Infinite, an All in comparison with the Nothing, a mean between nothing and everything. . . . Who will follow these marvelous processes?" Throughout these pages we have aspired to track these processes, wondering and marveling.

The source of the Christian investment in the anthropic principle is the conviction that the human person is created or made *in imago Dei et ad imaginem Verbi* (created in the image of God and toward the image of the Word [Logos]); thus a "from" and a "toward" is endemic to the formula. In the Genesis accounts of creation the human order has special standing and special obligation among all other creatures: it is the bearer of imperatives, is to name all other creatures and continue speaking them into existence and indeed to be the steward of divine dominion. But in the same mythological narrative almost as soon as the first human pair is created is it banished from the Garden of Innocence, exiled east of Eden, a banishment owed to human disobedience of divine injunction. Knowledge that is had in innocence, before the transgression of limiting taboos, is qualitatively different from post-transgressive knowledge. Just as developmentally there is no freedom in preadolescent human youth, only liberty to choose this and that, so in that freedom that is known only in its actual exercise—which involves the exclusion of certain potentiating possibilities as a kind of unintended fate—does freedom have a history in one's life that can be counted on. If the human person is made exhaustively *in* the image of God, the *what* (nature) of God is a critical matter. In classical theism God is the perfection of all virtues: perfected being (*ens perfectissimum*), the highest good (*summum bonum*). A person made in that image would have a nature "only a little lower than the angels." If one has renounced classical theism (as in this thought-experiment), has renounced equally every form of Marcionite gnosticism (two coeval gods, one of whom is good, the other evil), and has affirmed the reality of both evil and good in the human person, then one must conclude that the God in whose image ("from which") the human creature is made is both evil and good in unresolved tension. God has not finished becoming, or unbecoming, God; nor have we human creatures finished becoming and unbecoming not-God. The Good exceeds every modality of being "in dignity and power" (Plato), as it is the lure of every such mode.

Which leads us to the second part of the formula: "*ad imaginem*." Generally, the "from which" refers to what in nature has attained such relative stability as to allow generalizations, so that in Enlightenment modernity and its western revolutions (English, American, French), a table of "human rights" was affirmed to be universal, embodied "in nature," rooted in that nature's Creator. Those rights (such as "life, liberty, the pursuit of happiness") were held to be finished in principle, if not in fact. "In fact" in the case of human persons always includes not only what is but what it is *toward*, what is the *lure* of what is. *In imago* refers to the *extension* of human nature in nature; *ad imaginem* refers not only to that extension but particularly to the *intension* of human personhood: *this* human person, Sarah Coakley in Cambridge, David Tracy in Chicago. Throughout I have noted the logical relation of inversion that obtains between the extension and the intension of a term. Human life is between the extensions and the intensions of identified terms: the two nots, the two rooms of bicamerality, becoming and unbecoming.

I am well aware that in the formula the *ad imaginem* is not open-ended, is not something like "toward the image of the Lure. . . ." Rather, what the formula says is "made or created toward the image of the Word." No doubt the Word can be interpreted in a manner highly prejudicial to Christianity, but that is possible only if other Christian formulae are used to construe the word *Verbum*, translating the biblical Greek term *Logos*. First, in the formula held in view, I take the *Logos* to mean what it means in ordinary Greek: "word," hence language. In the hundred thousand or so years in which human attributes have been sorting themselves out, what is most charming and enthralling is the development, especially in the last two centuries, of human language well beyond species language (the sounds of alarm made to alert others in the species to predatory danger, but also sounds of joy, well-being, and contentment): the sort of subjects attracting the attention of structural linguists. More than that, it is not language as literal communication of relatively fixed states of affairs that charms, but rather expressive language comprising nondiscursive forms, language that intends not so much communication as apprehension of the saturated edges of things, the prehension of things as metaphors, as sites for carrying beyond and over, a kind of intraspecies reckoning with liminality. It is this kind of language that *ad imaginem Verbi* bears.

If this accounts for the first sense of *Logos* (*Verbum*) in the formula, the second related sense evokes a rationale or principle. In these ruminations I have used Logos interchangeably with Principle, and have asked whether Logos can be both principle and principal. In a Christianity with a high christology the answer has been yes. If Christianity is present in these pages, its christology is both low and heterodox. All theories of Logos, in their Christian utilization, are Greek in origin. In this respect, it is the pre-Socratic Heraclitus of Ephesus who has the best fit with my schema: among all the binaries, for him the Logos is the concert of the opposites or binaries.

Between Becoming and Unbecoming

We now essay one more foray into the territory of the individual person's "between," that between becoming and unbecoming. One's journey through time is a process of the simultaneity of growing up and growing down, the simultaneity of gain and loss, the simultaneity of desire and surfeit (and any number of other polarities a normal person metaxically inhabits). Since one's ontic-meontic *chora* (place) of habitation is between becoming and unbecoming, thus between a first and a second not, one's intellective soul aspires to make that dwelling in—and upon—a place of understanding, as to dwell there merely blindly were to be inhuman. The effort so to understand existence is very much like attending to the sonority of great music: one must somehow pierce the veil of its incubation (in the composer, in the orchestral rendition, in the reverberations set off in the hearer's soul). All philosophies not abandoning their "last" (métier) have intended the piercing of the veil of mystery surrounding the incubations of being and becoming, and from a philosophical theology we may expect no less, and that without attenuating the claiming power of the mystery itself, so that such understanding as is attained does not dispel the claiming power of the music itself, while at the same time appropriating that mystery critically through the mind's powers of mediacy.

Becoming

The territory of the human person's becoming is the entire range of her coming to be qua existent. Summarily (to this point): her becoming is initiated by e-mergence (first birth) from the first not, thus her existence as outstanding blank nothingness sheer. She was not but now, with birth, is; so the first mark of her becoming is indicative, formally inhering being qua existing, the very condition of all she shall come to be. By her birth, initiation into *being* qua existent, she is *individuated*, is *a* be-ing; distinct from other human beings, her *individuality* awaits further becoming (and unbecoming).

The ramification of these terse statements need not be extensive. In the dimension of the human body and its developmental stages, articulation would involve commonplaces about the human infant, known by every parent and indeed every child with the arrival of a sibling. No birth is a commonplace to parents and siblings; this birth is an incomparable joy, notwithstanding immediate attention to how this infant "looks like so-and-so" but still is unique in already obvious ways. So much so in every respect that in Christian conviction (at least since Augustine), each and every human person is a new creation,[30] is a creation *ab origine* however much his further becoming is a *creatio continua* engaging his own powers. Yet that uniqueness has no chance of development without a host of other conditions; hence the intersociality of even physical becoming. Among other mammals, the human infant has an exceptionally long period of dependence for its physical development, which development unfolds at an astonishing pace, willy-nilly. Indeed the physical becoming of the human infant could be said to be on autopilot, given the supply of nourishment, shelter, and protection, offered with care and love—but also with the necessary interdicts since, even though the human infant recapitulates all the phyla of ontogenesis, it has not the instincts for danger and threat of other infant mammals. Tough love, as the saying goes, is required for immature becoming. Enough commonplaces about what is anything but commonplace.

If one settles initially on the physical body in respect of becoming, that is because it is the most obvious and publicly visible form of human becoming, at least in roughly the first quarter of a normal life-span (as physical unbecoming is the most obvious and visible in the final period of life-span). Throughout the physical unfolding of a body there is apparent, especially until full physical stature has been attained, a certain necessity governed by one's individuated genetic code but also by economic and social and parental conditions. All human becoming, including the physical, is marked also by unbecoming although much less visibly; while no one individuated human life is necessary, once it is and becomes, it does so in necessary ways. There is no construction in the human body without destruction (as there is not in the whole of the cosmos, as presently known to us). Only as cells die can they be replaced with cells that live, a process that perdures as long as the body itself does. Of course a harmonious reciprocity is necessary between construction and destruction in normal physical becoming. If the destruction of cells gains such an upper hand that they are replaced by the "wrong" kinds of cells, we have the condition known as cancer.[31] In present oncological chemotherapy, the dial is turned up on unbecoming such that many if not all cells, good and bad, are destroyed in the hope of destroying the offending cells, and thus permitting the re-production of "right" cells. While we inhabit the interstices of becoming and unbecoming, that citadel of *metaxu* houses both what is salvific (literally, healthful) and perilous (death-dealing). Let the body, then, serve provisionally as metaphor for the *metaxu* ("between") of becoming and unbecoming.

For a person of average scientific sophistication nowadays all this is likely a commonplace, or is at least intuitively intelligible. But is that so in respect of the person's becoming a *psyche*, a soul, an intellective center of thinking and decision-making? The same person on the same knowledge base would not nowadays consider soul-mind and body to be radically distinct, for the brain is central to both. Neurological biology is in relative infancy itself, so one treads softly and carries no sticks large or small. Still, what is indistinct is susceptible of discriminability, which is of high importance in the incubation of what forms the personality, even the character, of an individual human person. When one thinks of a particular person (is there any other kind?), yes, an image of that person's body comes into play, but much more so a tonality and aura of mind, spirit, soul that distinguishes that person from any and every other. If "soul" may be stipulated as the placeholder for this complex (mind-spirit-soul), does the soul become with a necessity akin to that of the becoming of the body? Only if neurological signals are hard-wired by genetic code or otherwise, are not only determinate but determined without reference to the person's will, and only if "soul" is reducible exhaustively and without remainder to the electronics of the brain.

If it is important in theology to acknowledge *that* we don't know, and to acknowledge as much of the *what* of what we don't know as that *that* permits (as Augustine was at some pains to make explicit in the *Confessions*), it is equally important to own critically what we *do* warrantably know. And we *do* know something about the becoming of what people everywhere acknowledge to be the center of a person's *hecceitas* (uniqueness), here called soul. To be sure, the processes of becoming ensouled are much less obvious and public than those of becoming embodied, however interconnected those processes may be. With like surety we know that the becoming of a soul in its incubation is much more culturally influenced than is the physical maturation of the body, and that the soul's becoming requires at least as many conditions of nourishment and protection as does the body. All parents everywhere know that they have dual and interconnected responsibilities for setting the newborn on the path of becoming both souls and bodies. They do so by example and admonition, and by providing—often at the price of unbecoming what they themselves have become, thus sacrificially—the conditions under which their young can become exceedingly.

To speak of the becoming of a human soul—one's own center of thinking, deciding, judging, valorizing, loving, hating, receiving, entering and being a participant in the world—is to speak out of and toward a stipulated context that is more cultural than natural. If the life we live is Socrates's "examined life," it were well to meditate on the typical consequences of attending almost exclusively to human becoming (as is largely the American entrepreneurial way of becoming) to the neglect of unbecoming. One cannot overemphasize the donative and graceful character of one's existing at all; one is not in any way complicit in e-merging from nothingness, from the first not, yet there one is, among the things that already are, commissioned (as it were) to *become*. So one has his *is*, the *that* of formally inhering existence, as a *donatum*, a gift. In the dimension of becoming, can the human person become more or less existent (is not one *that* as big as another)? In the interlude above it was concluded that one cannot, that the facticity of every "this and that" is absolute, whether for a fly, a god, or a human person; there is neither expansion nor contraction of the being of any determinate "this or that" in respect of its *existence*. Equally as sure as one's standing out of the first not qua *existent* is the surety that one shall not so exist (hence the importance of the interlude's realization of this reality, "I exist, here, now."). There is, to be sure, *some* aggrandizement of indicative being for the human person: from an immature one becomes a mature human body, as from a nascent and potential soul one becomes a center of will, of discursive powers of thinking and speaking, a force of imagination and specular figuration, a responsible actor among other like becoming persons. But notwithstanding all the aids of the physical and cultural sciences, one cannot become so aggrandizingly as to make human existence endless. For the human person, there will be a then which has no now, a there where "there is no there there" (Gertrude Stein's famous characterization of Oakland, California), when the inventory of the universe will not include oneself. As noted already, the realization of this humanly omnipresent reality conduces to an agitated ontic humility, itself the very alembic for excogitating the person's coming to be *from* nothing *toward* nothing. To be *and* not to be is the problematic of human becoming.

One asks again the deeply human question, "Is this [the realization that one is now but shall not be] all there is for human being?" For *a* being being, thus existing participially in the only realm straightforwardly known to us experientially (namely, time and its horizons), does "being" harbor dimensions other than those of indicative being qua merely and only existing? What is to be made of classical western claims for the full-orbed coincidence of being, good, true, beautiful, sacred or holy? Is human indicative becoming wholly bereft of the good, the true, the beautiful, the sacred (for that matter bereft of the evil, the ugly, the *horror religiosus*)? These questions point us to a dimension of human existence other than but closely correlated with the indicative dimension, one in a different verbal mode (of the infinitive, *to be*), that of the imperative, and classically that of "essence," a potency (*potentia obedientalis*) no less immature in the human infant than body-soul, and subject to like becoming, and that notwithstanding my calling it unbecoming.

Unbecoming

Do not forget you are the nucleus of a rupture.
—EDMOND JABÈS, *THE BOOK OF QUESTIONS*

My eternal lot . . . between the black & white spiders.
— WILLIAM BLAKE, *THE MARRIAGE OF HEAVEN AND HELL*

If the becoming of the individual intensively is a process of the sharpening and rendering specific of the "this and that" of indicative being, unbecoming is a process that bears on the imperative *what* of the *that* the individual has become. The *time* of becoming and the *time* of unbecoming are coterminous, although they do not proceed at the same pace. Becoming (as previously noted in taking the body as metaphor) is continual but not continuous. It is not continuous for at least two reasons: first, the person's becoming terminates with the end of the *that* of existence, with death, with literal proceeding into the second not. And second, all human indicative existence is marked by interruptions, by ruptures, as in illness and near-death experiences. Unbecoming is neither continual nor continuous, is rather episodic, and is so because it engages the human will in response to the ruptures within one's ownmost existence. If becoming is taken to characterize the indicative *extension* of the human person as such (thus the growth and aggrandizement of human existence), unbecoming characterizes the imperative *intension* (thus the attenuation and diminution of merely indicative becoming) of an individual person. Thus one comes upon the heart of the problem in respect of the relation between human becoming and unbecoming: the *inverse* relation between extension and intension (the more one has of the range of being of the human person as such, the less one has of Jane Doe, and vice versa).[32] It remains to unpack these terse (and perhaps overly dense) affirmations.

As the *becoming* of the human person is an amplification of the first not, the distance one attains *from* the blank nothingness from which one has e-merged as *a* being be-ing, so *unbecoming* is an amplification of the second not, the very *quality* of willed progression toward when one shall not be, no longer *a* being be-ing.[33] *What* is it that one shall be, within the horizon of time, when one no longer exists?

I have spoken not only of the becoming of the body but also, although less extensively, of the becoming of the human soul and its powers (intellective mind, will, imagination). To speak more extendedly would entail more precise attention to contemporary cultural influences on the becoming of human spirit, influences more the métier of the social sciences than this thought-experiment can embrace. Yet it is a characteristic of some great works of art to capture the human spirit for an age, and to do so in the conjunction of prevailing arts and sciences. One such work is Robert Musil's *The Man without Qualities* (*Mann ohne Eigenschaften*), a twentieth-century classic novel at the dawn of a new millennium, one with as sure a grip on the forceps of fate as the vicissitudes of freedom in the formation of the human spirit.[34] Modern man is seated at and attached to Goethe's "roaring loom of time," resolved by the grip of fate to weave himself into a fabric of use to warm the body but above all to charm the salons of fashion, of *haute couture*. (Although Musil does not say or hint so, it would be beyond the pale for such a man to think of or imagine Penelope weaving by day and unraveling—unweaving—by night.) To such a person of industry it does not occur "that all our lives, we're somehow only half integrated with ourselves." Nor does it occur that "an act of the will is linked with a thought, that it is not a matter of acting on instinct. . . . It is the will that, in the process of the gradual development of the understanding and the reason, must dominate the desires and, relative to them, the instincts by means of reflection and the resolves consequent thereon."[35] There is always a personal decision to be taken, even if it be a decision taken against the indecision of the world around us.[36]

"The morality of our time," so Musil, is marked by a culture of *achievement*, "doing," action, success, entrepreneurship, "making something of ourselves." "Five more or less fraudulent bankruptcies are acceptable provided the fifth leads to . . ." (enter a list, most any list) being a patron of the arts (one need not understand them) or buying the election of one who will serve one's further achievements. Such "making something of ourselves" leads ineluctably to a loss of inwardness. For the reflective/reflexive person with a residual scintilla of inwardness that dramatizes the question: What does *outside* have to do with *inside*? Is there a frontier "between what goes on inside us and what goes on outside," and is there any communication across this frontier? Is the "inward" exhaustively only the dark underside of the "outward," itself driven only by the metaphysics of production as energized by the "morality of the 'next-step'"? Does not the ship of entrepreneurial morality bear only ballast, and not cargo? Ulrich, Musil's central character, lightheartedly but seriously proposed to a Viennese official that he establish a "World Secretariat for Precision and Soul" to address such questions.[37]

If the word *entrepreneur* could be shorn of the nuances it bears in Musil's novel, freed from the metaphysics and morality solely of production (which most likely it cannot in the late modern world), it could serve well the thinking of human being. *Entre-prenere*: to place in or between. But alas, language is abused by the forceps of fate (language so used and abused as to be used up); the entrepreneur as the word is now ordinarily used is placed altogether *in* the productivities of outward becoming, not *between* becoming and unbecoming. The entrepreneur's frenetic pace of accumulating the dots of "doing" leaves him no time to connect them in any correlation with his own inwardness, hence no "between" and thus no graph of his own being.

That there is no World Secretariat for Precision and Soul is scarcely to be lamented, as it would have only the longevity and usefulness of all such agencies launched to relieve us of the obligation to think for ourselves.

Indeed, there is little updated precision in respect of thinking "soul," of cutting the joints of the reality of the human person. In the philosophical-theological anthropology under development here, I have identified two such joints: *individuation* (the *that* of the e-mergence from the first not, the particularity of the bodily base and bias of *this* person) and *individuality* (the *what* of the pro-gression of this person toward the second not). It is with the third joint that precision is most difficult, what I have provisionally called "soul," and which most deeply pertains to the person's inwardness: the range of the uniqueness of the person's *synthesis* of her individuation and individuality. The point of all *analysis* (so Plato) is to understand the *synthesis* that is lived reality *realized*, that of the human person. As the word *soul* bears so much freight by use and abuse, arguably it were better to adopt and adapt the modern term *self* or *spirit* as the placeholder for this reality-joint in the human person.[38] For the human self/spirit, the ontic-meontic range intensively is *what* remains of the human person when she has entered the second not, when she is not, neither as she was existently nor as she was before existent. If the divine intention for the human creature is that she should leave more and better in the universe than she took from it, what is that?

What occasions inwardness, thinking oriented not to becoming alone, but to unbecoming what one has become, why Penelope and not Goethe (or vice versa) at "the roaring loom of time"? There is likely no saying, with any precision of general applicability to all human persons. To be sure, all persons at some point in their becoming are possessed of feeling hopeless, helpless, and superfluous, of a sense that ranges from lack or want, a conviction leaving one in a condition of lassitude or depression; but that state also extends to including surfeit and excess, thus the burden of bearing too much, and the consequent ennui of overwhelming "achievement" (rarely if ever does one read in obituaries the sometime real cause of death: overliving!). Nor can the occasioning of inwardness be plotted on a chronological graph, as though one becomes for a certain period in one's life and for the remaining period unbecomes; as with the body, one becomes and unbecomes simultaneously. Among the chattering classes, it is common now to speak of the midlife crisis. But who knows when life is at its middle? Life is always already at the middle: of the between. Would that the self-spirit were as attentive to itself as is the body. I have said that the body in its becoming is subject to interruptions, ruptures, wounds. In just such traumas are planted the spindly plants of inwardness, the very soil of the human self-spirit.

In and on such matters, one does well to recall Søren Kierkegaard, not as boundary but as beacon. For him time is the wound in which the residuum of Eternity perdures as trace, as the inwardness of self-spirit is the venue for energizing that trace. Any such energizing is itself enervated by the absolute inequality between time and eternity, so on guard. I say Kierkegaard as beacon, not boundary, because he never solicited his auditors/readers to have any regard for his *opinions* (if he had any they were his own; and if he did, none of them authorized others to make them their own).[39] What Kierkegaard invites is to put ourselves under the discipline of the dance, the dance of thinking human existence, in which the dance-partner is the thought of death, that paragon of inequality with eternity, the dance within the space of the wound of time. Among other things such a dance is not, it is not a *danse macabre*; it is a *danse libre*. Its motion by steps is the functional ontic-meontic equivalent of the hoary epistemic adage that "like knows like," while its rhythm is the "likening of unlikes." The *where* of this dance is between what I have called the two nots, and its cadence accelerates to the crescendo peaking in the being of an existing person made determinate by how he *realizes* emanating from nothing and going toward nothing. (In this Kierkegaard is at one with his old antagonist Hegel, who claimed that no thinking of Being could be creditable without tarrying over the "accidents" (wounds) of nothingness. The difference is that Hegel tarried too little, while Kierkegaard never ceased to tarry over the before and the after of nothingness in human existence; and another difference: Hegel thought it the right and power of Being to sublate each and every "accident" of nothingness. The likening of unlikes, the commensuration of incommensurables, is fraught with paradox, but that is the dance of partners who are not simulacra of each other. A must become less, or unbecome in some measure, that B can become more; B must become less, or unbecome in some measure, that A may not become so less as not to be A, and so on. So double negations on the part of each partner are involved in the dance that thinks human existence, in the dance that *lives* and *realizes* the existence thus thought.

Kierkegaard was brought to this our table not to reckon with his full-orbed thought but to address more directly the question: What occasions the eruption of inwardness in the human person such as to *realize* his unbecoming, and that in such a way as not to be reducible solely to the underside of his becoming? The larger context for this question is a reparsing of the *creatio ex nihilo*. The first being of an existing person is a consequence of e-merging from the first not, and is in this regard not different from anything in nature, and so can be said to belong to the order of *nature*. The second being, or modality of being qua human, depends on the quality of the second not, itself dependent on what the person does toward the determinateness of her life, and so belongs to the order of *history*, the order of *creatio continua ex nihilo*.

The principal occasion of that inwardness of self or spirit that gives food for thought is nothing more or less than the incitement of human freedom. Such inwardness of self is not mere subjectivity over against the outwardness of becoming. It is, to cite Kierkegaard once more, "the change of actuality brought about by freedom."[40] In mainline scholastic metaphysics, actuality was the transposition of potentiality into the key of full fruition. While the dancer of existence begins with the rhythms of actual music, the dance itself refunds the pool of potency from the freedom of partners in the motions of existence. The agent of "the change of actuality brought about by freedom" in the ballroom of existence is no longer just the self-spirit but the "I" (rather, in the dance, "we"); it is the I in the *chora* (space) of *ecstasis*. The dancer of inwardness is "beside" himself because "outside" himself, is the "ecstatic I" (as is his partner), outstanding both becoming and unbecoming through their simultaneity (for instance, the worldwide phenomenon of free-form rock music dancing).[41]

Freedom is never more misconstrued than when confused with *liberty* (as in the increasingly rampant libertarianism of the Ayn Rand variety in America), which is nothing more than license for the individual to choose anything whatever. Nothing is real without determinate limits, as every caring parent knows. If there is any consensus on freedom, it is that there is no freedom without constraints ("pricks against which one cannot kick"). Were anyone and everyone free to murder without let, no one would or could be free in any pertinent sense. Necessary limits are the necessity of freedom with its own propriety. No freedom can bind (*ligate*, oblige) that is not itself bound. Even so, as Hegel was wont to say again and again, to accept a limit is to be in reflection (and reflexion) beyond it, which is especially so in the case of freedom itself. Freedom for the human person is limited by death, the cessation of existence, and all of death's harbingers (illness, near-death experiences, and the like). Each and every such limit is a challenge to thought and action, and not for the religious in the way ordinarily taken, namely, what is there after death? What are the consequences for life before death, given the inexorable limit that death invariably is?

In the everydayness of existence one may very well lead a casually interim life between the two nots, relegating to one's "day job" the exigencies of becoming and to one's "night job" such reveries as may show themselves about what one is becoming and has become. A person does so, of course, within a custom-tradition or culture of expectation he has drunk in with his mother's milk. As the self's powers of introspection and circumspection mature commensurately with those of the body, one interrogates culturally inherited expectations and learns of expectations in other custom-traditions. While it is surely the case that freedom is not in the self as the body is in the world (is not a cosmic inventory item), that it must be aroused and incited to be a force of *dunamis* in actuality, it is also the case that freedom is always and everywhere exercised on and amidst *realia*. That is why freedom properly so-called (but not liberty, properly restricted to juveniles) is slow to be aroused, for it takes much experience of living and knowing for freedom to be aroused to demiurgic or dynamic force. Well did Eckhart say, as rightly as famously, "readiness and the giving of form occur simultaneously."[42] Only so can freedom come not too early, not too late. Who is ready to be formed by freedom?

Eckhart's insight is echoed in the modern sage Martin Buber: "everything is up to me, and I am up for disposition," which effectively says: I dispose (through freedom) but am disposed (through destiny, temporal necessity).[43] Elsewhere I have written extensively of the human person's situating or disposing under the category of "continuous ingredience," as I have of being situated or disposed under the category of "discontinuous ingression."[44] That the person has powers of latitude and discretion in disposing and situating, particularly in establishing "goals," seems essential to human freedom, but any person with experience in the exercise of freedom knows the limiting power of necessity, the constraint of being situated or disposed (for example, by nature, by other persons, by historical events).[45] One doubtless has affinities for "goals"—but which are effectively elective and which are not?[46] One cannot uncover or recover a moment when the self is unsituated or undisposed, as one cannot find a moment when the self *is*, exhaustively and without remainder, only or merely *a* situation. The there-being (*da-sein*) of the self is always enacted in a situation of interaction between situating and being situated (between, thus *metaxic*), of disposing and being disposed, of forming and being formed, or—as developed here—a situation of becoming and unbecoming. One sees then that in thinking oneself, as well as in thinking divinity reflexively, "one is neither oneself nor someone else."

Who is ready to think and live unbecoming? The matter is not so much "what have I become?" as "what is to become of what I have become and am becoming?" Such questions position one in the antechamber of that good which the "ecstatic I" *is* by the incitement of freedom. One stands on the threshold of the forecourts of what Nietzsche called "an ecstatic parable and a painful ardor."[47] Ecstatic because outside and beside the storied expectation that one is to secure one's being by becoming more and more—what?—Being itself?[48] Painful because the only being one knows at hand is that of existence, which, whatever betides it, is precious to us and is set between two nots; if becoming more and more cannot enhance existence toward the good, how can not-being? Can not-being enhance being? In Kierkegaard's terms, can the being preceding the second not be greater than that preceding the first not, and greater because of the negation of my own becoming? To think thus, more especially to live thus, were as painful as arduous.

In this anthropological sketch I have chosen not to think human existence only within the parameters of the custom-tradition of ontotheology. Within that tradition human becoming and unbecoming were located in a different "between," that of what Giorgio Agamben has called "a kind of diaphanous limbo between no-longer being and not-yet-being."[49] In such a crucible a person is positioned by her more or her less being, and her life project is to become more being than less being. In this thought-experiment, the person is thought otherwise. Theologically, the custom-tradition drawn upon here includes the expansive and largely subterranean body of western "mystics" (a placeholder for those contending against the regnant ontotheological tradition) who preserved the questionableness of being, and that particularly in relation to the *nihil* of *creatio ex nihilo* in construing the human creature and God.

The present subject is the unbecoming of the human person, which is now to be addressed more directly. What is to be unbecome is the determinateness of what one is becoming and has become by the passion of aggressive activity, whether of mind or body. Like all reversals, unbecoming is marked by irony, paradox, and the interplay of double negations. Here we may follow Hegel attentively, who said of irony and its human destiny that it is *ein Nichtiges, ein sich Vernichtiges*, a nothing, a self-annihilating nothing.[50] Applied to human existence as construed thus far, that existence comprises a double negation: to exist, to be at all, thus to become, involves the negation of the blank nothingness before the first not; the second not is the negation of the determinate being of the human person attained by becoming, the exit to nothingness. In neither the negation of the first not nor that of the second not is the human person complicit, for they are conditioned by the *creatio ex nihilo*. Whether the nothingness that preceded the first not is the same as that after the second not (and the meaning of the person's existence hangs on there being a difference) depends awesomely on the aroused freedom of the "ecstatic I." The limit that at once binds and frees her, the *quality* of the nothingness toward which she goes inexorably, is subject to her volition. To unbecome as determinately what she is becoming and has become determinately is to will another negation, a negation of the self in favor of the "ecstatic I," and to *live* that negation, to live oneself as nothing, a self-annihilating nothing. It is to become nothing one cannot, and does, unbecome. What does one's existence add to the total scheme of things, another way of asking, what is the meaning of one's existence? What one adds is one's ownmost nothingness to which, paradoxically as ironically, one subscribes one's own signature. To live an "unbecoming" life is to live the second not proleptically. Thus is the pool of potentiality replenished from which other human first nots will e-merge becomingly. So may one construe the words of scripture: "whoever wants to save his life will lose it" (Matthew 16:25). To which may be added that the life lived proleptically toward the second not requires a second innocence that, like all dimensions opened by an aroused freedom, must be earned and is much more demanding than the first (which seems to have been there without effort).

Unbecoming as Ascesis

Then you were yourself again after yourself's decrease.
—SHAKESPEARE, SONNET 13

I held it truth, with him who sings
To one clear harp in divers tones,
That men may rise on stepping-stones
Of their dead selves to higher things.
—TENNYSON, "IN MEMORIAM A. H. H."

A person's unbecoming is both a doing and a knowing, but a painful and arduous doing and knowing, because requiring self-conscious adjustments to ways of ordinary doing and knowing. A "doing" because the incitement of freedom is accompanied by an alerted passivity toward what we have actively made of ourselves and what our sociality has made of us. A "knowing" because, with the arousal of freedom, a tipping point is escorted into the venue of the imagination. Elsewhere I have argued that the imagination increases vastly the phenomenological range of the mind's intension and extension, focusing especially on their inverse relation.[51] Ordinarily what passes for imagination is passive toward conventioned doing and knowing and is essentially reproductive. Activated by the *realization* of unbecoming, imagination fixes upon the range of what is unfinished in human being. It does so not as *phantasy*, as playing with alternative ways of evading the second not, but so as to unfinish what we are becoming and have become, and thus to extend the range of potency for our ownmost looming not-being. Cognitively, this means the *realiza-*

tion of our own nescience. One recalls the injunction of Nicholas of Cusa, that one is to become "most learned in that very ignorance [nescience] which is peculiarly [one's] own."[52] Do we know ourselves in the fragility of our ownmost being? What unknowing is concealed in our ordinary knowing and awaits dis-covery?

The word *unbecoming* has multiple cognates that the reader is urged to recover from his or her own traditions. For present purposes a long list is not needed, as a few will do: detachment (Eckhart's *Abscheidung*), letting be, letting go of (Heidegger's *Seinslassen*), dispossessing (Nietzsche), disowning (Scharlemann), distancing from a given condition or state of affairs in the everydayness of existence.[53] All these cognates for *unbecoming* connote an exercise of inversion, reversal, and negation, that one may go bare, bereft of all extraneity, bearing only one's ownmost deliberate determinateness into the second not (and that as one's gift to the potency of its indeterminacy).

For all the connotations of these cognate terms for unbecoming I use the cover term *ascesis*. From the Greek verb *askein* (to work, exercise), ascesis is the work of self-discipline, normally that of self-deprival for higher ends than survival in the common course. Already noted is that nothing can be known that does not give itself to be known, that does not "appear." The "religious" know what many philosophers do not, that some things and their orders do not give themselves to be known, do not appear, save under the lash of discipline. Ritualized ascesis is the placeholder for such discipline. It is not by accident that they who commit themselves to such discipline are called "in orders," since they order their lives by ritual not episodically but continuously. In the Protestant Christian custom-tradition in which I stand, such a discipline is not the preserve of ecclesiastically set orders but is the vocation of all persons ("the priesthood of all believers"). I have said human becoming has its own interruptions and ruptures, which occasion food for thought about one's unbecoming. The ascetics, whether religious or not, are they who by the discipline of self-deprival deliberately occasion their own interruptions and ruptures (in a different metaphor) by stripping becoming of its accretive barnacles. In the self-inflicted wounds of ascesis, both of body and mind, grow the flowers of a new not-being, one's ownmost.

That said, there is significant risk (as with all figures) in speaking of ascesis. Mention asceticism and images pop into the mind: eremitic and cenobitic persons in the caves of the Egyptian desert, discalced monks in tattered robes flagellating themselves, yogis on their beds of nails, monks in saffron robes with their mendicant bowls, a gaunt Gandhi at his spinning wheel, a wizened Mother Teresa in the poverty-stricken streets of Calcutta; that there are such ascetics in most religious traditions is a fact. And it is the case that such figures do bias ascesis toward bodily unbecoming. But it is also true that most religious customs or traditions include ascetics of the mind: in Christianity, Pseudo-Dionysius the Areopagite, John of the Cross, Catherine of Siena, Julian of Norwich, Mechthild of Magdeburg, Nicholas of Cusa, Marguerite Porete and other beguines (nuns not in an order), Meister Eckhart, Jakob Böhme, to mention but a few. It is the full range of human becoming, body and mind, that is subject to the ascesis of unbecoming. It may have occurred to the reader to take these generalizations about human becoming and unbecoming to be a gloss on the Johannine injunction to be *in* the world but not *of* it.

Sacrifice

Paul Tillich claimed, famously, that religion is about what concerns us ultimately. To be sure, most human talk of gain and loss is about *proximate* gain and loss. Our talk here, however, is not about a proximate first not and a proximate second not (although their proximity must be ever *realized*), but is rather about the ultimate meaning of our existence between them. How do gain (becoming) and loss (unbecoming) figure in the ultimate reckoning of one's being and not-being in time? One has only to recognize the centrality of gain and loss in human narratives since time immemorial to understand why in all religions (known to me), in all times and everywhere, sacrifice has been the subject of thought and of ritual practice. It is a word-concept that falls quaintly, archaically upon the western post-Enlightenment ear. Without doubt it requires an agitated hermeneutical dehiscence that the pod of sacrifice may burst its seeds of incubation into the soil of contemporary imagination. The sedimented word *sacrifice* is so heavily laden with figure near its surface—the still-palpitating heart torn from a human body, the unblemished sheep on the pyre, Abraham with the knife poised over Isaac—as to make one recoil in ethical horror, notwithstanding "the teleological suspension of the ethical."[54] But then, have we forgotten—and forgotten that we have forgotten—the *horror religiosus*?

Sacrifice is a noun in which one can only with difficulty any longer overhear anything going on, any trace of verbal action. The heart of the substantive, as in most nouns central to the practice of religious adepts, is a verb. *Sacrificium* = *sacer* + *facere*, to make holy or sacred (and, depending on how the holy or sacred is understood, to *de*sacralize as well; see below). To *make* holy and to *unmake* the holy carry a host of assumptions chief among which is that the earth and all on/in it comprise planes or orders on the contingent intercalation of which human meaning and continuity depend and about which humankind has something ritually to *do*. To refer to Greek early chthonic and even later Olympian religion: The earth has had enough of the sacred in it to be fertile *this* year, but will it next? And its fruits this year are themselves sacred to the extent they are forthcoming, whereas we are profane and unfit to receive them, so the rite desacralizes the earth's bounty that we the unfit may receive it, and we ourselves require sanctification to deserve the earth's fertility: a ritual intercalation of planes (for a monotheistic custom or tradition, consider the Talmudic rule: "One may not taste anything until one recites a blessing over it."[55]) All ritual sacrifice involves the *likening* of radically unlike planes so that a plane suffused with sacred being or *mana* may overlay a plane empowered only by its positive absence (nothingness). Nor are these planes restricted, in some traditions, to the sacred and the profane; some rites of sacrifice pertain to planes *within* the sacred, as in deificatory sacrifices in which the god is "killed" that it may be "born" in a new plane of the sacred. There can be no question of offering here a fulsome catena of figures that would embrace the rites of sacrifice in all religions (if that were possible, which is doubtful), nor even of tracing the figures of sacrifice within a single tradition (which, in the case of Christianity, would surely include Hebraic roots). I am content rather to suggest that, for the human person existing between two nots in time, sacrifice offers the figural problem-space for the interrelation between being, nothingness, and the sacred; and that, specifically, rited sacrifice is the referential venue of unbecoming.

Sacrifice is surrender, release, dispossession of something prized for something to be prized more, for something having a claim superior to that of what is released or given up—often without knowing what that is, save by negative witness, by its lack. Sacrifice is driven by *desire*, as the rites of sacrifice embody desire as transmutations of *will*. The only plentitude sacrifice opens upon is that envisaged from the verges of a powered impoverishment. And impoverishment is never so misunderstood as when thought to consist solely having little or no physical or bodily means. (Jesus: "Blessed are the poor in spirit.") Too much—surfeit—is as impoverishing as too little.[56] Could one penetrate the conceptual traditions of being and nothingness in the West to their backlying *Schwärmerei* of figures, it would take a tin ear and a glazed eye not to overtake *kenosis* and *plerosis*, ascesis and excess, hunger and surfeit in the palpitations of ritual sacrifice. No great labor would be required to plot the correlation between the sedimentation (or reconditeness) of being and nothingness and the attenuation or decline of the rites of sacrifice in the western world. To speak of western modernity alone, nothingness began to bleed out of "God and the world" with the diminution of the rites of sacrifice in the quaint anti-rituals of the Enlightenment: the sacrifice of the formerly prized God for the now most highly prized humanity (the plenary humanity one got was from the verges of impoverished deity).

How would one make sacrifice of the soul's career with nothingness and being if the point of sacrifice were (as it always was) the ritual likening of incommensurable unlikes, an increase of ascesis or loss in the hope simultaneously of the reduction and increase of plenitude, the ritual intercourse of unlikelies? At this late hour of the western day such a sacrifice might well enfold the memory but would not itself be an extension of the modern project of *nihilation* (as notably in the great German identity-difference philosophers, especially Schelling). It would not be, anymore than it was in the case of Melville's Ahab, a lofting of "the imbecile candle in the heart of that almighty forlornness." The language of such a sacrifice would be the reflex of the listening of a nonpromethean ear, of harkening (as Alfred Kazin has said of Melville's *Moby-Dick*) "to the rock rather than to the hero trying to get his sword out of the rock."[57] One who listened thus, Melville's Ishmael (whose name means "God hears"), found in himself such language; and Melville, venting that language, cried out: "Bring me a Condor's quill! Bring me Vesuvius' crater for an inkstand!"[58]

"God hunt us all if we do not hunt Moby Dick," Ahab exhorted a crew overcome with the lassitude of chopping whale blubber for yet one more flicker of oil lamps in the salons of small talk in Boston's Back Bay. He hunted Moby Dick in the conviction that Moby Dick, thundering out of the headwaters of eternity, had always and everywhere hunted *him*. And this *burned* in him. As Buber has said, in words remarkably apt as applied to Ahab:

> For the Word burns in him. Ecstasy is dead, stabbed in the back by Time, which will not be mocked; but, dying, it has flung the Word into him, and the Word burns in him. And he speaks, speaks, he cannot be silent. . . . He knows that he cannot say it, yet he tries over and over again until his soul is exhausted. . . . This is his insurrection, the insurrection of a speaker: related to the insurrection of the poet. . . . This is the bending of the bow for the saying of the unsayable, an impossible task, a labor in the dark.[59]

If the Word burns in us late—and early—ones, our offering will be a *burnt* sacrifice, not seared flesh rising to the nostrils of deity but the word made flesh in a feverish tongue. Seething so voluptuously as to become the gesture of desire, our language would—how shall we say?—resist the domination of will by intellect? No, the discipline of will by desire imbued by pure intellect (Eckhart) would become *ritual* (in the nonpejorative sense). An offering of burnt words, themselves crisps of dehydrated silence. A symposium, a feast of sacrifice, hosted jointly by Heraclitus and the Levites, with Saint John (whether he of the Gospel or he of the Cross), where poet and priest conspire in the fire that consumeth not, neither Being nor Nothingness. The fiery ascesis of enacted language, the purification of small talk, the coal from the altar on the lips of Isaiah. Embered morsels of chthonic *logoi*, ash and spark, embers that dis-member and re-member, burnt words that are heat-seeking missiles of the Word. Burnt words, *Burnt Norton*; one recalls that T. S. Eliot prefaced *Burnt Norton* with passages from Heraclitus's fragments 2 and 60.[60] The conjunction of Augustine's "furnace of the tongue" and Jakob Böhme's claim: "In the enkindling of fire lies the entire ground of mystery."[61] Sacramental sacrifice is one of those rited acts in which the burnt words bleed into plurisignificance, in which the instituting words themselves are sacrificed. *Sacramental*: the rendering sacred of mind by dispossessing its *hybris*: the letting go of thinking what resists thought by entrusting it to its sacred *profundis*, the releasement of determinate thinking into the waters of indeterminacy.

So the burnt words of Job 26:7 read: "He stretches out the north over the void, and hangs the earth upon nothing"—a warning duly posted that to enter the Nothing, the Void, the Abyss is to trespass the very *chora* of Godhead, the place of the Holy One, an entrance severely forbidden or proscribed in western monotheisms. "Sin bravely!" was Luther's admonition, of course—to become the motto and mood of all successor aftermoderns? Trespassing in this region of ultimacy involves an ineluctable progression of three betweens: between the two nots of the human person, between the human person and God, and between God and Godhead. Simultaneous betweens that stand under the Cloud of Unknowing, the abysmal void of Nothingness, yet also the groundlessly renewing fount of Genesis.

Afterthinking Theology as Hermeneutics

O sages standing in God's holy fire
As in the gold mosaic of a wall,
Come from the holy fire, perne in a gyre,
And be the singing-masters of my soul.
—W. B. YEATS, "SAILING TO BYZANTIUM"

For the person undertaking this thought-experiment in thinking deity at mind's length, two overarching difficulties were addressed. The first had to do with construing God's self-generation, in effect the genesis of God godself: theogony. Critically at stake in this topic is whether all that is external to God (for example, the human creature) in its modality of existing is from the selfsame *nihil* as that from which God has God's ownmost modality of being—or not-being? In a first approach to this question, we emended the Christian formula *creatio ex nihilo et non se Deo* (creation from nothing and not out of God) to read *creatio ex nihilo, idem est, ex Deitate ipsa* (creation from nothing, that is, the nothingness of God godself). The second tasking problematic after that of God's self-generation concerned generation of what is not God or is otherwise than God, namely, cosmogony, the "creation" (which I disassociate from all fundamentalist "creationism"). Thus to be thought is the *a quo* of all that is and is not, or what it is *from*. Following the briefest review of the ancient formula *creatio ex nihilo*—adopted and adapted variously in the three western monotheisms—the present project was tasked to think the primordial *nihil*.

Although perhaps not evident at the time, the anthropological reflections of the third topos, anthropogony, closely correlated with creation or cosmogony, is also closely pertinent to the topic of the self-generation of God as already enfolding the critical distinction between Godhead and God. There, the two nots of human existence were brought under phenomenological circumspection: the nothing from which the creature comes and the nothing toward which she goes. Those circumspections ended with the question whether the nothing from which one comes is the same nothing as that toward which one goes. The person thinking deity can scarcely evade asking whether a like set of two nots is entailed in respect of the being and not-being of God, such that thinking "divine things" always involves a distinction within God: a distinction between God vis-à-vis eternity and God vis-à-vis time, or between Godhead (the eternal self-genesis of the same, itself temporally indeterminate) and God (temporally determinate in all relations with what is not God).

The Hermeneutical Spiral

The thoroughgoing ontic-meontic interconnectedness of theogony, cosmogony, and anthropogony argued here has led us along a progress of definition. *De-finition* is the rendering determinate of what is initially indeterminate—and may be so not only initially but enduringly, as with deity itself. Definition takes time because time itself is ingredient in definition. Thus the patient and wise inquirer asks for definitions not at the beginning but at the end, and asks at the end only to check her cumulative understanding of central terms for what has been progressively unfolded in their use, a check on what was enfolded in them from the outset but could not have been foreseen by stipulative definition. This approach allows for *sur-prise*, for being taken over by what cannot be taken in initially.

From its origins in Wilhelm Dilthey modern hermeneutics bore a stumble: that of the "hermeneutical circle." The figure of circle occasions more than a stumble; traversing it can only bring one back to where one started, with but slight enhancement of understanding where and with what one started. I have adopted a different figure; for the hermeneutical circle I have substituted the hermeneutical spiral.[1] The change has been required for two reasons. First, the hermeneutical *circle*, so named by Dilthey, had come to characterize the special difficulty one experiences in interpreting a *written* text. He described the difficulty thus: "Herein lies the central complexity of all hermeneutic. The whole of a work must be understood from its words and their relations, and yet the full understanding of individual words already draws upon the understanding of the whole."[2] The part-whole schema may well be the most appropriate one in which to cast the difficulty of interpretation, but the item up for interpretation may not be a written text; it may be anything at all, any datum that claims mindful attention: the fragment of a potsherd from an archaeological dig, a sharp pain in the chest, a crucifix or other icon, the cry of a child, the bewildered look on the face of a loved one, and so on. If a hermeneutic is to embrace such diverse things, it must extend to whatever puts itself forward to mind as comprising some significant union of knowing and not-knowing. Such an enterprise assumes, of course, that "meaning" as self-standing is not put forward as a datum (*un fait donné*), but rather that the enterprise of mind is to wrest meaning from the datum as claiming mindful attention, and that is achieved by executing the full hermeneutical spiral wherever it leads.[3]

A second reason spiral replaces circle as prevailing metaphor is that circle bears troubling connotations, as in a "vicious circle." The metaphoric figure of circle belies the responses of mind to those data (of the diverse sorts just mentioned) that set the mind in circumferential motion. A circle sets the mind in motion, and as that motion is circular, it remains in the same plane, thus returning mind to the selfsame point from which it set out. Such a circuit can yield neither an enhancement of the datum, which gave itself ("appeared") to be understood, nor an enhancement of the knowing/not-knowing with which it was received. Stated otherwise, the circle assumes a fixed relation between being/not-being and knowing/not-knowing, whereas the spiral is a figure that itself embodies hermeneutics as a thinking in which neither of the two terms nor their relation is fixed, but rather is unfinished because the circuiting motion proceeds through differing planes. This matter is best developed by turning directly to the hermeneutical spiral.

Thinking is protected against sterility of the given and infertility of mindful response only as it honors the relation between being/not-being and knowing/not-knowing as a relation which can be envisaged as that of a helical spiral. (A helical spiral is the curve assumed by a straight line drawn on a plane when that plane is wrapped around a cylindrical surface, especially a right circular cylinder, for example, a screw thread not coming to a tapering point, a distended wire spring, a circular staircase.) There is a circularity of motion as the wire of a helical coil goes around, but does not come back to the same point because its return is not in the same plane, and also because its return bears the cumulus of the circuit itself. Every spiral executed involves an enriched cognition of the field of something-given (at the outset), and every expansion of field furnishes impetus for another spiraling cognitive circuit: thus an expansion of knowing, interpreting mind and of the given, which is both a giving and a withholding of giving. Herein lies the mystery of every ontic or meontic "given" for the hermeneutical mind: it gives and withholds (conceals) simultaneously (whether the given is "divine things" or the troubled face of a beloved—and are such givings to be entirely dissociated?). All such givings Plato called "appearances" (*phainomena*), and the widest injunction he gave to philosophy was to "save the appearances" (!), as his injunction to philosophical theology was to save the appearances of "divine things."[4] The project of modern hermeneutics is indeed to save the appearances and a mindfulness adequated to them.

One other matter is essential if one is to understand and execute the hermeneutical spiral, namely, the rule in logic of the inverse relation between the intension of a term and its extension. This means that the more immediate and focal (the intension) of a datum as it claims mindful attention (the bewildered face of a beloved), the less the mediate extension of the datum (the multiply faced beloved). Hermeneutics, theories of interpretation, cannot avoid ontological and meontological discourse because any interpretable datum will have *intension* beyond its immediate presence to mind; neither can it avoid epistemological discourse because the datum will have *extension* beyond the power of mind to know immediately in a straightforward empirical sense. One cannot choose between the alternatives posed by Plato's Euthydemos: "What I know, is" or "What is, I know"; to accept either as exhausting the possibilities is to fail to understand the helical relation between knowing and being.[5]

This inverse relation between intension and extension is what makes the hermeneutical spiral move. The more we have of a datum's immediate presence (the spearhead of its internal unity) the less we have of its character (the whatness of its extension) in relation to the field in which it is presented, while the more we have of its character ("nature") in relation to the field in which it is presented, the less we have of its immediate presence. Knowledge, wrote Paul Weiss in an early article, "always involves a synthetic unification of externals, referring to an internal unity not had."[6] The mind begins its spiraling circuit from the datum's immediate claim around the arc, away from the immediacy of focal showing toward what the spearhead is *of*, the extension of its *what*.

Every modern philosopher of the scale of mental acts has had to reckon with the immediacy (determinacy) of what is offered by percepts through the "external senses," whereby the mind has something intensionally positive to think. At the same time, he has had to reckon with the mediacy (indeterminary) of what mind itself offers by concepts through inner sense, whereby the mind has something *more* (than the intensionally discrete) extensionally positive to think. Every modern philosopher standing in the lineage of the present thought-experiment had the aspiration, *pace* the rule of the inverse relation between intension and extension, to think the *coincidence* of intension and extension, particularly in the concept of God (for example, Hegel's concrete Absolute). We have the same aspiration, but in full recognition of the temporal determinacies of the hermeneutical spiral, and a robust recognition of the logical rule of inverse relations. In the preceding chapter the question whether God is a derivative idea or concept was broached, and we affirmed that it is. Now we can say (but only in part) what such a concept is derivative *from*: from the endless execution of the hermeneutical spiral and its attendant rule of inverse relations between the intension and extension of the term *God*. That means that God godself (*deitas*, Godhead) in extension is enduringly indeterminate, and that any presentation or re-presentation of God in intension, qua sign or trace, is temporally determinate and subject to both the ravages and the increments of time.

That only can be a datum for hermeneutical interrogation about which we *know* ourselves to be ignorant (to state it in the curious way one must). Knowledge can never be accounted for if it be assumed that the state prior to knowledge is absolute ignorance. No one ever found herself in such a state. One is always already at some point on the arcs of the spiraling circuit. In a way that the mind cannot leave alone, a hermeneutical datum both "gives" and "withholds" itself: it gives its immediate discrete intensional presence, withholds its mediate extensional range, its background and foreground, its "backfound" and "forefound." It gives by diverting the mind's attention from other datal claims to its own; it provokes or beckons the mind to search out along its own lines, a search that activates the apprehensive, synthetic, and creative machinery of mental powers. Such a datum withholds by its power to draw the mind back, to be sure to a novel but connected constellation in another plane, when all mediating concepts have lost all sense of its immediate presence. Without question, not all data are of a hermeneutical kind. The physicist is not thinking about nothing when she thinks of light, but she is not bound to her light bulb either. Physicists may well someday attain such an understanding of light that they will no longer be bothered by any delineated instance of it. In that case the light of a flashlight will be some sort of datum, but not a hermeneutical one. And what of an even more instructive case, that in contemporary astrophysics of dark energy, dark mass, and their relation to each other? Do these afford *data* in any ordinary sense? Or are they projections or ejections from an extended theory of the cosmos itself? Among many reasons why the macrophysical sciences are so exciting today is that they are driven more by what is not known than by what is known, or as presently verifiable.

Theology has much to learn from the sciences in this respect. Many if not most of the difficulties faced by professional academic theologians are rooted in their failure to acknowledge their ignorance of "divine things," something they should have learned long ago from Nicholas of Cusa's *De docta ignorantia* (*Of Learned Ignorance*), for in that acknowledgment is the beginning of wisdom. One has already said that the "meaning" of a datum does not appear to mind as does the datum itself; meaning is wrested from mind's engaging the datum through all disposable powers, however limited. Not being an item in the cosmic inventory, God ("divine things") does not appear, or show godself, as other ostensible *realia* do. Like "nothingness," or for that matter, like "being," God godself appears with an all but inconceivable indirectness (the classic example being God's showing of his hind parts in Exodus). If a datum itself is an appearing, a showing (*phainomenon*), God's appearing or showing is an epi-phenomenon of the datum: the datum's limns, edges, penumbrae, tracing signs of something "more" than the datum itself can bear within its determinate being and not-being, signs activating the full nondiscursive powers of mind.

In such a spirit, it is to Byzantium that Yeats would sail through tempestuous seas, the Byzantium whose *chora* was the Hagia Sophia, literally, the Saint of Wisdom. The Hagia Sophia was the grandest cathedral in Christendom for a millennium and to my mind is vastly more intriguing than its western parallel, St. Peter's Basilica in Rome. For a millennium the Hagia Sophia harbored within itself the *eikones* (icons); then when it became successively the Aya Sofya Mosque, the grandest mosque in Islam, the selfsame architectural structure sheltered the purest of iconoclasms. The largely same architecture outside sheltering successively different insides? Taking leave of historical fact and reflecting more systemically, reality never seems expansive enough to disclose its insides; rather, its insides seem more expansive than its outside. The icons—comprising mosaics ("Come from the holy fire, perne in a gyre"), each stone a simulacrum of a part of the exceeding inside—the icons require the iconoclast, the breach of the symbols. Only the broken symbol, the cracked icon, lets through the light. But light on what? On the self-aggrandizing darkness overcasting an inside no material outside can play host to—the re-veiling or concealment that accompanies all revelation and enlightenment: *deus revelatus et absconditus*. What to call this place, this *chora*? The novelist Richard Powers writes: "For God's sake, call it God. That's what we've called it forever, and it's so cheap, so self-promoting, to invent new vocabulary for every goddamned thing, at this late a date. The place where you've been unfolds inside you. A place so large it will surely kill you, by never giving you the chance to earn it."[7]

An Imperfect Conclusion

Jonathan Swift's warning that going too long is a cause of abortion as effectual—though not so frequent—as going too short holds true especially in labors of the brain. During the thirty or so years I have wandered the backroads of my mind, issuing in this book, there was no set arrival point, no goal-oriented thinking; spending more time would only mean spending more time. The attempt to conclude, like the essay to begin, inhabits the imperfect tense. Time itself is linear, at least in this sense: it runs out, for me, for everyone. Extensively, time will continue for human creaturehood as long as humans survive in the cosmos, but intensively my ownmost time will not; my existence has been between the extremities of extension and intension, and they are inversely related in meaning. Let us pause to ask what mental attitude (in German, *Stimmung*: mood, tone, humor) comports with the thinking here encouraged and under way. I find that the *humor* of such thinking is divided between two worlds, two "imaginaries," that are related to each other ironically and paradoxically.

One world with its own imaginary is that of the modern natural sciences. One cannot deny or otherwise ignore what one knows, nor can one tolerate cognitive dissonance. If God is not an item in the cosmic inventory, is not in any sense a cause, God does not intervene in the way that a physician intervenes in a situation of human illness. I will not add more to what I have already said about this religiously bleak world and its imaginary, except to affirm again that I am a fully consenting citizen in it.

The other world with its own imaginary is all but the opposite of the modern scientific one: it is the world of perennial human aspirations, may indeed be said to be the world of Matthew Arnold's "last enchantments"—which he thought to be eclipsed and irretrievable after the onset of the modern scientific worldview—redivivus. The imaginary of the recovered enchantments, however, is not that of the "lost" enchantments of eighteenth- and nineteenth-century Romanticism; these latter remain in the dustbin of history. An example of what has changed in the transition from the old to the new form of enchantments is exemplified by the change in *knowledge*: a change not only in the how but the *what* of knowledge. In a mood-world whose enchantments have been reinstaurated, one tarries over not what one knows but rather prehensions in the wake of knowledge, the reflex of knowledge: in short, one tarries over *being known*. Knowing and being known are different orders of knowledge (as Augustine trumpeted in the *Confessions*), and being known is the more significant one philosophically and religiously or spiritually. In the imaginary of the world of the modern scientist there are classes of "objects" (the divine, the natural, other human persons, animals, insects, plants, and so on). In the thinking of these by persons, none of these classes is thought to be exhaustively the product of thought. Each class is *real*, as real as is the cosmos itself. But much of their reality includes the claim to be *realized* in their *meaning*, not only extensively in the sciences but intensively in the arts and humanities—which finally comes around to their meaning to the individual, to me and my ownmost here, now.

Knowledge that is full-orbed in respect of its human meaning—resulting in the cognitive realization of the real—has its origin in a double acknowledgment: first, acknowledgment that one is obliged to know the designated subject extensively, and second, acknowledgment that one is obliged intensively *to be known* by and through what is known. This sounds odd in the imaginary of the scientific world but not in that of the reinstaurated enchantments. And it is perhaps less and less odd in the scientific world, especially if that is the world of Thoreau, the mid-nineteenth-century "naturalist" who was at the same time a poet. As a poet he not only talked to his garden beans but overheard talk among plants on his studied walks; so it happened also with animals, as one has only to stop in the woods, be unobtrusively silent, and animals will file by and introduce themselves to you. The single mullen in the pasture was solitary but not lonely because it was in converse with mullens in other sites, with dandelions, with Thoreau's beans; it is not only gardeners who talk to and are talked to by plants but also biological botanists. In the Anthropocene epoch, particularly between the hunter-gatherer and the settled agriculture of hominids, as some domestic animals came to be kept not primarily for food but as companions and pets, symbiotic relations led not only to being known but to *being known by*. To be known by is behavior-modifying for human persons: consider how different one's behavior is because of being known (thus loved) by *this* Cairn Terrier (Fiona), how different one's behavior because of being known (thus loved) by *that* Border Collie (Shep). And from behavior change it is safe to reason to a change in meaning.

Every knowing agent chooses what to attend to. Even if nowadays most persons have a vocation, a profession or calling to attend to a specified range of subjects and their tropes, for very few does one's profession exhaust one's attentiveness. Nor does one's attentiveness get divided neatly or evenly; a large percentage goes to professional subjects and x amount to "other." Attentiveness invariably involves multitasking. Attentiveness with the intent to know is presided over by the survey (overseeing) of its subject extensively. Attentiveness with the intent to be known is to acknowledge that in all one's uniqueness and idiosyncrasy, one's "idiocy," one is and always has been under a kind of surveillance. Such surveillance is a limit or check on self-deception, not a product of the self or its thought; it is at the same time an occasion of the unlimited, "the nurse of becoming," the filling in of the blanks of human "essence" with the hecceities of *this* person, here, now. This potency is by no means automatic; it depends upon our choices concerning what we are attentive to. I have no objection to naming this attentiveness to being known as *potentia obedientalis*, to recommission a hoary term from Thomistic theology (shorn of the supernaturalistic connotations it has in Aquinas). To be known is to be electively obedient to what is known only by *being known* in our relations with those dearest to us: by parents, life-mates, children, friends, even enemies, all of whom at once limit and open our behavior.[8]

This brief section began with the mental mood of the person who holds God and the human person at mind's length: it is a *Stimmung*, a voicing mood, of relinquishing and of releasement, in which one hears the receding sound of the relinquished, the tonality of releasement. One relinquishes the blind dogmatisms of the Abrahamic religions and, at the same time, one relinquishes the vain certitudes and certainties of the modern natural sciences.[9] This thought-experiment has recurrently sought to interrelate two mood-worlds—the one of the modern natural sciences, the other of the human religious enchantments redivivus *mutatis mutandus*—each with its own imaginary. Those imaginaries are related largely paradoxically and ironically. The thinker is released into the logos of their concert, their coincidence, which is more a cacophony than a symphony, a tonality of twelve-tone scale. It is to be released into the traces of primordial groundless *turba* that rumble in the basement of being and nothingness, even as the logos of divinity sifts down through the apertures of the cosmos.

What Did the Cartesian Cogito Establish as a Starting Point for Thinking the Human Being Who Thinks God?

In Topos 2: Cosmogony we spent some time on the injunction to be wary of backward thinking from "goals" (*ad quem*) to a starting point or points (*a quo*). In further amplification, in an extended pause, it is worth thinking not just the *a quo* of thinking divinity but also the *a quo* of the mode of being human, that is, oneself. Surely the latter has hope of achieving understanding that the former does not, at least ostensibly, as human being is the one mode of being each of us inhabits from the inside out. So the question of the *a quo*, the starting point of thinking the human does not arise because it is patently obvious: the human self, thinking? To disabuse oneself that this starting point *is* obvious and that an easy path lies ahead for it (or for that matter, behind it), one has only to recapitulate by *anamnesis* the philosophical history of it in modernity beginning with Descartes's cogito. What did the cogito (and its *ergo sum*) establish as a starting point for thinking human being?

Yes, I think; but who is the *I* who thinks? Can I be sure it is I, and not someone else? Some demon, some angel, some "ghost in a machine," some collective (the proletariat, the bourgeoisie, the church, the state)? If Descartes was able to clear the I's decks of these phantoms (as to his satisfaction he was), he was left with the I who indubitably *is* while thinking. So what of my existence when not thinking? Is it "gappy"? When I am asleep and ratiocinative processes are not in play (dreams are not "thinking" in the pertinent sense), do I exist? Yes, I do, because when I am not thinking I am *thought* (this, the very root of all modern idealisms)—by God. My existence (being-there) is not gappy but continuous by reason of God's ceaseless thinking (me) in my gappy stead. And what of the *what* I mostly think: the not-I, the other, nature, and so forth? Are these whats a secure *a quo* of thinking, a self-standing *Anstoß*? No. Just as the existence of "thinking substance" (that of the I) is gappy without its vesting in divine activity, so "extended substance" (matter, or mass) is gappy without a same or like vesting. We may leave to the side other questions occasioned by the Cartesian meditations. Such as: Does the cogito exhaust human mindfulness? Does discursive *thinking* comprehend the full range of human mind without remainder? What of sensing, feeling, imagining? Could one *live* humanely in Cartesian thought about thinking?

It may well be worth a brief excursion in pursuit of where such questions could and, in fact, did lead in continental philosophy since Descartes and Kant. In that period "since" there was a broad consensus that discursive acts of thinking (as in the cogito) do *not* exhaust without remainder the range of human mindfulness, and that the term accorded for the surplus was *imagination*. So saturated was the phenomenon of imagination, so plenary its phenomenological range, that post-Kantian German identity-difference philosophers contested whether imagination is essentially *synthetic* or *creative* ("productive").

One needs to understand why such thinkers were, and still are, called idealists, which to an English ear is grossly misleading. To such an ear *ideal* refers to something purposively perfect that is real, which is not the way the idealists use the term. The continental idealist distinguished between two orders: for every series of real events (or objects) there is a *Doppelgänger*, a series of ideal events or objects that engages the broadest range of mindfulness, which is the métier of continental philosophy. Especially German idealism, rooted as it is in Jakob Böhme (the "*philosophicus Teutonicus*"), who inaugurated the parallel universes of the real and the ideal. It is the failure to recognize and honor this distinction between the real and the ideal that tortures attempts at conversation between Anglo-American analytical and continental "idealist" philosophy to this day, notwithstanding the fact that, to take only the American case, pragmatic realism arose from initial American appropriations of Spinoza and Hegel by Peirce, James, Dewey, Santayana, and others.

Enter, abruptly, Jean-Paul Sartre, who illustrates both continuity and disruption in respect of thinking imagination. Like most French philosophical schoolboys, he had drunk in the Cartesian cogito with his mother's milk. But that milk was sour and produced in him a stomachache, as he claimed it did for all obsessed with the cogito and what it secured ineluctably, namely, the (real) existence of the thinker and the (real) existence of what the thinker thinks. For Sartre the certification of the *existence* of *realia* (the thinker, extended substance, God) was a disaster since every such rationally attested "given" was a prick against which one could not kick, thus was an offense to the free ideality of the human person. One might well summarize Sartre: everything *proved* is an offense to human freedom.

Sartre construes imagination essentially neither as synthetic nor creative but as negative, negational, or nihilizing. In a reversal of Descartes, one thinks imaginatively in order *not* to be. (In this Sartre is less novel than he thinks, for long ago Meister Eckhart, in the *Parisian Questions*, had elevated intellect over will (against his Franciscan inquisitors) because intellect imaginatively entertains not only what *is* (*realia*) but what is *not*, nothingness. Having negated or nihilized both the thinker and the thought in their *realia*, the thinker through imagination is freed of the strictures of the merely real, thus of its mere presentiment (as "given"), into the ideality of freedom, wherein the thinker is free to re-present the surplus of what is hidden or effaced by mere givenness. However convoluted such a move may be to technical philosophers, it has been enormously influential in the arts, as in the abstract expressionist painting of the twentieth and twenty-first centuries, wherein *realia* (fruit, flowers, water) are realistically represented but effectively effaced or negated by the presentiment of what is hidden by their mere existence, their infrastructure of surplus. Such art is a powerful instantiation of the positivity of nothingness.[1] And Sartre instances, if he does not inaugurate, *avant le fait*, that postmodern atheistic, nontheistic, or post-theistic brand of existentialism that was ascendant if not regnant in the twentieth century.

For the knowledgeable reader there is little point in pursuing further here anything like the full modern western history of the *a quo* and *ad quem* of thinking divinity from the rise of modernity to the so-called postmodern era in which we now live. In that respect all major modern philosophers in the West share some things in common. Their initial *a quo* was that of thinking from the *a quo* of the human mode of being and knowing and remaining with it until forced to regress or progress to an *a quo* that is Being, not a mode of being, whether human or otherwise. (I well realize this is a sweeping generalization and obtains only for those bent on keeping the ontotheological tradition viable, and further requires quali-fications *mutatis mutandis* in the case of individual thinkers.) Descartes's beginning with the human mode of being and thinking, and soon com-ing upon dis-ease, inaugurated a contagion that quickly spread among all the seventeenth-century continental rationalists (Leibniz, Spinoza, Berke-ley), with all regressing or progressing to a modern form of "substance" metaphysics. Here began also the modern philosophical preoccupation with foundationalism—the quest for the ground or sufficient and nec-essary reason as the *a quo* of all thinking whatsoever—a preoccupation pronounced by virtually all postmodernists in philosophy as utterly passé.

The eighteenth-century Enlightenment—transforming medieval "illumination," or light from "above," to light emanating from human reason—was effected by its giant, Immanuel Kant. He did so through a butting together of continental rationalist and English empiricist heads, displacing and replacing each with a transcendental sublation of both. His *a quo* was also the human mode of being and knowing, but to secure tran-scendental knowledge he had no need of recourse (or regression to) ratio-nalist "substance" or medieval ontological transcendentals. Cognitively, Kant's functional equivalent of Cartesian thinking substance was "the transcendental unity of apperception." This rudimentary a priori (thus the *a quo* of all thinking whatsoever) act of pure theoretical reason effects the unitary accommodation of raw sensory data (the proper matter of all ratiocination) derived under the forms of intuition, those of time and space, with the categories of human understanding. Hence the famous first line of the *Critique of Pure Reason* to the effect that while all veridical knowledge is through experience, none is derived wholly from experi-ence. All experience of cognitive value passes through the schematism of the transcendental unity of apperception whereby the *what* of thinking is subjected a priori to the discipline of the categories of the understanding. But, there are several buts.

Of the several buts (hesitations), it is worth lingering momentarily over at least two. (1) The first pertains to the deductions of pure theoretical (cognitive) reason and the questionableness of its primal "transcendental unity of apperception," especially the character and role of the imagination in that unity, a matter Kant bequeathed to all major nineteenth-century continental philosophers (the so-called idealists or identity-difference thinkers). (2) The second comprises Kant's like transcendental construal of pure practical (moral) reason (of which, more anon).

(1) Concerning the first, from the standpoint(s) of successors to Kant a primary problem was whether the unity effected by the imagination in apperception is *synthetic* or *creative*. Clearly, Kant stood in the tradition

(already in play in the Middle Ages) of construing imagination as an inter-
mediary between such mindful unlikes as the sensory manifold and con-
ception, but without imagination's having any cognitive force of its own.
Just as clearly, Kant intended that in the unity of apperception imagination performs a function that is essentially if not exhaustively *synthetic*,
the mindful con-forming of unlikes. Coleridge (largely from his reading
of Schelling) was among the first to question whether Kant's synthesis
exhausts the work of mind, whether that synthesis exhausts what reaches
the mind's entertainment. No doubt the Kantian synthesis establishes
and guarantees the reproducibility of mind's contents, but what about
the contents that mind as mind produces or creates, those functions of
imagination that extend the phenomenological range of what is given to
mind and by mind, for example, works of art?

Before elaborating briefly the view that imagination is essentially a *synthetic* act of mind, from a base largely in Kant but to some extent also in
Coleridge, it will be useful to remind ourselves of two observations made
earlier. First, all of modernity is marked by taking as the starting point
(*a quo*) of all thinking the human situation in respect of the limits of cognition, and abandoning that base for another only in the extremity of
de rigueur. Second is the importance of the historical milieu in which the
problem of the relation between imagination and synthesis arose in modernity.

Concerning that milieu, the problem of the relation between imagination and synthesis emerged as one of undeniable moment when continental rationalistic *substance* came under attack at the hands of English
empiricists in the seventeenth and eighteenth centuries. I do not mean to
suggest that the rationalist substance thinkers neglected the imagination
altogether, but rather that they did not ascribe to the imagination the
unifying, synthetic power critical for Kant in his determination to remain
solely within the domain of pure reason.[2] In those rationalistic doctrines
"substance" accounted for structure and unitary order, which veridical
intellection was thought to grasp directly. Exercising certain options in
Descartes, Locke inaugurated that venerable English empiricist tradition
which sought after unitary order not in the intuition of substantial being
but rather in the processes of the mind's operation, chiefly in the "association of ideas." In this tradition imagination came to play an important role
in the association of ideas, especially in the formation of "complex ideas."
Among the English philosophers of the seventeenth and eighteenth centuries only Berkeley seems to have discerned that, strictly on empiricist
terms, the associative power of imagination could not be construed as *necessary*. Berkeley therefore argued, in his *Siris*, that only those ideas can be

necessary which are ordered by and emanate from God (thus a recourse to something like substance).[3] Remove God from the system of Berkeley (or Malebranche) and one has left, as in Hume, the pure association of ideas by an imagination whose *propensity* (not necessity) is determined not by intrinsic rationality but by mere convention, or rather by the "constant conjunction" embedded in cultural mores.[4] One sees why it was, then, that it was Hume above all others among the English empiricists who famously awoke Kant from his rationalistic "dogmatic slumbers." While empiricism of the seventeenth and eighteenth centuries discerned a critical relation between imagination and synthesis, it was unable to ground the necessity of judgment in that relation.

So for Kant the problem of the relation between imagination and synthesis in the transcendental unity of apperception could be solved by recourse neither to the rationalist nor to the empiricist option. With the empiricists he agreed that synthesis would have to be accounted for from the side of mind alone; with the rationalists he agreed that no account of synthesis would be valid that did not lay bare the *necessary* character of judgment. Hence he aspired to transcend and sublate both rationalism and empiricism, an aspiration of all subsequent philosophers claiming the title of "critical."

For the "critical" philosophy of the Enlightenment, then, the primary if not exhaustive effect of imagination is one of synthesis (Kant), "esemplasy" (Coleridge),[5] or unity, an effect aptly captured in the German word for imagination: *Einbildungskraft* (the power for forming into one).[6] It is the function of synthesis to bring together disparate ingredients (the "many") into the unity (the "one") of cognitive consciousness. There are on Kantian terms three such ingredients, and to each of them corresponds a distinguishable level of synthesis. These ingredients are the sheer sensuous manifold (that is, phenomena considered in their material aspect), the pure forms of intuition (phenomena considered in their formal aspect of intuitability and reproducibility), and the categorical concepts of the understanding.

Already it will be clear that synthesis pertains not to the mere "association of ideas" (as per the English empiricists) but rather to that to which conceptual ideas refer. Assuming (as Kant does) that order is not imposed upon the sensuous manifold in the mind by the noumenal being of the mind's object (that is, as per the continental rationalists), the forms that the mind legislates through imaginative synthesis will not yield *knowledge* properly so-called unless the imagination operates according to necessary rule, such rule emanating from the mind itself. In short, imagination can be shown to be indispensable to all knowledge whatsoever only by showing that it is indispensable to *necessary* synthesis, itself essential to reliable knowledge of things in space and time. Utilizing Kant's terms from the context of his thought in the First Critique, we may summarize Kant on *synthesis* thus: the synthesis suffusing the transcendental unity of apperception, underlying and determining all knowledge, is pure, a priori, transcendental, and hence necessary. The synthesis achieved through imagination is pure because its origin is in the mind alone, in the sense that the form which imagination applies to the manifold, whether sensuous or a priori, derives from the mind alone; it is a priori because it is logically independent of experience; and it is transcendental because it is the condition of all experience whatsoever.[7]

One may conclude this cursory review of Kantian synthesis by developing in like brevity the levels or dimensions of synthesis corresponding to the ingredients of knowledge, just referred to above. Although the synthesis performed by the mind through imagination is essentially one, it has distinguishable dimensions or levels that are discerned in connection with apprehension, reproduction, and the categories of understanding. These will be taken up in Kant's order.

First, apprehension and imagination. Apprehension requires for its possibility a synthesis of intuition. Strictly speaking, there can be no representations of a manifold (that is, it cannot be apprehended through intuition alone, as in rationalistic "direct intellectual intuition") apart from its being "run through and held together" by the form of time (and in the case of sensuous intuition, space) (*CPR* 131–32). Space and time are not themselves unities but rather the forms of possible intuition; they must be wedded with the content of the manifold in order to yield unified representations. The "synthesis of apprehension" has to do therefore with the receiving, arranging, and connecting of representations.[8] It is the ordering into stable units of what otherwise would be a blind chaos of phenomena. Through its "schemata" the pure productive imagination arrests the chaos of phenomena by imposing upon it the forms of time and space, an *arrestation* that permits as well an "intellectual synthesis" by making possible the application to them of the mind's categories (of understanding).

Second, reproduction and imagination. The problem of the reproductive, empirical, or associative imagination is solved in principle by what was said in the preceding paragraph about "productive" imagination. Without some such theory or doctrine, the Humean empiricist and the transcendental idealist, both of them holding that cognitive contents are not ordered from the side of the object, have the problem that the reproductive imagination has nothing to refer to. According to Kant, this stable reference is furnished by the a priori synthetical unity of phenomena accomplished in the productive imagination. In this connection Kant writes: "If we can show that even our purest a priori intuitions yield no knowledge, save in so far as they contain a combination of the manifold such as renders a thoroughgoing synthesis of reproduction possible, then this synthesis of imagination is likewise grounded, antecedently to all experience, upon a priori principles; and we must assume a pure transcendental synthesis of imagination as conditioning the possibility of all experience." Indeed, experience presupposes reproducibility; for continuity of representations, whether those of objects or of the self, presuppose their having achieved such stability in "inner sense" as to allow association without loss of identity. But discrete impressions cannot become representations unless the manifold of the intuition of them, be it pure or empirical, is combined according to a rule of synthesis. That is, impressions cannot become ingredient in knowledge unless there is a necessary synthetic unity of them. Therefore the presupposition of the empirical, reproductive, or associative imagination is the productive imagination, or pure transcendental synthesis of imagination: "The synthesis of apprehension is thus inseparably bound up with the synthesis of reproduction" (*CPR* 133).

Third, category and imagination. A third dimension or level is the "synthesis of recognition in a concept." Knowledge is not possible without explicit consciousness that what we think now is the same as what we thought before. Such a "synthesis of recognition" cannot depend entirely upon a "synthesis of sensibility," the schematization of appearances through the forms of intuition by productive imagination. For recognition requires that schemata be subjected to a "synthesis of understanding" whereby they are informed by the universal categories of understanding—for Kant, a work of *pure imagination* (Kant's most explicit statement on pure imagination is found in *Critique of Pure Reason*, 146–47). In other words, the transcendental synthesis of pure (productive) imagination stands between and, so to speak, introduces to each other sensuous intuition and the concepts of understanding so that they bond perduringly, the compound of them comprising the irreducible fundament of all reliable knowledge whatsoever. It imposes the universal principles of synthesis contained in the pure categories upon appearances given under the form of time (and in the case of sensuous appearances, space). Therefore an object is recognizable universally and necessarily through the synthetic a priori concept of it.

For several pages now we have taken a side-trip excursion into the Kantian landscape in order to grasp his notion of "the transcendental unity of apperception," the cognitive equivalent of "substance" for the preceding continental rationalists, and the like equivalent of "the association of ideas" for the English empiricists. Having briefly addressed the three dimensions or levels of Kantian synthesis, the remaining matter is to consider the absolute transcendental condition of synthesis as such, and the relation of imagination to that condition. Since synthesis does not arise from the side of the object, or from the conventioned "association of ideas," it must, if it is to be universal and necessary, emanate from that which is numerically identical and continuous, and not itself in need of synthesis. This something is the formal unity of consciousness, the "abiding and unchanging 'I,'" the "I" of intellectual synthesis, or in Kant's technical phrase "the transcendental unity of apperception." Left to itself, imagination itself (although exercised a priori) would yield only a synthesis of sensibility; but apperception is combined (also a priori) with pure imagination "in order to render its function intellectual" (*CPR* 134, 146). This combination is indispensable to all knowledge (and experience) whatsoever.

But (always the buts!) the relation between the synthesis of pure productive imagination and the transcendental unity of apperception in Kant, or more simply the relation between imagination and human selfhood, is a notorious metaphysical problem of interpretation in Kantian studies. In the first of his critiques, Kant eschewed all metaphysical reference, reference to or even recognition of a *Ding-an-Sich*, a self-standing object or reality in itself, apart from human mind. As much was essential to distancing himself from the continental rationalists on one side, and on the other side distancing himself from the empiricists whose only unity was afforded by the regularities imposed on mind by various cultures (for Hume, *constant conjunction*).

Since it is no part of my intention to expose Kant's full doctrine of imagination here, not to mention adjudicating its difficulties in the light of the Second and Third Critiques, the "metaphysical" question may be laid aside (it will appear soon enough in his continental successors, and in the development of thinking divinity here in course). As for the *logical* relation between the synthesis of imagination and the transcendental unity of apperception, it is at all events safe to say that Kant held each to presuppose the other.

We may now summarize those features of the Kantian synthesis that have come briefly into view. From an undifferentiated field of phenomena the imagination selects, arranges, and connects, synthesizing units under the forms of time and space, effecting their intellectual wedding with the continuity of mind. It may be said the primary work of the imagination is to objectify objects; to arrest the blind rush of phenomena by amalgamating their contents with the forms of the mind. Neither content nor form is reducible to the creativity of the imagination. Such a view is realistic in the sense that the imagination *produces* schemata for the understanding only by *introducing* what are otherwise (logically) fixities or givens. Through this indissoluble combination, pure imagination forms the logical base for all acts of knowledge, as it gives to understanding a stable referent. By the same token, however, pure imagination has no cognitive efficacy in its own mode of operation. This is so because the synthesis of productive imagination is finally governed by the categories of the understanding. The intention of such a theory of imagination is to explain a "synthesis of imagination," not to afford cognitive contents to a "synthesis of imagination" or even to an "imagination of reason." Rather, on his view, pure imagination is made to serve a function of mediating synthesis; to ensure the applicability of categories to experience; to guarantee that percepts will not be empty and concepts will not be blind. In short, through all these dimensions of synthesis in which it is engaged, the transcendental imagination mediates order, structure, and regularity to nature (*CPR* 146–49).

Notwithstanding the emphasis laid on the synthetic character of imagination in all its dimensions, it is critical to recall Kant's recognition that that very synthesis must itself vest in what is not in need of synthesis, namely, the perduring "I" of the subject of cognition, in his technical term "the transcendental unity of apperception." These two logical primitives presuppose each other in his explicit language: he affirms that "the principle of the necessary unity of pure (reproductive) synthesis of imagination, *prior to apperception*, is the ground of the possibility of all knowledge"; then only a few paragraphs later he affirms that "the objective unity of all empirical consciousness in one consciousness, that of original apperception, is . . . the necessary condition of all perception" (*CPR* 143, 145).

There has been occasion already to question (however parenthetically) whether acts of mind centering in the imagination are exhaustively and without remainder *synthetic*. As just now noted, Kant clearly championed a pure, *productive* imagination, but only so as to afford the base of stable referents, themselves the basis of all *re-producibility*. A *productive* imagination, however, is not the same as a *creative* imagination, the latter construed either as having ontological potency or as the capacity of mind to entertain ontological emergence-y among its objects, principally those of nature.

Everyone knows that the origins of the modern sciences date to the late Renaissance and early modernity, and that they were the successor to "natural philosophy," whose central topic always was the "nature of Nature." In this long period there was a major paradigm shift, from the "organic" Middle Ages to the early-modern mechanistic worldview of nature. For the medieval person nature was thought to be constantly informed by the demiurge, prime mover, or first act (*actus purus*); nature possessed the structures in which creativity was going on, but not the consciousness of creativity; that is, nature was thought to be intrinsically intelligible but not *intelligent*. As for mind or spirit, it was conceived as that special instance of nature in which creativity is envisaged or apprehended.

When as in early modernity nature was given over to an absolute regularity of cycle and structure under the model of the machine, those philosophers who included theology in their purview were effectively deists. Spinoza offers a brilliant qualification in that he was a late modernist or even early postmodernist *avant la lettre* in his distinction between *natura naturata* (nature natured) and *natura naturans* (nature naturing), notwithstanding that this distinction, in a different sense, was of medieval origin. Kant is said to have effected a Copernican revolution, an apt and even strict analogy or metaphor: whereas in the previous astronomy the Sun (of this galaxy) revolved around planet Earth, with Copernicus the Earth revolves around the Sun. With Kant, whereas the structures of order and cyclicality had vested in the fixities of nature itself, such order vests for him solely in the mind's self-legislative constitution. Such a philosophy of mind, and it is a *quo* of all thinking whatsoever, afforded a secure basis for the sciences of the Enlightenment, but for the sciences of today, "How now, brown cow"? Between the Enlightenment and late modernity or early postmodernity has been interposed from the sciences themselves the so-called principle of indeterminacy, extended across the full spectrum of the sciences (physical, astrophysical, life sciences). From the vantage of the present and for as far as the eye can see, the effects of this principle are themselves indeterminate and arguably indeterminable. What could Kant possibly say about phenomena themselves extrapolations from data not themselves sensuously presented (to mind) in time or space, but in space-time (relativity theory)? What about the smallest things (and every small seems to yield to a smaller), the "particles," the "quanta"? Presently we know that the smaller things are, the weirder their behavior. Into nature, previously the bastion of order and regularity, is introduced ("discovered") disorder, disruption, instability; creation (or construction) is simultaneously destruction; and from behavioral economics theory (to touch the life sciences) we know that stability itself (whether in social-political organization or in nature) advances to a tipping point at which it produces instability, which offers yet another model of cyclicality in nature.

Not only is Kant challenged by the contemporary sciences; he was so by his immediate successors, the idealist cum identity-difference philosophers, and that on several counts. While committed to working through Kant, but around and beyond him, they found his reduction of the human self (the "I") and the *a quo* of all thinking to the cognitive unity of apperception wholly inadequate. Who, what, is this I, this "ego"? And what of the not-I: Is it wholly internal to the I (a not-I, projected by the I, to afford an *Anstoß* against which to hit and bounce off of, something to negate in the process of self-realization of the I?) Or is the not-I external to the I, such that it is equiprimordial with the I in the human condition? These questions (and many others) took the matter to be one of contention between Spirit and Nature. And theologically the matter was whether the realization of the Absolute was a function of Spirit or Nature or their coincidence—as of old, for example, in Nicholas of Cusa's coincidence of the absolute minimum and the absolute maximum.

At all events, none of the idealist-identity-difference successors of Kant could accept Kant's restriction of the imagination to its *synthetic* functions. The post-Enlightenment zeitgeist made clear to them that creativity and novelty had made manifest what Kant neither saw nor foresaw, whether in nature or in spirit. I prescind from commenting on Hegel and Fichte in this respect. It was above all Schelling who awoke Coleridge from his dogmatic slumbers of Kant in these respects. Just as it was Hume who awoke Kant, how ironic it was that an English Romantic who, from his reading of Schelling, was awakened from the new Kantian dogmatic, in which he was joined by many a continental Romantic. In this Coleridge joined Schelling, but well beyond Coleridge's ken. Schelling reckoned these matters not to reach closure, as did his old former roommate Hegel, but to keep them open to the potencies swarming the void of their source. He had established himself early on as a brilliant writer on nature, but he then fell silent publicly while working feverishly on an alternative to "positive philosophy," the net results of which he judged to be wholly negative. That alternative, *pace* Hegel, was a new theology sourced equally by "mythology" and "revelation."

Let us not pass over or dismiss Kant peremptorily, however; he is not judged a pivotal modern thinker for nothing. In fairness one must recognize his contributions to thinking all things ultimate, not least of them divinity. Certainly he is the key figure in consolidating the entire tendency of western modernity to take as the *a quo* of thinking divinity the full-orbed human condition, which for him comprised the three dimensions of reason (on each of which he offered a critique: theoretical, practical-moral, and aesthetic—and we have attended only the first). Thus, since Kant, it was characteristic of modern philosophical theology to set out from a base in anthropology; and for some successors who took that base to be exhaustive, theology could be little more than "projections" from the basic *a quo*, as with Feuerbach (who, however, was a Kantian only through a left-wing interpretation of Hegel).

But the whole of Kant, and the whole of the human condition, cannot be reduced to or exhausted by theoretical reason laid out in the First Critique. Just this was the fateful mistake of the so-called Marburg School of neo-Kantian interpretation (Cassirer, Natorp, Vaihinger, et al.), an *Arbeitskreis* all but totally preoccupied with a logic of the sciences, hence working from the base of the First Critique. The neo-Kantian opposers of the Marburg School were the so-called Southwest German–Badensian–Heidelberg School (Windelband, Rickert, et al.), an *Arbeitskreis* also all but exhaustively preoccupied with the metaphysics of moral life in the Kantian human condition, thus based on the Second Critique (of practical reason). One could easily plot graphs of actual theological options taken from the followers of each of these opposed neo-Kantian schools.

For example, one can see from the Marburg School why a certain agnostic pall has fallen over thinking divinity in much late-modern philosophical theology. From a base in the First Critique alone, one can see why that has been the case. Knowledge properly so-called relies on the *constitutive* process from the side of mind alone, in which the a priori schematism of reason effects the various levels of synthesis whereby the sensuous manifold received through the forms of time and space are unified and made subject to the universal categories of the understanding. What is not received through forms of sensible intuition cannot be known; hence the unknowability of anything in itself (*Ding-an-Sich*). The example of examples for such a thing-in-itself is and always has been God, at least in the monotheistic philosophical theologies. In being agnostic in respect of God in godself, Kant is by no means unique. No major western monotheistic theologian, whether based in reason or revelation, had claimed that God in godself was known or even knowable, was given rather to denial of same, and given rather to the "cloud of unknowing" ("the dark night of the soul") that hovers over the *ipseity* of the divine nature, a cloud that precipitates in the mystical "knowing not-knowing" (Nicholas of Cusa) of God. Kant is a modern participant in this tradition. But with important qualifications, of which only two shall be noted here.

First qualification: Kant's distinction between *knowing* and *thinking* was fundamental for him, as it is in the project of these pages, that of thinking divinity, as it is for his doctrine of the thing-in-itself. This distinction (between knowing and thinking) is itself the rough equivalent of that between constitutive and regulative acts of mind, the latter also the rough equivalent of the distinction between concepts and "ideas of reason." There can be no knowledge of things-in-themselves; nor can it be known whether the categories apply to them. When one *thinks* them they are purely formal, without empirical content; that is, are both empty and blind, are indeterminate in "meaning." Why, then, bother at all with "ideas of reason"? Because the human condition is not exhausted by the theoretical reason; beyond and distinguished from the latter is the practical-moral reason. While like the theoretical reason in that it is self-legislative, practical-moral reason is also *constitutive* of the human condition; but in its *use* the moral Imperative (which Kant takes to be an empirical fact with critical warrant) requires conditions not themselves having cognitive certainty. (The categorical imperative: "act so that you can at the same *will* that the maxim of your act shall be universalizable.") Just these conditions comprise the matter of the "ideas of reason," which have not a constitutive but rather a regulative function. For Kant the minimum of such regulative ideas as the condition for the employment of practical-moral reason comprises Freedom, Immortality, and God. *Freedom* because, on pain of being meaningless, the categorical imperative requires the capability of the human subject to obey or disobey it; and, ever the realist, Kant recognized the human condition to embrace radical evil, that, *pace* Plato, to *know* is insufficient to *do* the Good. *Immortality* because of the actual disparity between the absolute claims of the categorical imperative and the finite time of the fallible human subject. Kant's term for the extended "time" in which that disparity is rendered harmonious was *the Kingdom of Ends*, a time not our finite time. And *God* because only God godself is the guarantor of final harmony between the moral law and the means of its fulfillment as the good in the Kingdom of Ends. For all the reasons advanced, these three conditioning "ideas of reason" are not concepts; the mind's approach to them is rather one of *belief*. Beliefs are not less critical for that, but are to be formed with both vigor and rigor, and only with the justification warranted by the human condition of which they are themselves conditions. While Kant undoubtedly held that we cannot know what reality *is* (in itself), we also undoubtedly know what the reality (of the human condition) *ought* to be, as we are obliged by belief to think the conditions of our complicity in moral existence. Himself a pietistic Evangelical (the latter meaning, in Europe, Protestant) beginning to end, Kant was wary of all emotionalism and "enthusiasm," all that smacked of *Schwärmerei*, of all "religious experience" considered not subject to the strictures of all experience whatsoever, as he deemed such (religious) experience vulnerable to superstition and self-delusion, and as not only welcoming idolatry but as well displacing and substituting for the moral Law.

One is in position, then, to understand Kant's famous declaration that in respect of religion he had "destroyed knowledge in order to make room for faith," with faith construed in the sense of belief. Thus was set off a scramble among his successors in theology to elaborate a kind of cognitivity unique to faith, a tendency that took two palpable forms. In one, that among church dogmatic theologians, theology took the form of fideism, the most rigorous exclusivism of the *sola gratia, sola fides* principle since Luther and Calvin; and the one that found its champion in the twentieth-century Swiss theologian Karl Barth, especially his followers in the Anglo-American world. (And the one to say of philosophy: good riddance!) If this first form was only negatively neo-Kantian, the second theological form was positively neo-Kantian, and that in being based on Kant's metaphysics of morals. This form was embodied theologically in Germany in the school of Albrecht Ritschl and to a lesser extent in that of Ernst Troeltsch. Its principal "afterlife" has been in England and America, where, if theology is studied at all in the university, it is so as moral or ethical thought, and is inoculated against all speculative thought not required by its base.

Some pages back I noted that in fairness to Kant two qualifications were necessary. The first was what is at stake in the distinction between knowing and thinking, between the constitutive and the regulative, between concepts and "ideas of reason." We turn now to the second qualification, that pertaining directly to the thing-in-itself of theology itself: God. Concerning this second qualification, from what view of God's nature did Kant work? One cannot be certain, but it is safe to infer from the instruction in philosophy he received in the school of Christian Wolff, the secular rationalist and advocate of natural theology in the tradition of Leibniz—as one can infer from Kant's Copernican penchant for standing classical and scholastic metaphysics on its head. That scholastic metaphysics centered on God as *ens realissimum et perfectissimum.* One can easily see why this notion came into play in the composition of the *Critique of Pure Reason* when Kant entertained whether the ontological "proof" (God is that being than which no more perfect can be conceived) could serve as a regulative idea. Of course he rejected all arguments for the existence of God, but was most intrigued with the "ontological," if only because it offered the categories, themselves to be synthesized with the sensible manifold. The idea of God as *ens realissimum* is the notion of the sum of all ultimate, underivable predicates (categorical attributes); moreover, with the *et perfectissimum*, the predicates attributed to the *ens realissimum* are of the highest possible in degree (most perfect) and therefore are in eminent mode. All lower degrees of quality would then be limitations of the highest degree, as in the categories of human understanding per Kant's teaching in the First Critique.

Further, and this to my mind is critical, negative predicates were not included by Kant in the *ens realissimum et perfectissimum* on the grounds that they are derivative. Just this claim aroused contest and denial among Kant's speculative identity-difference successor philosophers, as it does in the thinking of divinity under way in these pages. If the aseity of Godhead-God is construed mindfully (in which construal Kant is a historically pivotal thinker), the paradigm of *ens realissimum et perfectissimum* is to be contested and denied as exhaustive of the self-generation of what God is and is not. Stated forthrightly, the sum of irreducible and nonderivative positive predicates of reality in eminent or perfect mode does not exhaust the being and/or nonbeing of God. The negative attributes (attributes in eminent mode negated) are equiprimordial with other nonderivatives in the realization of Godhead-God, as they are in all that *is* externally to God, thus for all creatures. The most real, most perfect God is not a finished storehouse of accomplished (actual) positive predicates but a process itself, a term (*a quo*) with a divine eschatological *ad quem*, in which *Homo sapiens sapiens* is complicit; that means that with the dismissal of ontotheology, one also dismisses the God of the classical *actus purus* tradition and its attendant *ens perfectissimum* correlate.

This brief review of modernity and incipient postmodernity ends with the posing of two critical questions: (1) In thinking God (deity, the sacred) at mind's length, what is indeterminate and what determinate? (2) In the idea or concept of God, what is derivative and what is not? The second question is addressed here as prefatory to the first. The first is addressed in Topos 1: Theogony, presupposing the treatment of derivatives here.

The modern consensus that theological thinking has its *a quo*, its starting point, in human modes of knowing and existence has carried the all but ineluctable consequence that its *ad quem*, God, would bear but the attributes of the *a quo*, attributes themselves "perfected" and intensified, thus that theology would be nothing more than anthropology in a loud voice (Ludwig Feuerbach to the left, Karl Barth to the right). In the tail wind of such a recognition there have been calls from many quarters for a deanthropomorphizing and a depersonalization of thinking deity (the sacred, the holy). At stake in these summons is the relation between *mediacy* and *immediacy* in thinking God. Just this relation is at the heart of the question concerning what is derivative and what is not in thinking God.

So let us think about *immediacy* for a moment (as even "for a moment" will become important). Nothing is more immediate than experience, which is what we call the state in which something is or things are sensuously "given" to us directly in the present. Virtually every major philosophy claims to begin from such a state (so Kant, as we have seen, and so Whitehead, as we shall see shortly) and to explain that state as critical for further thinking. At this point "for a moment" rears its head, for the moment of immediacy evaporates in an instant, yielding the "specious instant" long ago noted by Aristotle (*Physics* 6.234a). What was immediately given by perception in the present is "now" but the most recent entry into memory, thus is the presence of a given that is presently absent, has been taken up into the schematisms of *mediacy*. Immediate perception and the intellection of it therefore involve the absence of a given that is mediately present. There is no immediacy without the wholeness (mediacy) made possible by memory; there is no wholeness without the immediacy of the presence of the temporally absent. Without immediacy there is nothing to think; yet without mediacy there is no way to think what immediacy gives or yields. In *Unfinished Man and the Imagination* I claimed that the offices of imagination are engaged primarily in connection with the execution of mediacy or wholeness, wherever wholeness is executed, largely in memory, intention, and the potency of experience for expanding and contracting mindfulness, whether in philosophy, theology, or the arts.[9]

Enter the *theo-logic*. In its broadest sense, logic comprises a categoreal schema for coherently thinking the mediacy or wholeness of the immediacy of what is given to mindfulness. The same thing said otherwise: logic isolates irreducible logical primitives, themselves not derived, with and through which experience is schematized. If we assume that that experience is more or less constant in respect of its immediacy (which in the case of western and eastern experience is dubious), logics are not. Every major western philosopher has stipulated a logic in the broad sense as a propaedeutic to thinking experience at large, whether as visionary or revisionary.

The point can be illustrated randomly, in the West, in respect of a theo-logic. Plato's logical primitives were "division" (or separation, analysis, *analuein*, to cut) and "collection" (*synthesis*, a putting together again after requisite separation). For Plato God is not a logical primitive but an ontological one from multiple ontological (and meontological?) ones, and is that not as a Creator but as a *demiurgos* (Plato's fourfold schema is touched on in Topos 1: Theogony). For Aristotle God is formally a logical primitive among others, but whether God has effective standing among other Aristotelian primitives is unendingly contended among scholars of Aristotle. If the major thrust of Aristotle's logical primitives is to elucidate the experience of becoming, as most students of his thinking take it to be, his God could be removed from the list of logical primitives without net loss. His God, the first in the tradition of *actus purus*, is the unmoved mover, utterly and austerely transcendent of all becoming, himself assymetrically related to all becoming, thus but a formal placeholder of Being that does not move or become, a marker of final causality, a *telos* of other logical primitives.

As for Kant, from what has been said above and need not be repeated, it is clear that in the *Critique of Pure Reason* God is in no sense a logical primitive, and that if there is an idea or concept of God otherwise it will be derivative from the logics of the *Critique of Practical Reason* and the *Critique of Judgment*. And of course, one cannot omit from this brief random walk the great Hegel, arguably the most revisionist and radical of modern logicians (the very mention of whose name among some formal logicians will be thought scandalous). His logical primitives (in the sense used here) are developed in *The Science of Logic*, a book often skipped in rushing pell-mell to his magnum opus, *The Phenomenology of Spirit*. The latter cannot be understood without a comprehension of the former. In *The Science of Logic* Hegel unfolds and enfolds a logic of dialectics that is not susceptible of cryptic summation. Suffice to say that Hegel, while like others adopting a table of logical primitives, puts them into dialectical relation with each other, so that each is simultaneously affirmed and negated, yielding higher and higher sublations, so that each primitive expands the mediacy of its purview, thus transfiguring the mediacy necessary to understanding the immediacy of the experience of the full phenomenological range of mind or spirit (*Geist*).

For the fifth philosopher in this brief excursion on the derivative character of such ideas as God, and what is not derivative, namely, logical primitives, we turn to the twentieth-century Anglo-American philosopher Alfred North Whitehead, who is likely to be more accessible to anglophone readers than the continental figures just now examined, and that notwithstanding the fact that his language is riddled with multiple neologisms which take some living with to comprehend. If one is saying something new, old used (and often abused) words often will not serve; the constructive thinker must sometimes construct words, which then over time become used ordinarily, as in the "process" school of philosophy that followed in the train of Whitehead. It is important to remember several things about Whitehead. Before he emerged as a major constructive philosopher, he was a distinguished mathematician and logician, having published works on these subjects with Bertrand Russell. One needs as well to recall that his magnum opus *Process and Reality*, in which he laid out his logical primitives and major ideas, bore the subtitle "An Essay in Cosmology" (nota bene, *not* "An Essay in Theology"). Whitehead is famous for having said that all philosophy is a series of footnotes to Plato, that at bottom one is either a Platonist or an Aristotelian, and without question

Whitehead chose to be Plato redivivus. That precisely is ostensibly odd, is so because it was Aristotle who took *becoming* to be his widest purview, as Whitehead the cosmologist took the cosmos to be in *process* of *becoming*. Just as there is an argument among Aristotelians about whether God is essential to his (Aristotle's) system, so there is among Whiteheadians in respect of the standing of God in Whitehead's schema. It seems clear (to me) that his cosmology does not depend upon the idea of God, certainly not on the idea of God as *actus purus*. And that may well be the substantive reason that God is not listed among Whitehead's logical primitives. For him, God is a derivative idea or concept, derivative from the irreducible logical primitives themselves. (As noted many times in these pages: just as God is not an entity on the inventory shelves of the universe, so God is not an item in the list of logical primitives.) For Whitehead, the idea of God is derivative especially in the kind or nature of reality God *is*.

It is likely important to recall that the present examination of logical primitives in selected thinkers has been undertaken to make clear the proper context for reckoning the question whether the concept or idea of God is itself derivative. The question of the derivative character of the idea of God is not at all a genetic or developmental question; stated otherwise, it is not a psychological question but is rather a *logical* question. The teacher of theology knows well that both he and the student have genetic, developmental, and psychological personal histories in thinking God that are pedagogically important to keep in mind, but the subject taught, the idea or concept of God, has a logic independent of those histories. The supreme challenge in teaching (and in reading!) is to bring them into mindful conjunction.

Whitehead identifies and develops his logical primitives through his scheme of categories, which he takes to be further irreducible, in *Process and Reality* under the title "The Categoreal Scheme" (part 1, chapter 2).[10] He proceeds to name four sets of high generality, the first of highest generality being the "category of the ultimate." He then lists three sets of "more special categories," those of existence, explanation, and obligation. These do not exhaust Whitehead's table of logical primitives, but they form the basis for explicating others that are implicit in them, which is the project that is undertaken in the remainder of *Process and Reality*.

One notices at once that the fourfold categoreal schema does not include the term *God*. Nor is a concept of God included in the scheme by using some other referring expression, not even *the ultimate*, which is simply the matrix of the categorical scheme. No entity is designated as something to which are assigned the distinctive functions of God that Whitehead later develops systematically. Indeed, no *entity* whatsoever is mentioned in his categorical scheme. Of course this omission, like all other omissions, requires to be explained. That is precisely why, in the list of four basic categories, the category of explanation is included. The concept or idea of God is not deducible from the four most basic categories in their proper generality. Their very generality requires for their explanation "special" categories. The need for special categories is evident in explaining the ultimate, which, as noted, does not include the idea of God.

Whitehead cannot explain any one of the four categories of high generality without adding "special" categories that each of them presupposes. The explication of the basic category of the ultimate, for example, requires three special logical primitives: one, many, and creativity. As summarized by William A. Christian: "Whitehead cannot make a list of types of entities (that is, of logical subjects of systematic statements) in his categories of existence without presupposing the primitive notions of 'one' and 'many.' And he cannot supply categories of explanation that speak of 'process' and 'becoming' without drawing on the primitive notion of 'creativity.' The category of the ultimate is the matrix of the categorical scheme." The four basic categories are *superseded* by the special categories in all systematic explanation. No one of these categories is a fixed entity, but all are in play in the explanation of any entity claiming mindful attention in respect of its ostensible reality. One cannot think existing entities—that is, the logical subjects of systematic claims—without presupposing the logically primitive notions of *one* and *many*; nor can one supply categories of explanation concerning being or becoming without recourse to the primitive category of *creativity*. The primitive notion of *one* is superseded by the concept of an actual entity; the primitive notion of *many* is superseded by the concept of actual multiple entities; the primitive notion of *creativity* is superseded by the systematic account of how actual entities come into existence by concrescence. It comes to the same thing to say that logical primitives are pre-systematic. Whitehead's aim is "not to eliminate pre-systematic notions but to elucidate them."[11]

For present purposes one need not elaborate further Whitehead's list of logical primitives (categories). I have addressed this feature of his work to show how a major modern systematic logician and philosophical cosmologist understands God to be a derivative idea. I have not dealt here with many of the critical terms, beyond the categoreal scheme, essential to understanding Whitehead in the large: "actual entity," "subjective aim," "eternal object," "time as a perpetual perishing," "actual occasion," "nexus," "principle of concretion," and many others. These terms arise because something more than the categoreal scheme is needed to interpret the world in which we live, which is why, immediately following the chapter on "The Categoreal Scheme," he turns to "Some Derivative Notions," in which the idea of God appears. God does not appear out of the blue but in connection with thinking enduring things, despite their participation in time as perishing. We may skip over several important steps ("extension," the nexuses of "social order" and "personal order," the "subjective aim of a temporal actual entity," and others) to the problem of how such an actual temporal entity can satisfy the categoreal obligation of subjective unity. Such a satisfaction, so Whitehead avers, can only be in the constitution of a primordial and everlasting actual entity. This nontemporal actuality "is here termed 'God'; because the contemplation of our natures, as enjoying real feelings derived from the timeless source of all order, acquires that 'subjective form' of refreshment and companionship at which religions aim."[12]

These brief remarks on the role of logical primitives (categories) in thinking deity have been adduced only to reduce the ostensible oddness of a theologian's claiming and acknowledging that the very idea of God is derivative—or deeply recondite. Certainly logically primitive categories, their expansion, and their supersession in larger and larger frames are essential to construing and explaining *any* idea engaging the human experience of the cosmos. In this, the idea of God is not an exception, as Whitehead makes clear. Methodologically, logical primitives have not been adduced here as preface to a system, as they were by Whitehead, for this thought-experiment is not a system in any modern sense. For Whitehead, there is one respect in which the idea of God (namely, his own) is an exception: God is, for him, the only entity pertinent to the understanding and explanation of the cosmos that has both a primordial (eternal) and a consequent (temporal) nature. His distinction between the primordial and consequent natures of God has a family kinship with the distinction between Godhead and God developed in the preceding pages, especially in Topos 1: Theogony.

Fault and Fall in Human Existence

It is a tremendous act of violence to begin anything. I am not able to *begin*. I simply skip what should be the beginning. Nothing is so powerful as silence. It would never have been broken if we had not, each of us, been born into the midst of talk.

—RAINER MARIA RILKE, "THE YOUNG WORKMAN'S LETTER"

It is the character of metaphysical thinking to address the nature of the object thought, but the human person is not an "object" in any ordinary sense—not, for example, like an asteroid. To be sure, the living and lived reality of a human person is an intentional object of mind, and any such must have *some* kind of structure or nature that distinguishes it from everything else, or otherwise we have the problem of the identity of indiscernibles. Even if there is such a thing as human nature, knowing that nature will be insufficient to know my own nature or that of any Jane Doe. We come again, as we have before, to the inverse relation between the extension and the intension of a human person. The nub of this inverse relation is evident in this: that while the *will* may play a cardinal role in the nature of mankind as such—thus in "human nature"—that does not say how John Doe's will shapes his character, thus his and only his "nature." Accordingly, this section aspires to think the human person further, both extensively and intensively, in a larger framework.

As delivered by a virtually unbroken Christian theological tradition in the West, fault and fall are humanly intractable, inaccessible to revision, and so are intimately connected with creation itself. The character of that intimacy has been hotly disputed and is something of which we must speak, if but indirectly. If human fault and fall are indeed humanly intractable, are they not aboriginally embedded in the very structure of creation? That they are so embedded is the essential claim of all gnosticisms, which yielded a Manichaean cosmos and humankind, a view scarcely limited to late antiquity and that seems to have fired the most recent monstrous century—the twentieth—and to remain unabated at the dawn of the twenty-first. It is no accident that the notion of *creatio ex nihilo* arose in the second century of the Common Era in part if not in the main to contest the metaphysical coincidence of creation and human fault/fall. Not only in the modern secular world, but also in Christendom in all times and places, the Manichaean option has been rampant.

That says the *creatio ex nihilo* has not been sufficiently afterthought—or thought through—and so lays a strong claim upon the philosophical theologian. Such a thinking rehabilitates for the present the hoary medieval distinction between eternal and temporal creation and discriminates afresh *creatio ab origine* and *creatio continua* (as addressed in Topos 2: Cosmogony). Above all, such a thinking must accord the *nihil* of the *creatio ex nihilo* its due, both the nothing *from* which and *toward* which we are created, what I have called here the bicameral house of human being. Only such a thinking can end the conspiracy of silence about nonbeing or nothingness, which is no less regnant in the mainline ontotheological tradition in Christendom than it is in perennial philosophy—notably in all forms of Christian Neoplatonism—with its passion, in Gadamer's fine phrase, "to render nonbeing harmless."

A word about the difficulty of beginning, reflected in the Rilke epigraph above. The subject presently is fault/fall, not creation, but since the former is not unrelated to the latter in the tradition under examination, beginning on fault/fall entails thought that has already begun on Beginning *überhaupt*. The subject is fault/fall, not being and nothingness, but if the *nihil* in *creatio ex nihilo* is endemic to fault/fall, thought must have already begun on being and nothingness. Like Rilke, I must skip any absolute Beginning and maintain myself in discourse already under way in respect of extending the framework of the human person to include fault/fall and nature/nurture.

A reflective and contemplative anthropology, whether philosophical or theological, aspires to describe and explain what is made or "given," and what persons can and do make; what is up for human disposition and what is not. Just as the subject-person who is thinking a subject matter is now one, now diffused, so the stipulated subject matter is now one, now double or manifold, when the subject matter is "human nature." Even when unitary, the matter has a Janus double face. That is why the title of this section is neither just "fall" nor just "fault" but "fault and fall." Fault and fall are the fundamental distinctions to be made within the totality of the human phenomenon, and between them lies the *aporia*, the *metaxu*, between the two nots (addressed in Topos 3: Anthropogony). The hiatus is the dark center between two penumbral fields. The reason of the philosophical-theological mind, like that of the astrophysicist, is light-trained (alas, without the benefits of radiotelescopy) upon dark bodies verging upon a black hole. So, let us turn to our two *f*-words. First *fault*, then the real four-letter word, *fall*. At this late date, *fault* and *fall* probably cannot be dissociated from their Christian overtones. Although a philosophical theologian principally in the Christian traditions, I claim the reflective anthropology under development to be intelligible and indeed defensible without special theological appeals.

Fault. In the Romance languages one will hear the connections of *fault* with *fail*. In all uses of *fault* one hears the resonances of lack, of defect. In the moral sense, fault betokens culpable or blameworthy lack, failing, wrongdoing. As I shall use it here fault bespeaks in the first instance not the moral but the structural sense, that of defect, as evident principally in geology. Fault is crack, breach, rupture. In electricity talk it is the point of defect in a circuit that prevents the flow of current; in hunting it is a break in scent that throws the dogs off track; in tennis it is an error of service, a failure of service to the proper court. In geology fault is the zone of fracture in the plane of plates. Fault is not actual earthquake but is its subterranean possibility. What referent does the metaphor *fault* mark in the human person? It is the acute self-consciousness of ontological instability (which we have been at some pains to demarcate in preceding sections). Much western metaphysical ingenuity has been lavished upon attending the Richter scale of Being by graphing the rise and fall of tremors in a human reality that inhabits displacement.

In what does the ontological instability, the fragility of human being/becoming, consist? Absent external agency, a rock perdures what and as it is. But, leaving aside the complex matter of external agency bearing upon her, the human person is at perpetual risk of interior implosion. In starkest and plainest terms, the referent of fault in the human person is that she does not enduringly coincide with herself. She is a one-in-two, a two-in-one; rather, she is a one-in-many, a many-in-one. Since there must be at least two or more things to coincide or not coincide, what does not coincide with what? Here the classical distinctions come into play both in description and in explanation of the ontological-meontological instability of the human reality. The perennial candidates are all familiar: essence and existence, form and matter, substance and accident, identity and difference, presence and absence, and so forth. In any slice-specimen of what I am I find that I both am and am not what I am. My kind of being is a kind of becoming being but also a becoming not-being (or unbecoming), in that remarkable way whereby "I" am not lost but refound and refounded in swirling genesis. My form and matter, my essence and existence, are not wholly internally related but rather, to a degree I cannot anticipate or even learn, externally related. My body-matter expands and contracts in the course of birth, growth, and decay and so is vulnerable to different formations. The form of my existence is not laid up in some charter except as a dark limit to exceed or subvert, which would take me out of humanity; it rather is significantly vulnerable to cultural influence and to my own decisions. Add the prominence of *freedom* as the heart of what is at stake between internal and external relations for the human person and you have the crux of the person's ontological-meontological instability. This is especially so if one completes the picture, as we shall attempt when we turn to "fall," by the complications of freedom itself in what I have called simply "the human reality."

It says the same thing by elaboration to say that the fault line in human reality runs between the indicative and the imperative. In any given state of affairs I am one thing, but I intuitively sense that I should be other or more. I am the kind of being who knows himself not to be exhausted in what is at hand, who knows that I am not only *from* a state of affairs but also that I am vocated *toward*, that in any moment I am suspended between *from* and *toward*. What I am is not reducible to what is *made*; my being is not exhaustively and without reminder a *product*. Although I am biologically and culturally made, I am ever under summons to "make something" of what is made, and am the center of a contest between being made, self-making and self un-making. Martin Buber put the matter succinctly: "I am given over for disposal and know at the same time that it depends on myself."[1]

If I know this extensionally about every human person, thus of human existence, I must not forget it when I come intensively into the presence of another human person. Every individual human person as contrasted, say, with a rock, has a singularity and unsubstitutability of being. The disparity between human nature and *this* person, Mary, is qualitatively different from the disparity between rockness and *this* rock. In the case of the human person, the old rule in logic about the inverse relation between extension and intension (the more I have of human nature, the less I have of Mary; the more I have of Mary, the less I have of human nature *über-*

haupt) takes on ontological weight. What is precious about Mary I would not know merely from her extensional range, but only from her lived intensification of that range in her own story. While using the language of "summons" or "vocation," these remarks do not privilege a specifically religious or Christian reading of human ontological instability. They are consonant with diverse western metaphysical schemae, above all with Plato's fourfold ontological scheme in the *Philebus* (alluded to earlier in these pages). We do not know a person in her intensive reality until we know her *telos*, what she is *toward*, what she is *for*. For Plato all the ultimate factors were external to each other, so no one was reducible to another, and the Good was the lure or summons of all extensively.

Let us look at this matter of the ontological instability of the human person in a way that is demonstrated in William James's *Varieties of Religious Experience*. In his inspection of the human soul James finds in all such varieties something characteristic not only of his infamous "sick-minded" soul but of all souls. He calls this sentiment an uneasiness that "reduced to its simplest terms, is a sense that there is *something wrong about us* as we naturally stand."[2] For him no living sentiment can be kept alive by a merely metaphysical or theological scruple. We know a living universal sentiment not so much in its root as in its fruit. The fruit of uneasiness signals that we are not what we belong to, that what we most deeply long for signals what we belong to, that what we long for produces effects in another reality, namely, us as not yet realized, and "that which produces effects within another reality must be termed a reality itself."[3]

The faulted person is fallible, is "failable" in respect of being, even though she exists as absolutely as any other merely existent thing. What does the human person most deeply yearn for, long for? One might answer "infallibility," but that answer is useless because whatever infallibility might be it would not be human being, in which freedom means minimally the latitude of possible failure. The human person yearns for the finishing of her unfinished selfhood, for the complete coincidence of herself with herself. She longs to belong to a stability of being that does not annul the conditions of her fallibility but fulfills them through acceding to a claim upon her existence that is neither just heteronomous nor just autonomous but the coincidence of both.

What do immemorial affections of the human heart disclose about the deepest yearning for locative and durative stability? I think we find at least two aspirations that move counter to each other—and the cumulative effect of their countering is to establish fallibility even more firmly in the affections. I shall speak of the two as downward and upward aspirations. By *downward aspiration* I refer to the human affection for the *inanimate*, an emotion that arguably is a vestigial affective residue of "phylogeny re-capitulates ontogeny." I do not mean to slight the animate substratum of human being—one has only to remember the role that totem animals have played in the affections of religious cultures over time and place, the principal secular residue of which among us "civilized" ones is our pets, our dogs and cats. But nothing in the merely animate world can quite com-pare with the residual human admiration for the inanimate. Above all else in this respect is the immemorial human fascination with stone. A stone qua stone cannot fail to be what it is; wherever and whenever it is, it fully is all that it is. In the reverie of stability whether of locus or duration, the affections will be drawn to stone. Let the affections loose in eternity and they will fix on stone as its locus in time. Let the mind overhear genesis at rest in contemplation, through what Bergson called acts of "intellectual auscultation," and one hears the speech of stone. In stone form and mat-ter seem perfectly coincident, the one offering amplitude to the other. No one has understood the human reality, says E. M. Cioran, who does not envy a rock. From this vantage the history of religions is the story of the hermeneutics of stone. Where the instability of human reality peaks, there stand to counter it the Herms, the cairns, the pyramids, the Acropolises, the Gothic temples, the skyscrapers. Wander into the outbacks of the af-fections, often associated with geographical remoteness—the American prairies or deserts, rural Korea, the vastnesses of Siberia—and there will be found stones placed on top of each other, artifacts of human aspiration toward and through the inanimate. Of course, as with everything that human instability touches, we do not let stones be but press them into the service of our own aspiration, their being into the service of our becoming being, our not-being of what we have become. How much human life has been spent, in the title of a grand little book by Annie Dillard, *Teaching a Stone to Talk*?[4] Architecture and sculpture arose from and perdure in this instruction. Think of the masters at teaching stone to speak: Michelan-gelo, Rodin, Brancusi. Think of the stones that mark graves, that duratively and locatively mark the final instability of the human being that fails not only imperative essence but finally indicative existence as well, that un-derneath the stone disintegrates into elements that will finally sediment and start again the cycle eventuating in stone. All things that persist and recur, thought the Greeks, are divine. It would be empirically based and not merely jocular to say that who has a sense for the divine simplicity of coincidence has rocks in his soul, if not in his head.

A proclivity of the affections for downward aspiration to the inanimate, notably stone, is matched by a counter upward aspiration toward an inten-sification of the animate (animate: the souled). This upward aspiration is the *anagoge* of the human condition, the "leading up" of human fallibility. If an excess of human instability can and immemorially does lead downward to a stability seated in an excess of stability, as in the passions for inanimate stone, a like excess of instability can and immemorially does lead to a counterpassion for stability at the apex of the intensification of the animate. That apex marks the exacerbation of the imperative and is the very *anagoge* of the contest between what we are and what we ought to be. *That* we are and *that* we ought to be otherwise we know well enough. *What* we are and *what* we ought to be, if human history offers any clue, is known by contrast. Our very ordinariness—whether of baseness or nobility—is situated by contrast. Every human culture has its heroes, heroines, sages, saints, those exemplars of the *anagoge* of the human condition, those who at once position us in baseness and lure us toward nobility. The ordinary Greek warrior does not know the baseness of his ordinariness until, after the battle, the poet at the symposial banquet sings the nobility of the victor king into realization as hero. Each such *exemplatum* of humankind is not so much an archetype as it is a breakthrough, a new excess of the imperative. Such is the nobility of the hero or sage as to be characterized by no single metaphor—a giant tree at the center of the human condition, a sun whereby there is human day, a moon in cosmic darkness, their stone images bedecked in luminous precious stones, themselves the residuae of eternity in time. The saints are eternity's insomniacs in time. They arouse in us not only a sense of what we fallible ones are fallen from but vertigo before what we fall short of.

Aspiring to the upward limits of the imperative, this soaring from the contrarieties of human existence is a kind of natural grace. With the expanding knowledge of both animate and inanimate nature that the modern sciences have brought, we are less confident than earlier ages about breaks in the *scala perfectionis*—less sure where the animate bottoms and where it peaks. We know only that in us self-contestation marks our days and nights, and that both downward and upward aspirations are not to be explained exhaustively and without remainder by vestigial instinct. What would we not give to know whether dolphins and porpoises have heroes and heroines, sages and saints—and, above all, angels? We know that *we* have them; they are a human fact about human reality in all cultures and times, however embellished by traditions of a cumulative mythical imagination.

It is no accident that in the Middle Ages the anagogical crowned all other maneuvers of hermeneutics; the anagogical held superiority over both the literal and the allegorical senses for construing the human person. The apex of upward aspiration was not the saint—whether in Christianity, Islam, or Judaism—but rather was angels. Angels—unlike the saints and other holy ones who sought to transcend human fallibility but in the end could not—angels, in an absolute ascesis of existential contestation, were pure essences, the triumph of the stability of the imperative realized.[5] As such, angels have lost all individuation, are pure essences faced toward eternal creation, and, as such, even though they are in consequence not human, they are "guardian angels" of aspiring human souls in time. To be sure, angels were thought to be visible as such only in the power of what medievals called a supernatural grace. To the natural eye they were but stars, bodies in the heavens reflecting here dimly and there brightly the light of eternity in the darkness of time's night.

I have said that upward aspiration for us, in our much qualified *scala perfectionis*, and thus even without the apex of angels, is a kind of natural grace. As such it is not a straight line of ascent but a kind of undulation drawn by the combined force of yearning and an embodiment that is beyond our achievement hitherto, and probably ever. Upward aspiration is proleptic relief from the paroxysms of a temporally habituated individuation. We are solicited by and invited into a life not yet our own, but not absolutely discontinuous with it either, else we could not feel our baseness in relation to it. In the life of the other person, not yet our ownmost, in the higher plane—historical and mythical—we see the antinomies of our own existence subdued in that growing triumph of the imperative in a stability beyond our grasp but aspiringly within reach. Not quite the Sublime, it limns the Sublime, is the human saintly simulacrum of the Sublime.

If the saint, hero, or sage is incapable of the perduring rapture of ascending stability—whether of moral achievement or "enlightenment"—that is because she is not free of the rupture and displacement of *negation* and *negativity*. The more we penetrate the *mythos* and gain access to the biography of the saint or heroine, the more we know this to be the case. Negation dogs the heels of ascent because the rise is by reason of ascesis. In the saint we can peer but fleetingly into a negation that has lost its sting, that has lost its stench of irreparable loss. What every saint/hero discovers about himself—as we do in our own aspiration—is that he is faulted or flawed. That contestation and negation remain in the saintly exemplar and in our aspiration toward his kind of being signals that the abyss of human being is never left far behind. We cannot imagine a stone qua stone hanging over an abyss in respect of its being stone at all, which is perhaps why we envy it. So we are back to two primordial counteraspirations. Religions always and everywhere may be read as efforts to make sense of these counteraspirations: indigenous or "oral" religions with their stones and totem animals; Catholic and Orthodox Christianity with their saints and icons; Greek religion with its cultic heroes and heroines; Protestant Christianity, Judaism and Islam with their unremitting iconoclasms, the collision of two aspirations in a raid on all idolatries.

Let us recapitulate our course. Fallibility is the structure of the possible mode of human being, both becoming and unbecoming, a structure faulted. It belongs to the made character of her becoming and unbecoming that she is to make (of herself) something better, truer, more beautiful. Her being/becoming/unbecoming is unfinished. Fault is incorrigibly there, as is what lies to either side, a state of affairs and a not-yet state of affairs that obliges as lure or summons. We have considered immemorial aspirations to either side. But we are still in the realm of ontological-meontological possibility. How is faulted humankind actualized? To take up this question is to move to the other side of the slash, fault/fall, from fault to fall. In doing so, it will be useful to call up what has often been taken to be a surrogate for *possibility* (but really is not), namely, *potentiality*. Many things are possible, but not all things possible are potential since for a possible thing to be actual requires *potency*. Straightforwardly, no possibility can be actualized without power (*dynamis, energeia*). Fault in humankind pertains to power, but not in strict analogy with fault in the geological sense. In a geological fault line, the line will distribute and displace power, but the power itself resides in the shifting subterranean plates. It is of course an old metaphysical argument about where power vests in the becoming of all that is. For Plato the power to actualize what becomes is not limit (*peras*, the forms), not the unlimited (*apeiron*), not even their mixture, but rather is (in very different senses) the Soul and the Good. The remnant of Platonism that survives in Christian Neoplatonism is the vesting of power in the soul but, in the case of the human soul, ambiguously, and that by reason of the human soul's partition from the All-Soul (*demiurgos*): so that, in my terms, the human soul is a faulted actualizing power. In any case, from faulted possibility to fallen actuality, this is the trajectory now of our attention.

Fall. Fault and fall are not the same although they have the same range of reference and are related as possibility is to actualization. All metaphors have their faults, especially the metaphor *fault* in the geological sense. As I just now suggested, the power of an actual earthquake (as just occurred, as I write, in Haiti!) is wholly internal to its possibility. In the natural course of things, no externality has power over the actualization of an earthquake: one plate can only go over or under the other, and power is distributed to both sides (and thus to the surface of the earth above). But in the human person it is otherwise. If by reason of structural fault we are one-in-two, it is by reason of *will* that we are two-in-one, although will itself, by reason of its fall, *is a one-in-two*. The person's will is the power of relating her determinate possibilities as act, as "this or that," as actual concrete life. This will, the unitary *dynamis* of actualization, is, however, ambivalent. The very act of willing engages a doubleness, a trace of the two in the one: I cannot ask "will I?" without asking "nill I?"

To search for the root of "the fall" is like seeking the origin of bursting unaccountably into tears, is like seeking the taproot of a branching, deliquescent insomnia. The organon of fall, the will, is no structure, nor is it a component of structure, and so does not function as form, essence, or matter in human reality. Fault as sketched above can at best tell us only about the structural complication of human reality, of "human nature" in its extensive range. But extensive human nature is not intensive human narrative or biography. Human history is about events, largely events in which persons have been complicit, persons differentiated by their wills as the actualization of the *principium individuationis*. Fault is no one's history, is no one's intensive earthquake existence, but rather is one's determinate structural possibility. Fall is and cannot be a structure, hence is not embedded in creation. Fall's compossibility is indeed potentiated in the structure of fault—which is embedded in creation. We may say that fault belongs to *creatio ab origine*, fall to *creatio continua*, in which latter the human creature is complicit.

If some minimal theology has entered these remarks, that is not by accident. As Hannah Arendt has written in her magisterial *The Life of the Mind*, "the faculty of the Will was unknown to Greek antiquity," although *some* variant of the Fall was—which she does not say.[6] Not until the first century of the Common Era was the force field of the will and its freedom "discovered," immediately in Christianity—although derivatively from the Hebraic emphasis upon the will of God. Thus began the philosophically frenzied effort to "save the appearances" of both willing and thinking, of the *volo* and the *cogito*. Which shall be accommodated to which, Athens to Jerusalem (thinking to will) or Jerusalem to Athens (willing to think)? Does will infect thought, or thought will? Or are they parallel, noninteracting tracks in the doubleness of the human reality? Above all, how does the force field of human will overlay the ontological schemas of classical antiquity, wherein power of actualization was distributed ambiguously between Soul and the Good (so Plato), or less ambiguously and more directly in Greek religion to fate (*ananke*, *moira*)? Freedom, once "discovered," is the most intoxicating of ideas. And we should not forget that this discovery largely coincided with its Christian (and derivatively Judaic) explanatory framework: that of the *creatio ex nihilo*. According to this explanatory account, indeterminate Godhead is rendered determinate God the Creator, calling forth from *nothing* the determinate human creature who, as image of God, preserves a residuum of indeterminacy over which she is to preside (of course, within conditions themselves determinate—those of "fault").

Although he had heirs in this respect, it was arguably only Paul the Apostle on the early Christian side of the conjunction who was willing to think the *volo* apart from the Greek *cogito*. In the burst of freedom and its organon, with their concentration upon the inner human life, most of the Fathers established themselves in the conjunction of their interest in classical philosophy. Their interest was less in freedom as a postulate of ethics or any convention of laws, as modern moralists would have it, more in free volition (as Bergson put it) as an "immediate datum of consciousness." As such, acts of willing seem free of *necessity*, the darling of so much Greek and Roman thought, much more free than thinking, which, properly executed, is subject to such necessities as that of noncontradiction. Our awareness of freedom is made acute by the recognition that of the possible things we could have done, we could have left undone what we actually did. This is the blessing of a free will and at the same time the curse of thought reflecting on a life convoluted by actual choices that have come to count. The curse of the blessing is evident in Paul's lament—"that which I would I do not, and that which I would not, that I do" (Romans 7:19)—the scrambling of will in its exercise of freedom. Every exercise of will in the actualization of possibility, for which the human subject is responsible, restricts her range of possibilities for subsequent actualization. We see the stark difference between Greek necessity and responsible free will in Clytemnestra and Lady Macbeth. Both are complicit in the death of their husbands, but Clytemnestra is calm and remorseless, fate having run its course, whereas for Lady Macbeth not all the perfumes of Araby can remove the stench of blood from her hands.

The very organon of freedom, the will, not free and not free by its own exercise—can it be that the very power by which we actualize the possibilities of humankind serves to depotentiate, or repotentiate, the range of those possibilities? Does the very exercise of its freedom render the will less free, or more precisely, differently free? It is the exploration of such questions that is like seeking the unaccountable origin of bursting into tears, of a tearing insomnia. Our tears and our insomnia must have something to do with us and our doing, else why is it that it is we who weep and are sleepless?

In pursuit of such questions *the* thinker of the will *ne plus ultra* at the conjunction of Christian and classical motifs was Augustine of Hippo.[7] The Augustine to whom I refer is not the later, older Augustine of what could be called doctrinal closures, but rather the Augustine still recently converted from the cult of the Manichees to a profound blend of Neoplatonism and Christianity, one still dumbfounded by what he had become: I mean the Augustine of the *Confessions*. The *Confessions* were and are a project of *acknowledgment*. What Augustine wanted to know above all else was why and how he had become to himself a wasteland, to know his own complicity in wastrelness.[8] Through acknowledgment he would own up to his ownmost. In this he continues the old Socratic insight: acknowledging that I don't know is essential to knowing. "I know that I don't know" was no less a stunning recognition for Augustine than for Socrates. The affirmed knowing must have a different standing than that of the negative. For Augustine the affirmed knowing ("I know") vests not in a dim recollection of a mythological preexistent state in which the Forms were directly apprehended but in the presence of One by whom one is known. He is persuaded he can make no progress out of the "I do not know"—that is, come to know what he does not know, namely, himself—until he, the subject of the affirmed "I know," is himself known, until he knows himself as known, for the precise reason that his not-knowing infects all his knowing. This says that his knowing/not-knowing throughout his life hitherto was marked by self-aggrandizement; effectively his life hitherto had been a steady decrease of not-knowing in favor of a self-aggrandizing knowing. There is then in his acknowledgment a cry for a limit to self-deception, a cry to know *what* he does not know, what is ascribable only to himself. That is why his acknowledgment is made in the context of prayer, in which there is but one petition: let me know myself even as I am *known*—beyond the self-deceptions I practice upon myself, the deceptions I and my friends practice upon each other. A certain self-sacrifice of self-aggrandizing willfulness is necessary if the actualizations of will are to be recognized and reckoned with. One cannot come to one's ownmost without owning up to manipulations that cover up one's ownmost, the (at last) known knower.

Beyond these considerations, one may note without expansion two other presuppositions of Augustine's acknowledgments that signal his divergence from the classical tradition with which he is otherwise so congruent. First, he rejects out of hand what had previously held him in thrall in his addiction to the Manichees, the explanation of his wastrel existence that located the source of aberrant will in a cosmic source outside himself, and thus with *fate*. Second were his revolutionary meditations on *time* in the *Confessions*. For Augustine time is no longer the handmaiden of fate with its recurrences but rather is the arena of human freedom and its abuse. The past, what happened, is no longer cumulative fate, the unredeemable burden on my back. The past, *my* past, cannot be reversed or altered, that is true. It is a "made" not to be unmade, but it was a made in which my making was complicit. It is finished, but it is also crucially unfinished because I am not finished with it. To that extent, the past is unfinished, because I am unfinished. The past has a certain openness, that of what I am to make of it, what I am to make of the making I made. My past is not finished until every potentiality established in it is exhausted in one actualization of another, toward which actualization my own freedom is not free of claim. That says, among other things, that time is redeemable, and that the redeemability of time engages activated memory, which he understands to be "time present of things past."

While these presuppositions attend his meditative mediations, they are not immediately (in the *Confessions*) propaedeutic to a full-blown theory of human nature. In his *Confessions* Augustine is concerned with his intensive story. A certain incident in his adolescence, his complicity with boyhood chums in the theft of some pears, nags his memory, is something with which he is not finished. It remains there in his personal mass like a grain of sand in an oyster shell, an irritant attracting layer on layer of subtle accretion. If one could reverse the process of genesis, get back to the aboriginal irritant, one would have come upon a pearl of great price. At one level, the incident hardly warrants adult reflection. "But are you [the incident] anything at all, so that I could analyze the case with you?" (*Confessions*, trans. Outler, 2.6.12). After all, "boys will be boys," and who did not attest his adolescence by pranks and mischief? It's all a part of growing up, even if in adulthood such incidents are to be outgrown. But there's the hitch, the rub. In the pear-theft incident Augustine sees something not so much outgrown as ingrown, a disposition that was not born in this incident but riveted itself to his consciousness. The event of the theft of pears seems to be paradigmatic of the very eventfulness of his life.

So Augustine thinks that his will has delivered him into a wasteland, and he goes in quest of that first willing, which set him on the course he has taken. He has by now eschewed every source of actualizing power outside himself, and that because he senses himself altogether responsible for that course. But he is unable to recover any incident, including the pear theft, embodying his will as the first efficient cause of wastrelness. At the farthest tether of memory each incident seemed already to display a tendency to confirm a disposition in him. He saw that a profligate wastrelness invited incidents of a certain sort, which only served to establish him more and more in a wasteland, so that while he could not find in himself a wastrel *nature*, his incidental wastrel life was never without decisional *nurture*. Of the paradigmatic event itself Augustine asks: Why did I do it, since I could have left it undone? Surely there must be a reason I did it? Was it premeditated, something I had long planned? No. Was I hungry? No. Was I poor and in life-threatening need? No. Did I do it because I was swept up in a crowd-frenzy? Yes and No. I could have said: you guys go ahead if you wanna, but I'm not gonna, and the truth is I wanted to and derived a certain pleasure from doing the deed. The only reason Augustine could give himself was that he *could* do it and *wanted* to. But thinking Augustine knows that just because one *can* do something and *wants* to do it is neither a necessary nor a sufficient reason for doing it. One cannot deny, at least Augustine could not, that there is exhilaration in "taking liberties," in doing "just what I want." But all taking of liberties merely in the service of what I want is at the cost of freedom. It is not that taking liberties because I want to makes me less free and responsible, but such "taking" cumulatively restricts the subsequent range of possibilities over which my will may freely preside. Ask any drug or alcohol addict. Ask yourself. Ask a student: so you don't want to study, and blow it off, and blow it off, and pretty soon what you wanted to do didn't get you where you wanted to be. What, who, will deliver me from what I *want*? Taking leave of Augustine, we may say that at bottom we have come upon the residuum of indeterminacy in all desire or want, venting itself in "taking liberties," an exercise of will without regard to determinate possibility, an exercise that ironically serves only to render possibility ever more determinate.

If the remarks on Augustine help us understand the will as one-in-two, it remains to unpack a claim made at the beginning of this section on "fall," that the will is at the same time a two-in-one by reason of being ambivalent. In exegeting this ambivalence I shall adopt Hannah Arendt's felicitous phrase, the phenomenon of the "counter will" that accompanies every arousal of will itself.[9] I suspect all are tempted to think any one of us could have fashioned a more perfect creature than we in fact are, a person fully coincident with him- or herself. But could we, as we are, be such a person? Rather, could we design a fully coincident person whose actualizing power was *voluntary*? Augustine noted a curious thing about the will: I will to raise my arm, and (in a healthy body) my arm rises. But let the will address a command to itself, or receive a command, and something quite different happens: the emergence of a "counter will." The earliest developmental commands of our parents were arousals of the will. We were asked voluntarily to do or not to do. Whether the command was "you shall" or "you shall not," either sets up through the arousal of will its counter, its possible negation. To either I respond out of aroused will—will I? nill I?—and do so, as we say, willy-nilly. If in our earliest development there was a preponderance of "you shall nots," that owes perhaps to laying a logic of thinking upon what may loosely be called a logic of willing. As many a logician has pointed out, the affirmative can yield only itself whereas the negative can yield itself and the affirmative, the negation of negation being affirmative.[10] Everyone knows more or less that the Hebrew scriptures are suffused with "you shall not," and that the first command to the first persons in the Genesis myth was "you shall not eat of the fruit," the very condition of the arousal of the will, just as the Christian gospels are suffused with "you have heard it said that you shall not, but I say you shall. . . ." Either command, in the logic of the will, whether *to* the will or *by* the will, will arouse its counter. It is the very character of its willing that the will inhabits the *metaxu*, that it "falls" between Will I? and Nill I?, between counter wills, although every actualization must be one or the other. As such, ambivalent will is not in human nature as fault is, but it is my "second nature," freely nurtured for good or ill in a decisional intensive history or narrative.

There is yet another *metaxu* of the will to comment on. As a stand-alone word, *fall* carries with it the connotation of gravity, and indeed we might say that "the fall" is the specific gravity of *fault*. In the sense of weighted descent, *fall* was a favored word of pre-Christian Neoplatonists to characterize all partitive, privative existents, everything that has fallen away from the One and thus is manifold, everything that is a two without a one. In our ordinary usage, the meaning of *fall* is largely controlled by qualifying prepositions and adverbs. Fall in—in love is one thing, in rank is another. Fall out—a disagreement, or out of rank. It fell out—it happened. The fallout—the consequence of what happened. To fall for—to be infatuated, to be deceived, to be suckered. Taking the fall for—sacrificing oneself for—and so on; one's voice "falls away. . . ."

Prior to the will's taking of center stage in the human person, *fall* was all but exclusively "fall from." Virtually every human culture has had its paradise, its dreamtime of the race, an actualization in a time not our time, from which every actualization in our time is a declension. With the emergence in western consciousness of linear purposeful time, directly connected with the centrality of will in the person, there arose in addition to the primordial dream-time that of the eschatological end-time, in religion assuming various forms of messianism, in such secular equivalents as Kant's Kingdom of Ends, Hegel's temporalizations of Absolute Spirit, and Marx's classless utopia, to mention but a few. The self's willing and counterwilling is situated in the space-time between a mythical actualization lost, or fallen from, and a mythical actualization not gained, fallen toward but fallen short of. This *metaxu* is the trace or second nature of that *metaxu* remarked earlier in connection with fault, between downward and upward aspiration.

I close this section with a near-at-home (perhaps even homely) example concerning scholars and their Work of scholarship and thinking. To use some language from two contemporary French indwellers of sundry wondrous metaxies, Edmond Jabès and Maurice Blanchot, each of us is engaged in a lifework that depends for episodic and temporary closure upon the Book each is writing. But the Work and the Book never quite coincide. Willy-nilly, neither is an adequate carrier for the other. On the one hand, there is the lost Book, the Book that is the closure of the Work. Jabès, in *Livre des questions*, is preeminently the thinker of the lost Book, the Book in which my name is anonymously inscribed, to read which would coincide with my writing of the Book. This is not a matter of age, not a sentiment of the aged. Who has not felt when he has crafted the sentence that justifies a life that he has read it from a constituted text? Could he but find all the other lost sentences that go with it! He is a lucky one who gets a paragraph from the lost Book. The result of our Work at thinking and studying is at best a sighting now and then of the palimpsest text of the lost Book, to which we add our erasures and deformations. What we publish is yet another palimpsest, a further distancing, a further falling away from the Book.

On the other hand and at the same time, the Work is not alone nostalgia for the Book lost in a time not my time, but expenditure toward the Book not present because not now or ever written. You may think, you who are just starting out, that the palpitations of the "not yet" or that of the "falling short" beat more rapidly in the young than in the old; you have only to wait to be disabused. We start and end as much in falling toward and falling short as we do in falling from. In terms of William James's famous distinction, one is between the written but lost and unfound Book of the "sick-souled" and the unfound because unwritten Book of the "healthy-minded."[11] Given the optimism that has marked post-Enlightenment modernity, and the hold of time-consciousness upon late modernity and postmodernity, it is remarkable that so few have made good on the option of "healthy-mindedness," whether in philosophy or the arts.

Who gives herself over to "the agony of composition" without even the faintest guide from the lost Book will find her willing and counterwilling so overdetermined by desire that the Book fallen short of is dirempted by the Work: witness the consummate Work of Nietzsche, whose unwritten Book was released into the final troubled rest of clinical madness.

Such a one cries out with Franz Rosenzweig: "I wish I were a symphony in Beethoven or something else that has been completely written."[12] But neither would I file grievance against faulted human nature extensively, nor against its fallen "second nature" intensively, but would rather, as here, look at both as steadily as I can. Steadily, but not unflinchingly, for they look back—and I am the one who blinks.

Notes

1. For more on the modern philosophical background of the present thought-experiment, see Appendix A: What Did the Cartesian Cogito Establish as a Starting Point for Thinking the Human Being Who Thinks God?
2. Whether Buddhist emptiness (*sunyata*) and western nothingness are the same, or akin, is much mooted and bruited in the Kyoto School of Zen Buddhism (D. T. Suzuki, Keiji Nishitani). The western Eckhart scholar Reiner Schürmann has been active in this discussion; see his *Wandering Joy: Meister Eckhart's Mystical Philosophy* (Great Barrington, MA: Lindisfarne, 2011).
3. Plato himself was a pluralist, although not in the manner of Aristotle or his medieval and modern heirs; he clearly was not a monist, and became so only through the "Platonists"—who were really Neoplatonists—and (more egregiously) through the nineteenth-century German idealists. That Plato could and did source such radically different metaphysical alternatives accounts in part for the way Platonism early on fed into so much Christian reflection on God's creation of the world.
4. Was Böhme the last of the medieval hermeticists? The first theologian to accept the new Renaissance sciences, especially the new astronomy? The first radical Reformer? He was all of the above.
5. Unless, of course, zeitgeist is some ungainsayable temporal articulation of Absolute Spirit—a reading of Hegel (or Hegelianism) I find wrongheaded if not simpleminded.
6. How one wishes that W. H. Auden were incontestably right: "That love, or truth in any serious sense, / Like orthodoxy, is a reticence" (from "The Truest Poetry Is the Most Feigning," in *The Shield of Achilles* [New York: Random House, 1955], 46).

Lovers and truth-seekers *are* both emboldened and made reticent by their respective quarries; but the history of all orthodoxies, I fear, is the history of the diminution of thoughtful reticence, the reserve of thinking.

7. For this language about gift exchange and the subtle elaboration of it, both anthropologically and theologically, I am indebted to John Milbank, "Can a Gift Be Given? Prolegomena to a Future Trinitarian Metaphysics," *Modern Theology* 11, no. 1 (January 1995): 119–61. One appropriately responds to a gift with a gift; giving is intrinsically gift exchange (without the obligations of "contract"). But the return gift involves *delay* (the "prophetic" element in gift exchange): the giftee must assess what the gift says about the giver's "perception" of the giftee. And it involves "the non-identity of repetition"; one does not give back the same or identical gift, not because of the social gaucherie of doing so, but because the return gift embodies the difference the original gift has made in the giftee's "perception" of its giver. (Could we not, although Milbank does not, call the nonidentity of repetition the "wisdom" element in gift exchange, the element of indeterminacy?) Highly pertinent here is Elliot R. Wolfson, *Giving Beyond the Gift: Apophasis and Overcoming Theomania* (New York: Fordham University Press, 2014).

8. Wallace Stevens, "The Blue Guitar," in *The Collected Poems of Wallace Stevens* (New York: Knopf, 1964), 165.

9. Stevens, "The Snow Man," in *The Collected Poems*, 10.

INTRODUCTION: PRE-FACING THE DIVINE

1. Augustine, *Against the Academicians and The Teacher*, trans. Peter King (Indianapolis: Hackett, 1995).

2. Merleau-Ponty, *Signs*, trans. Richard C. McCleary (Evanston, IL: Northwestern University Press, 1964), 91.

3. Pseudo-Dionysius the Areopagite, *Mystical Theology*, 1001a, in *Pseudo-Dionysius: The Complete Works*, trans. Colm Luibheid (New York: Paulist, 1987), 137.

4. I use *fell* in the old Scots, Norse, Old High German, Middle English sense of the word: the high-country nesting upland moors, the upland country of both fascination and daunting dread (Rudolf Otto!).

5. Hegel, preface to *The Phenomenology of Spirit*, trans. A. V. Miller (Oxford: Oxford University Press, 1977), 18–19; compare also the translation in progress by Terry Pinkard, https://dl.dropboxusercontent.com/u/21288399 /Phenomonology%20translation%20English%20German.pdf.

6. While I do not remember learning to walk in infancy, I well remember learning to walk the second time. In the wake of an awful (and aweful) automobile accident now thirty years ago I was left unable to walk. In that state nothing was more astonishing (and indeed inspiring) than the ordinary, especially that of seeing people walk without effort. And nothing was more difficult in recovery than learning to walk again, this time altogether thinkingly

through a severely qualified body. I have no doubt that the reflections of these pages are sourced significantly in that experience of mindful body, and particularly since thinking that matters takes root in a wound (cf. Edmond Jabès). The reader will come to many references to the two nots in these pages: walking out of and from the first not was unconscious and largely physiological, but walking into and toward the second not is perforce mindful.

7. I have written extensively of the hermeneutical spiral in *Unfinished Man and the Imagination*, 60–68 and passim; see also the postscript to this book, "Afterthinking Theology as Hermeneutics."

8. Bachelard, though of peasant stock, was sophisticated in the modern sciences and philosophy and did his generative work living as a solitary in the remote French village Bar-sur-Aube, of which he was erstwhile postmaster. When his thinking attracted high notice he was elected to the Collège de France, but he never found La Sorbonne conducive to thinking; he left the academy as soon as he could, he said, so he could think.

9. Hannah Arendt, "Martin Heidegger at Eighty," *New York Review of Books* 17, no. 6 (October 21, 1971): 4. This is not the place to locate Heidegger's oeuvre in these pre-facings of thinking the divine. I can permit myself only a few remarks. In her review of her teacher's life and works Arendt attempts to explain one fact, that early on Heidegger attracted hordes of students simply because of rumors reaching them in the dark days following World War I that there was a philosopher at Freiburg who was attending not to the results of other philosophers (this was well before the publication of *Being and Time*) but rather to thinking itself and its matter. They knew him to be Husserl's most promising student, and carrying on Husserl's injunction "To the things themselves." But Heidegger carried on not in Husserl's way, namely, to establish philosophy as a rigorous science and thus to establish philosophy among the other rigorous academic disciplines. For Heidegger philosophy is not a science among sciences but is the discipline of thinking itself, above all thinking's subject matter. In this Heidegger was rebellious and was joined by but a few (Max Scheler and Karl Jaspers, for example), those who could and did distinguish between an object of scholarship and a matter of thought. It is no doubt unfortunate that this orientation was not self-evident in Heidegger's earlier published works. Only in his old age did he give a seminar on a text of his own, *On the Matter of Thinking* (*Zur Sache des Denkens* [Tübingen: Niemeyer, 1969]), which was a protocol for his *Being and Time*.

10. Parmenides as translated in Edward Zeller, *Outlines of the History of Greek Philosophy*, trans. Frances Alleyne and Evelyn Abbott (London: Longmans, Green, 1886), 61; see also Kathleen Freeman, ed. and trans., *Ancilla to the Pre-Socratic Philosophers: A Complete Translation of the Fragments in Diels, "Fragmente der Vorsokratiker"* (Cambridge: Harvard University Press, 1948), 41. Plotinus, *The Enneads*, trans. Stephen McKenna (Harmondsworth: Penguin, 1991).

11. Rudolf Otto, *The Idea of the Holy: An Inquiry into the Non-Rational Factor in the Idea of the Divine and Its Relation to the Rational*, trans. John W. Harvey (London: Oxford University Press, 1950). The English translation of the book's title is unfortunate since Otto's claim is that "idea" cannot comprehend the *what* of the divine. The German title is simply *Das Heilige* (the holy).

12. See particularly Rudolf Otto, *Mysticism East and West*, trans. Bertha L. Bracey and Richenda C. Payne (New York: Macmillan, 1932).

13. See Norman O. Brown, *Love's Body* (New York: Vintage, 1966).

14. Words borrowed from the French writer Antoine de Saint-Exupéry as a favorite mantra by John L. Hennessy, president of Stanford University, who did early pioneering research into RISC (reduced instruction set computing) processors as an alternative to the then more common CISC (complex instruction set computing) processors. His intention was the irreducible "simple" in instruction set theory for artificial intelligence, to do (one may suggest) for computer set instruction the equivalent of what medieval classical theology had done with the transcendentals as properties of God: to think the divine simplicity. Other epigraph sources: Heraclitus, *Fragments: The Collected Wisdom of Heraclitus*, trans. Brooks Haxton (New York: Viking, 2001), 7. Robert Musil, *The Man without Qualities*, trans. Sophie Wilkins and Burton Pike (New York: Vintage, 1996), 1:425. W. H. Auden, "September 1, 1939," a poem he wrote at the beginning of World War II in his quest for "an affirming flame," in *Another Time* (New York: Random House, 1940), 98. Leonard Cohen, "Anthem," on his album *The Future*, released in 1992. Kierkegaard, *Concluding Unscientific Postscript*, trans. David F. Swenson and Walter Lowrie (Princeton, NJ: Princeton University Press, 1944), 228. Eckhart, *Meister Eckhart: The Essential Sermons, Commentaries, Treatises, and Defense*, trans. Edmund Colledge and Bernard McGinn (New York: Paulist, 1981), 292.

15. Drawing on Paul Weiss and others, I have written of this inverse relation in *Unfinished Man and the Imagination*, 63–65.

16. Jason M. Wirth, foreword to F. W. J. Schelling, *Historical-Critical Introduction to the Philosophy of Mythology* (Albany: State University of New York Press, 2007). I am pleased to acknowledge my great debt to Wirth for his translations and commentaries, and especially for his capacious and sensitive work *The Conspiracy of Life: Meditations on Schelling and His Time* (Albany: State University of New York Press, 2003).

17. Heidegger, *Schellings Abhandlung über das Wesen der menschlichen Freiheit (1809)* (Tübingen: Max Niemeyer, 1971), 9; *Schelling's Treatise on the Essence of Human Freedom*, trans. Joan Stambaugh (Athens: Ohio University Press, 1985), 11. Cited by Jason Wirth in his foreword to Schelling's *Historical-Critical Introduction to the Philosophy of Mythology*, ix–xii.

18. Manfred Schroeter, ed., *Schellings Werke: Nach der Originalausgabe in neuer Anordnung* (Berlin: Beck'sche, 1927–1959 and 1962–1971), 1/7, 406.

19. Henry David Thoreau, *A Week on the Concord and Merrimack Rivers* (Boston: Osgood, 1873), 236.

20. It serves little purpose to list those philosophers who join in this acknowledgment, but the number is not inconsiderable. I may mention, among
philosophers before the Common Era, Plato, who accorded to priests of the
cult, poets both tragic and comic, and all "announcers of the gods" their
independence, and especially Plato because he coined the very word *theology*
to comprise the philosophical-critical evaluation of such independently
derived announcements and namings (see the postscript, "Afterthinking
Theology as Hermeneutics," for elaboration). As for a near-contemporary
twentieth-century philosopher, in respect specifically of Christianity,
Merleau-Ponty: "The Christianity that persists among us is not a philosophy; it is an account of and a meditation upon an experience of enigmatic
events which themselves call for several philosophical elaborations and have
not in fact stopped arousing philosophies, even when one of these has been
accorded a privileged position. Christian themes are ferments, not relics"
(Merleau-Ponty, *Signs*, 134).

21. Schleiermacher, *Über die Religion: Reden an die Gebildeten unter ihren Verächtern*
(1799), translated as *On Religion: Speeches to Its Cultured Despisers*, trans. and
ed. Richard Crouter (Cambridge: Cambridge University Press, 1988).

22. Mentioned in Rev. Dr. John A. McGuckin, "On The Mystical Theology of the
Eastern Church." Podcast and transcript posted February 5, 2014, http://www
.ancientfaith.com/podcasts/svsvoices/on_the_mystical_theology_of_the
_eastern_church#20045.

23. Proposition 7, the final sentence of Wittgenstein's *Tractatus Logico-
Philosophicus,* trans. D. F. Pears and B. F. McGinness (London: Routledge and
Kegan Paul, 1981), 189.

24. See Frank D. Macchia, "Sighs Too Deep for Words: Towards a Theology of
Glossolalia," *Journal of Pentecostal Theology* 1 (1992): 47–73. I am grateful to
Amos Yong for drawing my attention to this literature.

25. A thinking deracination of ordinariness is essential to thinking, and this is
sometimes best accomplished by a penetration of ordinariness itself—the supreme accomplishment of the parables of Jesus, and Kafka, and Borges—the
very astonishment of the ordinary, and here I interject a homely interlude:
this point can perhaps be understood by making (or participating in the
origin of) bread. When you make bread, though you know all the ingredients
independently (flour, water, leaven), you see how the origins of things advertise their essential mysteries without explaining them; you will not have
arrived at the foundation of bread. It does not suffice to know the properties
of yeast. Once you have made a loaf of bread from scratch, you can never
view bread again as merely a product. You saw everything that went into the
bread, except what made the difference—between this loaf and the previous.
Use the same ingredients again in the same measure and you get a bread
advertising its determinacy: the range of indeterminacy over which bread
presides differently determined in each occasion. Who eats the "same" bread
every day has no hand in making it, in participating its origins, has no taste

for either the same or the different. Some small part of the enigma of life is in the breadbox of our own filling.

26. William Desmond, "Being, Determination and Dialectic: On the Sources of Metaphysical Thinking," his 1995 presidential address to the Metaphysical Society of America, published in *Review of Metaphysics* 48, no. 4 (June 1995): 731–69, quote on 743.

27. Note 2 above; Merleau-Ponty, *Signs*, 91.

28. Is there a cross-species language? Many traditional, and typically nonliterate, religions think so, notably Native American religions, as in the vision quest for one's totem animal who bears specific messages from Wakan Tanka. The principal secular residuum of this conviction is evident in the unabated passion among persons for domesticated animals: one is understood by one's dog, cat, or horse better than by other humans. They understand our words (*parole*), but do they understand the *langue* in which our words are embedded? No doubt in part out of sheer human conceit, the communication is one-way: pets are disciplined to understand us, not us them. Probably there is a large literature in which linguists address the deep structures of cross-species language of which I am ignorant, as there is also probably a science-fiction literature that assumes the breaking of such a code, thus replete with multidirectional communication throughout the spirited (animal) realm, thus replicating the animal tales in the traditional religions that are as old as language itself.

29. One should remember the etymological meaning of the Hebrew-Assyrian-Babylonian place name Babel: the Gate of God. The Gate of God is closed to language? Or, the tower constructed with determinate language cannot reach that Gate?

30. In *this* exercise of language, the reader may recognize an adoption and adaptation of some language from Henry David Thoreau's *Walden*. See *"Walden" and Other Writings of Henry David Thoreau*, ed. Brooks Atkinson (New York: Modern Library, 1937), 289.

31. For an expanded treatment of the inverse relation between extension and intension, see my *Unfinished Man and the Imagination*, 63–65.

32. Of course to speak of "modalities" of nothingness is in itself already to risk nonsense, since that only can be modalized which is susceptible of discrimination, and the discriminable must be *something* of which the discriminated are parts. So, do I take this medicine? I do, as will be apparent below in the discussion of Wittgenstein. In respect of the nothingness bearing upon the human person, I discriminate between a first and a second nothingness and do so within a custom that governs reference, wherein both the first and second not refer to human "limit situations."

33. It is surely passing strange that some see a problem in speaking of nothingness or nonbeing, and no problem—or little problem—in speaking of being. Is it not the same problematic in speaking of either?

34. Note 29 above.

35. Ray Monk, *Ludwig Wittgenstein: The Duty of Genius* (New York: Free Press, 1990).
36. Letter to Norman Malcolm, November 14, 1944, cited by Monk, *Ludwig Wittgenstein*, 475.
37. "You can't hear God speak to someone else, you can hear him only if you are being addressed.—That is a grammatical remark." Ludwig Wittgenstein, *Zettel*, ed. G. E. M. Anscome and G. H. von Wright, trans. G. E. M. Anscome (Oxford: Blackwell, 1967), 124e.
38. Monk, *Ludwig Wittgenstein*, 468.
39. Monk, *Ludwig Wittgenstein*, 468–69.
40. Wittgenstein, *Remarks on the Foundations of Mathematics*, 6:21; cited by Monk, *Ludwig Wittgenstein*, 469.
41. Hence the enormous interest in Eckhart on the part of the Kyoto School of Zen Buddhism; see Keiji Nishitani, *Religion and Nothingness*, trans. Jan Van Bragt (Berkeley: University of California Press, 1982).
42. I do not use *grammar* as the term is used in linguistics—as I think Wittgenstein did not—and certainly not in the structuralist sense. I use it to refer to the rules that govern the sense that words can and do have in a public language.

TOPOS 1—THEOGONY

1. See Karen Armstrong, *The History of God* (New York: Knopf, 1993), and Jack Miles, *God: A Biography* (New York: Knopf, 1995). Miles's brilliant work, which essays to reconstruct God solely as the literary subject of the Hebrew Bible (*Tanakh*), like every good biography whets the appetite for an equally good autobiography. But also like the good biography it arouses the suspicion that the biographer—rather the texts on which he draws—knows more about the subject than the subject could say autobiographically. That is the case especially if, as Miles proposes, God both apprehends and constitutes himself importantly in interaction with his creation.
2. Ah and aha, that tortured Romanian-Parisian soul, so lethally and aletheically attracted to and repulsed by the saints, E. M. Cioran, *Tears and Saints* (Chicago: University of Chicago Press, 1995). The sum of reasons why the autobiography of God cannot be written is that we lack evidence, evidence that would *count* toward a definitive autobiography. Even on this front, however, the saints are a partial exception. Their evidence is gleaned from *prayer*, prayer that comprises speaking to and speaking by God, a kind of knowing that consists in being known: a flight from God to God *by* God through the capacity of the human soul for double personal agency, the capacities *imago Dei* and *ad imaginem Verbi*. What philosophical theologian would now write an essay entitled "Some Metaphysical Gleanings from Prayer"? See Julian N. Hartt, "Some Metaphysical Gleanings from Prayer," *Journal of Religion* 31, no. 4 (October 1951): 254–63.

3. "Therefore, every suffering that took place in the body of that man can be ascribed to the Word of God. So it is right to say that the Word of God—just God godself—suffered, was crucified, died, and was buried." (*Ergo omnis passio quae in corpore illium homnis facta fuit, potest Verbo Dei attribui. Recte igitur dici potest quod Verbum Dei, et Deus, est passus, crucifixus, mortuus et sepultus.*) *Summa Contra Gentiles*, 4.34.3704, in *Summa Contra Gentiles*, vol. 4: *Salvation*, trans. Charles J. O'Neil (Notre Dame: University of Notre Dame Press, 1975).

4. D. G. Leahy, *Novitas Mundi* (Albany: State University of New York Press, 1994) and *Foundation: Matter the Body Itself* (Albany: State University of New York Press, 1996).

5. See Deland S. Anderson, *Hegel's Speculative Good Friday: The Death of God in Philosophical Perspective* (Atlanta, GA: Scholars Press, 1996).

6. See especially *The Self-Embodiment of God*, which some intemperate wags have proposed is Altizer's autobiography, but which I would suggest rather is so many notes toward theology's aspiration to an autobiography of God.

7. Transparently a sweeping claim that, were this an essentially historical study, which it is not, could only be substantiated by getting down to cases. And some of those cases would entail qualifications and exceptions, themselves precursors of the theological thinking underway here.

8. Metaphysics as driven by the quest for the ground of mutable beings typically settles upon the Being of beings as that ground. But what determinate sense can be accorded Being without determinate beings? Is Being as ground rendered less vacuous by being identified with God if that God is not the divine God of theophantic manifestation? See Heidegger on the ground as the essence of metaphysical thinking: metaphysics thinks beings in the manner of a representational thinking that gives grounds. See "The End of Philosophy and the Task of Thinking," in Martin Heidegger, *Basic Writings*, ed. David Farrell Krell (New York: HarperCollins, 2008), 431–49.

9. An example is the widespread construal of Nietzsche's own death of God: understand the genealogy of the ideas of God and their gradual diminution or disappearance and you will understand the death of God as sociocultural fact—nothing if not a travesty of Nietzsche! Is it any accident that *Religionswissenschaft* and its centerpiece, the history of religions, arose about the time of Nietzsche or at the time of his discovery, in the conviction that it is sufficient to know what a religion is *about* to know the evolution and devolution of its ideas?

10. The lot has been cast here with the pursuit of genealogy rather than foundations, but we forewarn ourselves about the genetic fallacy: the peril of thinking we will know what is essential to a thing by knowing its origin. Thus duly forewarned, we nonetheless misunderstand if we do not in any way *participate* origin. Many a contemporary genealogy might not have gone wrong had this aspect of participation been resolutely held to. Case in point: the genealogies of the loss or absence of the self or subject. One notices that

a self (*some* self) or subject thinkingly arrives at self-loss: surely the affirmation is not that thoughts are thinking the lost or absent self. Thinking not *participated* is not thinking, not meaningful thinking anyway. Whatever Descartes got wrong, he got that right.

11. For the development of this notion, see the postscript, "Afterthinking Theology as Hermeneutics," below, and "Problematic and the Hermeneutical Spiral," chapter 2 of my *Unfinished Man and the Imagination*, 52–69.

12. The pollsters ask, "Do you believe in God?" and why shouldn't they put the question about God in this form? For that is the way they are taught to talk by the religious establishment.

13. The matter of reference for the art object and for the work of art and the bearing of that matter in analogy with the reference of revelation is elaborated and developed in my *Unfinished Man and the Imagination*, 254–66.

14. Schelling reckons with this complex of issues in *The Ages of the World*, trans. Jason M. Wirth (Albany: State University of New York Press, 2000), in the dense section "This organism of potencies is posited 'under the form of the past': the requirement of an (eternally posited) past in God itself," 38–46.

15. Cohen, "Revelation and Law: Reflections on Martin Buber's Views on Halakhah," in *An Arthur A. Cohen Reader: Selected Fiction and Writings on Judaism, Theology, Literature, and Culture*, ed. David Stern and Paul Mendes-Flohr (Detroit: Wayne State University Press, 1998), 128. I consider the greatest modern Jewish theologian to be Franz Rosenzweig, followed by Martin Buber and Arthur Cohen.

16. Far from being a Christian invention, the very word *theology* was coined by Plato, for whom the subject matter of theology was, simply, "divine things." As he had charged philosophy above all "to save the appearances," so Plato obliged theology to save the appearances of divine things. For Plato theology was not so much an attempt to construct a theory of God (gods, divine things) as it was an effort to abut critical mentality with the independent mythical-cultic traditions in the interest of an ordered state. Theology was essential to political education, the *paideia* (formation) of leaders of the polis, so a project serving statecraft (*Republic* 2:379a). Since philosophers as such produce no appearances but "save" them by unremitting critique, so theologians produce no appearances of divine things but save them by submitting them to the mind's searchlight (by, for example, submitting them to "division" and "collection" as in *Sophist*), so that they cohere metaphysically and ethically. Plato respectfully and fully acknowledged the independence of the Greek religions known to him, and of their priests, whom he called the "announcers" of the "appearances of divine things." It took many centuries before the term was used among Christian thinkers. *Theology* and its word-group (*theologia, theologein, theologos, theologikos*) are altogether lacking in the New Testament and the apostolic fathers; in the early Christian apologists they are rare. Not until the time of the Alexandrian Christian

thinkers did the term *theology* emerge in other than the Greek senses, and then sparsely and sparely. The term was used even less frequently in Latin Christianity; indeed it gained general currency only in the high Middle Ages. Readers interested in the fortunes of *theology* and its cognates may consult an excursus on the matter in my *Unfinished Man and the Imagination*, 390–402. The best historical study known to me is Gerhard Ebeling, "Theologie: Begriffsgeschichtlich," in *Religion in Geschichte und Gegenwart*, 3rd ed. (Tübingen: J. C. B Mohr [Paul Siebeck], 1962), 6:754–70.

17. In Wirth's decision to translate *Aufhebung*—commonly translated as "sublation," as in Hegel—with "sublimation," I understand him to take sublimation as a resetting of boundaries or pointing beyond boundaries, in any case, as an adjustment of limns.

18. Any thing is mixed. Beyond or in addition to the mixed itself as a factor, there are the two factors themselves party to the mixed, namely, limit (form, *peras*) and the unlimited (the womb of becoming, *apeiron*). There is the agent or cause of the imposition of limit upon the unlimited (soul), and there is the goal or intention the mixture is to subserve (the Good). No one of these factors is reducible to another, and all are necessary to account for any mixed. Aristotle roughly tracks this Philebean schema in his fourfold account of causality: formal, material, efficient, and final.

19. I have dealt at length with concentration in the context of the human self's continuous ingredience and discontinuous ingression in *Unfinished Man and the Imagination*, 138–62.

20. Not there in *which* there? A central irony in the scriptural nature of a sacred text—and this the Bible shares with nonscriptural literary arts in respect of characters—is that through its artful defaulting of language God is there in the there of the text but not in the there of what the text is *about*. The text is a watching brief.

21. And is why *sacrifice* figures prominently in Judaism and Christianity. By the default of language I mean in part the self-sacrifice of language that refers to God iconoclastically.

22. Nowhere more compellingly than in Heidegger's four-volume commentary on, analysis of, and polemic with Nietzsche. See especially "Nihilism as Determined by the History of Being," in *Nietzsche*, vol. 4: *Nihilism*, trans. Frank A. Capuzzi, ed. David Farrell Krell (New York: Harper and Row, 1982), pt. 2, pp. 199–250.

23. These ways of stating the *nihilo est sine ratio* are owed to Krell's helpful analysis in Heidegger, *Nietzsche*, 4:253–94.

24. Hegel says the same for being: as bare concepts, in advance of dialectical interpenetration, Being and Nothing are equally indeterminate, thus vacuous.

25. *Gottesfreunden im Oberland*: a shadowy body of largely lay folk in Europe from at least the fourteenth-century beguines on, persisting on the undersides of scholastic orthodoxies whether Evangelical, Reformed, or Counter-

Reformation Catholic, an underground forum for the study of Böhme and other proscribed mystics. Not even England was exempt from its reaches (providing a forum for Wyclif, for example), as is principally evident in the literary and graphic art of William Blake.

26. With a qualification already noted: whereas Aquinas clearly construed first cause in the sense of an efficient first cause, I claim that God the Creator is not in any sense within the chain of causality, is rather the Creator of the determinate conditions under which beings stand out of and into nothing.

27. I use *cathesis* in the etymological sense: a back-formation in which great mental-emotional energy is vested.

28. Böhme is one of the most important, if least studied, of Renaissance men, notwithstanding his being a relatively unlettered shoemaker. Astonishing is the fact that, against most of his Reformed detractors, he embraced fully the new astronomy while transmogrifying the received late-medieval alchemy. Alchemy was never about technics, about getting something spendable (gold) out of something cheap (base metals). It was about worrying the extraordinary out of the ordinary. If one may put it so, medieval alchemy had done this from the bottom of the scale up; Böhme saw in the nascent modern sciences a way of moving from the top (astronomy) down. He aspired to do the same for theology, in which top and bottom would cohere.

29. May one say that this groundless indeterminate turbic *energeia* is physically traced in the nuclear inferno of the big bang, the *a quo* instant when determinate Creator God renders the indeterminacy of Godhead cosmically nondeterminate, giving rise to the fusion and fission of elemental particles and the evolving-devolving determinateness of an expanding *ad quem* universe within space-time?

30. For an account of the broken character of symbols as astute as wide-ranging, see Robert C. Neville, *The Truth of Broken Symbols* (Albany: State University of New York Press, 1996).

31. These matters are addressed in high principle and low detail in my *Unfinished Man and the Imagination* throughout. On imagination in cognitive relation to wholeness and immediacy, see 238f.; on the ontological range of imagination, see 135f. and passim. The most serious and culpable defect of this study was its neglect of the imagination in relation to nonbeing, nothingness, the want of the *me*-ontological dimensions of the human and divine reality.

32. Desmond, "Being, Determination and Dialectic," 767; Robert P. Scharlemann, *The Reason of Following: Christology and the Ecstatic I* (Chicago: University of Chicago Press, 1991).

33. Annie Dillard, *Teaching a Stone to Talk: Expeditions and Encounters* (New York: Harper and Row, 1982), 18–19.

34. The Pole of Relative Inaccessibility is that imaginary point on the Arctic Ocean farthest from land in any direction. It is a navigator's paper point contrived to console Arctic explorers who, after Peary and Henson reached

the North Pole in 1909, had nowhere special to go. There is a Pole of Relative Inaccessibility on the Antarctic continent also; it is that point of land farthest from saltwater in any direction. See Dillard, *Teaching a Stone to Talk*, 18.

35. The subject, among others, of the great twentieth-century novel by Robert Musil, *The Man without Qualities*, 2 vols., trans. Sophie Wilkins and Burton Pike (New York: Vintage, 1996).

36. Epigraph sources: Jakob Böhme, *"De electione gratiae" and "Quaestiones theosophicae"* [On the election of grace and Theosophic questions], trans. John Rolleston Earle (London: Constable, 1930), 3.20, p. 39. Gerard Manley Hopkins, "To R. B." (a poem addressed to the poet Robert Bridges), in Catherine Phillips, ed., *Gerard Manley Hopkins* (Oxford: Oxford University Press, 1986), 184; in connection with what will be said about fire and Heraclitus, the reader may also want to review Hopkins's poem "That Nature Is a Heraclitean Fire and of the Comfort of the Resurrection." Friedrich Nietzsche, *Beyond Good and Evil*, trans. Helen Zimmern (Buffalo, NY: Prometheus, 1987), 73.

37. Böhme was by no means a systematic writer or thinker. After his first text (*Aurora*), he was placed under right-wing Lutheran scholastic interdict, but he managed to have his texts printed to meet the large demand from laity in the lowland countries of northern Europe and extended to England, where they were heavily influential on William Blake, who cites Böhme directly in *The Marriage of Heaven and Hell*: "without contraries is no progression." While the major motifs of Böhme's thinking are present in each of his texts, they vary in the order in which they are developed, and he nowhere puts them together such that they cohere. The texts on which my re-presentation depends, in addition to *On the Election of Grace* and *Theosophic Questions,* are *Six Theosophic Points, Six Mystical Points, The Earthly and Heavenly Mystery,* and *The Divine Intuition*. A reader approaching Böhme for the first time could not do better than read Nicolas Berdyaev's "Unground and Freedom," his long introduction to *"Six Theosophic Points" and Other Writings* (Ann Arbor: University of Michigan Press, 1958), v–xxxvi. Berdyaev has reminded us importantly that Böhme's "is a wisdom . . . grounded in . . . myths and symbols rather than concepts—a wisdom much more contemplative than discursive. Such is religious philosophy, or theosophy" (v). One can only lament that the grand old word *theosophy* has been ruined, probably beyond repair, by its association all but exclusively (in the United States at least) with Madame Blavatsky and the trappings of New Age spirituality.

38. The "mother" of both Being and Nonbeing was figured by Böhme as Virgin Sophia, venerated as the Mother of God in eastern Orthodox Christianity, the nondeterminate Wisdom of God (the *Abgrund* of Godhead), hence Berdyaev's acute interest in Böhme. One should note, more than parenthetically, that Böhme was not the only major Christian mystic to draw heavily on the Wisdom literature of the Hebrew Bible. Meister Eckhart took as texts for many of his vernacular sermons those from the same Wisdom literature,

a literature long acknowledged by biblical scholars to reflect a more direct Greek influence than any other segment of the Hebrew Bible.

39. Heraclitus: "That which is in opposition is in concert, and from things that differ comes the most beautiful harmony" (frag. 8 in Freeman, *Ancilla to the Pre-Socratic Philosophers*, 25).

40. Böhme, *Six Mystical Points*, trans. John Rolleston Earle (New York: Knopf, 1920), 2.1–8, pp. 119–20.

41. Böhme's preface to *Six Mystical Points*, 115.

42. Böhme writes: "As the mind of man in the understanding introduces itself by the senses into a counterstroke of an exact likeness, and by sense flows forth and disposes into images, which images are the thoughts of the mind, wherein the wills of the mind works, and thus by desire brings itself into a sharpness, as into a magnetic appropriations, from which joy and sorrow arise; so also in regard to the eternal mind of perceptibility, we are to understand that the outgoing of the one will of God has, through the Word, introduced itself into separability, and the separability has introduced itself into receptibility, as into desire and craving for its self-revelation, passing out of the Unity into plurality. Desire is the ground and beginning of the nature of perceptibility of the particular will. For therein is the separability of the Unity brought into receptibility, whence the separabilities of the wills are brought into the perceptibility of a self-hood. . . . For the will of the eternal One is imperceptible, without tendency to anything; for it has nothing to which it could tend, save only towards itself. Therefore it brings itself out of itself and carries the efflux of its unity into plurality, and into the assumption of selfhood, as of a place of a Nature, from which qualities take their rise. For every quality has its own separator and maker within it, and is in itself entire, according to the quality of the eternal Unity. . . . Thereby [by fire] the eternal power becomes desireful and effectual and [fire] is the original condition of the sensitive life . . . the separator in all the powers of the emanated being a steward of Nature, by whom the eternal will rules, makes, forms and shapes all things"; *On the Divine Intuition*, in *"Six Theosophic Points" and Other Writings*, 3.7–12, pp. 192–93.

43. Hegel, preface to *The Phenomenology of Spirit*, trans. Terry Pinkard (updated October 30, 2013), 9–10, https://dl.dropboxusercontent.com/u/21288399 /Phenomonology%20translation%20English%20German.pdf.

44. On will and the emergence of Being from potency (relative nonbeing), see Schelling, *Historical-Critical Introduction to the Philosophy of Mythology*, trans. Mason Richey and Markus Zisselsberger (Albany: State University of New York Press, 2007), 233.

45. It would be interesting to speculate on, though difficult to document, which has had the greater maieutic effect eventuating in Christianity's bringing again to mind the divine Nothing on its undersides: the late-modern philosophical and artistic discourses of nihilism, or western encounters with eastern, notably Buddhist, religious discourses of nothingness or emptiness.

46. Rationed not in the ordinary sense of parceling out a whole but in the sense of giving *ratio*, *archē*, or principle to what is otherwise indeterminate or chaotic.

47. Oh dear, lamentation and weeping, the ruination of words, perfectly good words, crippled beyond power to walk on their own legs. *Theosophy*, the wisdom of God, ruined by its association with those grown overly familiar with that wisdom, those who render its indeterminacy so determinate as to be trivial. And *mysticism*, too, now stands surrogate for obfuscation. Can these bones live?

48. By no means do I mean to suggest that Kabbalah encompasses the whole of Judaism. Much of rabbinic Judaism and the totality of Enlightenment Judaism declare against such a claim. My suggestion is modest: that the kabbalistic underside of Judaism is to Judaism as the mystical underside of Christianity is to Christianity, and that underside-thought in one tradition sparks underside-thought in another, and all undersides eventually and eventfully have their effective topsides. The modern Judaic figure I have in mind as a model is the great Franz Rosenzweig.

49. No doubt one should take care to acknowledge that one learns or should learn as much or more from what one resists as from what one admires. In my depreciating remarks about Gnosticism I do not intend to deprecate it *totaliter*. Such a deprecation would surely be to blink both its speculative and historical force in its stunning emergence in late antiquity, its persistence largely on the undersides of several western religious and philosophical traditions, and above all (if Eric Voegelin is right) its powerful reincarnation in modernity. The great scholar here is Hans Jonas in his *Gnosis und spätantiker Geist* (*The Gnostic Religion: The Message of the Alien God and the Beginnings of Christianity* [Boston: Beacon, 1963]). Unquestionably he is right in the claim that the Gnostics introduced the first great speculative theology in the frantic and speculatively undisciplined religiosity that superseded classical antiquity, a theology without parallel in either the Christianity or the Judaism of the time and a theology that shattered the ease of pantheism in which classical antiquity had rested. In this sense, Gnosticism was not a mere extension of paganism; if it was paganism at all, it was a radically different paganism. The core of Gnosticism was its speculative-mythical portrayal of the devolution of deity, an impairment in very Godhead that gives rise to an antidivine universe (creation), descending emanations that revolve around a devolving God, etc. While both Judaism and Christianity had simulacra of some of these notions deeply latent within them, neither had found its speculative feet. And while historical intercausality is notoriously difficult to establish, it can surely be no accident that Gnosticism emerged potently in the conjunction of Judaism, Christianity, and paganism in the intellectual air of late antiquity.

50. Heidegger of course claims that Being as such both summons thinking and repels it by the default (*Ausbleiben*) of Being as such, a repulsion that eventu-

ates fatefully in a modern inauthentic nihilism (see Heidegger's *Nietzsche*, vol. 4). Clearly for Heidegger Being as such is not God, but his insight on this matter seems to me a residuum of his early theological training, and had he written a theology—which he claimed he was tempted to do but never did—his position might not be radically dissimilar to the one elaborated here, though not the same, to be sure.

51. In raising the matter of the discursive placement of the *chora* I signal both its importance and my intention not to address it frontally. No doubt a fully un-reconstructed deconstructionist postmodern thinking would displace from types (genres) of being to types (genres) of discourse. See Jacques Derrida, *On the Name*, ed. Thomas Dutoit, trans. David Wood, John P. Leavey Jr., and Ian McLeod (Stanford, CA: Stanford University Press, 1995), 91.

52. *Philebus* 27c reads: "At the first I count the unlimited, limit as the second, afterwards in third place comes the being which is mixed and generated out of the two"; Plato, *Philebus*, trans. Dorothea Frede, in Plato, *Complete Works*, ed. John M. Cooper (Indianapolis, IN: Hackett, 1997), 415.

53. Paraphrases in this and succeeding paragraphs employ the translations in F. M. Cornford, *Plato's Cosmology: The "Timaeus" of Plato* (New York: Humanities Press, 1952).

54. This claim is set in the context of Plato's argument with his Milesian natural-ist predecessors, those who claimed that one or more of the primordial four elements (earth, air, fire, water) could account for the unity and all the diversity of the cosmos. Plato's point is that each of these elements has qualities by reason of its form—as such (to use a later language), their space is wholly universal (or utopic). Wherever fire is, it has such and such qualities. But where is the where of *this* fire? The space of fire itself is wholly indeterminate; *this* fire is wholly determinate. *That in which* this fire is is nondeterminate (to use my language, not Plato's).

55. And further, if the *ex nihilo* of eternal creation yields the indeterminate out of which all determinacy arises, temporal creation yields the nondetermi-nate that in which all determinacy is actualized. To this we return in Topos 2: Cosmogony.

56. The phrase is that of Derrida, *On the Name*, 146.

TOPOS 2—COSMOGONY

1. This chapter incorporates and modifies a few segments of my essay "God and Creature in the Eternity and Time of Non-Being (or Nothing): Afterthinking Meister Eckhart," in *The Otherness of God*, ed. Orrin F. Summerell (Charlottes-ville: University Press of Virginia, 1998), 36–59, and also draws occasionally on my exegetical study of Eckhart, "La négativité dans l'ordre du divin," and "Pensées d'après Eckhart," in *Voici Maître Eckhart: Textes et études réunis par Emilie Zum Brunn*, ed. Emilie Zum Brunn (Grenoble: Millon, 1994), 187–208, 473–78.

2. Henry David Thoreau, conclusion to *Walden*, in *"Walden" and Other Writings* (New York: Modern Library, 1950), 289.

3. Antonio Gramsci, *Quaderni del Carcere*, ed. V. Gerratana (Turin: Einaudi, 1975), 2:1363; *The Prison Notebooks: Selections*, ed. and trans. Quintin Hoare and Geoffrey Nowell Smith (New York: International, 1971), 324.

4. As E. M. Cioran thinks, and goads us to think; see, for example, *The Temptation to Exist*.

5. See Topos 3: Anthropogony for comments on the potentiality for nonsense in saying there is nothing in something, as in the statement "There is nothing in that tree."

6. Let us be spared a rehearsal of all the proofs for the existence of this or that— God, the ego, the extended world—on which so much ingenuity and energy have been expended. In their modern form (arguably different in their medieval forms), the "proofs" of existence are projects in what may be called the sacralization of consciousness: the existence of this or that is secured in the convincedness (certitude, not certainty) of consciousness.

7. Of course, the "speaking" of spirited beings is not bounded by vocables as in the case of mute human beings who speak by signing, gesture, and the like. No doubt too there is a scale of "spirited being," and the presumption that language is restricted to humans is likely a human conceit.

8. This is well understood (even if on its negative side) in those religions given to retributive practices, especially shunning: one effectively denies the existence of someone by refusing to speak to him or her. The extent of the denial of God in contemporary life coextends with the number (a vast number, no doubt) of people who, thinkingly or unthinkingly, decline to speak to God. It is a mark of those who refuse to speak *to* someone that they speak all but incessantly *about* him or her—an ironic if indirect attestation. In respect of God, academic theologians are skillful adepts in this professional vice!

9. My earlier book *Unfinished Man and the Imagination: Toward an Ontology and a Rhetoric of Revelation* was an essay aspiring to the desedimentation of this widely misunderstood and misused term, an essay in the constitution of the fundaments of theology; see especially chaps. 3–6.

10. On "appearing," "shining," and gold and water as catching and reflecting light, and on the conditions of perceiving all *phainomena*, "things that shine," as exemplars of these, the reader may profitably consult a remarkably prescient book by Curtis Bennett, *God as Form: Essays in Greek Theology* (Albany: State University of New York Press, 1976), 102–22.

11. I do not mean to suggest that there are no theologies apart from a "positive" religion. Manifestly, there are such theologies. Cases in point are the theologies of Spinoza and Whitehead.

12. In such generalizations one should be on guard against a certain Christian provincialism. Not to be ignored were Jewish readings of the same texts by Maimonides, Luria, and others and the independent preservation of them in

Islam: the magnificent "interreligious dialogue" of the Middle Ages largely ignored in contemporary amnesia.

13. The New English Bible renders: "I AM; that is who I am."

14. See Edmund Husserl, *The Crisis of European Sciences and Transcendental Philosophy*, trans. David Carr (Evanston, IL: Northwestern University Press, 1970). Meister Eckhart, "Another Sermon on Eternal Birth," in *Library of Christian Classics*, ed. John Baillie, John T. McNeill, and H. P. Van Dusen (Louisville, KY: Westminster John Knox, 2006), 189. Böhme wrote: "*Ein Principium is anders nichts als eine neue Geburt, ein neu Leben*" (A principle is nothing other than a new birth, a new life); *Beschreibung der Drey Principien Göttliches Wesens*, in *Sämtliche Schriften*, ed. Will-Erich Peuckert and August Faust (Stuttgart: Frommanns, 1955–61), 5.6, 2:49. An elaboration of the same point is made in Böhme's *Von der Menschwerdung Jesu Christi*, where it is said that a Principium is not a "thing" that ever was but rather as a "quality" (*Qual*) always emerges out of nothing. While Böhme treats of the relation of principles (*Prinzipia*) of self-constitution to the *principal* (the agent of act) in many places throughout his corpus, the three such principles he identified (which I call Logos, Sophia, Spirit) are most succinctly addressed in *The Way to Christ*, trans. and with introduction by Peter Orb (New York: Paulist, 1978), 205–24.

15. *Comm. John* 1.83; English translation in Bernard McGinn, ed., *Essential Writings of Christian Mysticism* (New York: Modern Library, 2006), 153. In this connection, one hazards yet another shot across the bow of the chattering classes in religious studies, who often aver that medieval theologians draw substantively on philosophy rather than "real" religion for their metaphysical distinctions and abstractions. It is a remarkable fact that, instead, such distinctions and abstractions were developed precisely in their commentaries on biblical texts. Meister Eckhart is a superb exemplar of this practice.

16. *Comm. John* 1.63: "In the abstract, 'to exist' is the most perfect of the three [modal wholes, identified above, holding out of view the fourth, the order of angels], because no mode or perfection of existing can be lacking to it [the creature]"; Edmund Colledge and Bernard McGinn, eds. and trans., *Meister Eckhart: The Essential Sermons, Commentaries, Treatises, and Defense* (New York: Paulist, 1981), 144.

17. The cognitive dimensions of the "hermeneutical helical spiral" and "extension" and "intension" as used here are developed in *Unfinished Man and the Imagination*, 60–68.

18. One may generalize that with respect to God and the creatures Eckhart's Latin commentaries and scholastic treatises are governed principally by *extension* and his vernacular sermons principally by *intension*, just as academic discourse is generally extensive and liturgical discourse (especially the homily) is generally intensive.

19. Especially pertinent here is the notion of *sin*, a peculiarly religious reality and category unknown in philosophy because, if mentioned at all therein, it is identified with evil, which it is not, although ambiguously not. Connot-

ing stain or pollution, sin can and does ambiguously characterize good no less than evil: the taint of inadequacy, of nonadequation, of separation, of distance, of uncleanness, of absence (postmodernity itself might be characterized as a phenomenology of sin). Philosophy hasn't even the rumor of the *holiness* of sin—in this it is equaled by most of orthodox Christianity, including its moralistic practitioners—a notion preserved and viable in Christianity and Judaism only on their heterodox-cum-heretical undersides. It is visible in Luther only before he gave rise to a new orthodoxy—in his admonition to "sin bravely!" The potency of sin, in extremity, to harbor holiness marks some nontheistic religions (as in Tantric Buddhism), which take determinate sin to such extremes as to explode into the excess of the determination process itself, but a different one: that of absolute emptiness or nothingness (*sunyata*). It is the singularly theistic, especially the monotheistic, religions that are challenged to relate manifold determinate sin to the unitary divine determination process.

20. Ritually considered, the triumphal association of God with Being rather than nothingness in mainline Roman Catholicism brought to the fore in its cumulative custom those ritual practices that center in the "restoration" (redemption) of errant being; thus the Mass ritually enacts the transformation of death into life, of one matter into another (transubstantiation), and so prefigures Resurrection for communicants. In the variant custom of radical Protestantism, by contrast, errant being is extended through exacerbation instead of being reversed, and so issues in the ritual practice of Crucifixion— surely part of the terrain of the grammar of nothingness.

21. I do not know when this emendation was made or at the instance of what person or body, and no historian of doctrine has been able to tell me. It seems to have been in effect since the sixth or seventh century CE. The emendation itself—*creatio ex nihilo et non sed* [or *se*] *Deo*—clearly implies that the nothing from which God creates is not sourced in God, but the Latin grammar of the emendation is faulty, leading one to suspect that it is not original and has been corrupted through transmission. The only study of the doctrine of *creatio ex nihilo* known to me is that of Gerhard May, *Creatio ex nihilo: The Doctrine of "Creation out of Nothing" in Early Christian Thought*, trans. A. S. Worrall (Edinburgh: T. and T. Clark, 1994), but it covers the formula only for the second and third centuries, thus does not reckon with permutations of the doctrine in the medieval, Renaissance, and modern periods.

22. See Sermon 16 in *Meister Eckhart: Die deutschen und lateinischen Werke; Herausgegeben im Auftrage der Deutschen Forschungsgemeinschaft* (Stuttgart: Kohlhammer, 1936–), 1:261–78; *Meister Eckhart: Sermons and Treatises*, ed. and trans. M. O'C. Walshe (Shaftesbury, Dorset: Element, 1979), 1:127; *Meister Eckhart: Mystic and Philosopher*, ed. and trans. with commentary by Reiner Schürmann (Bloomington: Indiana University Press, 1978), 102.

23. See Sermon 12 in Eckhart, *Deutsche Werke*, 1:190–206; Walshe, *Meister Eckhart*, 2:87; Colledge and McGinn, *Meister Eckhart*, 270.

24. Eriugena, *Periphyseon: Division of Nature*, ed. and trans. J. O'Meara (Washington, DC: Dumbarton Oaks, 1987), 3:680d–689b.

25. Eriugena, *Periphyseon*, 1:441a, 443c.

26. The editors of Karl Barth's *Church Dogmatics*, G. W. Bromiley and T. F. Torrance, assert that "the supreme problem of theology is not the existence of God, as natural theology supposes, but the independent existence of creaturely reality"; Karl Barth, *Church Dogmatics: The Doctrine of Creation*, ed. and trans. G. W. Bromiley and T. F. Torrance (Edinburgh: T. and T. Clark, 1958), 3.l, vii. In the same volume, Barth himself affirms as the first proposition of the *articulus fidei* (in the Apostle's Creed: "I believe in God the Father Almighty, Maker of heaven and earth") "that the whole reality distinct from God truly is. Negatively . . . it asserts that God does not exist alone; that the divine being is not the only one to the exclusion of others. And positively, it asserts that another exists before [vis-à-vis], near and with God, having its own differentiated being quite distinctly from that of God" (5).

27. Sermon 52 in Eckhart, *Deutsche Werke*, 2:486–527; Colledge and McGinn, *Meister Eckhart*, 199–203; Walshe, *Meister Eckhart*, 2:269–77; Schürmann, *Meister Eckhart*, 214–20.

28. Sermon 11 in Walshe, *Meister Eckhart*, 1:98: "All things that are in time have a *Why?*" (= Sermon 11 in *Deutsche Mystiker des vierzehnten Jahrhunderts*, ed. F. Pfeiffer, vol. 2, *Meister Eckhart* [Leipzig: 1857; reprint, Aalen: Scientia, 1962]; Sermon 49 in Meister Eckhart, *Deutsche Predigten und Traktate*, ed. and trans. J. Quint [Munich: Hanser, 1955]).

29. Sermon 32 in Eckhart, *Deutsche Werke*, 2:132–49; Walshe, *Meister Eckhart*, 2:55.

30. Sermon 56 in Pfeiffer, *Meister Eckhart*, 179–83; Sermon 26 in Quint, *Deutsche Predigten und Traktate*, 271–73; Walshe, *Meister Eckhart*, 2:80–81.

31. Eckhart is the most radical of Christian atheists, holding out of view his latest reincarnation, the American theologian Thomas J. J. Altizer, who, however, is also different by reason of his appropriation of Hegel, Nietzsche, Kierkegaard, and others—but that is another story. See Thomas J. J. Altizer, *Genesis and Apocalypse: A Theological Voyage toward Authentic Christianity* (Louisville, KY: Westminster John Knox, 1990).

32. The most comprehensive study known to me of Eckhart's *nomen nominabile, nomen omnenominabile*, and *nomen innominabile* is Vladimir Lossky, *Théologie négative et cormaissance de Dieu chez Maître Eckhart* (Paris: Vrin, 1960), chaps. 1–2.

33. See Sermon 87 in Walshe, *Meister Eckhart*, 2:271; Sermon 32 in Quint, *Deutsche Predigten und Traktate*, 305 (= Sermon 87 in Pfeiffer, *Meister Eckhart*).

34. Emilie Zum Brunn and A. de Libera, *Maître Eckhart: Métaphysique du verbe et théologie négative* (Paris: Beauchesne, 1994), 181.

35. The central claim of Parmenides is: "It needs must be that what can be spoken and thought is; for it to be possible for it to be, and it is not possible for what is nothing to be"; frag. 6 in J. Burnet, *Early Greek Philosophy* (New York: Meridian Books, 1958), 174.

36. Vladimir Lossky, *Théologie négative et connaissance de Dieu chez Maître Eckhart* (Paris: Vrin, 1960), chaps. 1–2.

37. See Meister Eckhart, *Parisian Questions and Prologues*, ed. and trans. A. A. Maurer (Toronto: Pontifical Institute of Mediaeval Studies, 1974), 45–46 (= *Quaest. Par.* 1, n. 4, in Eckhart, *Lateinische Werke*, 5:41): "The first of created things is being [existence]. . . . Hence as soon as we come to being [existence] we come to a creature." Eckhart never tires of citing Proposition 4 of the Neoplatonic *Liber de causis*, a book that draws extensively on Proclus's *Elements of Theology*: "The first of created things is being." See also "Selections from the Commentary on the Book of Wisdom," in *Meister Eckhart: Teacher and Preacher*, ed. Bernard McGinn (New York: Paulist, 1986), 148n21, 149n24.

38. See *Quaest. Par.* 1, n. 4 in Eckhart, *Lateinische Werke*, 5:40; Maurer, *Parisian Questions*, 45.

39. See *Quaest. Par.* 1, n. 9 in Eckhart, *Lateinische Werke*, 5:45; Maurer, *Parisian Questions*, 48.

40. Eckhart discusses the two graces in Sermon 25 in *Lateinische Werke*, 4:230–44; McGinn, *Meister Eckhart*, 216–19.

41. Eckhart is as inconsistent on the *in imago Dei* and the *ad imaginem Dei* as scripture is. Generally, he alternates between the two according to the context of what is to be explained. Typically, when speaking of the identity of the ground of the soul with Godhead, he highlights the *imago Dei*; but when he treats of the soul under the power of the *not*, that is, as separate and different from God, he centers on the *ad imaginem Dei*.

42. See Sermon 71 in Eckhart, *Deutsche Werke*, 3:211–38; Walshe, *Meister Eckhart*, 1:153.

43. Sermon 52 in Eckhart, *Deutsche Werke*, 2:486–527; Walshe, *Meister Eckhart*, 2:274.

44. Walshe, *Meister Eckhart*, 1:157–58. Walshe opines that this dream is "the record of Eckhart's personal experience.

45. Schürmann, in *Meister Eckhart*.

46. Rudolf Otto, *Mysticism East and West*, trans. B. L. Bracey and R. C. Payne (New York: Macmillan, 1970); Keiji Nishitani, *Religion and Nothingness*, trans. Jan Van Bragt (Berkeley: University of California Press, 1982), 61–68.

47. See Sermon 29 in *Deutsche Werke*, 2:73–92; Walshe, *Meister Eckhart*, 1:136.

48. Walshe, *Meister Eckhart* 1:1 (= Sermon 1 in Pfeiffer, *Meister Eckhart*; Sermon 57 in Quint, *Deutsche Predigten und Traktate*).

49. Walshe, *Meister Eckhart*, 1:121 (= Sermon 21 in Pfeiffer, *Meister Eckhart*; Sermon 17 in Quint, *Deutsche Predigten und Traktate*).

50. Walshe, *Meister Eckhart*, 1:5 (= Sermon 1 in Pfeiffer, *Meister Eckhart*; Sermon 57 in Quint, *Deutsche Predigten und Traktate*).

51. Walshe, *Meister Eckhart*, 2:82 (= Sermon 56 in Pfeiffer, *Meister Eckhart*; Sermon 26 in Quint, *Deutsche Predigten und Traktate*); Walshe, *Meister Eckhart*, 2:275 (=

Sermon 87 in Pfeiffer, *Meister Eckhart*; Sermon 32 in Quint, *Deutsche Predigten und Traktate*).

52. Nietzsche, *Thus Spoke Zarathustra: A Book for All and None*, trans. Walter A. Kaufmann (New York: Penguin, 1978), 3.16.1–7, pp. 228–31.

53. Walshe, *Meister Eckhart*, 1:123 (= Sermon 14 in Pfeiffer, *Meister Eckhart;* Sermon 16 in Quint, *Deutsche Predigten und Traktate*).

54. Walshe, *Meister Eckhart*, 1:124.

55. Walshe, *Meister Eckhart*, 1:43 (Sermon 59 in Quint, *Deutsche Predigten und Traktate*, 435); translation from *Meister Eckhart: A Modern Translation*, ed. and trans. R. Blakney (New York: Harper and Row, 1941), 121; Walshe translates: "But even if it were shared, so that you did the preparing and God did the working or the infusion—which is impossible—then you should know that God must act and pour himself into you the moment He finds you ready."

56. Here I prescind from two discussions that would be pertinent in this context. The first would acknowledge that there are at least two exceptions to my claim that Christianity temporalizes eternity: one being Eastern Orthodox Christianity, which clearly eternalizes time, although differently from Judaism, through a Greek understanding of the icon; the other being what Peter L. Berger has called the mythic mode, as in Eliade's retreat from "overheated time" to a primordial *in illo tempore*. The second discussion would essay some characterizations of modern time-consciousness, drawing chiefly on Hegel and Marx.

57. "Every foreign land is their [the Christians'] fatherland, and yet for them every fatherland is a foreign land"; *The Letter to Diognetus*, 5.5–6, in *Early Christian Fathers*, ed. C. Richardson (Philadelphia: Westminster, 1953), 1:217.

58. See note 32 to the introduction, above.

59. D. G. Leahy, *Novitas Mundi: Perception of the History of Being* (New York: New York University Press, 1980), 217–91.

60. Edmond Jabès, *The Book of Questions*, trans. R. Waldrop (Middletown, CT: Wesleyan University Press, 1987); Maurice Blanchot, *The Space of Literature*, trans. A. Smock (Lincoln: University of Nebraska Press, 1982); *The Writing of Disaster*, trans. A. Smock (Lincoln: University of Nebraska Press, 1986).

61. William James, *The Varieties of Religious Experience* (New York: Penguin, 1982), lectures 4–7, 78–166.

62. In discriminating Book from Work, I borrow from Maurice Blanchot, even if I do not do justice to his subtle and often puzzling senses of the terms. See Blanchot, *The Space of Literature*, trans. Ann Smock (Lincoln: University of Nebraska Press, 1982), and *The Writing of the Disaster*, trans. Ann Smock (Lincoln: University of Nebraska Press, 1986).

63. Cited by James, *Varieties of Religious Experience*, 137.

64. Suppose planet Earth, through human stupidity or cupidity or a cause entirely independent of human agency like planetary collision, should dissolve and disappear as other planets do. Would creation and its Creator

God coincidentally dissolve? By no means. Who knows with what God the Creator, *Deus sive natura*, has packed the trunks of the entire created universe, *naturatum*? What other nonhuman creatures, agents of finite determinateness and determinability, are there in the universe and what have been the epiphantic manifestations to them, bearers of the images *of* and *toward* God? But, further, let us suppose the end of the entire universe, of temporal creation, of the aeon of time-curved-by-space, of the time of the universe relativized by the space of the universe—by entropy, inversion of the big bang, or whatever. Would the end of the created universe be the end of God the Creator? Yes, the end of God the Creator of temporal creation, but not the end of eternal creation. From here on, only theological conjecture is possible. Two possibilities suggest themselves, and seem exhaustive. Either eternally triune God the Creator would create another universe, or in utter grief and suffering and abandonment of mutability, dissolve into the unitary, immutable indeterminacy of the abyss of Godhead. In the latter case, and based solely in faith in the grace of Godhead's trustworthiness, Godhead (because of the internal nisus to determinate expression of indeterminacy) would freshly self-generate the God of a new aeon of eternity.

65. Kierkegaard, *Philosophical Fragments*, trans. D. Swenson, rev. trans. H. V. Hong (Princeton, NJ: Princeton University Press, 1974), 25. The full context is as follows: "When one who has experienced birth thinks of himself as born, he conceives this transition from nonbeing to being. The same principle must also hold in the case of the new birth. Or is the difficulty increased by the fact that the nonbeing which precedes the new birth contains more being than the nonbeing which preceded the first birth?"

66. See Walshe, *Meister Eckhart* 1:1 (= Sermon 1 in Pfeiffer, *Meister Eckhart*; Sermon 57 in Quint, *Deutsche Predigten und Traktate*). Eckhart quotes Augustine: "What does it avail me that this birth is always happening if it does not happen in me? That it should happen in me is what matters."

67. The history of Incarnation—not the history of the *doctrine* of Incarnation, but the history of the Word made flesh, actualized in the flesh of time, the history of temporalized eternity—has not been written. Can it be written? However central Jesus may be to that history (and for the Christian he is), it would include many beyond the biblical frame, indeed, many beyond Christianity as a religion. It would of course be selective, as all history is, attending to those actualizations of the Word whose meaning belongs to the futures to which they have given rise.

68. Sermon 65 in Eckhart, *Deutsche Werke*, 3:95–107; Walshe, *Meister Eckhart*, 1:52. The translation is from Walshe, who notes, "I have followed Miss Evans's nice play on words here: though not in the original, it hits the sense most happily" (53).

TOPOS 3 — COSMOGONY

1. See my discussion of the self's continuous ingredience and the self's discontinuous ingression in *Unfinished Man and the Imagination*, 138–62.
2. I use *mythologies* in the sense employed by Mircea Eliade and others: myth deals with that which never was (in time) but always is temporally, in the sense that it "explains" what exists in time. The bulk of religious mythologies worldwide is disproportionately weighted toward the "before-not" (in my terms, the first not), the Not of archaic origins supervening upon every "is." This "before not" is the darling of the so-called perennialists, those who contend that the *telos* of human life is a "return" to a primordial unity. One can only be aghast that such a "before not" continues to enchant and seduce in the face of modernity's experience of the second not (to the extremity of nihilism), but there it is in popular interest in Joseph Campbell's nostalgic recovery of the primacy of the "before not," what I call the first not. But nothingness is not to be reduced or restricted to the "before not"—or in Shakespeare's phrase, quoted earlier, "the dark backward and abysm of time"—if human time is not to be cheated of the coincidence of the three *exstaces* of time (past, present, future) which alone ground a meaningful present. The mythologies of Christianity (and Judaism, I think) counterweigh the "before-not" with the "after-not" (the not of the future); and human existence and redemption of it are *between* them.
3. Again, I borrow the terms from Blanchot but use them more generally; see Topos 2, n. 62.
4. In a letter to his parents, from Munich, November 12, 1905, cited by Nahum Glatzer, *Franz Rosenzweig*, 2nd rev. ed. (New York: Schocken, 1961), 3.
5. Here I do not use the term *essence* in the same sense as in the main tradition of western metaphysics, namely, as a class-universal laid up in something like a Platonic form or as an eternal intention in the divine mind. From essence so conceived I would know only and abstractly the extremities of what counts as the *what* of humankind, not what my own *what* is. I have written of these matters, substituting for a fixity of essence (and now realize how awkward the language is!) "the imaginative, historico-personal *existentiale*," using *existentiale* in the German sense. While it is doubtless the case that there are fixed limits to the *what* of humankind, to breach which makes one inhuman or nonhuman, that *what* is only a negative *what* for an individual person. Any essence obliging all humankind has many blanks in it, which my own career of existing fills in in time as obliging *me*. This is another way of saying that *a* human being is unfinished. However one aspires "to be bound by being" (as Paul Ricoeur put it), I am unfinished as no one else is, not even those in closest proximity to my historico-personal situation. I put the question of being and truth which no one else can put for me; there is

something about myself I have to discover (and thus to occur, since discovery is occurrence), and since no one can do this in my stead, my own potency (situated by my career of existing) is the framework of what is ontically essential for my existence. Thus the *what* of every unique human existence is a form of *potentia obedientalis* (though, nota bene, I do not use this phrase in its Thomistic sense). See *Unfinished Man and the Imagination*, 170–75, 254–66.

6. Søren Kierkegaard, *Philosophical Fragments*, trans. David Swenson, rev. trans. Howard V. Hong (Princeton, NJ: Princeton University Press, 1974), 51n2. The sentence quoted is preceded by "In the case of factual being it is meaningless to speak of more or less of being" and followed by "Factual being is wholly indifferent to any and all variations of essence, and everything that exists participates without petty jealousy in being, and participates in the same degree." One may well cavil that Kierkegaard apparently does not know, and if he knows does not understand, the Neoplatonic-Augustinian notion of "degrees of being."

7. In my AAR presidential address I counterpose to Hamlet's ultimate question the question "to be *and* not to be"; see Ray L. Hart, "To Be *and* Not to Be: *Sit Autem Sermo (Logos) Vester; Est, Est, Non, Non*," *Journal of the American Academy of Religion* 53, no. 1 (1985): 5–22.

8. Kierkegaard, *Philosophical Fragments*, 26.

9. The full context is as follows: "When one who has experienced birth thinks of himself as born, he conceives this transition from nonbeing to being. The same principle also holds in the case of the new birth. Or is the difficulty increased by the fact that the nonbeing which precedes the new birth contains more being than the nonbeing which preceded the first birth?" Kierkegaard, *Philosophical Fragments*, 25.

10. Inscription in the autograph album of William Upcott, January 16, 1826; cited by Amelia H. Munson, *Poems of William Blake* (New York: Crowell, 1964).

11. Samuel Taylor Coleridge, *Biographia Literaria*, 2 vols., ed. Henry Nelson Coleridge, (London: Pickering, 1847), vol. 1, pt. 2, chap. 13, p. 297.

12. Curtis Bennett, *God as Form: Essays in Greek Theology* (Albany: State University of New York Press, 1976), 103.

13. Bennett, *God as Form,* 240. No sooner had I finished writing this quotation than I received word that a dear friend of fifty-five years, my graduate-school classmate Leon Pacala, had died. For me the quotation has immediate and poignant reference. Yes, I am made freshly aware of my own existence, here, now, but even more am I acutely aware of how my existence is diminished by his passing into the second not. Not ever again to see him and to be held by his eyes, never to hear his distinctive voice and his nuanced speech, never to touch him again is a diminution of my own existence. He, like every person, is unsubstitutable.

14. This might be called the poetic-fictive equivalent of what Peter L. Berger has termed "the sociology of knowledge."

15. I use *ontic* as the translators of Heidegger into English do (*existentiell*), refer-
    ring to the being of a concrete thing or person, whereas *ontological* refers to
    being-as-such participated by everything thing that is, or has being. Sacrifice
    is addressed further below.

16. I said above that artists are surer keepers of these matters than are philoso-
    phers. From many one could offer Fyodor Dostoevsky, that master of making
    concrete the ignominy of human life's snares. The voice of Ippolit in *The
    Idiot*, trans. Constance Garnett (New York: Bantam, 1958), pt. 3, chap. 7: "If I
    have once been allowed to be conscious that 'I am,' what does it matter to me
    that there are mistakes in the construction of the world, and without them
    it can't go on . . . it's all impossible and unjust" (423). "There is a limit of the
    ignominy in the consciousness of one's own nothingness and impotence
    beyond which a man cannot go, and beyond which he begins to feel im-
    mense satisfaction in his own degradation." These words from *The Idiot* (note
    that Dostoevsky used *idiot* in the Greek sense of idiosyncratic, unique to
    this individual) suggest that human degradation produces a force of *humil-
    ity*, an ontic humility that, within the world of *The Idiot,* is not or need not
    be related to *religious* humility. "Can't I simply be devoured without being
    expected to praise what devours me? Can there really be Somebody up aloft
    who will be aggrieved by not going on for a while longer? . . . [as though]
    all that's needed is my worthless life, the life of an atom, to complete some
    universal harmony; for some sort of plus and minus, for the sake of some
    contrast, and so on, just as the life of millions of creatures is needed every
    day as a sacrifice, as, without their death, the rest of the world could not go
    on" (422–23). If these quotations from *The Idiot* are negative on the implica-
    tions of degradation's ontic humility for *religious* humility, that is certainly
    not Dostoevsky's full view of the matter. There is no more rigorous excava-
    tor of the depths of the Russian soul and its adoration of the Mother of God
    (so different from the Latin Catholic veneration of Mary) than Dostoevsky,
    and it is certain that in other works (such as *Crime and Punishment* and *The
    Brothers Karamazov*) he does positively relate ontic humility of degradation to
    religious humility, as it is equally certain that he challenges classical western
    views of God (as does this study, if not precisely in the same way).

17. For a contemporary Proustian assault on the hegemony of the "now" by a
    distinguished American novelist, see Wallace Stegner, *Angle of Repose* (New
    York: Penguin, 1971): "I started to establish the present and the present
    moved on . . . Before I can say that I *am*, I was. Heraclitus and I, prophets of
    flux, know that the flux is composed of parts that imitate and repeat each
    other. Am or was, I am cumulative too. I am everything I ever was, whatever
    you . . . may think. . . . My antecedents support me here as the old wistaria at
    the corner supports the house" (15).

18. Stegner, *Angle of Repose*, 25.

19. The English word *imagination* is one of little internal resonance, of incom-
    parably less force than its equivalent in German, *Einbildungskraft*—a matter

much commented upon by Coleridge in his *Biographia Literaria* (see vol. 1, pt. 2, chap. 13). *Einbildungskraft* evokes the power, the force field of forming (*paideia*) the many toward the one.

20. Herman Melville, *Moby-Dick* (New York: Modern Library, 1982), chap. 118, 716–17.

21. Kierkegaard, *Concluding Unscientific Postscript,* trans. David F. Swenson and Walter Lowrie (Princeton, NJ: Princeton University Press, 1944), 228.

22. Mindful of the lines in the W. B. Yeats poem "A Prayer for Old Age": "GOD guard me from those thoughts men think / In the mind alone; / He that sings a lasting song / Thinks in a marrow-bone"; from *A Full Moon in March*, in *Yeats's Poetry, Drama, and Prose: Authoritative Texts, Contexts, Criticism*, ed. James Pethica (New York: Norton, 2000), 113.

23. One remembers Alfred North Whitehead: "Seek simplicity, and distrust it"; see *The Concept of Nature* (Cambridge: Cambridge University Press, 1926), 163.

24. Alas, English is a poor medium for ontological thinking. The point is less clumsily put in German, as is in Alois M. Haas's felicitous phrase "*das einzelhaft Seiend-Sein*." See his "Seinsspekulation und Geschöpflichkeit in der Mystik Meister Eckharts," in *Sein und Nichts in der abendländischen Mystik*, ed. Walter Strolz (Freiburg: Herder, 1984), 36.

25. While my preference as a fly-fisherman is to address trout with dry flies, I take Jesus's call to be "fishers of men" not to exclude "bottom fishers"!

26. If the bottom of the scale is marked by stability, we can extend Hyman Minsky's claim that stability itself conduces to instability to say that the higher modes are in the scale the more they are marked by instability.

27. In Topos 1: Theogony, I referred to such an indeterminate plane of sacrality as Godhead. To be sure, in any concrete religious tradition practiced by adherents such a plane is ritually determinate (usually by names).

28. I adopt the phrase "angle of repose" in its metaphorical use from Stegner, who applies it to the narrative account of his character's grandmother Susan Burling Ward.

29. Pascal, *Pascal's Pensées*, ed. and trans. W. F. Trotter (New York: Dutton, 1958), 17.

30. In Greek religion, as in many other archaic religious cultures, the number of mortal souls was thought to be fixed, so that a new human birth could occur only if the shade of a dead person could be persuaded to return from the region of the shades to ensoul another body in time. This conviction has a very long shelf life, as in those places where a Christian patina overlies indigenous religious cultures, such as in Africa and Latin America. I have myself been fascinated by the Day of the Dead, coinciding with the Christian festival of All Souls Day, in such cultures (the one I have experienced was in Mexico), when families stream to cemeteries bearing gifts and favorite foods for dead relatives to persuade them to return and be born again into the family. Anthropologists reckon with these matters under the conjoining of "food supply" and "tribe supply."

31. Becoming that does not turn off—simply grows and replicates endlessly until

the end of existence—is cancer of spirit/soul as well as of body. For cancer as metaphor of human existence, see Mark C. Taylor, *Field Notes from Elsewhere: Reflections on Dying and Living* (New York: Columbia University Press, 2009), 232ff.

32. As noted earlier, I have dwelt at length on the inverse relation between extension and intension in *Unfinished Man and the Imagination*, chap. 2, especially 63–65.

33. The distinction between the first and the second not is not without precedence in the custom-traditions drawn upon in this thought-experiment. One such precursor is the Neoplatonic metaphysician John Scotus Eriugena, who, however, developed the distinction not primarily in respect of the human person but as respecting the relation of the creature to God. Eriugena distinguished between the Nothing that is God (*nihil per excellentia*) and the nothing (in the human creature) as *nihil per privationem*. As I hope will become clear, I contend against his (and every other Neoplatonist's) view of nothingness as merely and exhaustively *privative*, since this cheats all nothingness of its force in the determinateness of human becoming and unbecoming.

34. Robert Musil, *The Man without Qualities*, 2 vols., trans. Sophie Wilkins and Burton Pike (New York: Vintage, 1996). Musil stands tall among the greatest of the Viennese intellectuals of the twentieth century; he worked on this book for many decades, and it was published only posthumously. Despite its widespread influence, I can count on fewer fingers than one hand the number of Americans I know to have read all 2,499 pages!

35. Musil, *The Man without Qualities*, 2:762–63.

36. Otherwise, Musil writes, "speaking of destiny: it's as if we had two destinies—one that's all superficial bustle, which takes life over, and one that's motionless and meaningful, which we never find out about!" (2:786).

37. Musil, *The Man without Qualities*, 2:806–7.

38. For the distinctions between individuation, individuality, and self/spirit, I acknowledge with gratitude the help received from Robert P. Scharlemann's work, marked as always by clarity of precision and depth of nuance. See *The Reason of Following: Christology and the Ecstatic I* (Chicago: University of Chicago Press, 1991), especially chap. 1.

39. Kierkegaard, *Philosophical Fragments*, chap. 1.

40. Kierkegaard, *Philosophical Fragments*, 96.

41. I use the term *ecstatic I* in the senses developed at length by Scharlemann.

42. Eckhart, "Another Sermon on the Eternal Birth," in *Late Medieval Mysticism*, ed. Ray C. Petry (Philadelphia: Westminster, 1957), 189.

43. Buber, *I and Thou*, trans. Ronald Gregor Smith (New York: Scribner, 1958).

44. See Hart, *Unfinished Man and the Imagination*, 138–62.

45. The primary name for constraints upon freedom in modernity has been "nature," the realm of nonspirited reality that limits spirited freedom. In the nineteenth century the previous consolidation of all considerations of

nature in *Naturphilosophie* was broken up, with the matter of the nature of "nature" being handed over almost entirely to the natural sciences, which is why philosophers and theologians now must attend the sciences. Is a person *free* to think if the neural wiring in her brain is skewed, the neural pathways clogged, diverted by drugs of "choice" or prescription? Can the will be effective if the brain misfires or miscues? Is freedom itself exhaustively a function of will? The questions are legion, and bear on the perennial pair: necessity and freedom.

46. I cannot recommend highly enough Goethe's subtle novella *Elective Affinities* (*Die Wahlverwandschaften*) for its reckoning with this range of issues, the sensitivity of which is superior to most discursive treatments in philosophical treatises. But then, that is Goethe's métier.

47. Nietzsche, *Thus Spoke Zarathustra: A Book for All and None*, trans. Walter A. Kaufmann (New York: Penguin, 1978), pt. 1, §20: "On Child and Marriage," 183.

48. In Nietzsche's case one would become more and more the *Übermensch*.

49. Giorgio Agamben, *The Man without Content*, trans. Georgia Albert (Stanford, CA: Stanford University Press, 1999), 53.

50. G. W. F. Hegel, *Aesthetics: Aesthetics: Lectures on Fine Arts*, vol. 1, trans. T. M. Knox (Oxford: Clarendon, 1975), 1:67.

51. Hart, *Unfinished Man and the Imagination*, especially 248–54.

52. Nicholas of Cusa, *Of Learned Ignorance* (London: Routledge and Kegan Paul, 1954), bk. 1, chap. 1. One notes as well the profound meditations of Jakob Böhme on a first and a second freedom. I correlate his "first freedom" with the first not, and the "second freedom" (that of the incited ecstatic "I") with the second not; see Böhme, *Six Theosophic Points*, and the introductory essay to this work by Nicolas Berdyaev, "Unground and Freedom."

53. Nietzsche, *Thus Spoke Zarathustra*, pt. 1, §11: "On the New Idol," 163; Scharlemann, *Reason of Following*, 135ff. In these pages Scharlemann develops the notion of the "ecstatic I" as the hamartetic self ("*hamartekios* from *hamartia*: missing the mark, or missing what is intended"). As distinguished from the inauthentic self of everydayness, the latter un-owns what (in my terms) it has become: "The hamartetic I is not an unowned but a disowned I. Its dialectic is that of an unending end rather than that of the self's coming to itself in the end" (135).

54. R. G. Hammerton-Kelly has offered interesting proposals for construing the Christian Cross (crucifixion) as the deconstruction and reconstruction of sacrifice in his *Sacred Violence* (Minneapolis, MN: Fortress, 1991).

55. *Tosefta Berakhot*, 4.1.A; Tzvee Zahavy, *The Mishnaic Law of Blessings and Prayers: Tractate Berakhot* (Atlanta, GA: Scholars Press, 1989), 80.

56. Goethe wrote, "The worst of torments we can suffer is to feel want when we are so rich"; *Faust I & II*, vol. 2 of *Goethe: The Collected Works*, trans. Stuart Atkins (Princeton, NJ: Princeton University Press, 1994), 284.

57. Alfred Kazin, "Introduction to *Moby-Dick*," in *Melville: A Collection of Critical Essays*, ed. Richard Chase (Englewood Cliffs, NJ: Prentice-Hall, 1962), 47.

58. The inkpot formed, of course, by the eruption of the Vesuvian rock itself, on the ashes of whose slopes grow the grapes from which is made the wine to this day called Lacrima di Cristo (tears of Christ); it was Paul Tillich's favorite.

59. Martin Buber, *Ecstatic Confessions* (Syracuse, NY: Syracuse University Press, 1996), 10.

60. Eliot, *Burnt Norton* (London: Faber and Faber, 1941). The Heraclitus fragments are quoted in Greek in Eliot's text; English translations by Kathleen Freeman read: "Therefore one must follow that which is common. But although the Law is universal, the majority live as if they had understanding peculiar to themselves" (frag. 2), and "The way up and down is one and the same" (frag. 60); see Kathleen Freeman, ed. and trans., *Ancilla to the Pre-Socratic Philosophers: A Complete Translation of the Fragments in Diels, "Fragmente der Vorsokratiker"* (Cambridge: Harvard University Press, 1948), 24, 29.

61. Böhme, *De Electione Gratiae*, 3:20; *On the Election of Grace*, trans. John Rolleston Earle (London: Constable, 1930), 39.

POSTSCRIPT: AFTERTHINKING THEOLOGY AS HERMENEUTICS

1. These matters are deliberated at length in "Problematic and the Hermeneutical Spiral," chapter 2 of my *Unfinished Man and the Imagination*, 52–68.

2. Wilhelm Dilthey, *Gesammelte Schriften* (Göttingen: Vandenhoeck and Ruprecht, 1958), 5:310.

3. *"Le sens n'est pas un fait donné, il est plutôt une tâche, une vision à conquérir,"* in the words of C. A. van Peursen, "Phénoménologie et ontologie," *Rencontre / Encounter / Begegnung: Contributions à une psychologie humaine dédiées au Professeur F. J. J. Buytendijk*, ed. M. J. Langeveld (Utrecht: Uitgeverij het Spectrum, 1957), 317.

4. Why, oh why, is the work of the great English humanist Owen Barfield, *Saving the Appearances: A Study in Idolatry* (New York: Harcourt, Brace and World, 1965), nowadays so little read and heeded?

5. In the later dialogues Plato himself came close to this point of view without, however, writing a treatise in explanation of it. Neither did he write a treatise on nonbeing—as he promised he would in *Sophist*—and surely the two unwritten treatises would have been critically interrelated? The understanding of the hermeneutical spiral presented here owes much to the later Plato and the early Paul Weiss. In addition to Weiss's article "Metaphysics: The Domain of Ignorance," *Philosophical Review* 43, no. 4 (July 1934): 402–6, see his book *Reality* (Princeton, NJ: Princeton University Press, 1938).

6. Weiss, "Metaphysics," 404.

7. Richard Powers's novel *Plowing the Dark* (New York: Farrar, Straus, Giroux, 2000), 414.

8. In these reflections on the bearing of attentiveness upon the fruit of cognition, of being known, I am aware of the vague influence of Simone Weil, who in her short conflicted, afflicted, and attentive life was, in my judgment, the greatest Christian mystic of the twentieth century. A second equally vague influence is Edmond Jabès, for whom the dialectic between knowing and being known is rooted in a wound or occasion of trauma. Though both Weil and Jabès were Jews, neither was religiously observant in any traditional sense. Weil repeatedly affirmed Christianity but vehemently refused baptism in the Roman Catholic Church because she would not deny the "pagans" whom she knew (living and dead) and by whom she was known: her beloved Greeks, her Vedic saints, her bodhisattvas, for example. A syndicalist and activist, working long hours alongside manual laborers, accepting no more than the most minimal rations, after hours she attended the unjustly imprisoned. From an advantaged family she secured a classical education in philosophy and was, so to say, afflicted with attentiveness to the afflictions of all her fellow humans—afflictions that were not alone physical. One is afflicted not only in body (hunger, malnutrition, disease, and similar) but in spirit; physical abuse is not always the most harmful abuse. What one cannot, does not, survive is an inattentiveness that amounts to indifference. To know and be known by those who have not been talked to or with, have not been spoken into singular existence, is to know humanity from its absence. In her short stringent life Weil was a negative witness to humanity, a humanity missed by not being known by those who embody just that lack.

9. This is confirmed by, among others, Carl Sagan, the popular historian of science, and Alan Lightman, the renowned MIT physicist; see Alan Lightman, *The Accidental Universe: The World You Thought You Knew* (New York: Pantheon, 2013).

APPENDIX A

1. By these cryptic remarks on Sartre, I by no means intend a summary of his full views on the imagination. For that I refer the reader to a fuller exegesis in *Unfinished Man and the Imagination*, 364–68. For my remarks above, I draw less on *Being and Nothingness*, more on *L'Imagination* (Paris: Presses Universitaires de France, 1950) in which Sartre essays a phenomenological investigation of the nature of imagination, and on *L'Imaginaire* (Paris: Gallimard, 1940). An English translation of the latter is *The Psychology of Imagination* (New York: Philosophical Library, 1948).

2. For the interested reader, I have written of the imagination in Descartes, Spinoza, and Leibniz in *Unfinished Man and the Imagination*, 335–37n1.

3. Berkeley, *Siris: A Chain of Philosophical Reflexions and Inquiries concerning the Virtues of Tar Water*, in *The Works of George Berkeley, Bishop of Cloyne*, vol. 5, ed. A. A. Luce and T. E. Jessop (London: Nelson, 1948–57).

4. I have written of Hume's understanding of the imagination, particularly of its propensive power in the formation of complex ideas, its tendency toward the creative rather than the synthetic functions of the mind's ordering of ideas, an epistemological consideration critical for understanding his work on "natural religion" (*Unfinished Man and the Imagination*, 346–51).

5. Concerning the word *esemplastic* Coleridge wrote: "I constructed it myself from the Greek words, εις εν πλαττειν, to shape into one; because, having to convey a new sense, I thought that a new term would both aid the recollection of my meaning, and prevent its being confounded with the usual import of the word, imagination"; *Biographia Literaria*, chap. 10, in *Selected Poetry and Prose of Samuel Taylor Coleridge*, ed. Donald A. Stauffer (New York: Random House, 1951), 191.

6. Coleridge on the German word *Einbildungskraft*: "How excellently the German *Einbildungskraft* expresses this prime and loftiest faculty, the power of coadunation, the faculty that forms the many into one—*in-eins-bildung!* Esemplasy or esemplastic power, as contradistinguished from fantasy, or the mirrorment, either catoptric or metoptric—repeating simply, or by transposition—and again, involuntary as in dreams, or by an act of the will." See George Whaley, *Poetic Process* (London: Routledge and Kegan Paul, 1953), 62.

7. My cryptic summary derives from Kant's own in the "Transcendental Analytic." See *Critique of Pure Reason*, trans. Norman Kemp Smith (London: Macmillan, 1953), 111–12. Hereafter this work is cited in the text as *CPR*.

8. "Appearances are only representations of things which are unknown as regards what they may be in themselves. As mere representations, they are subject to no law of connection save that which the connecting faculty prescribes. Now it is imagination that connects the manifold of sensible intuition; and imagination is dependent for the unity of its intellectual synthesis upon the understanding, and for the manifoldness of its apprehension upon sensibility" (*CPR* 173).

9. For this treatment of the relation between immediacy and mediacy, see *Unfinished Man and the Imagination*, 210ff., 238ff.

10. Alfred North Whitehead, *Process and Reality: An Essay in Cosmology* (New York: Macmillan, 1936). In what I contribute concerning Whitehead's categoreal schema, logical primitives, and related concepts, I gratefully acknowledge the influence of one of my Yale teachers some sixty years ago, William A. Christian. His most comprehensive study of Whitehead is *An Interpretation of Whitehead's Metaphysics* (New Haven, CT: Yale University Press, 1959), but his most helpful essay on matters discussed here is "The Concept of God as a Derivative Notion," in the festschrift for Charles Hartshorne entitled *Process and Divinity*, ed. William L. Reese and Eugene Freeman (Lasalle, IL: Open Court, 1964), 181–203.

11. Christian, "The Concept of God as a Derivative Notion," 182–83.

12. Whitehead, *Process and Reality*, 47.

1. Martin Buber, *I and Thou*, trans. Ronald Gregor Smith (New York: Scribner, 1958), 96. I am troubled by the common translation of his title *Ich und Du*, since *Du* is clearly familiar, as distinguished from polite or regal, and should be translated by the English "you." Buber's principal concern is to distinguish between *Du* and *Es* (it).

2. William James, *Varieties of Religious Experience: A Study of Human Nature* (New York: Penguin, 1982), 508.

3. James, *Varieties of Religious Experience*, 516.

4. Annie Dillard, *Teaching a Stone to Talk: Expeditions and Encounters* (New York: Harper and Row, 1982). See also two other of her earlier books, *Holy the Firm* (New York: Harper and Row, 1977) and *Pilgrim at Tinker Creek* (New York: Harper's Magazine Press, 1974).

5. It is not uncommon nowadays to illustrate the silliness of theology by saying it traffics in such questions as "How many angels can dance on the head of a pin?" As such the question only betrays the theological illiteracy of the questioner. In the Middle Ages, if the question was posed at all it was as a "trick" question. In the medieval worldview an angel is a pure essence. Having no body or any form of temporal or spatial determinacy, angels are not subject to number. The wise medieval student would have replied that the question itself is "a category mistake." Or he could have said "all, or none," since with angels all would be indistinguishable from none.

6. Hannah Arendt, *Willing*, vol. 2 of her *The Life of the Mind* (New York: Harcourt Brace Jovanovich, 1978), 5.

7. See the magisterial work of Charles Norris Cochrane, *Christianity and Classical Culture: A Study of Thought and Action from Augustus to Augustine* (New York: Oxford University Press, 1957).

8. Note that T. S. Eliot incorporated in his own *The Waste Land* a quotation from Augustine's *Confessions*.

9. In *Willing*, Arendt develops the "counter will" in her discussions of Paul the Apostle, Epictetus, Augustine, Nietzsche, and Heidegger.

10. These matters are worried at some length in my article "To Be *and* Not to Be: *Sit Autem Sermo (Logos) Vester; Est, Est, Non, Non*," *Journal of the American Academy of Religion* 53, no. 1 (1985): 14–18.

11. James, *Varieties of Religious Experience*, lectures 4–6.

12. *Franz Rosenzweig: His Life and Thought*, presented by Nahum N. Glatzer (New York: Schocken, 1961), 3.

Selected Bibliography

Agamben, Giorgio. *The Man without Content*. Translated by Georgia Albert. Stanford, CA: Stanford University Press, 1999.

Altizer, Thomas, J. J. *The Apocalyptic Trinity*. New York: Palgrave Macmillan, 2012.

———. *Genesis and Apocalypse: A Theological Voyage toward Authentic Christianity*. Louisville, KY: Westminster John Knox, 1990.

———. *The Genesis of God: A Theological Genealogy*. Louisville, KY: Westminster John Knox, 1993.

———. *Godhead and the Nothing*. Albany: State University of New York Press, 2003.

———. *The Self-Embodiment of God*. New York: Harper and Row, 1977.

Anderson, Deland S. *Hegel's Speculative Good Friday: The Death of God in Philosophical Perspective*. Atlanta, GA: Scholars Press, 1996.

Aquinas, Thomas. *Summa Contra Gentiles*. Vol. 4, *Salvation*. Translated with introduction and notes by Charles J. O'Neil. Notre Dame, IN: University of Notre Dame Press, 1975.

Aristotle. *Metaphysics*. 2 vols. Translated by Hugh Tredennick. Cambridge: Harvard University Press, 1956–58.

———. *Physics*. Translated by Philip H. Wicksteed and Francis M. Cornford. London: Heinemann, 1952–57.

Arendt, Hannah. *Willing*. Vol. 2 of *The Life of the Mind*. New York: Harcourt Brace Jovanovich, 1978.

———. "Martin Heidegger at Eighty." *New York Review of Books* 17, no. 6 (October 21, 1971).

Armstrong, Karen. *The History of God*. New York: Knopf, 1993.

Auden, W. H. *Another Time*. New York: Random House, 1940.

———. "The Truest Poetry Is the Most Feigning." In *The Shield of Achilles*. New York: Random House, 1955.

Augustine. *Against the Academicians* and *The Teacher*. Translated with introduction and notes by Peter King. Indianapolis, IN: Hackett, 1995.

———. *Confessions* and *Enchiridion*. Translated by Albert Cook Outler. Library of Christian Classics. Louisville, KY: Westminster John Knox Press, 2006.

Bachelard, Gaston. *Earth and Reveries of Will: An Essay on the Imagination of Matter*. Translated by Kenneth Haltman. Dallas: Dallas Institute of Humanities and Culture, 2002.

———. *The Poetics of Space*. Translated by Maria Jolas. Boston: Beacon, 1994.

———. *The Psychoanalysis of Fire*. Translated by Alan C. M. Ross. Boston: Beacon, 1964.

———. *Water and Dreams: An Essay on the Imagination of Matter*. Translated by Edith R. Farrell. Dallas: Pegasus, 1983.

Barfield, Owen. *Saving the Appearances: A Study in Idolatry*. New York: Harcourt, Brace and World, 1965.

Barth, Karl. *The Doctrine of Creation*. Vol. 3.1 of *Church Dogmatics*. Edited and translated by G. W. Bromiley and T. F. Torrance. Edinburgh: T and T Clark, 1958.

Bennett, Curtis. *God as Form: Essays in Greek Theology*. Albany: State University of New York Press, 1976.

Berdyaev, Nicolas. "Unground and Freedom." Introduction to Jakob Böhme, *"Six Theosophic Points" and Other Writings*, v–xxxvi. Ann Arbor: University of Michigan Press, 1958.

Berkeley, George. *Siris: A Chain of Philosophical Reflexions and Inquiries concerning the Virtues of Tar Water*. In *The Works of George Berkeley, Bishop of Cloyne,* vol. 5. Edited by A. A. Luce and T. E. Jessop. London: Nelson, 1948–57.

Blake, William. *Poems of William Blake*. Selected by Amelia H. Munson. New York: Crowell, 1964.

Blanchot, Maurice. *The Space of Literature*. Translated by Ann Smock. Lincoln: University of Nebraska Press, 1982.

———. *The Writing of Disaster*. Translated by A. Smock. Lincoln: University of Nebraska Press, 1986.

Böhme, Jakob. *"De electione gratiae" and "Quaestiones theosophicae"* (On the election of grace and Theosophic questions). Translated by John Rolleston Earle. London: Constable, 1930.

———. *Sämtliche Schriften*. 11 vols. Edited by Will-Erich Peuckert and August Faust. Stuttgart: Frommanns, 1955–61.

———. *Six Mystical Points*. 1620. Translated by John Rolleston Earle. New York: Knopf, 1920. Electronic edition: 2010, Martin Euser; meuser.awardspace.com /Boehme/SixMysticalPoints-JacobBoehme.pdf.

———. *"Six Theosophic Points" and Other Writings*. Translated by John Rolleston Earle. Introduction by Nicolas Berdyaev. Ann Arbor: University of Michigan Press, 1958.

———. *The Way to Christ*. Translated by Peter Orb. New York: Paulist, 1978.

Buber, Martin. *Ecstatic Confessions*. Syracuse, NY: Syracuse University Press, 1996.

———. *I and Thou*. Translated by Ronald Gregor Smith. New York: Scribner, 1958.

Burnet, John. *Early Greek Philosophy*. New York: Meridian Books, 1958.

Christian, William A. *An Interpretation of Whitehead's Metaphysics*. New Haven, CT: Yale University Press, 1959.

———. "The Concept of God as a Derivative Notion." In *Process and Divinity*, edited by William L. Reese and Eugene Freeman, 181-203. Lasalle, IL: Open Court, 1964.

Cioran, E. M. *Tears and Saints*. Chicago: University of Chicago Press, 1995.

———. *The Temptation to Exist*. Translated by Richard Howard. Chicago: University of Chicago Press, 1998.

Cochrane, Charles Norris. *Christianity and Classical Culture: A Study of Thought and Action from Augustus to Augustine*. New York: Oxford University Press, 1957.

Cohen, Arthur A. *An Arthur A. Cohen Reader: Selected Fiction and Writings on Judaism, Theology, Literature, and Culture*. Edited by David Stern and Paul Mendes-Flohr. Detroit: Wayne State University Press, 1998.

Coleridge, Samuel Taylor. *Biographia Literaria*. 2 vols. Edited by Henry Nelson Coleridge. London: Pickering, 1847.

———. *Selected Poetry and Prose of Samuel Taylor Coleridge*. Edited by Donald A. Stauffer. New York: Random House, 1951.

Conrad, Joseph. *The Heart of Darkness*. 4th ed. Edited by Paul B. Armstrong. Norton Critical Edition. New York: Norton, 2005.

Cornford, F. M. *Plato's Cosmology: The "Timaeus" of Plato*. New York: Humanities Press, 1952.

Derrida, Jacques. *On the Name*. Edited by Thomas Dutoit. Translated by David Wood, John P. Leavey Jr., and Ian McLeod. Stanford, CA: Stanford University Press, 1995.

Desmond, William. "Being, Determination and Dialectic: On the Sources of Metaphysical Thinking." *Review of Metaphysics* 48, no. 4 (June 1995): 731–69.

Dillard, Annie. *Holy the Firm*. New York: Harper and Row, 1977.

———. *Pilgrim at Tinker Creek*. New York: Harper's Magazine Press, 1974.

———. *Teaching a Stone to Talk: Expeditions and Encounters*. New York: Harper and Row, 1982.

Dilthey, Wilhelm. *Gesammelte Schriften*. Göttingen: Vandenhoeck and Ruprecht, 1958.

Dostoevsky, Fyodor. *The Brothers Karamazov*. 2 vols. Translated by David Magarshack. Harmondsworth: Penguin, 1958.

———. *Crime and Punishment*. Translated by David Magarshack. Harmondsworth: Penguin, 1951.

———. *The Idiot*. Translated by Constance Garnett. New York: Bantam, 1958.

Ebeling, Gerhard. "Theologie: Begriffsgeschichtlich." In *Religion in Geschichte und Gegenwart*. 3rd ed., 6:754–69. Tübingen: J. C. B. Mohr [Paul Siebeck], 1962.

Eckhart, Meister. "Another Sermon on the Eternal Birth." In *Late Medieval Mysticism*. Edited by Ray C. Petry. Translated by Raymond B. Blakney. Library of Christian Classics. Philadelphia: Westminster, 1957.

———. *Deutsche Predigten und Traktate*. Edited and translated by Josef Quint. Munich: Hanser, 1955.

———. *Meister Eckhart: A Modern Translation*. Edited and translated by Raymond B. Blakney. New York: Harper and Row, 1941.

———. *Meister Eckhart: Die deutschen und lateinischen Werke; Herausgegeben im Auftrage der Deutschen Forschungsgemeinschaft*. 13 vols. Stuttgart: Kohlhammer, 1936–.

———. *Meister Eckhart: Mystic and Philosopher*. Edited and translated with commentary by Reiner Schürmann. Bloomington: Indiana University Press, 1978.

———. *Meister Eckhart: Sermons and Treatises*. 3 vols. Edited and translated by M. O'C. Walshe. Shaftesbury, Dorset: Element, 1979–87.

———. *Meister Eckhart: The Essential Sermons, Commentaries, Treatises, and Defense*. Translation and introduction by Edmund Colledge and Bernard McGinn. Classics of Western Spirituality. New York: Paulist, 1981.

———. *Meister Eckhart*. Vol. 2 of *Deutsche Mystiker des vierzehnten Jahrhunderts*. Edited by Franz Pfeiffer. Leipzig, 1857; Aalen: Scientia, 1962.

———. *Parisian Questions and Prologues*. Edited and translated by Armand A. Maurer. Toronto: Pontifical Institute of Mediaeval Studies, 1974.

Eliot, T. S. *Burnt Norton*. London: Faber and Faber, 1941.

Eriugena, Johannes Scotus. *Periphyseon: Division of Nature*. Edited and translated by J. O'Meara. Washington, DC: Dumbarton Oaks, 1987.

Feld, Alina N. *Melancholy and the Otherness of God*: *A Study of the Hermeneutics of Depression*. Lanham, MD: Lexington Books, 2011.

Fitzgerald, F. Scott. *Tender Is the Night*. New York: Scribner, 2003.

Franke, William. *A Philosophy of the Unsayable*. Notre Dame, IN: University of Notre Dame Press, 2014.

Freeman, Kathleen, ed. and trans. *Ancilla to the Pre-Socratic Philosophers: A Complete Translation of the Fragments in Diels, "Fragmente der Vorsokratiker."* Cambridge: Harvard University Press, 1948.

Glatzer, Nahum. *Franz Rosenzweig: His Life and Thought*. 2nd rev. ed. New York: Schocken, 1961.

Goethe, Johann Wolfgang von. *Elective Affinities* (*Die Wahlverwandschaften*). Vol. 11 of *Goethe: The Collected Works*. Translated by Victor Lange and Judith Ryan. Princeton, NJ: Princeton University Press, 1995.

———. *Faust I and II*. Vol. 2 of *Goethe: The Collected Works*. Translated by Stuart Atkins. Princeton, NJ: Princeton University Press, 1994.

Gramsci, Antonio. *Quaderni del Carcere*. Edited by V. Gerratana. Turin: Einaudi, 1975.

———. *The Prison Notebooks: Selections*. Edited and translated by Quintin Hoare and Geoffrey Nowell Smith. New York: International, 1971.

Haas, Alois M. "Seinsspekulation und Geschöpflichkeit in der Mystik Meister Eckharts." In *Sein und Nichts in der abendländischen Mystik*, 33–58. Edited by Walter Strolz. Freiburg: Herder, 1984.

Hammerton-Kelly, R. G. *Sacred Violence*. Minneapolis, MN: Fortress, 1991.

Hart, Ray L. "God and Creature in the Eternity and Time of Non-Being (or Nothing): Afterthinking Meister Eckhart." In *The Otherness of God,* edited by Orrin F. Summerell, 36–59. Charlottesville: University Press of Virginia, 1998.

———. "La négativité dans l'ordre du divin," and "Pensées d'après Eckhart." Translated by Pierre-Emmanuel Dauzat. In *Voici Maître Eckhart: Textes et études réunis par Emilie Zum Brunn*, edited by Emilie Zum Brunn, 187–208, 473–78. Grenoble: Millon, 1994.

———. "To Be *and* Not to Be: *Sit Autem Sermo (Logos) Vester; Est, Est, Non, Non.*" *Journal of the American Academy of Religion* 53, no. 1 (1985): 5–22.

———. *Unfinished Man and the Imagination*: *Toward an Ontology and a Rhetoric of Revelation*. 2nd ed. Louisville, KY: Westminster John Knox Press, 2001.

Hartt, Julian N. "Some Metaphysical Gleanings from Prayer." *Journal of Religion* 31, no. 4 (October 1951): 254–63.

Hegel, G. W. F. *Aesthetics: Lectures on Fine Arts*. 2 vols. Translated by T. M. Knox. Oxford: Clarendon, 1975.

———. *The Phenomenology of Spirit*. Translated by A. V. Miller. Oxford: Oxford University Press, 1977.

———. *The Phenomenology of Spirit*. Translated by Terry Pinkard. Updated October 30, 2013. https://dl.dropboxusercontent.com/u/21288399 /Phenomonology%20translation%20English%20German.pdf.

Heidegger, Martin. "The End of Philosophy and the Task of Thinking." In *Basic Writings*, edited by David Farrell Krell, 431–49. New York: HarperCollins, 2008.

———. "Nihilism as Determined by the History of Being." In *Nietzsche*, vol. 4, *Nihilism*, edited by David Farrell Krell, translated by Frank A. Capuzzi, 199–250. New York: Harper and Row, 1982.

———. *Schellings Abhandlung über das Wesen der menschlichen Freiheit (1809)*. Tübingen: Max Niemeyer, 1971.

———. *Schelling's Treatise on the Essence of Human Freedom*. Translated by Joan Stambaugh. Athens: Ohio University Press, 1985.

———. *Zur Sache des Denkens*. Tübingen: Niemeyer, 1969.

Heraclitus, *Fragments: The Collected Wisdom of Heraclitus*. Translated by Brooks Haxton. New York: Viking, 2001.

Hopkins, Gerard Manley. *Gerard Manley Hopkins*. Edited by Catherine Phillips. The Oxford Authors. Oxford: Oxford University Press, 1986.

Husserl, Edmund. *The Crisis of European Sciences and Transcendental Philosophy*. Translated and introduced by David Carr. Evanston, IL: Northwestern University Press, 1970.

Jabès, Edmond. *The Book of Questions*. 7 vols. Translated by R. Waldrop. Middletown, CT: Wesleyan University Press, 1987.

James, William. *The Varieties of Religious Experience: A Study of Human Nature*. New York: Penguin, 1982.

Jonas, Hans. *The Gnostic Religion: The Message of the Alien God and the Beginnings of Christianity*. Boston: Beacon, 1963.

Joyce, James. *Finnegans Wake*. New York: Penguin, 1939.

Kant, Immanuel. *Critique of Pure Reason*. Translated by Norman Kemp Smith. London: Macmillan, 1953.

Kazin, Alfred. "Introduction to *Moby-Dick*." In *Melville: A Collection of Critical Essays*. Edited by Richard Chase. Englewood Cliffs, NJ: Prentice-Hall, 1962.

Kierkegaard, Søren. *Concluding Unscientific Postscript*. Translated by David F. Swenson and Walter Lowrie. Princeton, NJ: Princeton University Press, 1944.

———. *Philosophical Fragments*. Translated by D. Swenson. Revised translation by H. V. Hong. Princeton, NJ: Princeton University Press, 1974.

Kuhn, Thomas S. *The Structure of Scientific Revolutions*. Chicago: University of Chicago Press, 1962.

Lanzetta, Beverly. "Three Categories of Nothingness in Eckhart." *The Journal of Religion* 72, no. 2 (April 1992): 248–68.

Laughland, John. *Schelling versus Hegel: From German Idealism to Christian Metaphysics*. Burlington, VT: Ashgate, 2012.

Leahy, D. G. *Faith and Philosophy*. Burlington, VT: Ashgate, 2003.

———. *Foundation: Matter the Body Itself*. Albany: State University of New York Press, 1996.

———. *Novitas Mundi: Perception of the History of Being*. New York: New York University Press, 1980.

Lightman, Alan. *The Accidental Universe: The World You Thought You Knew*. New York: Pantheon, 2013.

Lossky, Vladimir. *Théologie négative et cormaissance de Dieu chez Maître Eckhart*. Paris: Vrin, 1960.

Louth, Andrew. *The Origins of the Christian Mystical Tradition: From Plato to Denys*. 2nd ed. Oxford University Press, 2007.

Macchia, Frank D. "Sighs Too Deep for Words: Towards a Theology of Glossolalia." *Journal of Pentecostal Theology* 1 (1992): 47–73.

McCullough, Lissa. *The Religious Philosophy of Simone Weil*. London: I. B. Tauris, 2014.

McGinn, Bernard, ed. *Essential Writings of Christian Mysticism*. New York: Modern Library Classics, 2006.

McGrath, Sean. *The Dark Ground of Spirit: Schelling and the Unconscious*. New York: Routledge, 2012.

McGuckin, John A. "On the Mystical Theology of the Eastern Church." Podcast and transcript posted February 5, 2014. http://www.ancientfaith.com/podcasts/svsvoices/on_the_mystical_theology_of_the_eastern_church#20045.

Melville, Herman. *Moby-Dick*. New York: Modern Library, 1982.

Merleau-Ponty, Maurice. *Signs*. Translated by Richard C. McCleary. Evanston, IL: Northwestern University Press, 1964.

Milbank, John. "Can a Gift Be Given? Prolegomena to a Future Trinitarian Metaphysics." *Modern Theology* 11, no. 1 (January 1995): 119–61.

Miles, Jack. *God: A Biography*. New York: Knopf, 1995.

Monk, Ray. *Ludwig Wittgenstein: The Duty of Genius*. New York: Free Press, 1990.

Motahari, Mohammad. "The Hermeneutical Circle or the Hermeneutical Spiral?" *International Journal of the Humanities* 15, no. 2 (2008): 99–111.

Murray, Gilbert. *Five Stages of Greek Religion*. Garden City, NY: Doubleday, 1955.

Musil, Robert. *The Man without Qualities*. Vol. 1: *A Sort of Introduction* and *Pseudo Reality Prevails*. Vol. 2: *Into the Millennium*. Translated by Sophie Wilkins and Burton Pike. New York: Vintage, 1996.

Neville, Robert C. *The Truth of Broken Symbols*. Albany: State University of New York Press, 1996.

Nicholas of Cusa. *Of Learned Ignorance*. Translated by Germain Heron. London: Routledge and Kegan Paul, 1954.

Nietzsche, Friedrich. *Beyond Good and Evil*. Translated by Helen Zimmern. Buffalo, NY: Prometheus, 1987.

———. *Thus Spoke Zarathustra: A Book for All and None*. Translated and with a preface by Walter A. Kaufmann. New York: Penguin, 1978.

Nishitani, Keiji. *Religion and Nothingness*. Translated by Jan Van Bragt. Berkeley: University of California Press, 1982.

O'Regan, Cyril. *Gnostic Apocalypse: Jacob Boehme's Haunted Narrative*. Albany: State University of New York Press, 2002.

Otto, Rudolf. *The Idea of the Holy: An Inquiry into the Non-Rational Factor in the Idea of the Divine and Its Relation to the Rational*. Translated by John W. Harvey. London: Oxford University Press, 1950.

———. *Mysticism East and West*. Translated by Bertha L. Bracey and Richenda C. Payne. New York: Macmillan, 1932.

The Oxford Study Bible: Revised English Bible with the Apocrypha. Edited by M. Jack Suggs, Katharine Doob Sakenfeld, and James R. Mueller. New York: Oxford University Press, 1992.

Pascal, Blaise. *Pascal's Pensées*. Edited and translated by W. F. Trotter. Introduction by T. S. Eliot. New York: Dutton, 1958.

Plato. *Complete Works*. Edited by John M. Cooper. Indianapolis, IN: Hackett, 1997.

Plotinus. *The Enneads*. Translated by Stephen McKenna. Harmondsworth: Penguin, 1991.

Porete, Marguerite. *The Mirror of Simple Souls*. Translated by Ellen Babinsky. Classics of Western Spirituality. New York: Paulist, 1993.

Powers, Richard. *Plowing the Dark*. New York: Farrar, Straus, Giroux, 2000.

Pseudo-Dionysius the Areopagite. *Pseudo-Dionysius: The Complete Works*. Translated by Colm Luibheid. Classics of Western Spirituality. New York: Paulist, 1987.

Richardson, C., ed. *Early Christian Fathers*. Philadelphia: Westminster, 1953.

Rilke, Rainer Maria. *Where Silence Reigns: Selected Prose*. Translated by G. Craig Houston. Foreword by Denise Levertov. New York: New Directions, 1978.

Sartre, Jean-Paul. *Being and Nothingness*. Translated and with an introduction by Hazel Barnes. New York: Gramercy, 1956.

———. *L'Imagination*. Paris: Presses Universitaires de France, 1950.

————. *The Psychology of Imagination*. New York: Philosophical Library, 1948.

Scharlemann, Robert P. *Inscriptions and Reflections: Essays in Philosophical Theology*. Charlottesville: University Press of Virginia, 1989.

————. *The Reason of Following: Christology and the Ecstatic I*. Chicago: University of Chicago Press, 1991.

Schelling, F. W. J. *The Ages of the World*. Translated by Jason M. Wirth. Albany: State University of New York Press, 2000.

————. *Historical-Critical Introduction to the Philosophy of Mythology*. Translated by Mason Richey and Markus Zisselsberger. Albany: State University of New York Press, 2007.

————. *Schellings Werke: Nach der Originalausgabe in neuer Anordnung*. Edited by Manfred Schroeter. Berlin: Beck'sche, 1927–1959 and 1962–1971.

Schindler, D. C. *The Perfection of Freedom: Schiller, Schelling, and Hegel between the Ancients and the Moderns*. Eugene, OR: Wipf and Stock, 2012.

Schleiermacher, Friedrich. *On Religion: Speeches to Its Cultured Despisers*. Edited and translated by Richard Crouter. Cambridge: Cambridge University Press, 1988.

Schürmann, Reiner. *Wandering Joy: Meister Eckhart's Mystical Philosophy*. Great Barrington, MA: Lindisfarne, 2011.

Sells, Michael A. *Mystical Languages of Unsaying*. Chicago: University of Chicago Press, 1994.

Stegner, Wallace. *Angle of Repose*. New York: Penguin, 1971.

Stevens, Wallace. *The Collected Poems of Wallace Stevens*. New York: Knopf, 1964.

Taylor, Mark C. *Erring: A Postmodern A/theology*. Chicago: University of Chicago Press, 1984.

————. *Field Notes from Elsewhere: Reflections on Dying and Living*. New York: Columbia University Press, 2009.

Tennyson, Alfred Lord. "In Memoriam A. H. H." In *Selected Poems*. Edited and with an introduction and notes by Christopher Ricks. Penguin Classics. New York: Penguin, 2007.

Thoreau, Henry David. *"Walden" and Other Writings of Henry David Thoreau*. Edited by Brooks Atkinson. New York: Modern Library, 1937.

————. *A Week on the Concord and Merrimack Rivers*. Boston: J. R. Osgood, 1873.

Turner, Denys. *The Darkness of God: Negativity in Christian Mysticism*. Cambridge: Cambridge University Press, 1998.

van Peursen, C. A. "Phénoménologie et ontologie." In *Rencontre / Encounter / Begegnung: Contributions à une psychologie humaine dédiées au Professeur F. J. J. Buytendijk*. Edited and with a foreword by M. J. Langeveld. Utrecht: Uitgeverij het Spectrum, 1957.

Weil, Simone. *Gravity and Grace*. Translated by Emma Crawford and Mario von der Ruhr. London: Routledge, 2002.

————. *The Notebooks of Simone Weil*. 2 vols. Translated by Arthur Wills. London: Routledge and Kegan Paul, 1956.

———. *Waiting for God*. Translated by Emma Craufurd. Introduction by Leslie A. Fiedler. New York: Harper and Row, 1973.

Weiss, Paul. "Metaphysics: The Domain of Ignorance." *Philosophical Review* 43, no. 4 (July 1934): 402–6.

———. *Reality*. Princeton, NJ: Princeton University Press, 1938.

Whaley, George. *Poetic Process*. London: Routledge and Kegan Paul, 1953.

Whitehead, Alfred North. *The Concept of Nature*. Cambridge: Cambridge University Press, 1926.

———. *Process and Reality: An Essay in Cosmology*. New York: Macmillan, 1936.

Wirth, Jason M. *The Conspiracy of Life: Meditations on Schelling and His Time*. Albany: State University of New York Press, 2003.

———, ed. *Schelling Now: Contemporary Readings*. Bloomington: Indiana University Press, 2005.

Wittgenstein, Ludwig. *Remarks on the Foundations of Mathematics, Cambridge 1939*. From the notes of R. G. Bosanquet, Norman Malcolm, Rush Rhees, and Yorick Smythies. Edited by Cora Diamond. Chicago: University of Chicago Press, 1975.

———. *Tractatus Logico-Philosophicus*. Translated by D. F. Pears and B. F. McGinness. Introduction by Bertrand Russell. London: Routledge and Kegan Paul, 1981.

———. *Zettel*. Edited by G. E. M. Anscombe and G. H. von Wright. Translated by G. E. M. Anscombe. Oxford: Basil Blackwell, 1967.

Wolfson, Elliot R. *Giving beyond the Gift: Apophasis and Overcoming Theomania*. New York: Fordham University Press, 2014.

Yeats, W. B. *A Full Moon in March*. In *Yeats's Poetry, Drama, and Prose: Authoritative Texts, Contexts, Criticism*. Edited by James Pethica. Norton Critical Edition. New York: Norton, 2000.

Zahavy, Tzvee. *The Mishnaic Law of Blessings and Prayers: Tractate Berakhot*. Atlanta, GA: Scholars Press, 1989.

Zeller, Edward. *Outlines of the History of Greek Philosophy*. Translated by Frances Alleyne and Evelyn Abbott. London: Longmans, Green, 1886.

Zum Brunn, Emilie. *St. Augustine: Being and Nothingness*. Translated by Ruth Namad. New York: Paragon, 1988.

———, ed. *Voici Maître Eckhart: Textes et études réunis par Emilie Zum Brunn*. Grenoble: Millon, 1994.

Zum Brunn, Emilie, and A. de Libera. *Maître Eckhart: Métaphysique du verbe et théologie négative*. Paris: Beauchesne, 1994.

Index